Lecture Notes of the Institute for Computer Sciences, Social Informatics and Telecommunications Engineering 285

More information about this series at http://www.springer.com/series/8197

Mahdi H. Miraz · Peter S. Excell ·
Andrew Ware · Safeeullah Soomro ·
Maaruf Ali (Eds.)

Emerging Technologies in Computing

Second International Conference, iCETiC 2019
London, UK, August 19–20, 2019
Proceedings

 Springer

Editors
Mahdi H. Miraz ⓘ
CFRED
Chinese University of Hong Kong
Hong Kong, China

Andrew Ware ⓘ
Faculty of Computing, Engineering
and Science
University of South Wales
Pontypridd, Mid Glamorgan, UK

Maaruf Ali ⓘ
University of Essex
Colcheser, UK

Peter S. Excell ⓘ
Glyndwr University
Wrexham, UK

Safeeullah Soomro ⓘ
AMA International University
Salmabad, Bahrain

ISSN 1867-8211   ISSN 1867-822X   (electronic)
Lecture Notes of the Institute for Computer Sciences, Social Informatics
and Telecommunications Engineering
ISBN 978-3-030-23942-8   ISBN 978-3-030-23943-5   (eBook)
https://doi.org/10.1007/978-3-030-23943-5

This Springer imprint is published by the registered company Springer Nature Switzerland AG
The registered company address is: Gewerbestrasse 11, 6330 Cham, Switzerland

Mahdi H. Miraz · Peter S. Excell ·
Andrew Ware · Safeeullah Soomro ·
Maaruf Ali (Eds.)

Emerging Technologies in Computing

Second International Conference, iCETiC 2019
London, UK, August 19–20, 2019
Proceedings

 Springer

Editors
Mahdi H. Miraz ⓘ
CFRED
Chinese University of Hong Kong
Hong Kong, China

Andrew Ware ⓘ
Faculty of Computing, Engineering
and Science
University of South Wales
Pontypridd, Mid Glamorgan, UK

Maaruf Ali ⓘ
University of Essex
Colcheser, UK

Peter S. Excell ⓘ
Glyndwr University
Wrexham, UK

Safeeullah Soomro ⓘ
AMA International University
Salmabad, Bahrain

ISSN 1867-8211   ISSN 1867-822X (electronic)
Lecture Notes of the Institute for Computer Sciences, Social Informatics
and Telecommunications Engineering
ISBN 978-3-030-23942-8   ISBN 978-3-030-23943-5 (eBook)
https://doi.org/10.1007/978-3-030-23943-5

This Springer imprint is published by the registered company Springer Nature Switzerland AG
The registered company address is: Gewerbestrasse 11, 6330 Cham, Switzerland

Preface

It is our great pleasure to introduce the proceedings of the Second Edition of the International Conference on Emerging Technologies in Computing (iCETiC 2019), held during August 19–20, 2019, at the London Metropolitan University, London, UK. This conference drew together researchers and developers from both academia and industry - especially in the domains of computing, networking and communications engineering.

The theme of iCETiC 2019 was "Emerging Technologies" as outlined by the Gartner Hype Cycle for Emerging Technologies, 2018.

iCETiC 2019 was organised by the International Association for Educators and Researchers (IAER) and technically co-sponsored by the UK and Ireland Section of the Institute of Electrical and Electronics Engineers (IEEE), the UK and Ireland Chapter and the Bahrain Chapter of the IEEE Communications Society, as well as the Chester and North Wales Branch of the British Computer Society (BCS).

The technical program of iCETiC 2019 consisted of 25 full papers in oral presentation sessions in the main conference tracks. The major conference tracks were:

- Track 1 - Blockchain and Cloud Computing
- Track 2 - Security, Wireless Sensor Networks and Internet of Things (IoT)
- Track 3 - FinTech
- Track 4 - AI, Big Data and Data Analytics

Apart from the high-quality technical paper presentations, the technical program also featured two keynote speeches and one invited talk. The two keynote speakers were Professor Andrew Ware, Professor of Computing, Faculty of Computing, Engineering and Science, University of South Wales, UK and Professor Garfield Southall, Executive Dean for the Faculty of Science and Engineering at the University of Chester, UK. The invited speaker was Dr. Mahmood Shah, Senior Lecturer in e-Business within the School of Strategy and Leadership, Coventry University, UK.

It was also a great pleasure to work with such an excellent organising committee, who put in very hard work in organising and supporting the conference. In addition, the work of the Technical Programme Committee is also greatly appreciated: they completed the peer-review process of technical papers and compiled a high-quality technical programme.

We strongly believe that the iCETiC 2019 provided a good forum for all researchers, developers and practitioners to discuss recent advancements in computing, networking and communications engineering. We also expect that the future iCETiC conferences will be as successful and stimulating, as indicated by the contributions presented in this volume.

May 2019

Mahdi H. Miraz
Peter S. Excell
Andrew Ware
Safeeullah Soomro
Maaruf Ali

Organization

Steering Committee Co-chairs

Maaruf Ali	International Association of Educators and Researchers (IAER), London, UK
Safeeullah Soomro	AMA International University BAHRAIN (AMAIUB), Bahrain
Mahdi H. Miraz	The Chinese University of Hong Kong, Hong Kong, SAR

Organizing Committee

General Co-chairs

Safeeullah Soomro	AMA International University BAHRAIN (AMAIUB), Bahrain
Ali Kashif Bashir	University of the Faroe Islands, Faroe Islands, Denmark

Technical Program Committee Co-chair

Mahdi H. Miraz	The Chinese University of Hong Kong, SAR

Web, Publicity, and Social Media Chair

Shayma K. Miraz	International Association of Educators and Researchers (IAER), London, UK

Publications Chair

Mahdi H. Miraz	The Chinese University of Hong Kong, SAR China

Local Chairs

Anowarul Karim	International Association of Educators and Researchers (IAER), London, UK
Emily Thomas	Wrexham Glyndwr University, UK

Track Chairs

Cloud, IoT and Distributed Computing Track Chair

Virginia N. L. Franqueira	University of Derby, UK

Software Engineering Track Chair

M. Abdullah-Al-Wadud	King Saud University, KSA

Communications Engineering and Vehicular Technology Track Chairs

Bhawani Shankar
  Chowdhry

Mehran University of Engineering and Technology,
  Pakistan

Mohab A. Mangoud

University of Bahrain, Bahrain

AI, Expert Systems and Big Data Analytics Track Chair

Christian Esposito

Università degli Studi di Salerno, Italy

Web Information Systems and Applications Track Chair

Seifedine Kadry

Beirut Arab University (UMB), Lebanon

Security Track Chair

Aniello Castiglione

University of Salerno, Italy

Database System and Application Track Chair

Basit Shahzad

King Saud University, KSA

Economics and Business Engineering Track Chair

Olga Angelopoulou

University of Hertfordshire, UK

mLearning and eLearning Track Chair

Garfield Southall

University of Chester, UK

General Track Chair

Andrew Jones

University of Hertfordshire, UK

Technical Program Committee

Ajith Abraham   Monash University, Australia
Renaud Lambiotte   University of Oxford, UK
Ajay K. Gupta   Western Michigan University, USA
Ljiljana Trajkovic   Simon Fraser University, Canada
Been-Chian Chien   National University of Tainan, Taiwan
Victor Preciado   University of Pennsylvania, USA
Lin Liu   Tsinghua University, China
Guanghui Wen   Southeast University, China
Nowshad Amin   Universiti Kebangsaan Malaysia and Solar Energy
                               Research Institute (SERI), Malaysia
Yalin Zheng   University of Liverpool, UK
AbdelRahman H. Hussein   Al-Ahliyya Amman University, Jordan
Ali Kashif Bashir   University of the Faroe Islands, Denmark
Rabie Ramadan   University of Ha'il, KSA
Vincenza Carchiolo   Università di Catania, Italy

Imran Mahmud	Daffodil International University, Bangladesh
Junaid Ahsenali Chaudhry	Edith Cowan University, Australia
G. Sahoo	Birla Institute of Technology, Mesra, India
Brenda Scholtz	Nelson Mandela University, South Africa
Fabiana Zama	University of Bologna, Italy
Wahab Yuseni	Technical University of Malaysia Malacca (KUIM), Malaysia
Jia Uddin	BRAC University, Bangladesh
Saad Alharbi	Taibah University, KSA
Aniello Castiglione	University of Salerno, Italy
Fazal Noor	Islamic University of Madinah, KSA
Bernhard Peischl	Technische Universität Graz, Austria
Anupama Prasanth	AMA International University BAHRAIN (AMAIUB), Bahrain
Christian Esposito	University of Salerno, Italy
Zainab Alansari	University of Malaya, Malaysia
Muzafar A. Ganie	University of Ha'il, KSA
Ruchin Jain	AMA International University BAHRAIN (AMAIUB), Bahrain
Abdul Rehman Soomrani	Sukkur Institute of Business Administration, Pakistan
Asadullah Shah	International Islamic University, Malaysia
Arcangelo Castiglione	University of Salerno, Italy
Suhail A. Molvi	University of Ha'il, KSA
Zahid Hussain	Technical University Graz, Austria
Mohammed Riyaz Belgaum	AMA International University BAHRAIN (AMAIUB), Bahrain
Trupil Limbasiya	NIIT University, India
Zahida Parveen	University of Hail, KSA
Marija Mitrovic Dankulov	Institute of Physics Belgrade, Serbia
Balakrishnan K.	Karpaga Vinayaga College of Engineering and Technology, India
Ahmed Ibrahim	Edith Cowan University, Australia
Asadullah Shaikh	Najran University, KSA
Ibrahim Kucukkoc	Balikesir University, Turkey
Faisal Karim Shaikh	Mehran University of Engineering and Technology, Pakistan
Cristóvão Dias	Universidade de Lisboa, Portugal
Morgado Dias	Universidade da Madeira, Portugal
Radoslaw Michalski	Wroclaw University of Science and Technology, Poland
Nor Badrul Anuar Bin Juma'at	University of Malaya, Malaysia
Samina Rajper	Shah Abdul Latif University, Pakistan
Amirrudin Bin Kamsin	University of Malaya, Malaysia
Adel Ahmed Hamed	IEEE Bahrain Section, Bahrain

Wafeeq Ajoor	IEEE Bahrain Section, Bahrain
Wasan Shakir Awad	Ahlia University, Bahrain
Yousuf M. Islam	Daffodil International University, Bangladesh
Prabhat K. Mahanti	University of New Brunswick, Canada
Massimo Ficco	Università degli Studi della Campania Luigi Vanvitelli, Italy
Rosa María Benito Zafrilla	Universidad Politécnica de Madrid, Spain
Syed Faiz Ahmed	British Malaysian Institute, Universiti Kuala Lumpur, Malaysia
Touhid Bhuiyan	Daffodil International University, Bangladesh
Anurag Singh	National Institute of Technology (NIT) Delhi, India
Mohammad Siraj	King Saud University, KSA
Anthony Chukwuemeka Ijeh	American University in the Emirates, UAE
José Javier Ramasco	Institute for Cross-Disciplinary Physics and Complex Systems (IFISC), Spain
Zi-Ke Zhang	Hangzhou Normal University, China
I-Hsien Ting	National University of Kaohsiung, Taiwan
Francisco Rodrigues	University of São Paulo, Brazil
Amir Rubin	Ben-Gurion University, Israel
Ahmed N. AL Masri	American University in the Emirates, UAE
Ahmed Bin Touq	United Arab Emirates University, UAE
Daniel Onah	University College London, UK
Oussama Hamid	University of Kurdistan Hewlêr, Erbil, Iraq
Souvik Pal	Elitte College of Engineering, Kolkata, India
Matteo Zignani	Università degli Studi di Milano, Milano, Italy
Stephen Uzzo	New York Hall of Science, NY, USA
Ali Hessami	IEEE UKRI Section and Innovation Director at Vega Systems Ltd., UK
Ezendu Ariwa	University of Bedfordshire, UK
Amirrudin Bin Kamsin	University of Malaya, Malaysia
Mohab A. Mangoud	University of Bahrain, Bahrain
Thamer Al-meshhadany	IT Consultant, Canada
Umair Ahmed	Gulf University Bahrain, Bahrain
Hafiz Abid Mahmood Malik	AMA International University BAHRAIN (AMAIUB), Bahrain
Hafeez Siddiqui	London South Bank University, UK
Valentina E. Balas	Aurel Vlaicu University of Arad, Romania
Mahmood Shah	Coventry University, UK
Aamir Zeb Shaikh	NED University of Engineering and Technology, Pakistan
Farhat Naureen Memon	University of Sindh, Pakistan
Ghulam Ali Mallah	Shah Abdul Latif University, Pakistan
Muhammad Mansoor Alam	University Kuala Lumpur (UniKL), Malaysia
Naveed Ahmed Shaikh	Management Sciences, Szabist, UAE
Fida Hussain Chandio	University of Sindh, UAE

Muhammad Yaqoob Koondhar	Sindh Agriculture University, Pakistan
Madad Ali Shah	Sukkur IBA University, Pakistan
Riaz Ahmed Shaikh	Shah Abdul Latif University, Pakistan
Muniba Memon	Najran University, Saudi Arabia
P. Vijaya	Waljat College of Applied Sciences, Oman
Mansoor Hyder Depar	Sindh Agriculture University (SAU), Pakistan
Jawdat Alshaer	AMA International University BAHRAIN (AMAIUB), Bahrain
Hamid Tahaei	University Malaya, Malaysia
Zohreh Dehghani Champiri	University Malaya, Malaysia
Md Tanvir Arafat Khan	Hanwha Q Cells America Limited, Palo Alto, USA
Afaq Ahmad	College of Engineering, Sultan Qaboos University, Oman
Abhishek Shukla	Dr A P J Abdul Kalam Technical University, Lucknow, India

Contents

Blockchain and Cloud Computing

Performance Analytical Comparison of Blockchain-as-a-Service (BaaS) Platforms

Md Mehedi Hassan Onik[1] and Mahdi H. Miraz[2,3(✉)]

[1] Department of Computer Engineering, Inje University, Gimhae 50834, Korea
hassan@oasis.inje.ac.kr
[2] The Chinses University of Hong Kong (CUHK), Sha Tin, Hong Kong
m.miraz@ieee.org
[3] Wrexham Glyndŵr University, Wrexham, UK

Abstract. Both blockchain technologies and cloud computing are contemporary emerging technologies. While the application of Blockchain technologies is being spread beyond cryptocurrency, cloud computing is also seeing a paradigm shift to meet the needs of the 4th industrial revolution (Industry 4.0). New technological advancement, especially by the fusion of these two, such as Blockchain-as-a-Service (BaaS), is considered to be able to significantly generate values to the enterprises. This article surveys the current status of BaaS in terms of technological development, applications, market potentials and so forth. An evaluative judgement, comparing amongst various BaaS platforms, has been presented, along with the trajectory of adoption, challenges and risk factors. Finally, the study suggests standardisation of available BaaS platforms.

Keywords: Atomic swap · Blockchain · Blockchain-as-a-Service · BaaS · Cloud computing · Distributed ledger technology · DLT · Lightning network

1 Introduction

Blockchain, as first introduced in 2008 by Nakamoto [1], as the technology behind Bitcoin, has now matured enough as a standalone technology. Applications of blockchain have reached far beyond cryptocurrencies [2]. Examples of non-monetary applications of blockchain include securities settlement [3, 4], supply-chain [2], HR management [5], Healthcare [2, 6], decision making [7], personal data management [8, 9] and so forth [10]. In fact, blockchain is not a completely new technology, rather it just a new incorporated mechanism utilising multifaceted existing technologies together – such as distributed ledger technology (DLT), mathematical hashing, distributed networks, asymmetric encryption techniques, digital signatures and programming [11] – for the system to perform seamlessly. A transaction in a blockchain ecosystem is triggered by the sending node, verified and validated by the other participating nodes and if a consensus is reached it is then added to the pool of "unconfirmed" transactions to form a 'block'. The creation of the block varies depending on the consensus algorithm (e.g. Proof-of-Work, Proof-of-Stake etc.) used. However, once a block is successfully formed, is then propagated to all the nodes in the network to be appended at the open end

M. H. Miraz et al. (Eds.): iCETiC 2019, LNICST 285, pp. 3–18, 2019.

of their existing copy of the chain. Thus, all the distributed copies of the database (ledger) is updated and synchronised. Because blocks are mathematically bound by cumulative hashes, altering a single transaction or even a single bit will invalidate that block and rebuilding block with a new hash will invalidate the following blocks. Thus, it acts as a "Trust Machine" [12] which brings immutability, security, eliminates single point of failure (SPF) as well as the need for a third-party for establishing trust.

Cloud computing has been defined differently by different bodies or professionals. However, the definition of cloud computing provided by the national institute of standards and technology (NIST), part of the U.S. Department of commerce—in its Special Publication 800-145 [13], is the widely accepted one. NIST [14] defines cloud computing as "*a model for enabling convenient, on-demand network access to a shared pool of configurable computing resources (e.g., networks, servers, storage, applications, and services) that can be rapidly provisioned and released with minimal management effort or service provider interaction.*" Further to this definition, cloud computing enables a model of IT service in any combination of IT resources – from a network accessible data storage to a fully-fledged virtual machines, from hosted application/service to application/service development infrastructure [15, 16]. A cloud consumer can simply avail the required resources from the pool through service orchestration. The resources are released and returned to the pool when the consumer no longer needs them. The cloud model functions analogous to regular utility services such as electricity. When required, a consumer plugs in the appliance into a socket and switch it on – in most cases without knowing the details of how electricity is produced and distributed. The consumers are only charged for whatever amount of electricity they have consumed. In a similar way, the cloud model abstracts the IT infrastructure for enabling the consumers to rent IT resources eliminating the associated costs and risks of owning these resources. However, the cloud is not limited to infrastructure, rather offers platforms, services and applications too making cloud service even more pervasive. Finally, cloud converts capital expenditure (CapEx) and operational expenditure (OpEx) making it popular among the small to medium enterprises.

One of the next generation cloud computing features is Blockchain-as-a-Service (BaaS) – a fusion of blockchain technology and the cloud computing model. BaaS enables offshoring the implementation of blockchain for any enterprise to the cloud environment, without needing any IT expertise. Thus, enterprises can benefit from BaaS as a utility service and serve their business need. BaaS relatively being a new addition to both blockchain and cloud technologies, this article conducts an extensive survey of relevant research literatures and projects as well as performs a performance analytical comparison of Blockchain-as-a-Service (BaaS) platforms- Mainly those provided by Microsoft, Amazon, Hewlett Packard (HP), Oracle and SAP. The paper also discusses future challenges, risk factors and trajectory of adoption.

2 Overview of Blockchain-as-a-Service (BaaS)

2.1 Overview

Blockchain: The blockchain technologies utilise decentralised distributed ledgers for recording the transactions across a peer to peer network. Without being dominated by any central authority and/or middle man for "trust", this technology can verify, validate and complete transactions being autonomously governed by the coded protocol and consensus approach powered by the nodes of the peer-to-peer networks. In fact, blockchain technology was first introduced in 2008 as a core technology for a cryptocurrency (i.e. Bitcoin) [1]. However, successful applications of BC in multifaceted other use-cases beyond cryptocurrencies have instituted it as one of the cardinal technologies of both the emerging and the upcoming industrial revolutions [2–10] evident by the forecasted business value creation of blockchain technology to exceed $3.1 trillion by 2030 [17]. Based on the level of write and read access to the ledger, blockchain can be categorised into three types: public (permissionless) blockchain – mainly for cryptocurrencies (e.g. Bitcoin, Ethereum), private (permissioned) blockchain – mainly for non-monetary applications within a closed network and Federated (consortium/hybrid) blockchain – a combination of both public and private mainly to be used within a consortium (e.g. Hyperledger). Anyone at any time can join and leave the public blockchain ecosystem enjoying full access to read and write (subject to consensus). Joining in a private blockchain is restricted - read and write access are controlled based on the roles of the nodes or other restrictions as imposed by the protocol. In a hybrid blockchain, joining is sometimes controlled by invitations only – while all the participating nodes enjoy read access as in public blockchain, write access is limited as in private blockchain.

Blockchain-as-a-Service: Blockchain-as-a-Service (BaaS) means of building, managing, hosting and using various aspects of blockchain technologies such as applications, nodes, smart contracts and distributed ledger, on the cloud. Such cloud-based service facilitates blockchain set-up, platform, security and other associated features. Thus BaaS introduces the blockchain service platform, supporting blockchain core features, based on cloud computing infrastructure with the integrated developing environment for both the developers and the consumers [18–20].

In fact, the key concept of BaaS is almost similar to that of Software-as-a-Service (SaaS). According to cloud computing orchestration, BaaS can function either explicitly utilising Platform-as-a-Service (PaaS) or implicitly via Software-as-a-service (SaaS). Based on how it is implemented, the locus of BaaS in a cloud computing environment may vary. Figure 1 demonstrates the location of BaaS in an on-premise local implementation. In such implementations, BaaS functions with the support of both SaaS and PaaS. While BaaS receives the technical services (software) from SaaS, it gets infrastructure support from PaaS. On-premise blockchain implementation is highly expensive. Users of such local implementation require investing a significant share of capital expenditure (CapEx) for maintaining the infrastructure and performance of the DLT. The alternative economical approach is BaaS – a user can enjoy full service of the blockchain technology even investing less. BaaS can manage blockchain consensus, forking, node validity, commodity exchange, backup, off-chain and on-chain synchronisation all by itself. Similarly, BaaS can also manage resource, bandwidth, internet connection and other associated services. However, BaaS provides the enterprises with the flexibility to emphasise on business logic and functional need of the blockchain. BaaS helps to create, develop, test, host, deploy and operate blockchain related applications on cloud infrastructure. BaaS implementation fully out-sources the technical overhead to the cloud service provider. Figure 2 shows the architectural overview of BaaS.

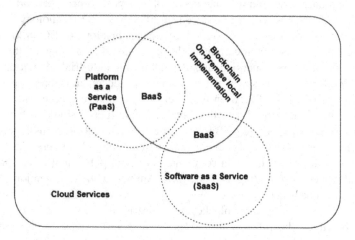

Fig. 1. Location of BaaS in compare with other cloud services

2.2   Advantages of BaaS

Real-world blockchain use cases are rapidly emerging, but the skills and resources required to build blockchain applications are neither widely available nor cheap. Therefore, BaaS possesses the potentials to address this aperture and make blockchain technology accessible to a broader audience. A few benefits of blockchain-as-a-service (BaaS) are discussed here:

- With already established cloud platform blockchain adopters can receive seamless service with far more fewer cost than actual (on-premise) implementation.
- In current blockchain architecture, several regulations and norms like node verification, node attachment, node deletion, forking must be taken care off. However, BaaS can take care of them without any intervention.
- Blockchain technology is being used beyond cryptocurrencies. Therefore, interaction with another platform, service, infrastructure has increased a lot in the last few years. Since BaaS blockchain technology is built utilising existing cloud infrastructure, PaaS, IaaS, SaaS and similar other aspects of the cloud remains native to BaaS – offering a higher degree of interoperability.
- Current blockchain implementation requires a moderate degree of knowledge in the domain of cryptography and distributed technologies. Alternatively, BaaS, which is

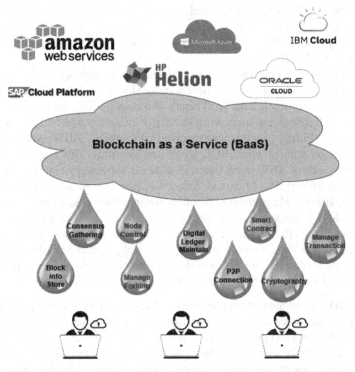

Fig. 2. Architectural overview of Blockchain-as-a-Service (BaaS)

offered as a complete service by the providers, allows deploying, managing and operating of enterprise blockchain technology without any technical knowledge.

3 Overview of Available BaaS Platforms

3.1 Microsoft Azure BaaS

During late 2015, Microsoft aligned with Consensys to offer Ethereum Blockchain-as-a-Service (EBaaS) [21]. As Microsoft corporation already possessed a widely used infrastructure and cloud platform (i.e. Azure), coupling up blockchain technology as a service on their existing Azure platform was a rational business move. In order to offer BaaS, 'Azure Blockchain Workbench' was introduced with two major tools: 'Microsoft Flow (Ether.Camp)' and 'Logic Apps (BlockApps)'. The aforementioned establish a scalable and integrated blockchain development environment along with a consortium Ethereum blockchain application development environment. Azure Blockchain Workbench (ABW) allows direct development of distributed applications (DApps) without worrying much about the underlying system services. With the available REST APIs, ABW facilitates the users to integrate other available services to interact with the newly created personalised application. ABW has the ability to connect available

Microsoft services like office 365, Excel, SharePoint, 365 CRM and other available services. More than 200 connectors are considered to provide a graphical user interface in 'Logic Apps' and 'Flow' which minimise end to end blockchain management complexity [20, 22, 23].

The ABW fully complement legacy Blockchain technology and provide core blockchain services. Identity management is ensured with the help of the Azure active directory. The Azure Blockchain Workbench also manage both the user roles and the smart contract. It allows the users to write their own access and business logic code (smart contract). Finally, for privacy-preserved data mining, ABW synchronised on-chain information with off-chain SQL server (on demand). This empowers the data analysing the scope of ABW many times. In addition, for seamless interaction amongst available software services, Microsoft Azure also provides Azure Blockchain Development Kit (ABDK). Microsoft ABDK offers linking interfaces, assimilating data and systems, deploying blockchain networks. ABDK can interact with legacy applications and protocols like FTP, Microsoft Excel, email data. Several legacy databases such as SQL, Excel, PowerBi and Azure Search service as well as other SaaS deployment such as SharePoint, Dynamics and office 365 can also be accessible by ABW though ABDK. Key advantages of ABW are as follows [20, 22, 23]:

- Using ABW, configuration, deployment and testing of any BaaS application in a consortium network can be performed by only a few clicks. ABW's by default ledger deployment and network infrastructure reduces infrastructure creation period.
- Overall blockchain technology development time and the cost are reduced by making proper use of Azure cloud services such as Azure Active Directory (AD) for easier sign-in and identity checking, storing private keys with Azure Key Vault, secure and easy messaging among blockchain nodes, off-chain and on-chain data synchronisation for privacy-preservation and visualisation.
- ABW facilitates easy integration between any business entity and the blockchain technology. With Microsoft's ABW and ABDK (REST-based API) interaction, messaging, verifying with blockchain nodes (clients) have become much easier than before.
- Finally, Microsoft acquires comparatively more platforms, services and infrastructures than any other cloud providers. This leaves a company with higher success and lower compatibility issues.

3.2 Amazon AWS BaaS

Initially, Amazon started providing blockchain by partnering with third parties (R3, Kaleido) [24, 25], however, it recently announced its own blockchain platform. Later, Amazon declares its own blockchain service based on Hyperledger in two different forms: Amazon Quantum Ledger Database (QLDB) and Amazon managed Blockchain. In addition, Amazon's AWS provides developers with a wide selection of blockchain frameworks with minimum pricing [24, 25].

Blockchain Amazon Quantum Ledger Database (QLDB): Amazon QLDB is a new database that provides the functionalities of a distributed ledger database without creating a ledger. Amazon QLDB mainly focused on developing an immutable and transparent ledger. This QLDB can create a distributed ledger application both with relational and blockchain database. To maintain both immutable (relational) and distributed (Hyperledger Fabric and Ethereum) databases simultaneously, individual blockchain node along with the network must be validated. In order to track every data exchange among blockchain nodes, QLDB maintains a ledger named Journal. It's an immutable transaction log where transactions are saved as a new block. In addition, the journal determines current and history of all the transactions [24, 25]. Figure 3 demonstrates the architecture of Amazon Quantum Ledger Database for BaaS.

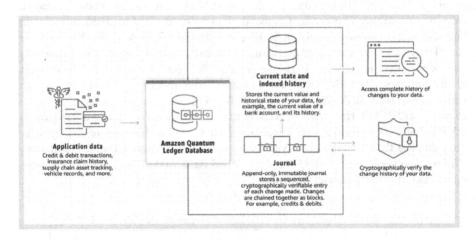

Fig. 3. Amazon QLDB (BaaS) [24–26]

Amazon Managed Blockchain: Amazon Managed Blockchain (AMB) is a blockchain network backed by the Hyperledger fabric. A full network can be installed within 10–15 min. It's a private network meant solely for blockchain based technologies. However, most of its functionalities are the same as QLDB [24–26]. Figure 4 presents the basic architecture of Amazon Managed Blockchain as a BaaS.

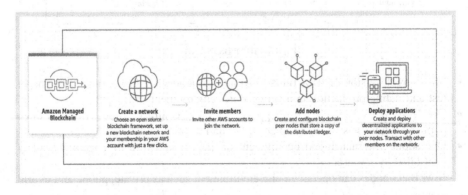

Fig. 4. Amazon managed Blockchain (BaaS) [24–26]

3.3   IBM BaaS

IBM revealed BaaS in the year of 2017 using the Hyperledger fabric on IBM cloud. This allows any private and public organizations to introduce private, public or consortium blockchain. IBM also introduced a 'SecureKey Technologies', a digital identity sharing key to protect the public-private key. IBM claims its 'blockchain-as-a-service' technology to be highly auditable and performs better than other SaaS services [27–29].

IBM provides SaaS through 'Bluemix' [27–29]. With the help of the 'Bluemix', developers are allowed to create blockchain application without any extra setup. With the aid of 'Bluemix', 'Hyperledger Fabric' and IBM cloud users can directly develop a DevOps and deploy Chaincode. Chaincode is a software used by IBM to maintain business logic (consensus) and can be written with Go and Node.js. IBM blockchain has 'Transactor's who are actually acting as clients using application programming interfaces (API) and software development kit (SDK). IBM also introduces the concept of the validating peer (VP) and non-validating peer (NVP). Only VP are able to participate in IBM SaaS directly. Alternatively, NVP can also be connected with the chain via REST API. However, for security reason, NVP can only forward a request to a VP rather than performing the actual work. High-level architecture of IoT applications that use IBM Cloud-based Hyperledger services is shown in Fig. 5. As of now, IBM has two versions of BaaS (1.0 and 2.0). IBM BaaS 2.0 [30] is comparatively more robust and offer the following benefits:

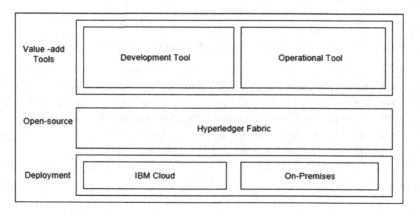

Fig. 5. IBM BaaS [30]

- The current version of IBM BaaS (2.0) allows large scale development, extensive test and public production in a single BaaS environment.
- The IBM Blockchain platform supports the smart contracts to be written in three popular languages such as JavaScript, Go and Java.
- Operation, governance and deployment of the blockchain components are solely controlled by the users.
- IBM BaaS nodes can operate in any environment such as private, public and hybrid clouds.

3.4   Hewlett Packard (HP) BaaS

Hewlett Packard Enterprise (HPE) introduced their first ever BaaS named 'Mission Critical Distributed Ledger Technology' (MCDLT) or DLT as a Service [31]. HPE's MCDLT includes higher scalability and SQL integration with blockchain technology. This solution includes replacing on-premise user infrastructure with public cloud environment or generic infrastructure. HPE partnered with R3 (software company) to establish a 100% fault tolerance blockchain application development platform for enterprise use.

3.5   Oracle BaaS

Oracle recently introduced Oracle Blockchain Cloud Service (OBCS) besides their already established Platform as a service (PaaS) and Software as a Service (SaaS) [32]. In order to start the internal blockchain (distributed ledger) project quickly, Oracle BaaS introduced two key concepts [33]. Firstly, OBCS possesses turn-key sandbox which is solely designed for the developers. Secondly, independent software vendors (ISV) facilitates easy deployment of blockchain technology regardless of their vendor (Fig. 6).

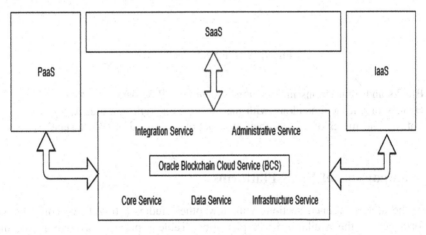

Fig. 6. Oracle BaaS [33]

3.6   SAP BaaS

A great addition to BaaS is SAP Blockchain [34]. SAP introduced both SAP-Cloud-Platform Blockchain Service and SAP HANA Blockchain Service. SAP HANA connects any SAP HANA database to the most popular enterprise blockchain platforms [35]. This provides very interesting capabilities that were previously unheard of in the blockchain ecosystem.

SAP HANA blockchain (BaaS) connects the SAP HANA database with distributed ledger technology (DLT). SAP HANA supports stellar consensus protocol (SCP) blockchain within it. SCP blockchain can be hosted on any third-party cloud and local infrastructure. In addition, SAP HANA cloud services are only available if it is hosted on SCP. SAP HANA is not a blockchain node, rather it configures the connection properties of SCP. SAP HANA BaaS maintain the blockchain transaction details in 3 types of SAP HANA database tables, as shown in Fig. 7:

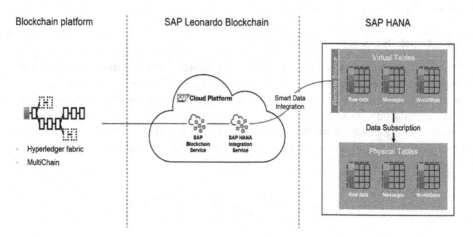

Fig. 7. SAP HANA BaaS [34]

- Blocks and transactions information is saved as 'Raw data'.
- History of transactions along with the messages is kept in a ledger.
- Latest valid tuples of a blockchain transaction are saved in 'Worldstate'.

4   Comparison of BaaS Platforms

From the aforementioned sections with few other studies [36–41], we compare the performance of the available BaaS platforms. Table 1 provides availability of the several blockchain hosting platforms by top BaaS platforms:

In Table 2, other aspects are compared to available BaaS services. Available partners, major users, authentication mechanism, pricing, blockchain access type, development facility and scalability factors are compared amongst key BaaS platforms.

In summary, as Azure and AWS have already established cloud infrastructure, they are in a strong position than other services. Alternative, an increase of on-premise (local database) use intensify the usage of Oracle, IBM and SAP services. However, service provided by Azure and AWS is costly while SAP provides relatively cheaper service. As BaaS platforms' security, cost and efficiency are changing rapidly, a stable release of enterprise BaaS platforms will open more scopes for comparison. Next section will discuss the future scopes, research directions and recommendations to help choosing efficient BaaS platform.

Table 1. BaaS platform vs Hosting platform availability comparison

	Ethereum	Quorum	Corda	Hyperledger fabric	Multichain	Digital asset
AWS	√	√	√	√		
Azure	√	√	√	√	√	
Google	√			√		√
HPE			√			
IBM				√		
Oracle				√		
SAP				√		

Table 2. Comparison of BaaS platforms

	Azure	AWS	IBM	Oracle	SAP
Major partner	Corda, Blockapps, GoChain, Consensys	Cisco, Intel, Keleido, Corda, R3, Blockapps	SecureKey Technologies, Canadian banks	Tron, Aurora, Steemit, Pantera	Intel, UPS, HPE, Airbus
Major user	Xbox, 3 M and Insurwave	T mobile and Guidewire	Arab Jordan Investment Bank, CargoSmart, Certified Origins, Intelipost, Nigeria Customs	commercial bank Banco de Chile, Circulor, SERES, and CDEL, HealthSync	
Authentication and authorization	Active Directory	Identity and Access Management	IBM Secured Services Containers	Identity federation	Service Key
Pricing	Subscription plan and pay as per sue	Pay as per use	Monthly Subscription, Free trial	$0.75 pay as you go	
Blockchain type	Permissioned	Permissioned	Permissioned	Permissioned, Consortium	Permissionless
Development facility	High with Microsoft development kit	Medium, limited only with AWS kit	IBM Bluemix development platform	Hyperledger Fabrik SDK	Not yet Released
Scalability	High with all Microsoft products	Provide API for quick node creation	IBM Smart Cloud only		

5 Future Research Challenges and Risk Factors

Three major problems of blockchain technologies, as inherited in its architecture, are lack of scalability [3, 42], lack of interoperability [3, 43] and its antithetic stand against the notion of green computing [44, 45]. On the contrary, despite its widespread adoption, cloud computing also suffers from varies limitations such as lack of standardisation leading to vendor lock-in, security and privacy concern as well as data ownership and locality issue. While both the technologies are relatively immature, integration of both may give birth to new complexities in terms of technical aspects.

Blockchain highly suffers from scalability problem due to its capped transaction latency as well as consensus approach – as injected in its architecture to provide better security and to eliminate double spending problem [42]. Many research have been conducted so far to overcome this issue, keeping the base technology unaltered as it has already been proven to be highly secure. Recent advancement in the development of Bitcoin's lightning networks (LN) and similar technologies forecasted to play a vital role in addressing this issue. In a LN [42], direct transactions between two parties can take place in a tête-à-tête fashion, via a payment channel constructed in a separate (second) layer on top of the base layer of the chain. These transactions are considered as intermediate transactions which are not subject to normal consensus approach. As a result, the transactions are "instantaneous". That being said, they are still relatively slow compared to fiat currency transactions such as those facilitated by Visa. While the intermediate transactions broadcasted to the nodes of the peer-to-peer network for consensus, the final balance needs to be validated and verified by the nodes for settlement on the base chain once a channel is closed. With the help onion style routing, it is possible to perform LN transactions amongst the peers who are not "directly" connected by any LN channel between themselves, while maintaining the same level of privacy. However, the success of LN depends on the level of future technological maturity as well as the rate of adoption. BaaS can play an important role in this regard, by implicitly increasing the LN adoption trend.

Because tokens or coins exist only on their respective native chains, there is no straightforward method to swap two different tokens or coins or (transaction) data of different blockchain ecosystems. However, the recent development of Atomic Swaps [43] holds the potentials of addressing the interoperability problem to some extent. The term "Atomic" has been taken from database systems where atomicity means an operation (i.e. swap of two different cryptocurrencies in this case) will happen either completely or not at all. LN network powered atomic swaps also support off-chain scaling. Thus, both LN and Atomic Swaps together – if the technologies mature as expected – possess great potentials to accelerate BaaS adoption.

Most of the blockchain consensus approaches, including the most widely use Proof-of-Work (PoW), demand a tremendous amount of power consumption. Thus, its antithetic stand against the notion of green computing is highly critiqued [44]. However, if the tasks associated to consensus are outsourced from the cloud nodes via BaaS, which are already being run anyway, can save the "extra" demand of electricity needed for this purpose [45].

One of the major problems of cloud computing, as stated above, is the lack of standardisation leading to vendor lock-in i.e. lack of interoperability and portability. A vendor lock-in takes place when altering the cloud service provider becomes either impossible or highly expensive. Such situations mostly happen when there are non-standard proprietary services offered by the cloud service providers or if there are no viable alternatives. With the maturity of the cloud technology, while "generic" cloud services today is far more standardised than it was in the past, this is not the case for specific cloud services such as BaaS. Thus, lack of standardisation may still remain as a major challenge and risk factor for BaaS. While technologies like atomic swaps may be applied to address this problem, the viability has not yet been measured and it remains uncertain concerning to what extent atomic swaps can help.

Since BaaS is not primarily aimed to facilitate cryptocurrency transactions, rather the targeted applications are in the domain of non-monetary data transactions and storage, it is not going to be a subject to money-laundering or other financial regulations. However, both blockchain and cloud computing being distributed in nature, they are subject to data ownership, data localisation and data privacy regulations, especially in regards to EU General Data Protection Regulation (GDPR) and similar other regulations in various legal jurisdictions [42, 43].

To surmise, cloud computing, blockchain technologies and the fusion of both i.e. Blockchain-as-a-Service (BaaS) are still considered as immature technologies. Thus, the fusion possesses significant risk factors and the future adoption trend of it significantly depends on many aspects including legal and regulatory ones.

Finally, the study suggests the following key considerations while choosing a BaaS platform:

1. Feasibility of the BaaS platform to solve real-world problems.
2. Scalability of the BaaS platform to host ever-increasing hosts (nodes).
3. Availability of the community support of a BaaS platform.
4. Feasibility of the BaaS platform from coding or modification perspectives.
5. Adaptability with the existing technologies.
6. Accessibility (public, private or consortium) of a BaaS platform.
7. Security and privacy of a BaaS platform.

6 Conclusions

By briefly introducing both the blockchain and the cloud computing technologies, the paper then presents the concept of Blockchain-as-a-Service (BaaS) – the fusion of both the technologies. A comprehensive survey of the current status of BaaS in terms of technological development, applications, market potentials and so forth was also presented. To form an evaluative judgement, the paper also compared various BaaS platforms such as Microsoft Azure Ethereum Blockchain-as-a-Service (EBaaS), Azure Blockchain Workbench - Microsoft Flow (Ether.Camp) and Logic Apps (BlockApps), Amazon AWS, Amazon Quantum Ledger Database (QLDB), Amazon Managed Blockchain, IBM BaaS, Hewlett Packard (HP) Mission Critical Distributed Ledger Technology (MCDLT), Oracle Blockchain Cloud Service (OBCS), SAP-Cloud-Platform Blockchain Service and

SAP HANA Blockchain Service. The paper also attempts to forecast the trajectory of adoption of BaaS and its challenges as well as risk factors. Finally, future research directions are outlined.

In future, our goal is to establish an access control aware personal information access platform with BaaS architecture. In addition, future studies will consider R3, HPE R3, BitSE, Blocko, PayStand, Blockstream and other BaaS platforms. In our future studies, energy efficiency and privacy preservation in blockchain technology will be our main concern.

References

1. Nakamoto, S.: Bitcoin: a peer-to-peer electronic cash system, October 2008. http://www.bitcoin.org/bitcoin.pdf
2. Miraz, M.H., Ali, M.: Applications of blockchain technology beyond cryptocurrency. Ann. Emerg. Technol. Comput. **2**, 1–6 (2018). https://doi.org/10.33166/AETiC.2018.01.001
3. Donald, D.C., Miraz, M.H.: Restoring Direct Holdings and Unified Pricing to Securities Markets with Distributed Ledger Technology. Chinese University of Hong Kong Faculty of Law Research Paper (2019)
4. Miraz, M.H., Donald, D.C.: Application of blockchain in booking and registration systems of securities exchanges. In: IEEE International Conference on Computing, Electronics & Communications Engineering (IEEE iCCECE 2018), pp. 35–40. IEEE, University of Essex, Southend (2018). https://doi.org/10.1109/iCCECOME.2018.8658726
5. Onik, M.M.H., Miraz, M.H., Kim, C.-S.: A recruitment and human resource management technique using blockchain technology for industry 4.0. In: Proceedings of the Smart Cities Symposium (SCS-2018), pp. 11–16. IET, Manama, Bahrain (2018). https://doi.org/10.1049/cp.2018.1371
6. Onik, M.M.H., Aich, S., Yang, J., Kim, C.-S., Kim, H.-C.: Blockchain in healthcare: challenges and solutions. In: Big Data Analytics for Intelligent Healthcare Management, pp. 197–226. Elsevier, London (2019). https://doi.org/10.1016/B978-0-12-818146-1.00008-8
7. Yang, J., Onik, M., Lee, N.-Y., Ahmed, M., Kim, C.-S.: Proof-of-familiarity: a privacy-preserved blockchain scheme for collaborative medical decision-making. Appl. Sci. **9**, 1370 (2019). https://doi.org/10.3390/app9071370
8. Al-Zaben, N., Onik, M.M.H., Yang, J., Lee, N.-Y., Kim, C.-S.: General data protection regulation complied blockchain architecture for personally identifiable information management. In: International Conference on Computing, Electronics & Communications Engineering 2018 (iCCECE 2018), pp. 72–88. IEEE, Southend (2018). https://doi.org/10.1109/iCCECOME.2018.8658586
9. Onik, M.M.H., Kim, C.-S., Lee, N.-Y., Yang, J.: Privacy-aware blockchain for personal data sharing and tracking. Open Comput. Sci. **9**, 80–91 (2019). https://doi.org/10.1515/comp-2019-0005
10. Onik, M.M.H., Ahmed, M.: Blockchain in the era of industry 4.0. In: Mohiuddin Ahmed, A.-S.K.P. (ed.) Data Analytics: Concepts, Techniques, and Applications, pp. 259–298. CRC Press, Boca Raton (2018)
11. Miraz, M.H., Ali, M.: Blockchain enabled enhanced IoT ecosystem security. In: International Conference on Emerging Technologies in Computing 2018 (iCETiC 2018), pp. 38–46. IEEE, London Metropolitan University, London (2018). https://doi.org/10.1007/978-3-319-95450-9-3

12. Miraz, M.H.: Blockchain: Technology Fundamentals of the Trust Machine. Machine Lawyering, Chinese University Hong Kong, 23 December 2017. https://doi.org/10.13140/RG.2.2.22541.64480/2
13. Mccallister, E., Grance, T., Scarfone, K.: Guide to Protecting the Confidentiality of Personally Identifiable Information (PII) Recommendations of the National Institute of Standards and Technology (2010). https://doi.org/10.6028/NIST.SP.800-122
14. Mell, P., Grance, T.: The NIST definition of cloud computing (2011)
15. Ali, M., Miraz, M.H.: Cloud computing applications. In: Manikandan, A. (ed.) Proceedings of the International Conference on Cloud Computing and eGovernance, pp. 1–8. Internet City, Dubai, United Arab Emirates (2013)
16. Ali, M., Miraz, M.H.: Recent advances in cloud computing applications and services. Int. J. Cloud Comput. (IJCC) 1, 1–12 (2014)
17. The Global Market for Blockchain (2018–2023): Projected to Expand at a CAGR of 80.2% - ResearchAndMarkets.com | Business Wire. https://www.businesswire.com/news/home/20181210005600/en/Global-Market-Blockchain-2018-2023-Projected-Expand-CAGR
18. Samaniego, M., Deters, R.: Blockchain as a Service for IoT (2016). ieeexplore.ieee.org
19. Rimba, P., Tran, A., Weber, I., Staples, M., Ponomarev, A., Xu, X.: Comparing blockchain and cloud services for business process execution (2017). ieeexplore.ieee.org
20. Lahiri, S.K., Chen, S., Wang, Y., Dillig, I.: Formal Specification and Verification of Smart Contracts for Azure Blockchain (2018)
21. Blockchain Technology and Applications | Microsoft Azure. https://azure.microsoft.com/en-us/solutions/blockchain/
22. Philip, J., Shah, D.: Implementing signature recognition system as SaaS on microsoft azure cloud. In: Balas, V.E., Sharma, N., Chakrabarti, A. (eds.) Data Management, Analytics and Innovation. AISC, vol. 808, pp. 479–488. Springer, Singapore (2019). https://doi.org/10.1007/978-981-13-1402-5_36
23. Azure Integration Opens Blockchain Firm Kaleido to 80% of Cloud Market – CoinDesk. https://www.coindesk.com/azure-integration-opens-blockchain-firm-kaleido-to-80-of-cloud-market
24. Blockchain on AWS. https://aws.amazon.com/partners/blockchain/
25. Everything Enterprises Need to Know About Amazon's Blockchain as a Service. https://media.consensys.net/everything-enterprises-need-to-know-about-amazons-blockchain-as-a-service-9bd740e09276
26. Buyya, R., Ranjan, R., Calheiros, R.N.: InterCloud: utility-oriented federation of cloud computing environments for scaling of application services. In: Hsu, C.-H., Yang, L.T., Park, J.H., Yeo, S.-S. (eds.) ICA3PP 2010. LNCS, vol. 6081, pp. 13–31. Springer, Heidelberg (2010). https://doi.org/10.1007/978-3-642-13119-6_2
27. Narayanaswami, C., Nooyi, R., Raghavan, S.G., Viswanathan, R.: Blockchain Anchored Supply Chain Automation (2019). ieeexplore.ieee.org
28. IBM Blockchain Platform | IBM. https://www.ibm.com/blockchain/platform
29. IBM Blockchain Platform locations. https://console.bluemix.net/docs/services/blockchain/reference/ibp_regions.html#ibp-regions-locations
30. IBM Blockchain Platform 2.0 Beta: Run your blockchain N/W in 10 Simple Steps. https://medium.com/@mailganesh/ibm-blockchain-platform-2-0-beta-run-your-blockchain-n-w-in-10-simple-steps-5a549f8cc09e
31. Hewlett Packard Enterprise Introduces Blockchain as-a-Service Solution for Enterprises NYSE:HPE. https://www.globenewswire.com/news-release/2017/11/10/1184733/0/en/Hewlett-Packard-Enterprise-Introduces-Blockchain-as-a-Service-Solution-for-Enterprises.html
32. Blockchain Cloud Service | Oracle Cloud. https://cloud.oracle.com/en_US/blockchain/features

33. What is a Blockchain Oracle? – Leon Johnson – Medium. http://medium.com/@leon. johnson/what-is-a-blockchain-oracle-8d7b94d55bf
34. SAP Blockchain Applications and Services. https://www.sap.com/products/leonardo/block-chain.html
35. SAP HANA Blockchain: Technical Overview | SAP Blogs. https://blogs.sap.com/2018/08/28/sap-hana-blockchain-technical-overview/
36. Kotas, C., Naughton, T., Imam, N.: A comparison of Amazon Web Services and Microsoft Azure cloud platforms for high performance computing (2018). ieeexplore.ieee.org
37. Sefraoui, O., Aissaoui, M., Eleuldj, M.: Comparison of multiple iaas cloud platform solutions. In: WSEAS (2012). wseas.us
38. Fowley, F., Pahl, C., Jamshidi, P., Fang, D., Liu, X.: A classification and comparison framework for cloud service brokerage architectures (2018). ieeexplore.ieee.org
39. Khelaifa, A., Benharzallah, S., Kahloul, L., Euler, R., Laouid, A., Bounceur, A.: A comparative analysis of adaptive consistency approaches in cloud storage. J. Parallel Distrib. Comput. **129**, 36–49 (2019)
40. Singh, I., Lee, S.-W.: Comparative requirements analysis for the feasibility of blockchain for secure cloud. In: Kamalrudin, M., Ahmad, S., Ikram, N. (eds.) APRES 2017.CCIS, vol. 809, pp. 57–72. Springer, Singapore (2018). https://doi.org/10.1007/978-981-10-7796-8_5
41. AWS vs AZURE vs Oracle Blockchain Solution Offering: Comparison. https://101block-chains.com/aws-vs-azure-vs-oracle-blockchain/#prettyPhoto
42. Miraz, M.H., Donald, D.C.: LApps: technological, legal and market potentials of blockchain lightning network applications. In: Proceedings of the 3rd International Conference on Information System and Data Mining (ICISDM2019). ACM, University of Houston, USA (2019)
43. Miraz, M., Donald, D.C.: Atomic cross-chain swaps: development, trajectory and potential of non-monetary digital token swap facilities. Ann. Emerg. Technol. Comput. **3**, 11–18 (2019). https://doi.org/10.33166/AETiC.2019.01.005
44. Miraz, M.H., Excell, P.S.: Evaluation of green alternatives for blockchain Proof-of-Work (PoW) approach. In: International Conference on Green Communications and Computing (MIC-Green 2019), Istanbul, Turkey (2019)
45. Onik, M.M.H., Al-Zaben, N., Phan Hoo, H., Kim, C.-S.: MUXER—a new equipment for energy saving in ethernet. Technologies **5**, 74 (2017). https://doi.org/10.3390/technolo-gies5040074

A Discussion on Blockchain Software Quality Attribute Design and Tradeoffs

John M. Medellin[✉] and Mitchell A. Thornton

Darwin Deason Cyber Security Institute, Southern Methodist University, Dallas, TX 75275, USA
johnmedellin@verizon.net, mitch@lyle.smu.edu

Abstract. The blockchain design pattern has many variations and is a concept that will continue to lead many implementations in the years to come. New design and implementation patterns are frequently being announced and the choices available continue to expand. The design patterns imply tradeoffs which are reviewed.

We begin by describing the components of a blockchain; network nodes, blocks and consensus in a concept. We further elaborate on the key characteristics of the various design areas that are available adding emphasis to those used in private blockchains.

The individual components can be designed in different ways and imply tradeoffs between such quality attributes as performance and security or availability. We conclude with an initial tradeoff matrix that identifies the quality attributes that one should look for in designing these software systems.

Keywords: Blockchain · Cyber-attacks · Secure software architectures · Software architecture attributes · Software design tradeoffs

1 Introduction

Blockchain has become a common "house-hold" word in the vocabulary of almost all technology. This relatively new pattern of data sharing and encapsulated validation has impacted many public and private organizations. What started with simple exchange in values through crypto-currencies has become a veritable eco-system of different design and implementation choices. An experienced designer must still consider the far-reaching implications of selecting one course of action over another.

From its roots, deep in distributed operating systems and databases through current implementation, the pattern for information hiding through encryption and sharing of that information with other parties has continued and is continuing to evolve through requirements that are sometimes unknown until implementation. The pattern has been made famous by the implementation of bitcoin, a crypto currency. In a primary objective, the pattern allows for transferring value between the peers through consensus and encryption of results in a cumulative event ledger.

However, in addition to exchanging value concepts, the pattern is also very useful for sharing secrets or other information between participants. This particular sharing has been adopted by researchers and industry advocates for transmitting sensitive or

M. H. Miraz et al. (Eds.): iCETiC 2019, LNICST 285, pp. 19–28, 2019.

private information between trusted parties in a group [1]. An example of this particular sharing is the transmission of PKI (private key infrastructure) keys in a network where only the intended receiver can decode such a transmission and by virtue of the blockchain pattern cannot repudiate (negate receipt) of that specific information. Furthermore, a block is mathematically bound with subsequent blocks through progressive hashing. The cumulative effect of this is to make the transaction a permanent one in the event registry.

This objective of this paper is to segment the key software quality attributes and associated tradeoffs a designer should consider when architecting a solution with this pattern in mind. As mentioned above, the standard is evolving and will continue to do so for the foreseeable future. We discuss our assessment of these key tradeoff patterns and provide a matrix that identifies the ones that should be especially considered in software design. We however do remind the reader that these are only considerations not to be omitted in addition to consideration of all software quality attributes for any solution design.

2 Related Work

Many variations have been had to the famous Nakamoto [2] paper; the precursor to the famous bitcoin series of crypto currencies. This first paper on the nature of exchange of value through the blockchain design pattern has been adopted and now constitutes several billion currency units of value in over 700 crypto exchanges around the world; bitcoin being the most famous.

Since Nakamoto in 2008, most of the implementations of blockchain have had crypto currency as their target. However, in recent studies, the design pattern has begun to be adopted as a means to transmit data while preserving the key attributes of privacy and encryption. Indeed, many technology implementations have begun to look at this design pattern as a means to protect private exchange of information between interested parties [3, 4].

A significant difference in implementation patterns exists when a private blockchain is implemented versus a public blockchain [5]. In a public blockchain environment, parties do not necessarily have to know or trust each other in order to exchange value. Rather they can exchange by creating a block that is cryptographically validated by others in the network known as miners who are incented to validate by receiving shares of crypto currency for the one that validates the block first.

In contrast in a private exchange of data, the parties wish to know and trust each other before the exchange happens. Some examples of private blockchains include distribution of sign-on credentials [1] or authentication of agents delivering content on a home [6]. In these cases, the "value" to be exchanged is a secret or information that is only known to the sender and receiver [7] and potentially to other trusted parties in the closed network of operation for the blockchain.

As previously mentioned, significant amounts of intellectual capital have been spent on public blockchains. However, our focus is the private blockchain as a means to guarantee key properties of secure transmission models. We have written about usage of this design patterns in previous work and have focused mostly on the consensus architecture requirements and implementation [8].

Our previous work was dedicated to modeling different consensus algorithms and their impact on resource consumption. Most of the literature compares those algorithms to the Byzantine General's Problem [9] since it has become a pseudo-standard for measuring performance characteristics in newer algorithms. In this work however, we expand the scope of our discussion to include the other aspects of the blockchain architecture requirements in relation to Private exchanges. In a later section we discuss the block, smart contract, network, consensus and cryptography aspects.

3   Design Considerations

There is some variability in the definition of components required for a successful implementation. However, there is general agreement that the components required for the pattern to work include:

- A block architecture; the contents and specifications of the actual block of data to be transmitted [10].
- The scope and specifications of the smart contract; a smart contract is a reference to a set of procedures that the block will operate or has been operated in an offline fashion [11].
- The consensus model; the process whereby the participants agree in adding the new block to the chain [12].
- The network of participants; the group of valid members that can perform the basic operations of exchange and validation [13].
- The cryptography algorithm; the method for encrypting the block by carrying forward necessary information, a mathematical formula result and a unique number a "nonce" or number that is only used once [14].

3.1   General Architecture Requirements by Component

A brief description of each component was previewed above, this section discusses them in more detail.

1. Block: this is the specific unit of information that is "chained" by reference to the prior block. The block must be able to contain the following components (Fig. 1 below from ethereum.org):
   a. A mathematical reference to the prior block, usually in a part of the encryption result from that prior block.
   b. A mathematical reference to a unique number included as input into the block encryption algorithm (the "nonce").
   c. A mathematical reference to the actual data being encrypted.

The result of the encryption algorithm (for example RSA, or SHA-512 or SHA-256 [15]) as required by the overall parameters of the implementation and combining the three previous components.

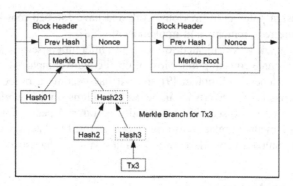

Fig. 1. Blockchain architecture.

2. Smart Contract: this is an optional item but one which is quite popular in business transaction processing. The smart contract is a block that defines a set of procedures in the actual data payload or a reference to another part of the blockchain with those references. The smart contract, when invoked by a special block-type, will produce a result that operates on the input data of that other block. The smart contract may contain the algorithm for processing the additional data or may reference a specific location for those instructions [16].
3. Network: Network in this context means the group of members that are on-boarded, validated, able to operate and off-boarded in the blockchain [17].
4. Consensus Model: This is the method whereby sufficient proof of validity is provided by a given set of participants in order to append the block and commit it to permanent storage in the chain. The two most popular ones appear to be Proof of Work (PoW) [18] in public blockchains and Byzantine Fault Tolerance Consensus (BFTC) [19] in private. Discussion of these details is beyond this paper but in a succinct explanation is that PoW deals with presentment of sufficient available computation usage to validate the block while BFTC deals with validation of voting by valid voter nodes [13].
5. Encryption Method: This pertains to the mathematical technique used to encapsulate the block into a number that is computationally inefficient to derive before the next block is appended to the chain [20].

Next, we will describe each one of the above components in light of variations that can be included in the implementation of those blockchains.

3.2   Key Variability Parameters by Architecture Component

Each of the architecture patterns has a variety of choices that ultimately influence the achievement of objectives in the blockchain implementation. The major component variabilities and impacts are discussed below.

1. Block: the block architecture itself is a major influencer on the objectives. On one hand, the block needs to be sized appropriately in order to include the necessary data. On the other however, if the block is too large the impact is felt in encryption

computation and latency of transmission [18]. Still on the other hand, a large block provides by definition a larger cyber-attack surface.

2. <u>Smart Contract</u>: The nature of the smart contract has a very large impact on both performance and attack resilience. By including a smart contract in the implementation complexity and additional overhead is acquired [13]:

   a. If the contract is wholly contained in the design then by definition, some of the prior blocks will need to be modified. A wholly contained smart contract is a type of block that is mutable as it processes and receives the effect of transactions.

   b. If the contract has a reference to a third location, the attack surface is expanded, performance could be impacted by additional steps to be taken in retrieval and update of external entities and finally, for subsequent block encryption, this result must be taken into consideration so the cryptography rules can continue unimpaired.

3. <u>Network</u>: the variability in the network aspect is the rules for adding/processing/deleting nodes/actors in the chain. This might seem to be the most secure but it is where Impostor and Sybil [7] attacks have most frequently come from. The variability in private blockchain comes as a function of the complexity to join versus the usability of the method. A strict adherence to high trust necessitates high complexity to belong in most cases. That additional overhead needs to be balanced with the usability of the blockchain.

4. <u>Consensus Model</u>: this is the area of highest variability in the implementation design. There are several dozen consensus models that have both computational overhead and complexity required to ensure agreement without tampering. Several discussions on these algorithms are out there [21, 22].

5. <u>Encryption Method</u>: most of the blockchain patterns defined will use accepted methods of cryptography and these are well documented [15]. The biggest issue identified has been the potential for quantum computing usage to break those algorithms. Several studies exist on post-quantum cryptography and we strongly suggest incorporating some of those initial rules into the design [23].

3.3 Software Architecture Quality Attributes

The Software Engineering Institute (SEI) has published guidelines for designing software systems with emphasis on architecture [24]. They are as follows:

1. <u>Availability</u>; the system is there and ready for interaction.
2. <u>Modifiability</u>; the system is able to be altered.
3. <u>Testability</u>; includes facilities for validation of results.
4. <u>Interoperability</u>; able to interact with other systems.
5. <u>Security</u>; resilience to cyber-attack.
6. <u>Performance</u>; achieves SLA targets.
7. <u>Usability</u>; user able to use system for designated purpose.
8. (Optional) <u>Extensibility</u>; able to extend functionality beyond its original enterprise level scope.

These attributes are key in determining the quality of the software system and usually work against each other (for example, performance vs security). Our main contribution in this paper is the focus of our next section; how do these tradeoffs work to enhance or deter each other.

4 Quality Attribute Tradeoffs

Software Quality Attributes will drive decisions that will shape the final solution [25]. In this section, we discuss the overall tradeoff process while also elaborating on the tradeoffs that are more prevalent in the blockchain design pattern.

4.1 Architecture Design Implies Tradeoffs

Architecture design implies tradeoffs between quality attributes in order to deliver a solution that reasonably complies with stated requirements. Quality attributes are typically in conflict with each other, for example, the testability attribute which includes verbose output might be in conflict with the security attribute which aims at hiding the attack surface (verbose output implies additional code that may be turned on to describe what's happening but this code could also be attacked). Another example would be the conflict between interoperability and performance. If a system is designed with very high level of interface abstraction and cohesion it might cause the system to use more cycles and impact performance requirements. These tradeoffs are even more specific for blockchain design and are discussed in the next section.

4.2 Key Blockchain Architecture Tradeoffs

These are some of the more important tradeoffs in blockchain architecture design. They are complemented further from the list provided by [26–28]:

1. Storage vs Computation: the amount of storage required by the block will affect the computation requirements; a larger block will require more computation to encrypt since there are more elements to encrypt. The design tradeoff in this case is *Usability vs Performance*.
2. Anonymity vs Trust: if the parties do not know each other they most likely need to verify proper identities through the use of public/private keys. This additional step will require a different design pattern. The design tradeoff in this case is *Interoperability vs Security*.
3. Incentive variations: by definition, the pattern requires distributed validation before blocks can get appended. Participants are usually incented to validate in order to carry out this function. In public chains, this means allocation of value to those participants which implies tracking value in the network. Similarly, in private, the incentive schemes vary, in the simplest form it could mean that the participant must validate prior blocks before theirs gets appended. The design tradeoff in this case is *Extensibility vs Usability*.

4. Degree of Distribution: In traditional Nakamoto patterns, the participants keep copies of the blockchain. However, there are different patterns which may require that smart contracts reside offline, on the chain in a centralized or other node. The design tradeoff in this case is *Interoperability vs Extensibility*.

5. Scalability vs Latency: These two attributes are closely tied into performance. In most cases, systems are designed for fulfilling a certain return time to users that is specified in requirements. When those limits are exceeded by larger scale (more volumes) the processing of blocks begins to lag, in some cases well beyond the expected requirements. The design tradeoff in this case is *Availability vs Performance*.

6. Immutability vs Process Functionality: This happens mainly on implementation of smart contracts. One of the key tenants of the architecture is that it is a permanent record. The inclusion of smart contracts can either violate (by having data offline or modifying previous blocks) or preserving it (by restating the smart contract, previous states and the of new state). The design tradeoff in this case is *Security vs Usability*.

7. Consensus Algorithm Selection: This tradeoff relates to the selection of the consensus approach to validation. In Nakamoto for example, the PoW constitutes both a security approach (51% of the omputation) and validation of the block (encryption/finding the "nonce") while in other approaches, this could be varied to provide a level of accuracy and protection that may not be as computationally intense. The design tradeoff in this case is *Security vs Performance*.

4.3   Architecture Tradeoff Matrix

We next proceed to defining the tradeoff attribute matrix. The numbers in cells refer to the discussion number in 4.2 above.

	Availability	Interoperability	Modifiability	Performance	Security	Testability	Usability	Extensibility
Availability	X			5				
Interoperability		X			2			4
Modifiability			X					
Performance	5			X	7		1	
Security		2		7	X		6	
Testability						X		
Usability				1	6		X	3
Extensibility		4					3	X

Fig. 2. Key architecture quality attribute tradeoff matrix

5 Tradeoff Discussion

Bearing in mind that a holistic view of all quality attributes is best practice [24] one should design for all quality attributes (by usage of patterns that facilitate them and embed in design [29]). However, some quality attributes are key in different architectures and will typically require additional tradeoff analysis to solve [30]. Figure 2 above depicts the major quality attribute tradeoffs identified in earlier sections of this document.

5.1 Key Attribute Tradeoff Discussion

From a purely numeric perspective, it is evident that performance, security and usability are the most impacted attributes. This intuitively makes sense since performance is taxed by adding requirements for security and usability (both of which require additional resources and potentially more design impacting performance decisions). Interoperability and extensibility are a close second in this tradeoff analysis. This also intuitively makes sense since blocks are dependent on each other to deliver functionality and the variety of design patterns requires extensibility to enable design those additional features. Finally, availability (although only one tradeoff is noted) is a very important quality attribute since if the blockchain system is unavailable or underperforms (as in the case of some crypto currencies) it will render the system unusable.

The modifiability and testability attributes do not seem to have specific tradeoffs (beyond those normal software systems require). This also intuitively makes sense since to our knowledge there are no specific requirements to modify code or test that code beyond what would be required in normal transactional or other types of systems.

5.2 Use of the Key Attribute Tradeoff Matrix

As mentioned above, all attributes should be considered in the design decisions (most design patterns incorporate them [31]). The objectives of this document are to convey which quality attributes seem to be more important from our research. The matrix should be used as an additional checkpoint to ensure these key issues are considered by the designer of blockchain systems.

References

1. Li, D., Du, R., Fu, Y., Au, M.H.: Meta-key: a secure data-sharing protocol under blockchain-based decentralized storage architecture. IEEE Netw. Lett. 1(1), 30–33 (2019)
2. Nakamoto, S.: Bitcoin: A Peer-to-Peer Electronic Cash System. www.bitcoin.org. Accessed 19 Mar 2019
3. Dinh, T.T.A., Wang, J., Chen, G., Liu, R., Ooi, B.C., Tan, K.-L.: BLOCKBENCH: A Framework for Analyzing Private Blockchains. https://arxiv.org/pdf/1703.04057.pdf. Accessed 19 Mar 2019

4. Dorri, A., Kanhere, S.S., Jurdak, R.: Towards an optimized blockchain for IoT. In: 2017 IEEE/ACM Second International Conference on Internet-of-Things Design and Implementation (IoTDI), pp. 173–178 (2017)

5. Medellin, J., Thornton, M.: Simulating resource consumption in three blockchain consensus algorithms. In: MSV 2017 International Conference on Modeling, Simulation & Visualization Methods, pp. 21–27 (2017)

6. Dorri, A., Kanhere, S.S., Jurdak, R., Gauravaram, P.: Blockchain for IoT security and privacy: the case study of a smart home. In: 2017 IEEE International Conference on Pervasive Computing and Communications Workshops (PerCom Workshops), pp. 618–623 (2017)

7. Salman, T., Zolanvari, M., Erbad, A., Jain, R., Samaka, M.: Security services using blockchains: a state of the art survey. IEEE Commun. Surv. Tutorials 21(1), 858–880 (2019)

8. Medellin, J., Thornton, M.: Performance characteristics of two blockchain consensus algorithms in a VMWare hypervisor. In: 2018 International Conference on Grid & Cloud Computing and Applications "GCA 2018", pp. 10–17 (2018)

9. Lamport, L., Shostak, R., Pease, M.: The byzantine generals problem. ACM Trans. Program. Lang. Syst. 4(3), 382–401 (1982)

10. Liang, X., Wu, T.: Exploration and practice of inter-bank application based on blockchain. In: The 12th International Conference on Computer Science & Education (ICCSE 2017), pp. 219–224 (2017)

11. Christidis, K., Devetsikiotis, M.: Blockchains and smart contracts for the internet of things. IEEE Access 4, 2292–2303 (2016)

12. Ongaro, D., Ousterhout, J.: In search of an understandable consensus algorithm. In: Proceedings ATC 2014 USENIX Annual Technical Conference. USENIX (2014)

13. Muralidharan, S., Murthy, C., Nguyen, B., et al.: Hyperledger Fabric: A Distributed Operating System for Permissioned Blockchains. https://arxiv.org/pdf/1801.10228.pdf. Accessed 19 Mar 2019

14. Ferguson, N., Schneier, B., Kohno, T.: Cryptography Engineering Design Principles and Practical Applications. Wiley Publishing Inc, Indianapolis (2010)

15. Stallings, W.: Cryptography and Network Security, Principles and Practice, 7th edn. Pearson Education Limited, London (2018)

16. Daniel, F., Guida, L.: A service-oriented perspective on blockchain smart contracts. IEEE Internet Comput. 23(1), 46–53 (2019)

17. Xia, Q., Sifah, E.B., Asamoah, K.O., Gao, J., Du, X., Guizani, M.: MeDShare: trust-less medical data sharing among cloud service providers via blockchain. IEEE Access 5, 14757–14767 (2017)

18. Fullmer, D., Morse, A.S.: Analysis of difficulty control in bitcoin and proof-of-work blockchains. In: 2018 IEEE Conference on Decision and Control (CDC), pp. 5988–5992 (2018)

19. Golosova, J., Romanovs, A.: The advantages and disadvantages of the blockchain technology. In: 2018 IEEE 6th Workshop on Advances in Information, Electronic and Electrical Engineering (AIEEE), pp. 1–6 (2018)

20. Johnsonbaugh, R.: Discrete Mathematics, 8th edn. Pearson Education Inc, New York (2018)

21. Ehmke, C., Wessling, F., Friedrich, C.M.: Proof of property – a lightweight and scalable blockchain protocol. In: 2018 IEEE/ACM 1st International Workshop on Emerging Trends in Software Engineering for Blockchain (WETSEB), pp. 48–51 (2018)

22. Ceccetti, E., et al.: Solidus: Confidential Distributed Ledger Transactions via PVORM CCS 2017, pp. 1–23, 30 October– 3 November 2017

23. Li, C.-Y., Chen, X.-B., Chen, Y.-L., Hou, Y.-Y., Li, J.: A new lattice-based signature scheme in post-quantum blockchain network. IEEE Access 7, 2026–2033 (2019)

24. Bass, L., Clements, P., Kazman, R.: Software Architecture in Practice: The SEI Series in Software Engineering, 3rd edn. Addison Wesley, Upper Saddle River (2012)
25. Cervantes, H., Kazman, R.: Designing Software Architectures; A Practical Approach: The SEI Series in Software Engineering. Pearson Education, Boston (2016)
26. Scriber, B.A.: A framework for determining blockchain applicability. IEEE Softw. **35**(4), 70–77 (2018)
27. Xu, X., Weber, I., Staples, M., Zhu, L., et al.: A taxonomy of blockchain-based systems for architecture design. In: Proceedings 2017 IEEE International Conference on Software Architecture, pp. 243–252 (2017)
28. Zheng, Z., Xie, S., Dai, H., Chen, X., Wang, H.: An overview of blockchain technology: architecture, consensus, and future trends. In: 2017 IEEE International Congress on Big Data (BigData Congress), pp. 557–564 (2017)
29. Booch, G.: Object-Oriented Analysis and Design with Applications. Addison Wesley Longman, Inc., Reading (1994)
30. Tian, J.: Software Quality Engineering; Testing, Quality Assurance and Quantifiable Improvement. IEEE Computer Society (2005)
31. Larman, C.: Applying UML and Patterns: An Introduction to Object-Oriented Analysis and Design and Iterative Development, 3rd edn. Pearson Education Inc, Upper River (2005)

An Efficient Peer-to-Peer Bitcoin Protocol with Probabilistic Flooding

Huy Vu[✉] and Hitesh Tewari

Trinity College Dublin, Dublin 2, Ireland
{vuhu, htewari}@tcd.ie

Abstract. Bitcoin was launched in 2009, becoming the world's first ever decentralized digital currency. It uses a publicly distributed ledger called the blockchain to record the transaction history of the network. The Bitcoin network is structured as a decentralized peer-to-peer network, where there are no central or supernodes, and all peers are seen as equal. Nodes in the network do not have a complete view of the entire network and are only aware of the nodes that they are directly connected to. In order to propagate information across the network, Bitcoin implements a gossip-based flooding protocol. However, the current flooding protocol is inefficient and wasteful, producing a number of redundant and duplicated messages. In this paper, we present an alternative approach to the current flooding protocol implemented by Bitcoin. We propose a novel protocol that changes the current flooding protocol to a probabilistic flooding approach. Our approach allows nodes to maintain certain probabilities of sending information to their neighbours, based on previous message exchanges between the nodes. Our experimental evaluation shows a reduction in the number of duplicated messages received by each node in the network and the total number of messages exchanged in the network, whilst ensuring that the reliability and resilience of the system were not negatively affected.

Keywords: Bitcoin · Peer-to-Peer · Flooding · Cryptocurrencies · Information propagation

1 Introduction

Cryptocurrencies, of which Bitcoin is the most popular, have risen greatly in popularity in recent times. With the popularization of cryptocurrencies comes an increase in daily users. As a result of this increase in daily users, countless more transactions are made within the network leading to an increase in network resources and power consumption by the systems in order to maintain the cryptocurrencies. For example, Bitcoin between 2011 and 2012 averaged approximately 7,000 transactions per day, but at the time of

This work was supported, in part, by Science Foundation Ireland grant 13/RC/2094 and co-funded under the European Regional Development Fund through the Southern Eastern Regional Operational Programme to Lero - the Irish Software Research Centre (www.lero.ie).

writing, Bitcoin currently averages approximately 270,000 transactions per day, with the daily trading value estimated at approximately $700 million[1].

Bitcoin uses a publicly shared distributed ledger known as the *blockchain* to maintain the transaction history in the network. Transactions in the network are grouped together and placed in *blocks*. Bitcoin uses proof-of-work (PoW) as its consensus mechanism [1]. In PoW, participants in the network are challenged to solve a computationally difficult problem, from which blocks are produced when solved. By successfully completing the PoW puzzle, the newly created block is then added to end of the already existing chain of blocks. The linking of the blocks to create the chain of blocks ensures a serial and chronological ordering of transactions, allowing all the nodes in the network to agree on a common ordering of transactions. The blockchain is maintained in a decentralized manner by all the nodes participating in the network.

As the Bitcoin network is structured as a decentralized peer-to-peer network (P2P), information is disseminated across the network through *gossip-based flooding* [2]. Nodes participating in the network do not have an entire view of the network. Instead of having an entire view of the network topology, nodes are only aware of the other nodes that they are directly connected to, known as their *neighbours*. Due to the decentralized nature of the network, if a node wants to broadcast new information across the network, they must follow Bitcoin's implementation of the flooding protocol. By following the flooding protocol implemented by Bitcoin, nodes will broadcast their desired information to each of their connected neighbours. Once received, the node's neighbours will then in turn broadcast the newly received information to their neighbours, who will then broadcast it to their neighbours until eventually the information is received by all the peers in the network [3]. However, this flooding protocol for information dissemination is wasteful, producing a large number of redundant and duplicated messages.

1.1 Our Contributions

In this paper, we present a novel protocol that aims to change the current flooding protocol implemented by Bitcoin. The proposed protocol changes the flooding protocol implemented by Bitcoin to a probabilistic flooding approach. The proposed probabilistic flooding approach is based on the idea that nodes in the Bitcoin network have a wide variance in the number of neighbours they are connected to. Therefore, if a node's neighbour is well-connected in the network, they are likely to already have the transaction that the node was going to transmit to it, making the message redundant. However, if a node's neighbour is less connected in the network, they may likely not have the transaction and may need the transmitting node to broadcast the transaction to them. As a result of the wide variance in the number of neighbours a node may have, we propose a probabilistic flooding approach where a node maintains a "probability of sending" for each of their neighbours based on previous message exchanges between the node and the neighbour. The main objective of the change in protocol is to reduce

---

[1] https://www.blockchain.com/charts/estimated-transaction-volume-usd?daysAverageString=7timespan=all.

the number of redundant and duplicated messages being generated in the network whilst ensuring that the reliability and resilience of the system is not negatively affected by the change in protocol.

1.2 Paper Structure

The remainder of the paper is structured as follows: Sect. 2 presents an overview of Bitcoin, Sect. 3 discusses the Bitcoin network and Information Propagation, Sect. 4 discusses related work, Sect. 5 presents our probabilistic flooding protocol, Sect. 6 evaluates our protocol and Sect. 7 concludes the paper.

2 Bitcoin Overview

Bitcoin was proposed in 2008 and launched in 2009, under the pseudonym Satoshi Nakamoto in their paper entitled "Bitcoin: A Peer-to-Peer Electronic Cash System" [1]. The objective of Bitcoin is to create a means of exchange, without dependence on a central authority, that could be transferred electronically in a secure, verifiable and immutable way. The most important attribute of Bitcoin is the decentralization nature of it - the lack of dependence on a central server or trusted parties. As mentioned in a forum post shortly after Bitcoin was launched, Satoshi wrote that "The root problem with conventional currency is all the trust that is required to make it work"[2].

In the following subsections, we will describe the main building blocks of the Bitcoin system.

2.1 Transactions

Transactions are the most important part of the Bitcoin system. Everything else in Bitcoin is designed so that transactions are able to be created, propagated, validated and added to the global distributed ledger used in Bitcoin (also known as the blockchain).

At an abstract level, a transaction essentially transfers bitcoins from one or more source accounts to one or more destination accounts. Each account is created from a public/private-key pair using public-key cryptography [3]. A *Bitcoin address* is derived from the public key of an account. The Bitcoin address is used to uniquely identify an account and is used as the destination account when receiving payment from other users. Ownership of the *private key* allows full control of the Bitcoin address associated with that private key. The private key can be used to move funds associated with the corresponding Bitcoin address by creating the digital signature that is required by transactions.

Transactions can be broken down into *transaction outputs*, *transaction inputs* and the *transaction ID*. The transaction inputs are the accounts of the payers and the transaction outputs is where the bitcoins are being sent to i.e. the payee's account. The transaction ID uniquely identifies each transaction [3]. Transaction outputs are fundamental in Bitcoin

---

[2] http://p2pfoundation.ning.com/forum/topics/bitcoin-open-source.

transactions. Transaction outputs are indivisible chunks of Bitcoin currency that are recorded on the blockchain and are seen as valid and spendable by the Bitcoin network. Unspent Transaction Outputs (*UTXO*) are available and spendable transaction outputs. A user's Bitcoin "balance" is the sum of all the UTXO associated with the user's Bitcoin address.

Transactions consume UTXO which in turn creates new transaction outputs that can be spent by the payee. Every output of a transaction will also contain one or more inputs that indicates where the Bitcoin originated from before the transaction.

In order to transfer bitcoins to an account, the public key of the payee's account must be listed as the destination of the transaction. The payer must also sign the transaction. They do this by digitally signing a hash of the previous transaction and the public key of the next owner [1].

In order for a transaction to be valid, the following criteria must be fulfilled by the outputs claimed and created:

– An output may be claimed at most once.
– New outputs are created solely as a result of a transaction.
– The sum of the values of the inputs has to be greater than or equal to the sum of the values of the newly allocated outputs[3] [3].

2.2 Blocks, Mining and Proof-of-Work

A block is a data structure that is composed of a set of transactions and a block header. Blocks on the blockchain are identified via the block header hash. When a new transaction is propagated through the Bitcoin network, it is stored in each node's local mempool. The Bitcoin mempool is a pool of unconfirmed transactions in the Bitcoin network. Each node has their own mempool. The transactions in the mempool may be valid transactions but are not yet confirmed by the Bitcoin network. The transactions are not seen as confirmed transactions until they are included in a block that is on the blockchain. The process in which transactions are taken from the mempool and included in blocks is known as *mining*. As more miners join the network, the difficulty of the PoW gets harder and harder[4], in such a way the average time to mine a block is approximately every 10 min [4].

The process of mining a block is a computationally difficult process. The nodes which attempt to mine a block, known as miners, must find the solution to Bitcoin's PoW problem. The PoW problem consists of finding an integer value, known as a *nonce*, that when combined with the block header, will provide a hash with a given number of leading zeroes, known as the difficulty [3]. As cryptographic hashes are a one-way function [5], the only solution for miners to find the nonce that will satisfy the difficulty of the block is to use a brute-force approach, testing different values for the nonce until a suitable hash is found. The nonce which satisfies the difficulty check of

---

[3] If the inputs are greater than the required outputs, miners may collect the difference as a transaction fee or may be sent back to the payee's address as change.

[4] It may also decrease in difficulty, depending on the average block creation rate of the previous 2,016 blocks.

the block, known as the golden nonce, is therefore very difficult to find but once found, is straight-forward to verify it.

Nodes within the network may sometimes have an inconsistent view of the blockchain due to the decentralization nature of the Bitcoin network. This inconsistency may occur when two nodes in the network discover and propagate different blocks at approximately the same time. The two different blocks will propagate through the Bitcoin network, arriving at nodes at different times. The nodes will accept the first block that they received and reject but save the other block when they eventually receive it [1]. Nodes in the network will now have a temporary inconsistent view of the blockchain, as there are now two blocks claiming to be the blockchain head. In order to resolve this inconsistency, nodes can work on either branch of the fork but are likely to work on the block that they received first [7]. The fork would likely be decided when the next block is mined and one branch becomes longer than the other. The longer branch will become the legitimate one and nodes working on the other branch will then switch to the longer one. This occurs as nodes always consider the longest chain to be the legitimate one and will keep working on extending it [1].

2.3   The Blockchain

Thus far, when blocks are mined and transactions are placed in the blocks, the blocks do not offer any synchronization or chronological ordering of the transactions. However, this changes when blocks are linked together sequentially, creating a chronological ordering over the blocks and therefore the transactions in the blocks [3]. This sequential formation of blocks is known as the blockchain [8]. When a block is created and propagated through the network, it is added to the blockchain by creating a reference to the latest block (the previous block) on the blockchain. The chaining of each block to the previous block is what creates a chronological ordering of transactions in the network. The referenced previous block is known as the *parent* block. Blocks may only have one parent block but can temporarily have multiple children during a blockchain fork. As every block references the previous block, the blockchain is made up of a single sequence of blocks from the first block, or the genesis block, to the latest generated block [8]. The distance between a block and the genesis block is referred to as its *block height*, and the block that is furthest away from the genesis block is known as the *blockchain head* [3] (Fig. 1).

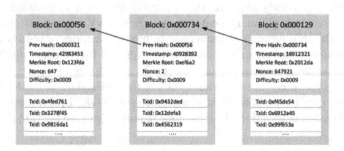

Fig. 1. Blockchain representation example [6]

3 The Bitcoin Network and Information Propagation

The Bitcoin network is structured as a decentralized P2P network. In a P2P network, nodes participating in the network are seen as peers. Peers are all treated as equal, with shared responsibility in providing network services. The Bitcoin network consists of over 10,000 nodes [9]. Each node in the network implements a version of the Bitcoin protocol through the use of a Bitcoin client. Although there are several Bitcoin clients available to use, the Bitcoin client used by the majority of the nodes in the network is Bitcoin Core, also known as the reference client or the Satoshi client.

Although all the peers in the network are equal, they may have different roles based on the different functions they support. For example, simplified payment verification (SPV) nodes do not keep a copy of the full blockchain and do not participate in mining. They are lightweight nodes that integrates the wallet and routing function, designed for peers with limited resources. In contrast, full nodes may be either a full blockchain node when it includes routing and full blockchain functions, or a solo miner when it includes routing, the full blockchain and mining functions [9]. However, in order to participate in the Bitcoin network, nodes must implement a routing function[5]. The routing function includes network discovery of new peers, establishing inbound and outbound connections, validating transactions and blocks and propagating information through the network [9].

When new transactions or blocks are created in the Bitcoin network, they must be broadcasted to the entire network to inform the peers in the network of the new transactions/block. As the Bitcoin network is a decentralized P2P network, there is no central authority to distribute the transactions/blocks to every peer in the network. As nodes in the network are only aware of their directly connected neighbours, Bitcoin implements a gossip-based flooding protocol to propagate transactions and blocks across the network.

When propagating information across the Bitcoin network, a node maintains a message queue for all of their connected neighbours. This message queue may contain different types of messages that a node may want to send to their neighbours, such as transaction hashes or block hashes etc. Along with the message queue, there is a timer associated with each neighbour. All the messages within the message queue will be sent to the associated neighbour when the timer elapses. The time-out is calculated using a Poisson distribution [10].

In order for a node not to send the same transactions or blocks that their neighbouring peers may already have, transactions and blocks are not forwarded directly to their neighbours. Instead, an **INVentory** message or **INV** message is sent to their neighbours. The INV message transmits one or more inventories of objects known to the transmitting peer and are now available to be requested from the transmitting peer if the receiving node is missing one or more of the inventories of objects in the INV message [3]. If the receiving node requires any of the transactions or blocks within the INV message, they will respond to the sender node with a **GETDATA** message, which contains the hashes of the information the node requires. Once the GETDATA message

---

[5] Users may turn off the routing function in Bitcoin Core if desired.

is received, the sender node will send the requested block or transaction via individual *block* or *tx* messages [3]. However, if a node receives an INV message that contains transactions and blocks that the node already possesses, the node will simply ignore the INV message, and not respond with a message to the sender node.

Although sending INV messages to neighbouring peers will prevent the peers from receiving duplicate transactions, peers may still receive duplicate INV messages for the same transaction. This occurs as a node's neighbours does not know which transactions the node currently has or is missing. Therefore, if a node's neighbour recently received new transactions, they will add it to the INV message that will be sent to the node as they assume the node might not have the transactions they just received. As every node's neighbours may think the same, a node may receive an INV message for the same transaction from all of their connected neighbours (125 worst case) whereas 1 INV message would have sufficed to send the transaction to the node (Fig. 2).

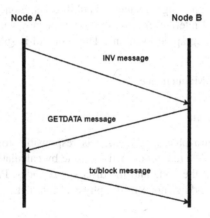

Fig. 2. Messages exchanged between two nodes for information propagation

4 Related Work

Fadhil et al. present a new protocol, Bitcoin Clustering Based Super Node (BCBSN) as a mechanism to speed up information propagation in the Bitcoin network [13]. In this protocol, the Bitcoin network is divided into geographically diverse clusters. Within each cluster, there is a cluster head or super node responsible for maintaining the cluster. Each peer is connected to a cluster head, and each cluster head is connected to other cluster heads. The claim is that this would reduce the propagation delay as it reduces the number of non-compulsory hops that blocks, or transactions require to reach all the peers in the network. Nodes at each cluster are geographically localized, with the hope of reduction in the link latencies between nodes at each cluster. The BCBSN protocol resulted in a reduction of the transaction propagation time variances, compared to that of the normal Bitcoin network. Possible limitations of the BCBSN protocol may include a successful attack on a cluster head. By successfully attacking a cluster head, the nodes in the associated cluster are unable to connect to connect to the rest of the network as the cluster head was their means of contact to the rest of the network. If the cluster head was infiltrated by a malicious node, they have essentially partitioned the nodes within the cluster from the rest of the network and may carry out an eclipse attack [15]. As nodes in the clusters are geographically localized, this may make the network highly prone to partitioning.

Following on from BCBSN, Fadhil et al. proposed a proximity-aware extension to the current bitcoin protocol, named Bitcoin Clustering Based Ping Time Protocol (BCBPT) [14]. Based on their previous work BCBSN, which placed nodes in clusters based on their geographic location, BCBPT will place nodes in clusters based on their ping latency. Nodes that are geographically close could be quite far away from each other on the physical internet [14]. The results of BCBPT show that the protocol maintains an improvement in variances of delay over their previous work, BCBSN. This may be due to the fact that in BCBSN, clusters are based on geographic location, meaning they could be close geographically but far away on the physical internet. By creating clusters based on ping latencies, Fadhil et al. concluded that proximity awareness in the physical internet improves delivery latency with a higher probability than clusters based on geographic locations. The protocol is split into two phases:

1. Distance Calculation
2. Cluster Creation and Maintenance

4.1 Distance Calculation

In the distance calculation phase, each node is responsible for gathering proximity knowledge regarding discovered nodes. This is done by calculating the distance in the physical internet between the node and the discovered nodes. Proximity is defined as how far a node is from another node in the physical internet.

4.2 Cluster Creation and Maintenance

When joining the network for the first time, a node N will learn about other available Bitcoin nodes in the network from a list of DNS services. The node N will calculate the proximity distance to each of the discovered nodes. The node N will then send a JOIN request to the closest node K of the discovered nodes. Once node N establishes a connection with node K, it will receive a list of IPs of nodes that is in the same cluster as node K. Node N will then connect to all the nodes in the cluster. If node N discovers a node that is physically closer than the current cluster, node N will leave to join the nearer cluster.

Although the transaction propagation time and variances are lowered in the proposed protocol, the same issues from BCBSN can be applied to the proposed protocol. As mentioned by Fadhil et al., they identify that eclipse and network partition attacks have great potential due to the clustering based on countries. An attacker might concentrate a number of bad peers within a cluster in order to create a malicious cluster on the network [14].

Marcal [10] proposes a new protocol for the dissemination of transactions in the Bitcoin network. The protocol proposes a bias to disseminate transactions to neighbours that are more likely to reach miners quickly, as miners are the nodes that need knowledge of the transactions in the network as they are responsible for placing the transactions in blocks, and subsequently placing the block on the blockchain.

The protocol encompasses three changes to the Bitcoin dissemination protocol:

1. Nodes maintain for each of their neighbours, a list of transactions sent by their neighbour and how long it took for these transactions to be included in a block.
2. Nodes maintain for each of their neighbours, the time it took to disseminate a new block to the node.
3. Use the metrics collected above to rank their neighbours and prioritise the dissemination of transactions based on the rankings.

The proposed protocol was able to reduce the bandwidth usage by 10.2% and reduce the number of messages exchange in the network by 41.5%. Some issues with the aforementioned protocol is that the commit time of transactions may increase as transactions are reaching miners, but may not necessarily reach the miner who is going to mine the next block [10].

Other related works focus on exploiting the current dissemination protocol in order to gain an advantage for the attacker or put the victim at a disadvantage. For example, Courtois and Bahack [11] indicate miners could have a specific mining strategy known as *selfish mining*. In selfish mining, nodes purposely withhold mined blocks from the network, only revealing the mined block(s) in a selective way which benefits the selfish miners. Eyal and Sirer [12] show that through the use of selfish mining, the selfish pool's reward exceeds its share of the networks computational power.

5   Probabilistic Flooding

As described in Sect. 3, when propagating a transaction through the network, an INV message will be sent to the node's neighbours 100% of the time. This flooding mechanism implemented by Bitcoin produces many duplicated INV messages being received by nodes in the network.

The solution and protocol change that we propose changes the current flooding mechanism approach that was described above to a probabilistic flooding approach. Our approach aims to maintain a probability for each of the node's neighbours. This probability is the probability that a node will send an INV message to the associated neighbour. The probability is calculated based on the number of INV messages sent to the neighbour and the number of GETDATA messages received in return from the neighbour.

Formula for Calculating a Neighbours Probability

$$neighbour\,Probility = \frac{total\,ttet\,Data\,From\,Neighbour}{total\,Inv\,sen\,to\,Neighbour}$$

The idea of sending INV messages based on probability is centered around the fact that nodes in the Bitcoin network have a large variance in the number of connected neighbours. A node may be well-connected, and in the best case, have 125 neighbours whereas another node may have as low as 8 neighbours. The node with 125 neighbours is more likely to have already received the transactions contained in the INV message that it received and therefore will not reply to the INV message with a GETDATA message. The idea of the protocol change to a probabilistic flooding approach is based on the criteria that well-connected nodes will already have the transactions contained in an INV message and will not need to receive an INV message 100% of the time, whereas a node that is less connected may need to receive an INV message the majority of the time.

For example in Fig. 3, node *A* will send an INV message to node *B* with a higher probability than sending an INV message to node *C*. This is due to the fact that node *B* has a total of three neighbours and is less connected than node *C*, who has a total of five neighbours. As node *C* is more well-connected, it is more likely that node *C* may already have the transactions contained in the INV messages, whereas node *B* is less likely to have the transactions as it has two less neighbours than node *C*. The probability is based on previous message exchanges between the nodes. Node A may have previously sent 54 INV messages to node *C* and may have only received 34 GET-DATA messages in return. In this case, the probability that node A will send an INV message to node *C*, based on the formula mentioned above, will be 63% (34/54). The probability of sending an INV message from node *A* to node *B* is also based on the exchange of previous messages between the two nodes. In this case, node *A* sent 77 INV messages to node *B*, whilst receiving 64 GETDATA messages in reply. Based on the formula of calculating neighbour probability, the probability node *A* will send an INV message to node B will be 83% (64/77).

From the example, node *B* replies to INV messages more times than node *C*, and therefore will have a higher probability of receiving an INV message in the future from node *A*. The higher probability can be attributed to the fact that node *B* only has three neighbours and is not as well-connected as node *C*, who has five neighbours. As node *B* has fewer neighbours, this leads to fewer options for which it may receive an INV message for certain transactions in the network, leading to a higher GETDATA response rate when it receives an INV message. Conversely, node *C* is better connected than node *B*, having five neighbours. This leads to more avenues for which node *C* may receive INV messages, therefore leading to a lower response rate to INV messages. As node *C* has more neighbours, this leads to a higher probability that they have already received the transactions contained in the INV message.

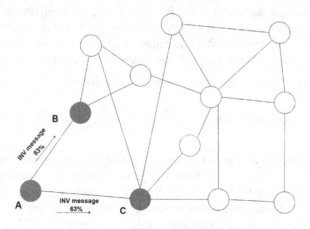

Fig. 3. Probabilistic flooding example

6   Evaluation

In order to test our protocol changes we ran a number of simulations. *Joao Marcal's bitcoin-simulator*[6] [10] supports the newest versions of Bitcoin and recorded a number of important metrics that would be vital to compare and contrast the current Bitcoin protocol, and the proposed probabilistic flooding approach. The metrics recorded by the Bitcoin simulator were as follows:

- Average number of INV messages sent per node
- Average total number of sent messages per node
- Percentage of duplicated messages received per node
- Total transactions created
- Percentage of transactions created and committed
- Total number of forks created

The simulator is an event-driven simulator, where the behaviour of each node in the network is defined by a deterministic state machine, that consumes events and produces events. Each cycle in the simulation represents a second in real-time. The default settings and the settings for which the results are formed are based on the following configurations:

- Number of nodes in the network - 625
- Number of miners - 5
- Minimum neighbourhood size of each node - 8
- Number of cycles - 208800

Algorithm 1 represents how the probability of sending an INV message to a specific neighbouring node is calculated.

Algorithm 1. Function to calculate the probability of sending INV message to each neighbouring node

---

1: **function** get probability(*myself, neighbouring_node*)
2:      *total_inv sent* ← *get total inv sent*(*myself, neighbouring node*)
3:      *total getdata received* ← *get total getdata received*(*myself, neighbouring node*)
4:      *probability_to send* ← *total getdata received/total inv sent*
5:      **return** *probability to send*

Algorithm 2 is the function that will determine whether or not a node will send an INV message to its neighbouring node. Algorithm 2 is called every cycle for every node, as long as the adjusted probabilistic flooding mechanism is enabled in the simulation. Algorithm 2 will firstly get the current time of the simulation. For each of the node's neighbours, the algorithm will receive the calculated probability of sending an INV message to that specific neighbour based on Algorithm 1. Associated with each neighbouring node is a timer which is calculated using a Poisson distribution [10]. The node will receive the timer for the neighbouring node and will determine whether or not the

---

[6] https://github.com/JoaoBraveCoding/bitcoin-simulator.

timer elapsed for sending a message to the neighbouring node, based on the current time received at the start of the algorithm. If the timer elapses and the probability of sending an INV message is satisfied, the node will send the INV message to the neighbouring node and increment the INV messages sent to that neighbour counter. This is to ensure that the data used in Algorithm 1 to calculate the probability of sending an INV message to neighbouring nodes is up to date. However, if the timer elapsed but the probability of sending is not satisfied, the INV message scheduled to be sent to the node is ignored.

As each cycle represents a second in real-time, the experiments were run for a simulation time of 58 h. The first five hours and the last five hours of the simulation were discarded in order to study the system in a stable state. The simulator is tuned to generate blocks at the Bitcoin desired rate of 1 block per 10 min, as well as creating 2 transactions per second.

Algorithm 2. Broadcast Inventory Messages

```
 1: function broadcast invs prob flooding(myself)
 2:     now ← get current_time()
 3:     for neighbour in neighbourhood do
 4:         probability to send ← get probability(myself, neighbour)
 5:         time to send ← get time to send(neighbour)
 6:         timeout ← now > time to send
 7:         send inv based on prob ← random.random() < probability to send
 8:         if timeout and send inv based on prob then
 9:             sim.send(myself, neighbour, IN V message)
10:             myself.increaseInvSentT oN eighbour(neighbour)
11:         if timeout and not send inv based on prob then
12:             myself.increaseIgnoredMessagesCount()
```

The most relevant and important metrics when comparing the two protocols are:

- **Percentage of Committed Transactions** is the most vital metric when comparing the two protocol changes. The percentage of committed transactions indicates whether or not every transaction that was created during the simulation period was eventually committed into a block. As Bitcoin is the most popular cryptocurrency and has a market cap of approximately 72$ billion, it is essential that every transaction that is created is eventually committed in a block to maintain the reliability of the system. The main objective of the protocol change is to reduce the number of redundant messages being exchanged on the network. However, if the protocol change negatively impacts the percentage of committed transactions, reducing the 100% commitment rate of transactions then regardless of the potential reduction of redundant messages, a less then 100% committed transactions rate would be detrimental to the system and unacceptable.
- **Total Number of Messages Sent Per Node** is an important metric when comparing the two protocols. As the main objective of the probabilistic flooding approach is to reduce the number of redundant messages exchanged on the network, comparing the total number of messages sent per node between the two protocols would indicate exactly how many messages were saved as a result from the protocol.

– **The Commit Time of Transactions** is also an important metric to consider when comparing the two protocols. The commit time represents the time between when a transaction was created to when it was placed in a block. As commit times of transactions is an extremely important aspect in cryptocurrencies, having an increased commit time when implementing the proposed probabilistic flooding approach may not be worth the trade off in potential messages saved within the network.

6.1 Percentage of Committed Transactions

As mentioned previously, the most important metric when comparing the proposed probabilistic flooding protocol to the current Bitcoin flooding protocol is the percentage of committed transactions. Both protocols produced a 100% transaction commitment rate, committing every transaction to a block during the simulation period. We can conclude from these results that the adjustment of the flooding protocol to a probabilistic flooding approach did not have an adverse effect on the number of committed transactions during the simulation. A 100% transaction commitment rate ensures that the system remains reliable when the probabilistic flooding approach is implemented.

6.2 Transaction Commit Time

Another important metric that was previously discussed when comparing the two protocols is the time taken to commit a transaction. Figure 4 represents the average time taken for a transaction to be committed into a block for the two protocols. As you can see from Fig. 4, the time taken to for a transaction to be committed into a block for both protocols were very similar. The small difference between the two protocols is negligible. This is very important as the results indicate that changing the flooding protocol to a probabilistic flooding approach does not have a negative effect on the transaction commitment time. As transaction commit time is an extremely important aspect for cryptocurrencies, if there was a significant increase in transaction commit time when changing to the probabilistic flooding approach, the potential reduction in redundant messages may not be worth the trade-off in increased transaction commit time.

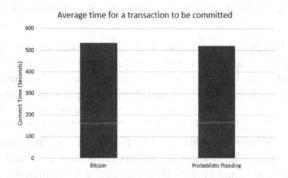

Fig. 4. Average time taken to commit a transaction.

6.3   Total Sent Messages

As mentioned in Sect. 1, the main objective of changing the current Bitcoin flooding protocol to the probabilistic flooding approach is to reduce the number of redundant and duplicated messages that are currently being generated in the Bitcoin network. Figure 5, represents the number of total sent messages gathered from our simulations for the two protocols.

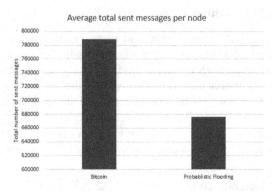

Fig. 5. Average total sent messages per node.

The results show that when running the probabilistic flooding approach, there was a significant decrease in the total number of messages sent per node during the simulation. When running the Bitcoin flooding protocol, the simulation showed that there was approximately 790,000 total messages sent per node, whereas when the simulation was run with the probabilistic flooding protocol implemented, there was approximately 675,000 total sent messages per node. This results in a **15%** reduction in the total number of messages sent per node during the simulation period. As the 115,000 reduction in messages mentioned are the amount of messages saved per node, the total number of messages saved throughout the entire network can be estimated at approximately **70** million messages as there are 625 nodes participating in the network during the simulation. Figure 6 represents the aforementioned statistics between both protocols.

The limitations of using simulations when testing the proposed protocol are as follows:

- The current simulator does not take into account other factors that may affect transactions being included into blocks such as incentives i.e. transaction fees.
- Each node in the simulation network has a wide variance of the number of neighbours they are connected to, with 8 neighbours being the minimum. However, an important characteristic of the Bitcoin P2P network is that nodes are able to join and leave the network as they desire. A node may receive a low probability of being sent an INV message as they are highly-connected in the network, however, many of their neighbours could potentially leave the network. This leads to the node still receiving a low probability of being sent an INV message, even though they may be less-connected than before. An area of future work could be to run further simulations.

	AVG INV SENT PER NODE	% OF DUPLICATED INV	AVG TOTAL SENT MESSAGES PER NODE	% OF TRANSACTONS ADDED TO BLOCKS	Transaction Commit Time (Seconds)
Full Bitcoin Protocol	270,633	8.33%	789,220	100%	534
Probabilistic Flooding Approach	191,335	7.45%	677,222	100%	519
Difference	-79,278	-0.88%	-111,988	0%	-15
Total Network Savings	49,548,750		69,992,500		

Fig. 6. Table representing the aforementioned statistics.

- where the probabilities of each neighbours are reset after a certain period of time. This allows for nodes who were initially well-connected but then as their neighbours leave the network, become less-connected, and vice versa, to receive updated probabilities from each of their peers.
- The simulator is tuned to create 2 transactions per second (TPS), leading to a daily average of 172,800 transactions, which were the number of daily transactions created when the simulator was created. However, Bitcoin can handle up to 7TPS [16] but currently has a daily trading volume of approximately 4TPS[7].

7 Conclusion

In this paper, we proposed a novel protocol that aims to reduce the number of redundant messages being generated by the current flooding protocol. The proposed protocol changes the current flooding protocol implemented by Bit-coin to a probabilistic flooding approach. The proposed probabilistic flooding approach presented in this paper is based on the idea that well-connected neighbours will more likely not respond to an INV message compared to a node that is less-connected, therefore the probability of sending an INV message to a less-connected node is higher than that of a well-connected node.

As we have shown in Sect. 6, the proposed protocol is able to significantly reduce the total number of messages being exchanged on the network, whilst maintaining the reliability of the system. The number of INV messages sent per node and the total number of messages sent per node decreased by **29%** and **14%** respectively when running the probabilistic flooding protocol. During the 58 h simulation period, the total number of messages saved when running the probabilistic flooding approach when compared to the current flooding protocol was approximately 70 million messages.

---

[7] https://www.blockchain.com/charts/n-transactions.

The proposed protocol met the objectives that it aimed to achieve - reducing the number of redundant messages on the network whilst maintaining the reliability and resilience of the system. We have shown that the current flooding protocol implemented by Bitcoin for the dissemination of information across the network is inefficient and wasteful, and have proved that the mechanism can be improved upon whilst maintaining the reliability and integrity of the system. This leads to many possible, alternate flooding solutions to the current flooding protocol for future work.

References

1. Nakamoto, S., et al.: Bitcoin: a peer-to-peer electronic cash system (2008)
2. Essaid, M., Kim, H.W., Park, W.G., Lee, K.Y., Park, S.J., Ju, H.T.: Network usage of bitcoin full node. In: International Conference on Information and Communication Technology Convergence (ICTC), pp. 1286–1291. IEEE (2018)
3. Decker, C., Wattenhofer, R.: Information propagation in the bitcoin network. In: IEEE P2P 2013 Proceedings, pp. 1–10. IEEE (2013)
4. Ghimire, S., Selvaraj, H.: A survey on bitcoin cryptocurrency and its mining. In: 26th International Conference on Systems Engineering (ICSEng), pp. 1–6. IEEE, December 2018
5. Zheng, Y., Pieprzyk, J., Seberry, J.: HAVAL — a one-way hashing algorithm with variable length of output (extended abstract). In: Seberry, J., Zheng, Y. (eds.) AUSCRYPT 1992. LNCS, vol. 718, pp. 81–104. Springer, Heidelberg (1993). https://doi.org/10.1007/3-540-57220-1_54
6. Sharkey, S., Tewari, H.: Alt-PoW: an alternative proof-of-work mechanism. In: IEEE International Conference on Decentralized Applications and Infrastructures (DAPPCON), San Francisco, California, USA, 5–8 April 2019
7. Bonneau, J., Miller, A., Clark, J., Narayanan, A., Kroll, J.A., Felten, E.W.: SoK: research perspectives and challenges for bitcoin and cryptocurrencies. In: IEEE Symposium on Security and Privacy, pp. 104–121. IEEE (2015)
8. Liu, Y., Chen, X., Zhang, L., Tang, C., Kang, H.: An intelligent strategy to gain profit for bitcoin mining pools. In: 10th International Symposium on Computational Intelligence and Design (ISCID), vol. 2, pp. 427–430. IEEE (2017)
9. Deshpande, V., Badis, H., George, L.: BTCmap: mapping bitcoin peer-to-peer network topology. In: IFIP/IEEE International Conference on Performance Evaluation and Modeling in Wired and Wireless Networks (PEMWN), pp. 1–6. IEEE (2018)
10. Maral, J.E.: Adaptive information dissemination in the bitcoin network (2019)
11. Courtois, N.T., Bahack, L.: On subversive miner strategies and block withholding attack in bitcoin digital currency. arXiv preprint arXiv:1402.1718 (2014)
12. Eyal, I., Sirer, E.G.: Majority is not enough: bitcoin mining is vulnerable. Commun. ACM 61(7), 95–102 (2018)
13. Fadhil, M., Owenson, G., Adda, M.: A bitcoin model for evaluation of clustering to improve propagation delay in bitcoin network. In: IEEE International Conference on Computational Science and Engineering (CSE) and IEEE International Conference on Embedded and Ubiquitous Computing (EUC) and 15th International Symposium on Distributed Computing and Applications for Business Engineering (DCABES), pp. 468–475. IEEE (2016)
14. Owenson, G., Adda, M., et al.: Proximity awareness approach to enhance propagation delay on the bitcoin peer-to-peer network. In: IEEE 37th International Conference on Distributed Computing Systems (ICDCS), pp. 2411–2416. IEEE (2017)

15. Heilman, E., Kendler, A., Zohar, A., Goldberg, S.: Eclipse attacks on bitcoin's peer-to-peer network. In: 24th USENIX Security Symposium (USENIX Security 2015), pp. 129–144 (2015)
16. Miraz, M., Donald, D.C.: Atomic cross-chain swaps: development, trajectory and potential of non-monetary digital token swap facilities. In: Annals of Emerging Technologies in Computing (AETiC), vol. 3 (2019)

Economic Impact of Resource Optimisation in Cloud Environment Using Different Virtual Machine Allocation Policies

Bilal Ahmad[1]([✉]), Zaib Maroof[2], Sally McClean[1], Darryl Charles[1], and Gerard Parr[3]

[1] School of Computing, Ulster University, Coleraine, UK
ahmad-b@ulster.ac.uk
[2] National Defence University, Islamabad, Pakistan
[3] University of East Anglia, Norwich, UK

Abstract. Exceptional level of research work has been carried in the field of cloud and distributed systems for understanding their performance and reliability. Simulators are becoming popular for designing and testing different types of quality of service (QoS) matrices e.g. energy, virtualisation, and networking. A large amount of resource is wasted when servers are sitting idle which puts a negative impact on the financial aspects of companies. A popular approach used to overcome this problem is turning them ON/OFF. However, it takes time when they are turned ON affecting different matrices of QoS like energy consumption, latency, consumption and cost. In this paper, we present different energy models and their comparison with each other based on workloads for efficient server management. We introduce a different type of energy saving techniques (DVFs, IQRMC) which help toward an improvement in service. Different energy models are used with the same configuration and possible solutions are proposed for big data centres that are placed globally by large companies like Amazon, Giaki, Onlive, and Google.

Keywords: Cloud computing · Energy optimisation · Resource optimisation · Economic impact · Service quality · Green computing · Virtualisation

1 Introduction

Cloud Computing is growing day by day with the development of IT services. The reason for this development is improving cost effectiveness and quality of experience from a user's perspective. The IT industry is becoming adaptable to cloud computing technologies for the achievement of improved service intelligence and good user experience. The cloud generally has three types of services SaaS (software as a service), PaaS (platform as a service) and IaaS (infrastructure as a service). Along through provisioning of enhanced quality of service cloud providers can move towards more

The authors would like to acknowledge partial support from the BT-Ireland Innovation Centre (BTIIC) and, Ulster University.

© ICST Institute for Computer Sciences, Social Informatics and Telecommunications Engineering 2019
Published by Springer Nature Switzerland AG 2019. All Rights Reserved
M. H. Miraz et al. (Eds.): iCETiC 2019, LNICST 285, pp. 46–58, 2019.
https://doi.org/10.1007/978-3-030-23943-5_4

profits by saving resources e.g. energy, bandwidth consumption, cost effectiveness etc. In a cloud environment, servers have a significant part in the design of cloud infrastructure in addition of resource allocation. The quality of cloud service primarily depends upon economic resource allocation and scheduling which servers perform during their operation. If servers have advanced resource allocation and scheduling algorithms services could be improved automatically [1].

All types of resource allocation and scheduling is related to a server's physical design and resource allocation policies. A system designer's major task is to determine trade-offs between quality of service factor and energy consumption [6]. Idle servers can be turned off for power saving purpose and expense to profit ratio can be improved. However, this can also hamper the quality of service factor i.e. latency when they must be turned on as requested by the users. To date, many suggestions and ideas have been proposed for energy consumption for jobs arriving in cloud servers. The quality of cloud service depends upon how much stable resource allocation is provided to the user requesting the service. For the achievement of this goal virtualisation is carried out by the service providers. Large scale data centres consist of thousands of hosts and nodes resulting in the consumption of a large amount of energy. As a result, cloud servers are being designed in such a way that they become automatically adaptable to the service requested by the users [2]. Dynamically scaling up or down is carried out by the servers and virtual machines are created and destroyed depending upon the load servers are receiving from users across the globe. This dynamic approach helps to maintain a quality of service while managing the resources efficiently from both perspectives i.e. user and service providers. Techniques require to be developed and deployed on the cloud servers that support elastic management of tasks that are being run on the server with different workloads (gaming, big data and internet of things, web hosting, social networking, etc.). These applications are quite challenging depending upon the user's location, service requests, time, weather and interaction patterns. Hence, to attain a good quality of service and experience dynamic, provisioning techniques are required to be designed and implemented by researchers that are compatible across the globe. However, so far resource allocation is still a challenge in terms of video streaming, gaming in which data is streamed online globally [3].

Recent advances that are being made around the world have turned the idea of cloud gaming into reality. The use of elastic resource utilisation and globally placed servers has made it possible for users to enjoy service on a pay as you go basis. Issues related to a bulk amount of data streaming to cloud servers are being addressed resulting in improvement of user experience. User satisfaction has been mainly improved because of dedicated servers that are placed globally for solving latencies and data offloading issues. High definition 3D issues related to gaming have been addressed over the cloud environment which makes it a reality for gamers to enjoy single and multi-player games over the cloud environment. The basic architecture design of cloud gaming consists of a game that is hosted on the cloud server which is located globally. The player whether in single or multi player mode streams the game scenes in the form of video by using the internet as a communication media. The player sends the commands over the cloud environment and these commands are processed by the graphical processing unit and are sent back to the user through a thin client. All these actions are required to be executed in an order of milliseconds therefore, a service provider has a small margin of error [4].

Several factors are required to be managed for hosting of gaming application over the cloud environment. In a virtual cloud environment factors like quality of service, energy consumption and cost need to be managed. An efficient energy solution is required for power saving in big data centres. Certain types of techniques e.g. dynamic voltage frequency scaling, virtual machine migration and load balancing are required to be designed and implemented by researchers. By implementing these techniques not only improved value of facility be provided, it can also decrease of carbon dioxide emission from the servers [5]. The rest of the paper is organised as follows: Sect. 2 (Cloud Computing Background and Platforms), Sect. 3 (Related Work), Sect. 4 (Experimentation), Sect. 5 (Experimental Framework), and Sect. 6 (Results and Discussion) with a Conclusion at the end.

2   Cloud Computing Background and Platforms

There are number of advantages of using services over the cloud environment from which a normal user can benefit e.g. facilities and designer tools. People carrying out the research work can benefit from these tools without any device limitations. These devices could be in any form from a small tablet to large computer servers that could be placed in a commercial environment for development purpose. The emerging field of Cloud Computing where servers are placed globally provides its user with immense advantages as compared to old technologies. This include concept of working anywhere any time without limitation of devices, storage, cost and virtualization concept.

In the era of development and progress in this century still many people around the globe are unable to enjoy these services for number of reasons e.g., (a) Restricted capability of electronic devices (performance, swiftness, visuals) (b) System limitations (bandwidth, topographical location) (c) Delay of service from core computers (weak networks) [6]. Consequently, to accommodate these problems simulation platforms (Cloud Sim, iFog Sim, Green Cloud, iCaroCloud, Cisco, Cloud Analyst, Network Cloud Sim, iCanCloud etc.) have been developed which provide users with a means to overcome the problems they are facing. The cloud architecture is in the form of layers. Each layer has a defined functionality and is interconnected as shown in Fig. 1. The service provision of IaaS and PaaS is performed using middleware whereas, SaaS services are provided by lower layer services using physical resources in a cloud environment. Third-Party service providers develop and provide SaaS/PaaS services in the cloud environment. Different cloud layers and their functionality [7] are discussed below (Fig. 1).

CloudSim is a rich platform that provides it users with the ability to simulate and calculate energy consumption of large servers by using the Dynamic Voltage and Frequency Scaling (DVFS) technique. The input parameters are used as host for the cloud environment and energy calculations are provided as an output results. In this way, a researcher that is carrying an investigation towards green computing can measure amount of energy which will be required for calculation of designed tests. This platform is very flexible and provides its user with the leverage of dynamic experimentation [2].

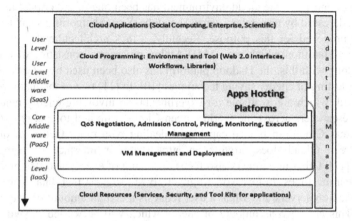

Fig. 1. Cloud computing layered architecture.

3 Related Work

The IT industry is evolving day by day from the domain of grid, parallel and distributed computing. With the ongoing development of the industry different simulation software tools have been developed for cloud-based environments e.g. GridSim, CloudSim, Green Cloud, iCan Cloud etc. This software help researcher around the world to design and test their algorithms and techniques for improvement of the quality of service and quality of experience [3]. Present research shows that distributed computing is more advantageous towards economical resource provisioning. It can provide centralised access, tolerance and coordination capability. It also allows cloud developers to manage and provision resources as desired. Quality of service is maintained by the broker which is present between user and server and is located globally. In this model, resources are provisioned to the users depending upon their requirements. e.g. Amazon EC2 server [7]. Ahmad, B., et al., uses the concept of static load and allocates resources based on under or overloaded hosts. Energy consumption comparison is performed by using different virtual machine allocation policies based on host workload. The results are analysed and compared with the DVFS technique. Dynamic allocation of resources helps in saving more resources as compared to static allocation. The experimentation is performed in the CloudSim environment and configured using Eclipse Luna and Java IDE [13]. The authors focus on the basic of resource optimisation and proposes an algorithm that manages resources for efficient performance. Resource optimisation requires service providers to manage resources in such a way that no user should be denied resources when requested. The work focuses on one of the non-preemptive resource allocation technique i.e. a game-based approach. Different trade-offs are also required to be carried that may hamper the quality of service at the user end. A game based resource allocation model has been suggested but lacks the experimentation results whether it is feasible for cloud gaming or not [8].

Saving of energy in the cloud environment has been one of the critical factors that have been addressed by researchers across the globe. Several algorithms and techniques have been proposed for this purpose. Recently, a rack architecture design has been suggested by Hamilton which uses AMD Athlon processors consisting of low power devices. Along with this, the Hadoop platform has also been used by Atiewi, S. and S. Yussof. for testing of energy saving techniques [10]. In [11] two of the major platforms are discussed, which are available for experimentation involving energy relating scenarios by researchers across the world. Green Cloud is limited to energy experimentation whereas CloudSim is also capable of dealing with other factors of quality of service. Green Cloud does provide an attractive user interface as compared to CloudSim [11]. Other researchers also focus on saving of energy and this involves the use of virtual machines. In this work, Nguyen, B.M., suggest that data images should be maintained on servers and when a user requests a certain amount of data it can be provided. This can save an amount of energy which will be wasted in switching the servers ON and OFF again and again [10]. The authors focus on energy consumption issues in a cloud data centre that are located globally and are providing services to users 24/7. The suggestion is limited to small data workload applications based upon hardware requirements (server, memory and network). A further study emphases that many techniques that are implemented in cloud servers work towards reliable availability of services when requested by users [4].

Ahmad et al., uses the concept of changing energy and time scaling technique. Based on this energy consumption is analyzed for observation of quality of service. A gaming workload is used, and optimum energy solution is suggested. Results show that DVFS behaves better as compared to non-power aware techniques for the same test scenario [9]. Many techniques are being used in the mobile gaming world for reduction of power. Song J. et al., propose that if a platform embedded with a GPU (graphical processing unit) is used with dynamic voltage frequency scaling algorithms, energy consumption can be reduced. It defines the frame complexity model that recognises the importance of GPU and its working efficiency towards the energy cost saving problem. However, the approach lacks the practical capability for testing the ideas on real gaming servers like Onlive and Gaikai [12]. In an approach based on the switching of machine states is used i.e. active and inactive states. This algorithm works based on the calculations that are performed about waiting time of jobs which are present on the servers and uses queue theory for energy resource optimisation. This work suggests working based on two states of servers i.e. ON/OFF. The algorithm is efficient for small jobs but can be overloaded when jobs are long. Back draw is that it results in high energy consumption and latency. Servers need a lot of power to come active gain when requested by users [10].

4   Experimentation

The experimentation has been carried in CloudSim and measures one of the service parameters i.e. energy for data centers. The economic impact of energy consumption has been analysed and tested by using different techniques, e.g. interquartile range, changing power and time scrambling and non-power aware for the same workload. The tests scenarios that are designed will be implemented and tested using the CloudSim platform. The platform is combination of software and platforms and is built using Java IDE along with Eclipse Luna. In this simulation platform number of methods have been implemented for calculation of power consumption. The workload that has been used for testing purpose consist of popular game World of War Craft. The workload consists of data traces from servers which are located over three continents and has runtime of 1107 days, 660723 sessions, 91065 avatars. The approach compares the used power levels, service provisioning and excellence of facility by using a gaming workload for testing the behaviour of the proposed technique [9].

4.1   Dynamic Voltage Frequency Scaling

DVFS one of the methods that helps big servers to save energy. It uses the frequency scaling technique. In DVFS the CPU power consumption is directly proportional to the workload which is provided to it. Therefore, if the CPU has more load, it will consume more power and vice versa. This allows it to consume less power in the idle state. This does not affect additional features of the server (I/O devices, random access memory, bandwidth etc.) as they are dependent upon CPU frequency. DVFS provides the user with four states that are available for the user. These states allow the device to select its operation depending upon the workload e.g. G0 (power ON), G1 (partial sleeping), G2 (partially OFF but still being powered by the power supply), G3 (power off state). These states provision users to have their algorithms designed according to the workload [9].

4.2   Inter Quartile Range

Inter Quartile Range is a statistical dispersion metric that calculates the different the third $Q3$. It dynamically calculates the threshold level of CPU utilizations by the following equation:

$$IQR = Q3 - Q1 \qquad (1)$$

$$T(n) = 1 - sf \times IQR \qquad (2)$$

Whereas, 'sf' is the protection factor. It defines the maximum safe limits for the user in a cloud environment. Its minor values signify maximum acceptance level of fluctuations in central processing unit [14].

4.2.1 Maximum Correlation VM Selection Policy

The concept behind maximum correlation relates to how resources are being used on the servers. If an application running on servers have a higher correlation with resource usage then the chance of servers overloading will be increased. Therefore, VM performance is analysed and VMs having high correlation with CPU utilization are migrated to other VMs in the system. Thus, multiple correlation is used for this purpose which evaluates the quality of independent constants [14].

4.2.2 Minimum Migration Time Policy

After overloaded system detection, virtual machines migration is carried out for resource optimization (power usage) and to refrain from the low service quality standards. In this algorithm only those VMs are migrated that need minimum time for migration from the system. This is done on the basis of bandwidth consumption of every virtual machine that is allocated for each individual user [15]. Therefore, VMs that are required to be moved across the network can be calculated by the following equation,

$$\left(\frac{RAM_u(v)}{NETj}\right) \leq \left(\frac{RAM_u(a)}{NETj}\right), \quad v \in Vj | \forall a \in Vj, \tag{3}$$

Whereas, Vj shows total number of VMs with host j, $RAM_u(a)$ is the amount of RAM that is used by the virtual machine (a), $NETj$ equals available bandwidth from host 'j' [13].

4.2.3 Minimum Utilisation Selection Policy

Due to the resource consumption, a virtual machine can be migrated in overloaded hosts. This technique will migrate VMs from underutilized or over loaded hosts to reduce the overhead caused in CPU utilization. This migration of virtual machines allows the systems to meet SLA violation and helps in saving of unwanted energy consumption [13].

5 Experimental Framework

There are two main techniques that have been used in this experimentational framework one of which is called nonpower aware and second one is called dynamic voltage and frequency scaling technique. These two methods differ from each other based on resource allocation phenomena they use. Dynamic voltage and frequency scaling technique adjusts the amount of power required for each host based on the level of the workload which is present. In the power adjustment and optimisation other elements of the system including random access memory, storage, bandwidth allocation remains same throughout the testing [9]. If changing power level are used within the central processing unit energy usage for all parts of the system can be reduced. Central processing unit within any computer system has limitations therefore its states are limited for current and frequency. Therefore, results that are achieved after experimentation are better than other simpler methods used in general. As a result when system will be implanted using dynamic power management lot of energy will be wasted as compared to dynamic frequency scaling approach [13]. In this experimental setup, broker plays a key role which is responsible for resource allocation and virtualisation. This consist of 800 hosts that are physically present on the system along with 1000 virtual machines. These virtual machines are assigned to the hosts dynamically depending upon the load present. The system constitutes of HP ProLiant model having two Xeon 3040 and Xeon 3075 standards.

Both these systems are dual core and have a processing speed of 1860 MHz and 2660 MHz [13]. Detailed parameters are given in Table 1. All the users that are present in this system will be adjusted based upon usage of central processing unit. Random access memory used is four giga bytes with a bandwidth rate of one giga bits per second for each system.

Table 1. System specification.

System (HP ProLiant)	Host MIPS	Host RAM	Host Bw	Host PE (s)	Hard Disk
ML110G4 (Xeon3040)	1860	4096 MBs	1 Gbit/s	02	1 GB
ML110G5 (Xeon3075)	2660	4096 MBs	1 Gbit/s	02	1 GB

The system is tested using a workload that consists of modern multiplayer game called world of war craft. This dataset has been collected over 1107 days and consist of different features and values. The data set specification consists of traces of avatars, sessions and data size. The data provides information of game location, time when it was played and for how long it was played, game positions information, level of graphics it used etc. for analyzing quality of services [16]. The time which is required by each to execute is provided based on energy consumption levels. The time-shared policy is being used to fulfill this scenario. In this experimentation, all the instructions are executed at one speed and total speed is sum of all the instructions that are executed. Therefore, to have good user experience better quality of service is required to provided [15].

All the resource allocation and virtualization is done on priority basis i.e. a virtual machine which requires immediate service it will be treated first and all resources will be allocated to it. If this condition is ignored quality of service and quality of experience is hampered and this leads to bad user experience. It provides service provider with higher level of violations and drops the standard of service. Therefore, a good mechanism is required that provides switching of resource when required urgently by the hosts with immediate service requirement. performance level causing SLA violations. Therefore, service quality can be met if two matrices are kept in mind i.e. number of violations and each hosts performance per unit time [16].

6 Results and Discussion

The system has been evaluated based on the performance of the designed model which is verified with diverse virtual machine placement and selection policies. The performance of the systems has been analysed based on the comparison with different energy saving techniques e.g. DVFS, Non-Power Aware, Inter Quartile Range (IQR) technique. Further, interquartile range uses three different virtualisation policies i.e. maximum correlation selection policy (MC), minimum migration time selection policy (MMT). IQR performs CPU utilization based upon these algorithms and does virtual machine allocation deallocation based upon the available workload. The virtual machine allocation has been performed using MC and MMT selection policy. Based upon these allocations and selection policies, simulation has been performed in CloudSim for the designed data centre. This facilitates analysis and assessment of different parameters such as energy efficiency, service provision level and its violations, how many violations occur every second and time it takes to shut down the server after processing.

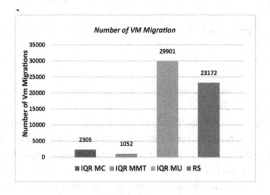

Fig. 2. VM migration.

System performance has been observed by using different virtual machine allocation and placement algorithm. From the results (Fig. 2) it becomes obvious that IQR MMT performs minimal virtual machine migration which leads to minimum downtime probability. However, when it comes to SLA violations MMT performs minimum violations leading to the best quality of service (Fig. 3). System performance has been observed by using different virtual machine allocation and placement algorithm. From the results (Fig. 2) it becomes obvious that IQR MMT performs minimal virtual machine migration which leads to minimum downtime probability. However, when it comes to SLA violations MMT performs minimum violations leading to the best quality of service (Fig. 3).

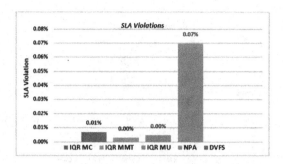

Fig. 3. Number of SLA violations

In (Fig. 4), performance degradation of virtual machines can be analysed, and it becomes clear from the results that by using MU approach a minimum number of degradations is performed at the virtual machine level. On the other hand, maximum correlation selection policy has the highest value of service level agreement violations. Minimum Utilisation involves a smaller number of virtual machines leading to less SLA violations for the system.

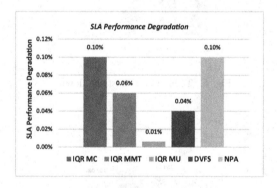

Fig. 4. SLA performance degradation.

MMT has better service quality and results and less violations are performed for every second of execution (Fig. 5). After performing the desired tasks, the hosts that are created are closed. The highest number of host shutdowns is performed by MU thus leading to better reliability of the system (Fig. 6).

Energy consumption has also been analysed in all these algorithms. It has been observed that MC has minimum energy utilisation when it comes to interquartile range algorithm (Fig. 7). Thus, by using our approach, energy could be saved and quality of service can be improved by adjusting other service parameters, i.e. service level agreements, service level agreement violations, number of hosts created and shutdown etc.

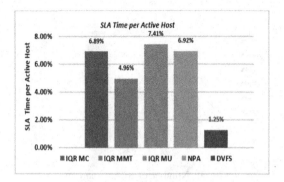

Fig. 5. SLA time for active host.

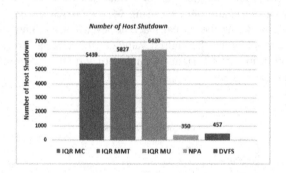

Fig. 6. Total sum of host shutdown.

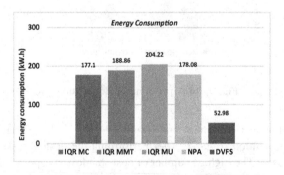

Fig. 7. Energy consumption comparison.

From the above results, it can be deduced that minimum energy consumption is dependent upon two factors, minimum virtual machine migration and maximum number of host shutdowns. It can also be noted that energy consumption by the physical host and service level agreement violations are indirectly proportional to each other. When the hosts use more energy, they have a smaller number of service level agreement violations and vice versa. Therefore, better quality of service and resource optimisation could be performed if these factors are controlled in the real time computing world. Dynamic frequency scaling techniques provides better results as we can demonstrate using the interquartile virtualisation technique.

7 Conclusion

In this paper, tests have been carried out in relation to different factors that affect resource optimisation in cloud computing. Virtual machine migration is done based on under or overutilization of resources, service level agreement that are achieved and which are violated. The economic impact of servers in terms of the energy efficiency factor has also been considered for resource optimisation. Implementation of interquartile range algorithm shows that MMT has a minimum number of virtual machine migration and service level agreement violations which lead to better resource optimisation of quality of service. Therefore, the suggested scheme can be expanded and implemented for virtualised cloud servers, leading to better efficiency, cost saving and better quality of service. Therefore, the dynamic frequency scaling technique can save more energy when used on a bigger scale as demonstrated using interquartile virtualisation.

References

1. Chen, K.T., Huang, C.Y., Hsu, C.H.: Cloud gaming onward: research opportunities and outlook. In: IEEE International Conference on Multimedia and Expo Workshops (ICMEW) (2014)
2. Long, S., Zhao, Y.: A toolkit for modeling and simulating cloud data storage: an extension to CloudSim. In: International Conference on Control Engineering and Communication Technology (2012)
3. Calheiros, R.N., et al.: CloudSim: a toolkit for modeling and simulation of cloud computing environments and evaluation of resource provisioning algorithms. Softw. Pract. Exper. **41**(1), 23–50 (2011)
4. Shuja, J., et al.: Survey of techniques and architectures for designing energy-efficient data centers. IEEE Syst. J. **10**(2), 507–519 (2016)
5. Yannuzzi, M., et al.: A new era for cities with fog computing. IEEE Internet Comput. **21**(2), 54–67 (2017)
6. Alsaffar, A.A., et al.: An architecture of IoT service delegation and resource allocation based on collaboration between fog and cloud computing. Mobile Information Systems **2016**, 15 (2016)
7. Rawat, P.S., et al.: Power consumption analysis across heterogeneous data center using CloudSim. In: 3rd International Conference on Computing for Sustainable Global Development (INDIACom) (2016)
8. Godhrawala, H., Sridaran, R.: A survey of game based strategies of resource allocation in cloud computing. In: 3rd International Conference on Computing for Sustainable Global Development (INDIACom) (2016)
9. Ahmad, B., et al.: Analysis of energy saving technique in CloudSim using gaming workload. In: Proceedings of the Ninth International Conference on Cloud Computing, GRIDS, and Virtualization, IARIA (2018)

10. Nguyen, B.M., Tran, D., Nguyen, Q.: A strategy for server management to improve cloud service QoS. In: IEEE/ACM 19th International Symposium on Distributed Simulation and Real Time Applications (DS-RT) (2015)
11. Atiewi, S., Yussof, S.: Comparison between Cloud Sim and green cloud in measuring energy consumption in a cloud environment. In: 3rd International Conference on Advanced Computer Science Applications and Technologies (2014)
12. Song, J., et al.: FCM: Towards fine-grained GPU power management for closed source mobile games. In: International Great Lakes Symposium on VLSI (GLSVLSI), pp. 353–356 (2016)
13. Ahmad, B., et al.: Energy optimisation in cloud servers using a static threshold VM consolidation technique (STVMC). In: Proceedings of the 13th International FLINS Conference on Data Science and Knowledge Engineering for Sensing Decision Support (FLINS2018) (2018)
14. Abdelsamea, A., et al.: Virtual machine consolidation enhancement using hybrid regression algorithms. Egypt. Inform. J. **18**, 161–170 (2017)
15. Theja, P.R., Babu, S.K.K.: Evolutionary computing based on QoS oriented energy efficient VM consolidation scheme for large scale cloud data centers. Cybern. Inf. Technol. **16**(2), 97–112 (2016)
16. Lee, Y.-T., et al.: World of warcraft avatar history dataset. In: Proceedings of the Second Annual ACM Conference on Multimedia systems, pp. 123–128. ACM, San Jose (2011)

SOSE: Smart Offloading Scheme Using Computing Resources of Nearby Wireless Devices for Edge Computing Services

Ali Al-ameri[(⊠)] and Ihsan Alshahib Lami

School of Computing, The University of Buckingham,
Buckingham MK18 1EG, UK
{ali.al-ameri,ihsan.lami}@buckingham.ac.uk

Abstract. Offloading of all or part of any cloud service computation, when running processing-intensive Mobile Cloud Computing Services (MCCS), to servers in the cloud introduces time delay and communication overhead. Edge computing has emerged to resolve these issues, by shifting part of the service computation from the cloud to edge servers near the end-devices. An innovative Smart Cooperative Computation Offloading Framework (SCCOF), to leverage computation offloading to the cloud has been previously published by us [1]. This paper proposes SOSE; a solution to offload sub-tasks to nearby devices, on-the-go, that will form an "edge computing resource, we call SOSE_EDGE" so to enable the execution of the MCCS on any end-device. This is achieved by using short-range wireless connectivity to network between available cooperative end-devices. SOSE can partition the MCCS workload to execute among a pool of Offloadees (nearby end-devises; such as Smartphones, tablets, and PC's), so to achieve minimum latency and improve performance while reducing battery power consumption of the Offloader (end-device that is running the MCCS). SOSE established the edge computing resource by: (1) profiling and partitioning the service workload to sub-tasks, based on a complexity relationship we developed. (2) Establishing peer2peer remote connection, with the available cooperative nearby Offloadees, based on SOSE assessment criteria. (3) Migrating the sub-tasks to the target edge devices in parallel and retrieve results. Scenarios and experiments to evaluate SOSE show that a significant improvement, in terms of processing time (>40%) and battery power consumption (>28%), has been achieved when compared with cloud offloading solutions.

Keywords: Offloading · Edge computing · Cooperative ·
Mobile cloud computing

1 Introduction

The Smart Phone (SP) is continually being improved to have more and more computational resources and connectivity, amongst many others such as memory, display, sensors, battery, etc. Nevertheless, SP's are still lacking behind in terms of performance and battery capacity, which are the main desired features for SP subscribers [2]. SP's are now being used for running resource intensive MCCS, such as tracking humans or

M. H. Miraz et al. (Eds.): iCETiC 2019, LNICST 285, pp. 59–73, 2019.

animals in crowd sensing scenarios, or "manipulating blind persons" via IoT Sensors [3]. Some of these MCCS require machine learning and AI algorithms to be executing live. Current SP's will run out of puff processing, and the battery will run flat when running such MCCS.

We believe that there will always be a big gap between SP resource offerings and developers of intensive processing MCCS. To fill this gap, many offloading solutions exist that ship the processing of such MCCS to a central server in the cloud. This will create large traffic in an already crowded spectrum. I.e. offloading the computation to servers in the cloud, introduces time delay and communication overhead cost. Edge computing has emerged to resolve these issues, by shifting the computation from servers in the cloud to servers near the edge, to reduce both delay and communication cost. However, edge computing servers normally are planned as part of the infrastructure of the cloud in the vicinity. SOSE overcomes this limitation! SOSE; a scheme that forms an edge computing resource to execute such MCCS on-the-go, from cooperative nearby edge devices. SOSE offloads the sub-tasks for computation, from the MCCS host device/SP to a network of nearby SP's/devices. Figure 1 shows SOSE end2end scheme. It shows that, the cloud server is used to host SOSE_INTELLIGENT; an intelligent engine to recruit cooperative end-devices and authenticate their availability when needed. Also, SOSE_INTELLIGENT engine provides the end-device with decisions of the best scenario to partition and offload, to achieve a low processing time and reduce the battery power consumption. It also shows the newly formed SOSE_EDGE computing resource network, (dotted circle in the diagram).

The Offloader will ask SOSE_INTELLIGENT engine for decisions of nearest device, that has the lowest load and the highest resources of processing and battery capacity, as well as the best network connectivity to use. Then the Offloader will generate VMs, (bundle them as APKs and JAR files), of all the partitioned sub-tasks and will establish connectivity with all available Offloadees, as advised by SOSE_INTELLIGENT engine. Finally, the Offloader will offload the VM's to the Offloadees and retrieve the results.

The novelty contributions of this paper are:

- Introduces SOSE; a unique scheme that forms the edge computing resource, on-the-go, from nearby devices and share the execution of the MCCS in parallel among them, via short-range wireless connectivity.
- The offloading between the devices of SOSE_EDGE is done intelligently by an SOSE_INTELLIGENT engine based in the cloud. SOSE_INTELLIGENT engine recruits cooperative device resources, monitors (processing capability, battery status, and availability), and authenticates (access key, session key and engagement status), so to advice on available device nearby when the Offloader needs to form the SOSE_EDGE.

The rest of this paper includes: Sect. 2 that summarizes the recent literature on edge computing implementations, while Sect. 3 presents the development of SOSE. Section 4 presents the experiments, results and analysis. Finally, Sect. 5 presents the conclusion and future work.

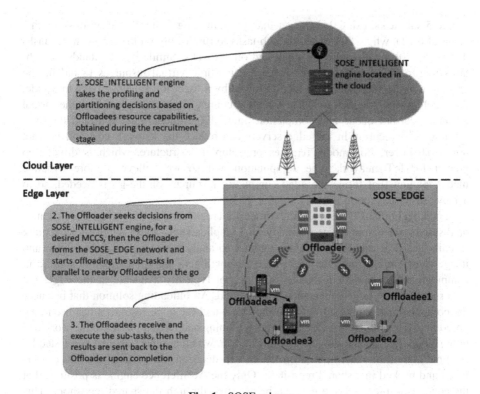

Fig. 1. SOSE scheme

2 Recent Literature of Edge Computing Implementations

Review of solutions that perform offloading to a centralised server in the cloud has been published in our previous paper [1]. This review focuses on implementations/ solutions, that consider IoT intensive applications, which offload to nearby pre-setup infrastructure of edge servers. SOSE proposes to deploy the SOSE_EDGE solution on-the-go when needed. This is achieved by recruiting a group of available nearby processing resources/devices in a local network, to form a cooperative sharing environment using SOSE_INTELLIGENT engine.

IoT deployments have increased the amount of data generated to the cloud; the amount of data hosted in 2018 is equal to the data gathered in all prior years [4]. This has necessitated that data-handling tasks are shifted to the edge nearer to the IoT sensors network, and so typical existing solutions focus on offloading between the edge servers and the cloud. Running these services on cloud servers can have a negative impact on the offloading process, due to network cost and bandwidth traffic. Therefore, an advantage of edge computing is to provide resources near end-users/devices, so to reduce long execution time and battery power consumption. A solution that facilitates offloading the service from a SP to an edge computing server, has introduced a model that provides the use of virtual resources in edge servers [5]. It achieves this, by shifting the service sub-tasks from a SP to the edge server automatically, by dividing a single task to 5 sub-tasks, using 0–1 integer liner programming. It marks the sub-tasks with a value of (0, 1), where "0" stands for sub-tasks to run locally on the SP, such sub-tasks that access SP local features or input and output tasks. Similarly, "1" stands for sub-tasks to run on an edge server, which has multiple virtual resources to handle the execution of the sub-tasks. This then followed by a "decision solver" engine to decide, on which virtual resource to select for the incoming 5 subtasks, based on the virtual resource "current queue and completion time". Experiments have affirmed that performing the execution in the edge servers can reduce the network cost and internet traffic. However, this model requires pre-setup infrastructure, which is difficult to predict for IoT network type computation and so we believe a more dynamic model/solution that forms the edge computing resources on-the-go is needed, so to achieve faster execution time.

Tracking humans or animals with drones in crowd sensing scenarios, like volcanos or disasters are examples of nowadays IoT applications. These applications require machine learning and AI algorithms engines to analyze streams of audio, video and image data coming from many sensors. Such intelligent algorithms require significant computational/processing resources that are not typically available at the edge, but rather available in large data centers in the cloud. An offloading solution that balances the computational workload between the cloud and the edge resources has been proposed in [6]. It achieves this, by shifting the training and testing phases of the workload to the cloud. I.e. the end-device will upload data, which are then labelled and tested by multiple algorithms, then, based on the chosen decision, the model is retrieved, sterilized and packed in a shared repository. Only the AI inference engine is positioned at the edge, as a micro service that can be accessed through the shared repository. This model is impressive in that it sends less data to the cloud, which reduces network cost and bandwidth traffic. However, it lacks a dynamic partitioning algorithm that decides if a task is executed in the cloud/edge servers, but rather depends on a pre-processing developer analysis to decide where to execute every task. We believe that the concept of letting the cloud be responsible of the overall decision-making in splitting the computation workload between the edge and the cloud is commendable. We shall deploy a similar concept, SOSE uses AWS services to perform the creation of the DB and recognition using AWS rekognition service [7]. Only the recognition results of the extracted faces are saved in a local DB shared repository using SQLite.

A solution that enhances the above offloading model, by including a dynamic partitioning algorithm of tasks moved between the cloud and the edge, is achieved by including an "optimal virtual machine selection technique" and a "dynamic task partitioning algorithm" [8]. These two algorithms offload the intensive tasks from end-device to the edge server and/or the cloud server. It achieves this by (1) sort algorithm that topologically analyze a "task graph", to partition the tasks between edge and cloud servers, to achieve a low computational complexity. (2) Then it ranks the available virtual machines, based on the time it takes to execute. (3) Finally, it selects the appropriate virtual machine and utilize the dynamic task partitioning algorithm, to compute the minimum completion time for the executed task. However, it only considers execution time as a metric to evaluate the proposed model, we believe other metrics like, battery power consumption, communication and efficiency must be considered in the evaluation. We deploy a similar concept to execute the sub-tasks in parallel on the nearby edge devices, so faster execution time can be achieved.

Some IoT apps required deep learning algorithms to extract accurate information for classification, especially for IoT devices deployed in complex environments. Nevertheless, such algorithms require a significant amount of processing, (i.e. each deep learning extra layer can bring extra processing among its multilayer structure). Therefore, Efficient scheduling mechanisms are needed to decide on how many layers can run on the edge servers. A solution that facilities offloading to optimize the performance of deep learning for IoT at the edge, has introduced a model that provides offline and online scheduling mechanism [9]. It achieves this by, monitoring each server capacity to decide how many layers each server can handle. I.e. the first input layers are consisting of many processing compute layers, therefore, it is more beneficial to run such layers in the cloud server. Then, when the dimension of the deep learning network is reduced, and the size of the intermediate layers becomes smaller than the input layer. This allows moving the processing of these lower layers to the edge server. This proposed model uses AlexNet deep learning model which consists of 8 layers, the first 5 layers are deployed in the cloud server and the last 3 layers are deployed in the edge server. This model is unique in that it can generates less data transfer and reduces the response latency. This inspired us to form SOSE, by forming a network of resources from end-devices and schedule the sub-tasks among them. I.e. SOSE_INTELLIGENT engine schedules the sub-tasks and selects the device with the lowest load and has the highest resources, in terms of processing power and battery level.

Offloading the intensive processing tasks and sharing the end-user data to the cloud or edge servers lead to an unsecure deployment inviting malicious activities. A solution that proposes to secure the offloading process has introduced a model, that secures the data being shared between the edge servers during offloading [10]. It achieves this by (1) it segments and offloads the tasks to the edge server in a sequence order. (2) It syncs to the edge server through a middleware that handles the communication. (3) It provides a security manager interface to encrypt, exchange security keys and verify the data before offloading. It is responsible to monitor the offloading process and generate alerts if a breach occurred, by observing all the edge devices. Despite the fact that, to the best of our knowledge this proposed model is the first to addresses security issues when offloading to the edge server. Nevertheless, it lacks details of the used mechanism nor experiments to approve the novelty. Being said that, SOSE introduces; (1) a SOSE_INTELLIGENT engine based in the cloud server that (monitors and approve) the nearby end-devices for qualifying as being secure and fit before offloading. (2) Partitions the tasks and distribute the sub-tasks among a variety of nearby edge devices, so the shared data cannot be retrieved or invoked as a package, and so stealing the sub-task will not impact the overall security of offloading. (3) We are using AWS rekognition service, which is a highly secure service that uses access and secret keys to authenticate the nearby devices. (4) We used nearby peer2peer API protocol [11] to communicate the nearby devices, which is a secure middleware that provides fully encrypted P2P data transfer between nearby edge devices.

3 SOSE Architecture

There are two distinct engines that make SOSE function. The SOSE_INTELLIGENT engine and the SOSE_EDGE.

3.1 SOSE_INTELLIGENT

This engine is based in the cloud. Its main functions are:

1. Identify and recruit suitable devices that can be used when needed by SOSE_EDGE. This process is continuous, and we envisage that such devices, as a principle, are SP's that are willing to contribute to help other SP's when running demanding MCCS. We propose that such devices are assigned certain credits that they will be able to use when running the MCCS. A suitable arrangement for controlling this will need to be in place as in [12], but out of the scope of this paper. Therefore, this engine will have a database of such devices, their local localisation, their resources, typical usage, availability and current load.

2. When contacted by the SOSE_EDGE Offloader, this engine will: (a) perform profiling and partitioning of the MCCS, if not already done in a previous request. (b) Try to establish if such MCCS has been run elsewhere to learn from that experience, (resource required, time to execute, and dependency between tasks). (c) Provide a list of potential available SPs/devices near the location of the Offloader together with their capability. (d) Advice the Offloader with the MCCS profiling and partitioning decisions. This information will help the Offloader to generate the Virtual Machines (VMs) that will form the sub-tasks to be offloaded to nearby devices.

3.2 SOSE_EDGE

This engine performs various stages resulting in forming the edge computing resource, that will execute the MCCS and is led by the SP that is hosting the MCCS (named the Offloader here). Any participating device in helping to run the sub-tasks are named the Offloadee. The process of SOSE_EDGE is as follows:

1. The Offloader will generate VMs (bundle them as APKs and JAR files) of all the partitioned sub-tasks, based on the instructions provided by the SOSE_INTELLI-GENT engine. Note that, the choice of having the profiling and partitioning of the MCCS in the cloud was to save battery of the Offloader, and source knowledge of the MCCS provided by the developer is more accessible to the cloud.

2. The Offloader will establish connectivity with all available Offloadees as advised by the SOSE_INTELLIGENT engine. Note that, the connectivity will be wireless, and that SOSE_INTELLIGENT engine will advise on the best wireless technology to use (e.g. Wi-Fi or BT, or Cellular) for each Offloadee device.

3. The Offloader will offload the VM's to the Offloadees and communicate the results from this process appropriately, including the termination of the contact.

4. The Offloader will also be executing its own share of the sub-tasks, as when it is not busy with the other sub-tasks.

5. When the MCCS run is completed, a summary record of this experience is feedback to SOSE_INTELLIGENT engine, to train and update it for future execution if needed by any other Offloader.

Details of each of these steps will be detailed as part of the experiments we have done to prove the concept of SOSE. For example, all wireless connectivity is done on a peer2peer protocol, etc.

4 Experiments, Results and Analysis

The following experiment scenarios is used to prove that SOSE_EDGE can provide an on-the-go (dynamic) edge resource from available nearby devices, and will perform as good as, or better than, a structured pre-setup edge computing server. The details of the implementation of SOSE_INTELLIGENT engine and the automation of the process will be documented elsewhere as being not the focus of this paper.

4.1 MCCS Choice: Face Detection Service (FDS)

FDS is chosen to demonstrate the computational complexity and the benefits of offloading, (typically used by police or at an airport mobile search activities). It involves a variety of complex tasks, including face detection and feature extraction. We developed FDS using Android studio platform and Dlib library, which is an open source library for image detection and recognition. It obtains a face bounding box using coordinates of the face in the image. Then it detects and draw 68 coordinators in the face, and finally, it extracts the face features. Asysnc class is basically used to run the heavy part of FDS algorithm on another thread so no pressure on the main thread that is also handling the GUI. FDS uses mface.train function to train the algorithm to perform the face detection process. Then it uses recognizeAsync function to execute the algorithm. Full details about the specification and experimental devices are illustrated in Sect. 4.2.

To illustrate more sub-tasks, we developed a complex version of FDS, we named it; FDSC. This includes recognition functions. As shown in Fig. 2, the main GUI of FDSC contains three main buttons, which are Offloader, Offloadee and server. The Offloader button is to specify whether to run the tasks locally on Offloader or remotely on Offloadees. It shows a drop-down list of Offloadees (0–3), (we used up to 4 devices in this experiment, (note that the maximum number of devices to be used is 7, because the BT protocol only allows 7 actual devices to connect to one master node [13])). The "0" means the tasks run locally on the Offloader, while (1–3) specify the number of Offloadees. The Offloadee button is to represent the participated Offloadees. The server button is for running the tasks remotely on the server, (we have decided to use 2 servers in this experiment, the first one is a cloud AWS EC2 server, and the second is a local Edge WAMP server), it requires a server IP address to start the connection.

We developed a simple algorithm to distribute the images among the Offloadees and the servers. Firstly, we divide the number of images (n) equally among the total devices. After that we find the remaining number of images, if the remaining images

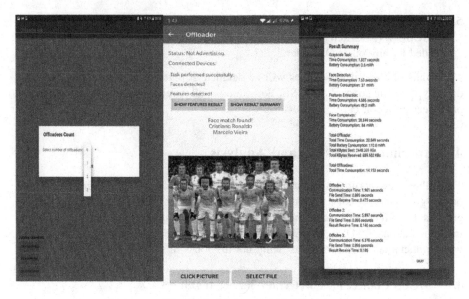

Fig. 2. Screenshots of FDSC

are equal to 0, then the algorithm starts distributing the images. If the remaining images are > 0, then it distributes the remaining images one by one to the Offloadees. (For example, if the number of connected devices = 4, number of images = 10, then 10/4, so initially each device gets 2 images, then for the remaining 2 images, it assigns one by one to the devices, so Offloader = 2, Offloadee1 = 3, Offloadee2 = 3, Offloadee3 = 2 and so on).

We used a third-party tool (AWS rekognition service) that uses storage-based API operations to create the DB, to compare with the Offloader new images. It gets the images from FDSC local repository root, then it calls Detectface request, call-FaceDetails, and Detectfeatures functions to build a client-side index.

4.2   Experimental Scenarios

In this section, the various scenarios for the experiments that have been done to illustrate the overhead of forming the edge resource are described. The aim of these scenarios is to examine the benefit of SOSE when offloading in terms of processing time, and battery power consumption, when FDS & FDSC sub-tasks are executed by various devices together with the Offloader. In the experiments, we have focused on comparing the processing time of sub-tasks, as well as battery power consumption for this period, as being the quality of service parameters along with the accuracy and efficiency of SOSE. Full details about the processing time cost and battery power consumption cost, with the equations can be found in our SCCOF paper [1]. There are many equations developed that calculate offloading time as a whole, based on the above and including amount of computation and communication [14, 15]. However, we did not find a significant impact of all these parameters on the trend of the described experiments as explained in Sect. 4.3. These scenarios are referred, as Edge Server Scenario (ESS), Edge Offloadees Scenario (EOS) and Cloud Server Scenario (CSS), in this paper, as shown in Fig. 3.

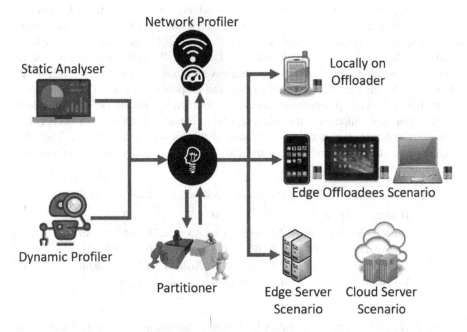

Fig. 3. SOSE architecture

4.2.1 The Offloader Sends (FDS & FDSC) Sub-tasks to a Local Edge Server (ESS)

In this scenario, we have created a WAMPSERVER 3.1.0, which acts as a local nearby edge server. Both Offloader and server are connected through an IP address. If the decision is to run the tasks on ESS, the decision engine triggers the distribution algorithm to partition the images between the Offloader and ESS. The Offloader generates a serializable interface and decides on the images to be offloaded. Then it invokes the remote manager, to connect to the server using IP address and post API and offloads the images in parallel. The edge server waits and listens to any incoming tasks, it runs the requested sub-tasks when receives the images, records the time, converts it to JSON format, and sends the results back to the Offloader as will be stated later in Sect. 4.3. We used BroadbandChecker tool [16] to profile the network and make sure it is stable when offloading.

4.2.2 The Offloader Sends (FDS & FDSC) Sub-tasks to Nearby Edge Offloadees (EOS)

In this scenario, we performed offloading to cooperative nearby edge-devices on-the-go. We used one Offloader and a maximum number of 3 Offloadees, full specifications of the conducted devices are shown in Table 1. All the devices are connecting through nearby API, which is a peer2peer networking API that allows apps to connect, share, and exchange data in order to communicate over a local area network. We have used nearby connections type, since it offers unlimited payload to be shared and it supports sensitive data, by encrypting the data for secure payload exchange. We have defined 5 classes to establish the communication between edge Offloadees, these are; Start Discovery (), Start Advertising (), Endpoint Discovery Callback (), Request Connection (), and Payload Callback (). When the device is selected as an Offloadee, the Offloader starts accepting incoming connections, (the number of incoming connections is equal to the number of the Offloadees). When we select more than 0 in the drop-down list, the Offloader starts advertising itself to accept incoming connection from nearby Offloadees. The Offloadees then discovers the Offloader and sends a request to connect. The Offloader accepts the connection and adds the incoming Offloadee to the connected devices list. Then the connection is established, and devices are ready to exchange images between them.

Table 1. Experimental (Offloader & Offloadees) specifications for EOS

Devices specification	CPU	RAM	OS	Battery
Samsung S2 Sm-T710	1.3 GHz	3 GB	Android 7.0	4000 mAh
Lenovo TB-7304F tablet	1.3 GHz	1 GB	Android 7.0	3500 mAh
LG Nexus 4	1.5 GHz	2 GB	Android 5.1.1	2100 mAh
LG Nexus 4	1.5 GHz	2 GB	Android 5.1.1	2100 mAh

We developed a simple algorithm to distribute the images among Offloadees, as explained in Sect. 4.1. (For example, if the Offloader selects 20 images to execute, each device executes 5 images in parallel and performs the required sub-tasks, then each device sends the results back to the Offloader). The Offloadees wait and listen for any incoming tasks, run the sub-tasks, record the time and send the results back to the Offloader. A total of 100 images to perform offloading between a variety of edge devices are used. The images are set to have the same resolution (700 × 700), and have a maximum size of 300 KB, and tests are repeated 5 times to examine stable and unstable network when offloading. The results are calculated (an average of 5 runs) in terms of processing time, battery power consumption, and offloading gain as illustrated in Sect. 4.3.

4.2.3 The Offloader Sends (FDS & FDSC) Sub-tasks to a Cloud Server (CSS)

In this scenario, we have created a server in the cloud using Amazon AWS services, namely t2.micro Amazon Linux 2 AMI EC2 server. We created the credentials (secret, access, and IAM keys), to authenticate the server with (FDS & FDSC), so it can connect and push images to the cloud server. We have also used FileZilla and Putty tools to install and migrate the necessary PHP files to the server. We created a S3 bucket to save the offloaded images, if needed for future execution and/or to train SOSE_INTELLIGENT engine. If the decision is to run the tasks on the server, the Offloader connects to the server and starts to offload the images through an IP address and POST API. The server waits and listens to any incoming tasks, it runs the requested sub-tasks when receives the images, records the time, converts it to JSON format, and sends the results back to the Offloader as will be stated later in Sect. 4.3.

4.3 Results and Discussion

This section presents all the results achieved from the conducted various experiments for the scenarios we designed to illustrate the concept of this SOSE solution.

Figure 4 shows the processing time of executing FDS for ESS, EOS and CSS we described in Sect. 4.2. Offloading to ESS and CSS has reduced the burden on the Offloader by 83.4% due to their unlimited resource capability. Note that the results are testimony that having an edge server is the correct decision, since it will be less overhead when communication traffic is taken into consideration. It is also clear that offloading to a single Offloadee is costly with an increase of 14.3%, due to the overhead not meeting the crossover point of being advantageous. However, offloading to >1 Offloadee has significantly improved the Offloader resource capability (21.3% & 40.2% for 2 & 3 Offloadees respectively).

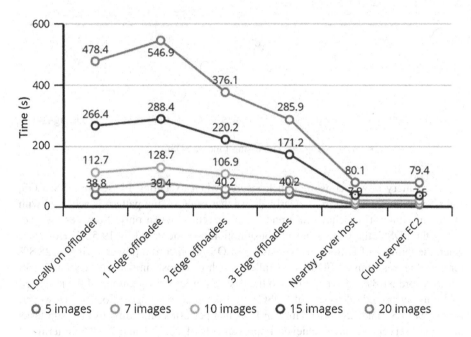

Fig. 4. Processing time of FDS

Figure 5 shows the processing time when running FDSC for ESS, EOS and CSS. It shows an increase of the complexity of the FDC, by adding more intensive sub-tasks, such as matching the extracted features with a DB. This highlights the importance of SOSE, where the processing time became liner for all ESS, EOS and CSS. This means that the overall cost of SOSE is much less than having the offloading done to the cloud, without the network traffic caused by transporting the data to the cloud. For 20 images with 4 edge end-devices, we achieved 10.13% in comparison to running the sub-tasks locally, while 12.1% for the cloud scenario, which indicates that, SOSE will outperform offloading to the cloud solution when complex sub-tasks are executed on more participated edge end-devices.

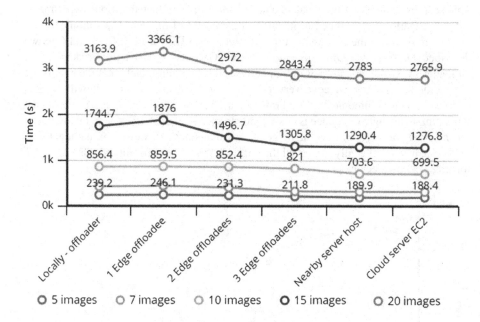

Fig. 5. Processing time of FDSC

The battery power consumption measured when executing FDSC for ESS, EOS, and CSS is shown in Fig. 6, it clearly shows that same saving pattern is achieved with processing time. The behavioral trend we observed is, when only 2 devices are executing the FDSC, the battery power consumption cost increased by 19.52%. However, when the number of Offloadees increases in EOS, we record a power saving of 28.8% for 4 Offloadees running FDSC in parallel, which is almost similar with ESS and CSS which record 31.8% power saving. To the best of our knowledge, none of the reviewed solutions performed offloading of FDSC sub-tasks to nearby edge offloadees. However, to compare ESS and CSS with Thinkair [17], that performs offloading of FDS sub-tasks to a cloud server, we have achieved improvements of 12.48% and 38.4%, in terms of processing time and battery power consumption respectively.

Figure 7 shows the processing time of FDS sub-tasks for ESS, EOS, and CSS, it shows that the feature extraction task is the most intensive task compared to other tasks. Also, it shows, the processing time dropped down continuously, almost up to 81.2% saving when more Offloadees run FDS. To measure the accuracy of SOSE, we used Rekognition confidence score of similarity. The confidence score is between (0–100), that expresses the probability of the detection, if the face is predicted correctly. We achieved up to 99% accuracy as almost all the selected images are recognized successfully. We compared the accuracy rate achieved by SOSE, with the work in [18], that used facial recognition service. We achieved an increase of 23.75%.

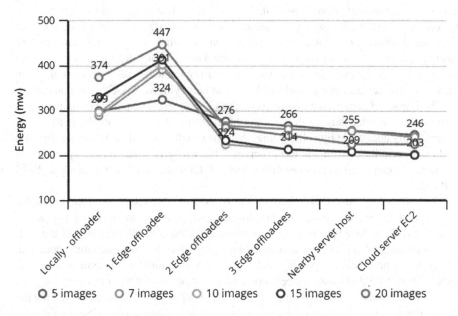

Fig. 6. Battery power consumption of FDSC

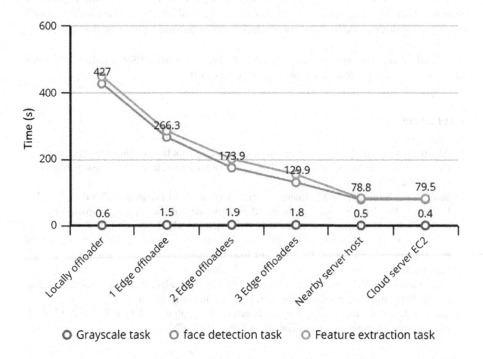

Fig. 7. Processing time of FDS sub-tasks

5 Conclusion and Future Work

The discussion and analysis of the experiments in the above section concludes that we can form a network of Offloadees on-the-go as needed, that will, even small number of devices of 4 Offloadees will perform as good as an edge computing server with unlimited resources. Our future study on this thread will focus on the granularity and partition of the sub-tasks, so to maximize the benefit from the Offloadees without having to run their battery to the ground or increasing the local connectivity traffic with them. For sure having only a single Offloadee to help with the MCCS is not an option.

The impact of connectivity between our local edge resource network and the cloud is significant and depends on the location of the Offloader. For example, if the cloud server is only accessible by cellular link, then the overheads will be 10x more than if a Wi-Fi connectivity is available to the server. This will give much more importance to SOSE as we can form P2P connectivity with all Offloadees, including using a Wi-Fi P2P link.

For automating all the decisions on the offload or not, sub-tasks sizes, Offloadee choices and so on, an automatic partitioning and profiling are required instead of manual profiling. As a next step, we will implement the controller engine, all the end-devices connect to the engine, and exchange a report of features including; location, battery level, processing capability, etc. In CloudSim simulator, the broker role is to decide where to offload the service workload, based on simple broker policies such as nearest VM, fastest VM or dynamic VM. We shell deploy our engine as so, to take the broker policy in deciding where and what to offload, based on SOSE assessment criteria as described in Sect. 3. An intelligent engine is very important to achieve efficient offloading. The various variations for the type of intelligence algorithms, (such as genetic algorithm and/or Markov model) is the next study phase of this project.

Acknowledgment. Gratitude to the University of Basra, and MOHESR (Ministry of Higher Education and Scientific Research) for sponsoring this work.

References

1. Al-ameri, A., Lami, I.A.: SCCOF: smart cooperative computation offloading framework for mobile cloud computing services. In: the 8th Annual International Conference: Big Data, Cloud and Security (2017)
2. Saad, S.M., Nandedkar, S.C.: Energy efficient mobile cloud computing (2014)
3. Elmannai, W., Elleithy, K.: Sensor-based assistive devices for visually-impaired people: current status, challenges, and future directions. Sensors **17**(3), 565 (2017)
4. Dwivedi, A., et al.: Internet of Things' (IoT's) impact on decision oriented applications of big data sentiment analysis. In: 2018 3rd International Conference on Internet of Things: Smart Innovation and Usages (IoT-SIU). IEEE (2018)
5. Wei, X., et al.: MVR: an architecture for computation offloading in mobile edge computing. In: the IEEE International Conference on Edge Computing (2017)
6. Calo, S.B., et al.: Edge computing architecture for applying AI to IoT. In: 2017 IEEE International Conference on Big Data (Big Data). IEEE (2017)

7. Amazon Rekognition: Developer Guide. http://docs.aws.amazon.com/rekognition/latest/dg/rekognition. Accessed January 2019
8. Chen, X., et al.: Thriftyedge: resource-efficient edge computing for intelligent IoT applications. IEEE Netw. **32**(1), 61–65 (2018)
9. Li, H., Ota, K., Dong, M.: Learning IoT in edge: deep learning for the internet of things with edge computing. IEEE Netw. **32**(1), 96–101 (2018)
10. Ko, K., et al.: DisCO: a distributed and concurrent offloading framework for mobile edge cloud computing. In: 2017 Ninth International Conference on Ubiquitous and Future Networks (ICUFN). IEEE (2017)
11. Nearby Connections API. https://developers.google.com/nearby/connections/android/exchange-data. Accessed July 2018
12. Wang, X., Chen, X., Wu, W., An, N., Wang, L.: Cooperative application execution in mobile cloud computing: a stackelberg game approach. IEEE Commun. Lett. **20**, 946–949 (2016)
13. Sirivianos, M., et al.: Dandelion: cooperative content distribution with robust incentives. In: USENIX Annual Technical Conference, vol. 7 (2007)
14. Thu, M.S.Z., Htoon, E.C.: Cost solving model in computation offloading decision algorithm. In: 2018 IEEE 9th Annual Information Technology, Electronics and Mobile Communication Conference (IEMCON). IEEE (2018)
15. Kumar, K., Lu, Y.-H.: Cloud computing for mobile users: can offloading computation save energy? Computer **43**, 51–56 (2010)
16. BroadbandChecker. http://www.broadbandspeedchecker.co.uk. Accessed November 2017
17. Kosta, S., Aucinas, A., Hui, P., Mortier, R., Zhang, X.: ThinkAir: dynamic resource allocation and parallel execution in the cloud for mobile code offloading. In: 2012 Proceedings of the IEEE INFOCOM (2012)
18. Luzuriaga, J., et al.: Evaluating computation offloading trade-offs in mobile cloud computing: a sample application. In: Proceedings of the 4th International Conference on Cloud Computing, GRIDs, Virtualization (2013)

Security, Wireless Sensor Networks and Internet of Things (IoT)

Securing Big Data from Eavesdropping Attacks in SCADA/ICS Network Data Streams through Impulsive Statistical Fingerprinting

Junaid Chaudhry[1] , Uvais Qidwai[2] , and Mahdi H. Miraz[3,4(✉)]

[1] Duja Inc., Perth, Australia
chaudhry@ieee.org
[2] Qatar University, Doha, Qatar
uqidwai@gmail.com
[3] The Chinese University of Hong Kong, Shatin, Hong Kong
m.miraz@ieee.org
[4] Wrexham Glyndŵr University, Wrexham, UK

Abstract. While data from Supervisory Control And Data Acquisition (SCADA) systems is sent upstream, it is both the length of pulses as well as their frequency present an excellent opportunity to incorporate statistical fingerprinting. This is so, because datagrams in SCADA traffic follow a poison distribution. Although wrapping the SCADA traffic in a protective IPsec stream is an obvious choice, thin clients and unreliable communication channels make is less than ideal to use cryptographic solutions for security SCADA traffic. In this paper, we propose a smart alternative of data obfuscation in the form of Impulsive Statistical Fingerprinting (ISF). We provide important insights into our research in healthcare SCADA data security and the use of ISF. We substantiate the conversion of sensor data through the ISF into HL7 format and define policies of a seamless switch to a non HL7-based non-secure HIS to a secure HIS.

Keywords: Cyber security · SCADA/ICS networks ·
Healthcare SCADA systems · Health Level Seven ·
Impulsive Statistical Fingerprinting · Data obfuscation · Encryption ·
Context-aware security · IEEE 11073

1 Introduction

Healthcare data has superior black market cyber value compared to financial data as noted by Trend Micro [1]. With an increasing number of personal healthcare records being digitised, for obvious reasons, the number of cyber-attacks on Health Information System has increased dramatically in the past few years [2].

The ISO/IEEE 11073 Personal Health Data (PHD) is a family of standards that enables medical/healthcare data to be exchanged between medical/healthcare/wellbeing devices and external computing systems. The Health Level Seven (HL7) has been

© ICST Institute for Computer Sciences, Social Informatics and Telecommunications Engineering 2019
Published by Springer Nature Switzerland AG 2019. All Rights Reserved
M. H. Miraz et al. (Eds.): iCETiC 2019, LNICST 285, pp. 77–89, 2019.

providing data modelling and standardization support for almost 30 years. The successor of HL7 is the Fast Healthcare Interoperability Resources (FHIR) draft specification [3]. However, The FHIR specifications and its implementation are not within the scope of this paper. Rather, we chose to use HL7 due to its maturity. In fact, HL7 stays as the most widely accepted and adopted healthcare information sharing standard.

The ISO/IEEE 11073 and HL7 have successfully played a key role in enabling the medical devices to exchange data amongst themselves. Due to privacy and security issues, this data needs to be protected. Since medical devices are not typically computationally very proficient and the standards advocate lightweight communications, a cryptographic data security scheme is not an ideal solution to go ahead with [4]. In order to address this problem, we propose to use the statistical fingerprinting as data obfuscation method.

The Impulsive Statistical Fingerprinting (ISF) was used by Crotti et al. to classify the network traffic for anomaly detection [5]. When network traffic shows an atypical pattern and skewness from the "normal" traffic pattern, this is raised as an anomaly to the system [6]. We use the ISF to prevent leaf sensors from broadcasting the actual readings. Since the ISO/IEEE 11073 allows the flexibility to transmit metadata in the HL7 packet, we calculate the statistical model proposed in this paper to calculate the obfuscated values from sensors before translating the communication in the HL7 format.

The statistical model proposed in this paper assumes that the devices are already connected and configured in a network. An initial handshaking between PHDs and IP network provide the baseline values for mean calculation that will help in recalculating back to original values of the sensor data. From the results reported in [7] we learn that the PHDs send periodic metric report containing time stamp, and status value which reports device errors and alarms. The time stamps received from the devices helps keep both the TCP session [8] and time series data consistent. Using the statistical method proposed in [9], which assumes that the time series data is stationary, we consult to the history of the PHD values. We use the algorithm proposed in [9] and apply autoregressive integrated moving average models to find the best fit of the time series model to past values of the time series. An adversary, who is using a Man-in-The-Middle (MiTM) attack, needs to know considerable amount of time series data to predict the future values.

Following are the advantages of using statistical fingerprinting:

(1) There is virtually no extra overhead in the existing infrastructure,
(2) Adoption to the new solution is typically fairly straightforward and
(3) The obfuscation of the patient data complies with privacy laws of both Australia [10] and Qatar [11], where the test-beds are planned for implementation and trial purposes.

2   Paper Organisation

Section 3 provides relevant definitions and background information on PHDs as well as the security and privacy goals. Section 4 delivers the circumstantial account on the proposed method. Section 5 of the paper comprises a meticulous breakdown of the state-of-the-art in PHD security and privacy research. The concluding remarks have been discussed in Sect. 6 whereas the future works have been ventilated in Sect. 7.

3   Background and Definitions

Recent advances in the embedded technologies and their usage in the field of medicine [12] have increased the benefits of integrated digital patient data to the highest levels. Seamless availability of medical data through interconnected systems has been made possible through the presence of standards [13]. These standards have evolved over time and have served as the key driving force in advent of PHD clusters at one/different HISs.

3.1   PHD Clusters and Inter/Intra Cluster Communication, Translation, and Addressing

According to ISO/IEEE 11073 standard [13], the Personal Healthcare Devices (PHDs) communicate through IEEE 11073 agents with the 11073 manager through a plethora of communication interfaces. These communication interfaces may range from IPv6 enabled Low powered Personal Area Networks (6LowPAN), Zigbee, Bluetooth, or 802.11x etc. [14]. The point to point communication among the PHDs has been left on user settings i.e. as per needed. The devices communicate to the outside world through a hierarchy that includes device agents that are associated intern with the agent managers. This helps in scaling the device clusters in a better way.

3.2   Healthcare Data Security: Needs and Wants

There has been a tremendous growth in breaches into medical and healthcare data [1]. Healthcare data consists of patients' personal physical condition, financial information, private location information, images, videos, peers information, etc. Due to unavailability of legislation on collection of personal data in a HIS settings in the past and increasing availability of healthcare archives, there is a great amount of unfiltered data in healthcare databases. The IEEE 11073 assumes very little responsibility of privacy and security of user data. The standard assumes that each user agent communicates with only one manager and each of them is free to keep their own copy of the data. The presence of these copies makes the layered architecture proposed in IEEE 11073, a vulnerable data network architecture.

3.3   Data Obfuscation in Healthcare Information System

Since data is kept archived in its original form at different layers of communication, the risk of data loss and corruption increases exponentially. There is a growing need for a data security protocol which secures the data in transit and in archives. Because the IEEE 11073 encourages interoperability of heterogeneous devices and simplicity of the infrastructure, it is impractical to get the whole industry to agree on a set of encryption scheme. The PHDs have high diversity in computational power among themselves. Different encryption algorithms have different computational power [4]. We identify that there is a need for a lightweight data obfuscation scheme.

3.4   Statistical Fingerprinting

Due to the constant data stream that is periodically transmitted by the PHDs and inability of agreement to one encryption scheme, we propose to apply linear time series data aggregation algorithms to predict the next value [15] to calculate the autoregressive moving averages of the values that are generated by the PHDs. Using this statistical method, there is no need to change standards or manufacturer's device specifications.

4   The Proposed System

According to the IEEE 11073, the disease management devices fall in the 10400–10439 domain of standards. The PHD agents typically have limited capabilities i.e. RAM, ROM, CPU, etc., connection to a single PHD manager, limited resource in power, they are fixed in their configurations, and unreliable connection to the managers. On the other hand, PHD managers are higher in abstraction layer to the PHD agents with multiple connections, richer power resources, and higher processing capability. The Fig. 1 shows a typical PHD cluster scenario:

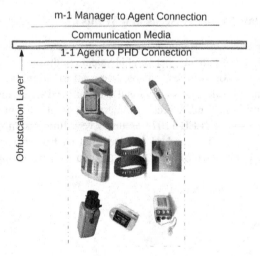

Fig. 1. The Organisation of PHDs, Agents, and Managers in an IEEE 11073 compliant cluster.

As shown in Fig. 1, the obfuscation layer that we propose in this paper resides between the agent and manager. We believe that the placement of obfuscation layer is critical considering the constraints posed by the device and the practice of data archiving as discussed in the previous section.

Let k be the PHD value at a given time t_k.

Where, we have an array of values that a PHD generates and those values are interrelated through a common source or by a common noise $k_i \in k[I]$. So the range of values that are generated from the PHD initially is the sample base for the statistical forecasting model that works on time series data. This series is generated by:

$$R_n = \sum_{i=0}^{i=n} K_i/t$$

Since it is well known, the variance, $\sigma^2 = (\overset{i \to 0}{\Sigma} k_i - \mu)^2 /n$. We can derive that if $K[I]$ be a numerically-valued discrete random variable with sample space Ω and distribution function $m(x)$.

Now, if σ^2 is added with the mean of the time series values, the original value can be obtained: $O_v = \sigma_2 + O[I]_{mean}$. The expected value $E(X)$ at PHD Agent is defined by $E(k[I]) = \sum_{x \in \Omega} xm(x)$. The proposed scheme shall be considered valid if and only if $t_k = (\gamma \cdot E(X))/\beta$.

Where γ and β are coefficients of consistency within the tolerance ranges of error.

4.1   The Testbed

We use the testbed presented in [16]: a testbed for monitoring the long term bedridden patients. The testbed consists of pressure sensors that generate events (pressure readings) which generate time series data & triggers the IEEE 11073 compliant video camera and can communicate to the PHD agent. There are 25 force sensitive sensors that are placed under the bedsheet in 5×5 strips manner. Each row of sensors is supported by the enamelled wiring and sown in a row into fabric for patient comfort. The sensors are arranged in the form of a matrix on the bed. The position of the sensors is adjustable according to the morphology and physiological features of the patient. The intensity of pressure/force on the sensors by a patient's posture on laying position in bed is measured by the voltage amplitude. The implementation of the PHD agent is performed on the Arduino board that is attached with wires to the sensors (Fig. 2).

The intensity of pressure/force on the sensors by patients' posture on laying position in bed is measured by voltage amplitude. The implementation of the PHD agent is performed on the Arduino board that is attached with wires to the sensors. The matrix of force sensors provide uniform data series. In order to achieve closeness to the

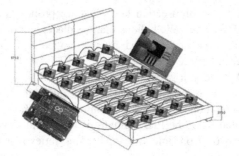

Fig. 2. Matrix of sensors in the long term bedridden patients and an Arduino board with PHD agents implementation and a host to the obfuscation layer algorithm.

real time environment, we introduce an event triggered digital camera. The data feed from the digital camera is routed to the IP network through the Arduino board (Fig. 3).

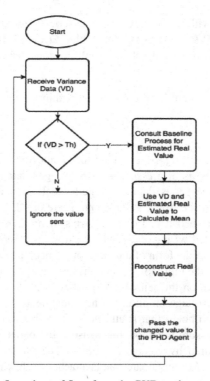

Fig. 3. The flow chart of flow from the PHD to the agent and back.

In Fig. 4, we present the sequence flow diagram of the protocol proposed. We propose that the PHD transmits the baseline values at initial handshake. This is achieved after initial DHCP. After the acquisition of the baseline values, the PHD starts sending variance of the values with respect to the previous value transmitted. This way, the burst frequency is reduced which will result into lesser network traffic and if the sensor values stay the same, the network will carry packets with zero data values in it.

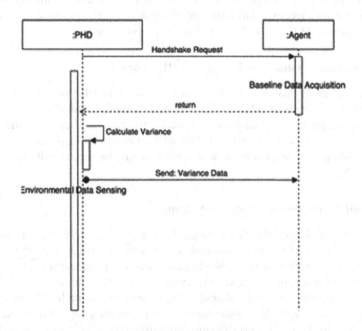

Fig. 4. The sequence diagram of the protocol proposed.

4.2 Multisensor Data Obfuscation Through Statistical Fingerprinting

The continuous time series data that PHDs send through PHD agents to the PHD managers is in plain format in the conventional HIS. We propose that instead of sending sensor values, the variance from the previous value is sent. In [17], the algorithm for calculation of variance from an incoming data stream is reported. Using the stream of data carrying variance of sensor readings and mean from the baseline sensor readings, one can calculate the original sensor reading. This way, the data in transit stays obscure to the intruders.

The initial handshake in the system is based on trust. That is the devices that are newly configured to the system, share their 'native' sensor readings with the agents: residing on the Arduino. It is only after a sizable sample, in our case 50 samples, or native values are stored as demonstrated by the authors in [9]. An interesting debate on the usability of Kalmans filter and statistical methods are found in [9] which assisted us in choosing the statistical methods for this particular scenario.

The following notations describe the method of calculating the forecasted value for the time series under consideration using the statistical methods. This calculated value shall be used as the confidence value against packet injection attacks in a PHD networked environment. Although the statistical methods have their shortcomings [18], we believe that an alternative incorporation of input verification method shall greatly benefit the security in the PHD based networking environment.

4.3   Conversion of Obfuscated Data into HL7 Format

From [19], we learnt that conversion of data streams into HL7 format requires the policy engine that generates XML documents when provided with data source. In the current scenario, we have two series of data streams for the policy engine: 1- time series data to be kept as a baseline sample for the statistical model, 2- Variance data as time series data. We plan to implement a new version of the conversion software into the Weka tool [20].

4.4   Threat Model for the Proposed Scheme

In this section we discuss the threat model for the proposed scheme. As discussed earlier, that the ISO/IEEE 11037 standards encourages the transit of healthcare data through various networked devices. Mostly, this data is in plain text format. This data in transit, while unencrypted, is a serious security and privacy threat.

Let's assume that Alice is an attacker who wants to steal the healthcare data. In conventional environment, Alice will spoof network packets, or spoof IP of the PHD-Agent and request the latest sensor reading from the PHD. If the method proposed in this paper is adopted, the attacker will have the following scenarios to attack and steal the data.

Through Packet Capture: If an attacker captures the packet that contains the PHD data, the attacker shall get variance from the data packet, which will not be of any use unless the attacker knows the mean of over the range of the values.

Through Spoofing PHD-Agents IP Address: This type of attack is typically classified as Man in The Middle (MiTM) attack. If Alice sends a decoy packet to the PHD agent and an association request, unless Alice has the statistical model, she cannot generate the mean from the baseline values and hence the attack will only be valid for the amount of time it takes to generate baseline values.

5   Empirical Analysis and Discussion

In our experiments, we extracted a sample set of 1400 readings from embedded temperature sensor hosted on the Adruino. The following diagram shows the dataset: (Fig. 5)

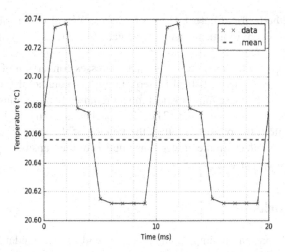

Fig. 5. The sample data set.

Lemma 1: Whether we can constitute the original value from variance and mean?

We extracted the mean and variance of the sample values which were 20.65627 and 0.00233 respectively. We determined that the reconstructed value was an exact match with the real value at the sensor. Whether this condition will still hold true for change in variance? - we rest this argument for the future work (Fig. 6).

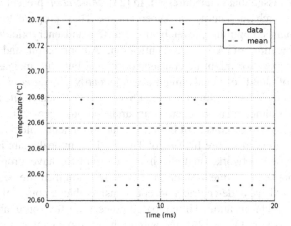

Fig. 6. Comparison of the original value at sensor and recalculation of original value at PHD agent.

Lemma 2: Whether the predicted value from the statistical model matches with the real value?

In our observation, we noticed that the variance values for each sensor value predicted filled in perfectly in the gaps between the estimated value and the real value at the sensor. In future, we aim at investigating the effectiveness of the statistical fingerprinting methods for different types of traffics. We also aim at testing these methods in different environments and investigate the effects of multi-sensor data fusion environments.

In past, we proposed the method in [19] that addresses conversion of the healthcare data into HL7 format. Using statistical fingerprinting, the volume of traffic is reduced by 66.75%. This is so because the statistical model requires two previous neighbouring values to serve as a reference point. The HL7 packet is going to hold additional statistical value within the packet to reflect the volume of the sample and variance of the values. This also reflects in the power consumption of the transmitting nodes which is not within the scope of this paper.

6 Related Works

Martinez et al. [21] present the implementation of an end-to-end standard-based patient monitoring solution. They demonstrate that their implementation is incompliant with X73 and EN13606 standards. However, data security in the system proposed by Martinez et al. rely on the security strengths of its components i.e. database security. The data in transit and cache stored at each level, according to the IEEE standard, stays vulnerable. The authors of [22] have enumerated the threat space for the medical devices. They go on to state that despite the vulnerabilities in the communication technologies, the data in transit is still vulnerable to attacks. Lee et al. [14] enumerate the interoperability challenges in the personal healthcare devices and also list that the data in transit as an issue that is unaddressed. In [23], Marc et al. present the case study of hospital image archive security on super clouds. They propose to use network services as the main computing power behind transfer and encryption/decryption of secure data. Delegation of AAA (Authentication, Authorization and Accounting) functions to the hypervisor might be considered rational but with increase in network volume, the idea of clouds of clouds might get in jeopardy. Zheng et al. [24] illustrate the application of blockchain technique in the PSN-based healthcare. The application of the blockchain in healthcare environment is unparalleled but since healthcare networks are hybrid in nature i.e. they consist of both thick and thin clients, blockchain might be overkill. An application of secure Internet of Things (IoT) in healthcare is proposed in [25]. On an IP-based network, on thin clients, the authors have proposed hashing messages and propose to use the hashing time as verification measure between the two processes. Since IoT is a de-centric concept, considerable amount of energies are invested in clock synchronisation. Timing-based process verification in absence of a/or two master clock(s) is risky. In [26], the authors have implemented a standard com-plaint prototype. They have discussed the plug and play capabilities derived from X73 standards. In compliance with ISO11037, the authors have not discussed the issues like security of data in transit, security of data in storage, device security, connection security, etc. They have relied on the inherent security features of TCP/IP.

Zhang et al. [27, 28] used statistical fingerprinting to detect peer-to-peer botnets through host-to-host traffic analysis. In [29], Trevor et al. is the RF fingerprinting for feature selection in Zigbee emissions and in [30], Sucki et al. use spatial fingerprinting to improve security in wireless networks. The statistical fingerprinting provides an in-vivo baseline to match the anomaly against, which is one of the most research areas in anomaly detection research. The foremost advantage of this non-crypto-based data obfuscation scheme proposed in this research paper is the lightweightness, portability, scalability, with very nominal overhead costs. Lee *et al.* [31] discussed several cases where anomaly detection is hard in health care networks because attackers mask their traffic with the normal traffic. In this situation, signature-based or traffic pattern based anomaly detection is near impossible. They emphasize on the use of verified transactions in the network which is an unrealistic assumption in large networks such that of health care networks. Zhenyu *et al.* [32] and in [33, 34] addressed large-scale internet of things and its application in health care through fog computing. Having considered the rapid volumetric increase in the IoT technology, unless the underlying flaws of the supportive technologies are fixed, the cyber security is going to stay as a major cause of concern [35, 36].

The ISO/IEEE 11073 Personal Health Data (PHD) is a family of standards that enables medical/healthcare data to be exchanged between medical/healthcare/wellbeing devices and external computing systems. The Health Level Seven (HL7) has been providing data modeling and standardization support for almost 30 years. The successor of HL7 is the Fast Healthcare Interoperability Resources (FHIR) draft specification [3]. However, The FHIR specifications and its implementation are not within the scope of this paper. Rather, we chose to use HL7 due to its maturity. In fact, HL7 stays as the most widely accepted and adopted healthcare information sharing standard.

7 Concluding Remarks

In this paper we presented our research using statistical fingerprinting before transformation of the healthcare data into HL7 format. We demonstrated that the statistical fingerprinting not only adds a semantic layer of security to the data, it can be performed locally at the data acquisition site without considerable overhead. The process of ISF is performed at the presentation stage of the data which means that the integrity of data is ensured. After the ISF is performed, the data is converted into HL7 format using the converter built in Java. If the data packet containing fingerprinted data is intercepted, an adversary will not be able to predict the value of the sensor unless s/he is physically present at the sensor site or has been present throughout the lifetime of the sensor sending the fingerprinted data. We believe that the research presented in this paper is of significant value because it advocates for seamless of HIS into a more secure HIS without considerable overhead or changes to the existing infrastructure.

8 Future Works

We aim at presenting a comprehensive comparative analysis of various encryption techniques, data obfuscation techniques, and the scheme proposed in this paper in an HIS setting. This tasks requires analysis of "key-driving variables" in a Health Information System (HIS), foresighted strengths and weaknesses of cryptographic schemes, and development of context in order to choose the right data security scheme. We also plan to develop an adversarial model for the scheme proposed.

References

1. Trend Micro Threat Intelligence Report 2016. http://www.trendmicro.com.au/vinfo/au/security/research-and-analysis/threat-reports. Accessed Jan 2017
2. Symantec Internet Security Threat Report. https://www.symantec.com/content/dam/symantec/docs/reports/istr-21-2016-en.pdf. Accessed Jan 2017
3. Namli, T., Aluc, G., Dogac, A.: An interoperability test framework for HL7-based systems. IEEE Eng. Med. Biol. **13**, 389–399 (2009)
4. Parmar, P.V., Padhar, S.B., Patel, S.N., Bhatt, N.I., Jhaveri, R.H.: Survey of various homomorphic encryption algorithms and schemes. Int. J. Comput. Appl. **91**(8) (2014)
5. Crotti, M., Dusi, M., Gringoli, F., Salgarelli, L.: Traffic classification through simple statistical fingerprinting. ACM SIGCOMM Comput. Commun. Rev. **37**(1), 5–16 (2007)
6. Boero, L., Cello, M., Marchese, M., Mariconti, E., Naqash, T., Zappatore, S.: Statistical fingerprint-based intrusion detection system (SF-IDS). Int. J. Commun. Syst. (2016). https://doi.org/10.1002/dac.3225
7. Hoffman, R.M.: Modeling Medical Devices for Plug-and-Play Interoperability. MIT Press, Cambridge (2007)
8. Santos, D.F.S., Almeida, H.O., Perkusich, A.: A personal connected health system for the Internet of Things based on the Constrained Application Protocol. Comput. Electr. Eng. **44** (C), 122–136 (2015)
9. Chatterjee, S., Brad, J.F.: A Comparison of Box-Jenkins time series models with autoregressive processes, IEEE Trans. Syst. Man Cybern., 252–259 (2012)
10. Department of Prime Minister and Cabinet, Australian Cyber Security Strategy. https://cybersecuritystrategy.dpmc.gov.au/assets/pdfs/dpmc-cyber-strategy.pdf?q=270716. Accessed Jan 2017
11. Ministry of Information and Communication Technology, Qatar National Cyber Security Strategy. http://www.motc.gov.qa/sites/default/files/national_cyber_security_strategy.pdf. Accessed Jan 2017
12. Clerk Maxwell, J.: A Treatise on Electricity and Magnetism, vol. 2, 3rd edn., pp. 68–73. Clarendon, Oxford (1892)
13. IEEE Healthcare IT Standards 11073, https://standards.ieee.org/findstds/standard/healthcare_it.html, Last Accessed Jan 2017
14. Lee, Y.-F.: Personal medical monitoring system: addressing interoperability. IT Prof. **15**(5), 31–37 (2013)
15. Box, G.E.P., Jenkins, G.M., Reinsel, G.C.: Time Series Analysis: Forecasting and Control, 3rd edn. Prentice-Hall, Inc., Englewood Cliffs (1994)
16. Qidwai, U., Ilyas, S.K., Al-Sulaiti, S., Ahmed, G., Hegazy, A.: Intelligent integrated instrumentation platform for monitoring long-term bedridden patients. In: IEEE EMBS Conference of Biomedical, Engineering and Sciences (IEEE-EMBS 2016) (2016)
17. Lin, X., Zhang, Y.: Aggregate computation over data streams. In: APWeb 2008, pp 10–25 (2008)
18. Talluri, K.T., van Ryzin, G.J.: The Theory and Practice of Revenue Management. Kluwer Academic Publishers, Boston (2004)
19. Chaudhry, J., Qidwai, U., Malrey, L.: Dynamic Health Level Seven Packetizer for on-the-fly integrated healthcare enterprises in disaster zones. Neural Inf. Process. **7663**, 432–438 (2012)
20. Weka 3: A data mining software in Java. http://www.cs.waikato.ac.nz/ml/weka/. Accessed Jan 2017

21. Martinez, I., et al.: Implementation of an end-to-end standard-based patient monitoring solution. IET Commun. **2**(2), 181–191 (2008)
22. Aragues, A., et al.: Trends and challenges of the emerging technologies toward interoperability and standardization in e-health communications. IEEE Commun. Mag. **49** (11), 182–188 (2011)
23. Lacoste, M., et al.: User-centric security and dependability in the coulds-of-clouds. IEEE Could Comput. **2**(5), 64–75 (2016)
24. Zhang, J., Xue, N., Huang, X.: A secure system for pervasive social network-based healthcare. IEEE Access **4**, 9239–9250 (2016)
25. Yeh, K.-H.: A secure IoT-based healthcare system with body sensor networks. IEEE Access **4**, 10288–10299 (2016)
26. Martínez, I., et al.: Implementation of an end-to-end standard-based patient monitoring solution. IET Commun. **2**(2), 181–191 (2008)
27. Zhang, J., Perdisci, R., Lee, W., Luo, X., Sarfraz, U.: Building a scalable system for stealthy P2P-botnet detection. IEEE Trans. Inf. Forensics Secur. **9**(1), 27–38 (2014)
28. Zhang, J., Perdisci, R., Lee, W., Sarfraz, U., Luo, X.: Detecting stealthy P2P botnets using statistical traffic fingerprints. In: Proceedings of IEEE/IFIP 41st International Conference on DSN, pp. 121–132, June 2011
29. Bihl, T.J., Bauer, K.W., Temple, M.A.: Feature selection for RF fingerprinting with multiple discriminant analysis and using ZigBee device emissions. IEEE Trans. Inf. Forensics Secur. **11**, 1862–1874 (2016)
30. Suski, W.C., Temple, M.A., Mendenhall, M.J., Mills, R.F.: Using spectral fingerprints to improve wireless network security. In: Proceedings of IEEE Global Telecommunications Conference (GLOBECOM), pp. 1–5, November/December 2008
31. Lee, W., Kim, S., Jeon, H., Kim, H.: Detecting an abnormal traffic on healthcare network. In: International Conference on IT Convergence and Security (ICITCS), October 2015
32. Wen, Z., Yang, R., Garraghan, P., Lin, T., Xu, J., Rovatsos, M.: Fog orchestration for Internet of Things services. IEEE Internet Comput. **21**(2), 16–24 (2017)
33. Ahmad, A., Ahmad, M., Habib, M.A., Sarwar, S., Chaudhry, J.: Parallel query execution over encrypted data in database-as-a-service (DaaS). J. Supercomput. **75**, 2269–2288 (2019)
34. Habib, M.A., Ahmad, M., Jabbar, S., Khalid, S., Chaudhry, J.: Security and privacy based access control model for internet of connected vehicles. Future Gener. Comput. Syst. **97**, 687–696 (2019)
35. Miraz, M.H., Ali, M., Excell, P., Picking, R.: A review on Internet of Things (IoT), Internet of Everything (IoE) and Internet of Nano Things (IoNT). In: The Proceedings of 2015 IEEE International Conference on Internet Technologies and Applications (ITA 2015), Wrexham Glyndŵr University, UK, pp. 219–224. IEEE, 8–11 September 2015. https://doi.org/10. 1109/itecha.2015.7317398. Print ISBN: 978-1-4799-8036-9. http://ieeexplore.ieee.org/xpl/ articleDetails.jsp?arnumber=7317398
36. Miraz, M.H., Ali, M., Excell, P.S., Picking, R.: Internet of nano-things, things and everything: future growth trends. Future Internet **10**(8), 68 (2018). https://doi.org/10.3390/ fi10080068. http://www.mdpi.com/1999-5903/10/8/68

A Trust Based Mutual Authentication and Data Encryption Scheme for MANET Security

Mansoor Ihsan[✉] and Martin Hope

The University of Salford, Manchester M5 4WT, UK
{m.ihsanl,m.d.hope}@salford.ac.uk

Abstract. MANET are self-configurable wireless network where the nodes do not have fixed infrastructure, no centralized mechanism, nodes are fully cooperative, highly mobile and dynamic. There is no inherent security between the nodes for secure communication and data exchange. One of the huge security challenges is authentication of nodes in such environment in general and peer communicating nodes in particular where nodes are communicating for the first time.

The proposed scheme presents a novel solution to authenticate peer nodes (source and destination) with no prior trust and security associations. As no pre-established trust exists before the MANET is initialized therefore, in MANET, nodes present a huge challenge of authenticating communicating peer nodes. The proposed scheme provides a solution to authenticate the sending and receiving nodes using trust based scheme as the sender and receiver doesn't have first-hand information about these trust values as they could be at the opposite end. Thus, the trust is calculated by nodes for all their neighbours and is send to peer communicating nodes when requested before peer nodes initiate communication. We refer to this process as authentication through trust. Lastly, to ensure end to end data encryption, the mutual trust scheme is combined with Diffie-Hellman Elliptic Curve DHEC Key Exchange. This allows nodes pair to exchange data securely by using shared secret keys to encrypt data.

Keywords: MANET · Network security · Trust-based scheme ·
Trust-based authentication · Cryptography · Asymmetric key exchange

1 Introduction

One of the vulnerabilities of MANET is the lack of secure communication mechanism between nodes and protection against various threats. The minimum requirement of implementing security in any system is achieving the security goal of Availability, Integrity, Authenticity commonly referred to a CIA. This paper is concerned with the using trust to achieve authentication in MANET nodes. This can only be achieved by forming a secure channel between the communicating nodes. The algorithm used is a combination of trust based scheme as a framework and available efficient cryptographic techniques to achieve the above security goals. The scheme is divided into three steps. The first step of the algorithm is to build the trust factors which provide a secure

M. H. Miraz et al. (Eds.): iCETiC 2019, LNICST 285, pp. 90–105, 2019.
https://doi.org/10.1007/978-3-030-23943-5_7

platform for the later steps of the protocol that uses the trust values to authenticate peer node. Lastly, a secure key management scheme to secure communication between nodes in the network is also proposed to provide data encryption.

The trust calculation can be achieved using any trust threshold scheme proposed [1–7]. Once the trust is established between neighbour nodes, the trust values can be used to validate communicating peer nodes in the second step. The scheme addresses the issue of authenticating peer communicating nodes that could be far apart and one-to-one trust value exchange is not possible. Thus, step-one is a framework to provide the level of security required in the form of a trust and step-two can be used to authenticate nodes based on those trust values.

2 MANET Security Completed Work

Routing protocol in MANETs such as AODV were designed without taken security considerations into account therefore, it is prone to number of security threats as mentioned earlier. There are number of attacks that has been identified and studied in MANET. The type of attack also depends on which network has been targeted. We will discuss more advanced attacks that could affect MANET. Some of the types are Blackhole [7], Greyhole [8], Wormhole [9, 11] that are classed as Denial-of-Service (DoS) attacks. Other types of attacks are Byzantine [12], Flooding [13], Grayhole [10] and Rushing [14].

Extensive research has been done and various security protocols have been proposed by the researchers in an attempt to secure different aspects of MANET. The mobility of nodes and constantly changing topology makes availability challenging in MANET. It is essential to the network operations. MANETs are vulnerable to attack on any level of the open system interconnection OSI model including physical attacks such as Denial of Service DOS or wireless jamming techniques as well as attacks on higher-level services such Key Management services [10]. We will briefly discuss and analyze some of secure routing protocols developed for MANETs such as SAODV [15], SEAD [16], TESLA [17], Ariadne [18], SAR [19], Security Aided Adhoc Routing [20] and ARAN [21].

- Secure Adhoc On-demand Distance Vector SAODV [15] routing protocol is used to secure the routing messages for the original AODV. Basically the SAODV uses digital signature, a branch of symmetric cryptography, to authenticate non-mutable fields and using hashing algorithm such as hash chain to authenticate the mutable field i.e. hop count for both route request RREQ and route reply RREP message [16].
- Authenticated Routing for Adhoc Network ARAN [21] is another type of MANET security protocol that uses digital signatures to protect the non-mutable fields of the routing messages and uses Open SSL library for certification. This is thought to be time consuming and generate a lot of overhead.
- Security Aware Routing protocol SAR [19] is a trust based reactive protocol. It uses trust values and relationships with the nodes which form the basis of its routing

decisions. Only trusted nodes can participate in the routing. The protocol does not provide high-end security.

- Another protocol proposed called Security Aware Aided Adhoc Routing SPAAR [20]. It's a location aware protocol which uses geographical information to secure routing information and uses asymmetric cryptography i.e. the use of public key infrastructure for routing.
- Hu et al. [16] proposed Secure Efficient Ad Hoc Distance Vector SEAD and used a protocol, which is based on the design of DSDV [20]. SEAD is designed to prevent attacks such as DoS and resource consumption attacks. Also uses One-Way Hash Chains to secure routing.
- Ariadne also developed by Hu et al. [17] which is based on the operation of DSR [22]. Ariadne [18] uses message authentication code (MAC) and secret key shared between two parties to ensures point-to-point authentication of a routing message. Ariadne is a secure on-demand routing protocol and uses symmetric cryptographic operations. The protocol provides security against one compromised node and prevents many types of denial-of-service attacks. However, it relies on the Timed Efficient Stream Loss-tolerant Authentication TESLA [17]. This is not suitable for MANET as it requires clock synchronisation.

3   Trust Based Scheme

Trust based routing protocol works by adding Trust parameters to the nodes. Nodes operate in promiscuous mode and hear the conversations between other nodes in transmission range. Trust can be computed by taking into account different factor such as packets sent, received, acknowledged and forwarded by various nodes in the network. Therefore, nodes representing high trust can be selected as best path for communication. Trust schemes are used to mitigate security attacks and identify malicious nodes in the network as an alternative to cryptographic methods due to special characteristics of MANET. Extensive research has carried out on the use to trust threshold schemes in MANET. In the next section we will discuss some of trust based schemes proposed.

Several techniques have been proposed to detect and eliminate malicious nodes in the network such as [23–31]. One of the earliest techniques proposed was Watchdog and Pathrater. The Watchdog technique identifies misbehaving nodes while Pathrater technique calculates path avoiding misbehaving nodes [24]. The Pathrater rates every path in its cache and select a path that best avoids misbehaving nodes. In [27] the author used the concept of incentives called beans to forward packets. Each node in return for participating in packet forwarding earns beans. The packet is automatically dropped when the packet run out of beans. A credit-based scheme known as Sprite was proposed by [30] in which the receipts of all packets send and received are kept and reported to Credit Clearance Services CCS when there is an internet connection. The CCS can make decision based on its report about the individual nodes. Scheme called Ex-watchdog proposed by [32] was proposed to address the weaknesses of watchdog scheme by discovering malicious nodes which can partition the network by generating false reports. Another Intrusion Detection System proposed by [5] relies on watchdog technique to overcome deficiencies in the original watchdog scheme by introducing end-to-end acknowledge called TWOACK. Another trust based scheme called Adaptive Acknowledge scheme (AACK) [27] is an attempt to reduce detection overhead while increasing detection efficiency through detecting misbehaving node rather than link proposed in TWOACK [5]. Muhammad et al. [1] proposed Adaptive Trust Threshold Strategy for detecting and isolating misbehaving node. The main difference between this and other schemes proposed is that it adapts to changes in topology and therefore, its threshold against which the trust is measured and compared is a dynamic value.

Confident scheme was proposed by [26] which is also a reputation based scheme. It has four major components Monitor, Reputation System, Path and Trust Manager. Monitor performs watchdog function, Reputation deals with node rating, path is about path rating and Trust deals with alert messages.

4 Our Proposed Scheme

Trust based routing protocol works by adding trust parameters to the nodes. Nodes operate in promiscuous mode and hear the conversations between other nodes in its transmission range. Trust can be computed by taking into account different factors such as packets sent, received, acknowledged and forwarded by various nodes in the network. Therefore, nodes representing high trust can be selected as best path for communication. Trust schemes are used to mitigate security attacks and identify malicious nodes in the network as an alternative to cryptographic methods due to special characteristics of MANET. Extensive research has been carried out on the use of trust schemes for security in MANET. The next section will discuss some of trust based schemes proposed.

The proposed mutual authentication scheme can be implemented on top of any trust based scheme. There have been number of trust schemes proposed [1–6] that can be used as a framework for the proposed scheme in step-one.

For instance, the Watchdog technique identifies misbehaving nodes while Pathrater technique would calculate path avoiding misbehaving nodes [24] using trust values. Another example of a scheme using static trust is Adaptive Acknowledge scheme (AACK), [27] is an attempt to reduce detection overhead while increasing detection efficiency through detecting misbehaving node rather than link proposed in TWOACK [5]. All these schemes use trust in some shape and form to represent trust in the nodes.

4.1 Neighbour Nodes Trust Calculation

According to the above schemes [1, 4, 6], trust is generally calculated by nodes listening in promiscuous mode to the packets send and received by its corresponding neighbours. Our scheme relies on this information collected by neighbour nodes as being first hand is used to authenticate peer nodes. The trust is represented as Average Trust and calculated using Eq. 1 below.

$$\text{Average Trust } T = \frac{\sum \text{Packets Sent/Recvd}}{\sum \text{TotalPackets}} \tag{1}$$

Once the node trust is calculated using trust schemes mentioned above then the trust is compared against an arbitrary static trust threshold to determine the final trust of a node (κTa) using Eq. 2. The Average trust (T) In most of the cases the trust is calculated by neighbour nodes as they operate in promiscuous node and can listen to the packets send and received by its neighbour.

4.2   Mutual Trust Authentication Scheme Structure

We have used AODV as a reference to compare our scheme. AODV is modified to embed our scheme and comparisons are drawn to validate our findings. There are four types of messages RREQ, RREP, RERR and RACK defined by AODV protocol. Our scheme only uses the RREQ message at destination node and RREP at the source node for implementation.

According to this stage, once the Trust values received from neighbors of corresponding peer nodes then, the trust values are combined as shown in Eq. 2, to calculate the peer node trust.

$$\kappa Ta = \frac{1}{N} \sum_{i=0}^{N} Ti \tag{2}$$

Where T is Average Trust value calculated by each neighbor node, N is Total number of neighbors, K is the trust of node a and i is the Node index.

Once the trust values are received from all the corresponding neighbor nodes then the trust values are evaluated to calculate final trust value by using Eq. 2. The peer node is authenticated if the trust threshold is above certain static predetermined threshold or authentication fails if the trust threshold calculated is low. The Algorithm-1, represents how the node trust is calculated using trust based schemes and the node is declared as trust or malicious as a result of the computation. The Algorithm 1 shows how the trust is calculated in the majority of research work presented so far.

```
Begin
Compute Node Trust
Compute Static Trust
        If Node Trust >= Threshold then
                Trusted
    Else
                Not Trusted
    End
```

Fig. 1. Trust threshold scheme algorithm

4.3   Mutual Authentication Process at Source Node *S*

The source node S waits for a route reply RREP after sending a RREQ in order to communicate with the destination node D. When it received a RREP from destination node D, the source node S then repeats the same process performed by the destination node. Source node also requests the trust values from all the neighbours of the destination node. Upon receiving the trust values of destination neighbours, the source compares the trust values and authenticates the destination node to establish communication. As both nodes S and D have no security association with one another to exchange data, hence the proposed scheme provides that layer of security by using trust to authenticate destination node. The Fig. 1 shows the steps in AODV, when the Mutual Authentication scheme is implemented and the trust is requested by source node. The steps highlighted in the end, where the source receives the RREP, it requests the trust from destination's neighbours followed by DHEC, which constitutes the last step.

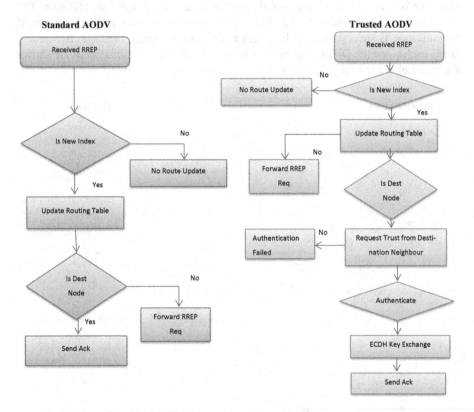

Fig. 2. Source node DFD standard versus mutually authenticated trusted AODV

4.4   Mutual Authentication Process at Destination Node *D*

This section describes how AODV can be used to implement the proposed mutual authentication scheme. When a source node S wishes to communicate with destination

Node D, and doesn't have a route to destination node D, it sends a RREQ. In the normal AODV operation the destination node sends a reply to the source node with the valid root when the RREQ reaches the destination node D and the last action performed is a |Send Reply| message sent. After the AODV operation is complete and before any data communication is performed by both nodes, the authentication and authorization stage begins which concludes the first phase of the proposed scheme.

According to this stage, the destination node requests trust values from source S and all its neighbour nodes. Once the trust values are received from all the corresponding neighbour nodes of S then the trust values are evaluated to calculate final trust value. The node is authenticated if the trust value is equal to and higher than the values received from all neighbours, and authentication fails if the trust value is low. The same process is repeated by the source node S to authenticate destination node by requesting source and its neighbours trust values recorded for the source node.

The AODV process at destination node is shown in Fig. 3. The Fig. 3 presents the difference between standard and AODV process based on Mutual authentication. The authenticated AODV requests the trust values from source neighbour node and if authentication is successful, a reply is sent in the form of RREP message. Before any data is exchanged the DHEC algorithm is implemented. The additional steps are shown at the end of trusted AODV in Fig. 3.

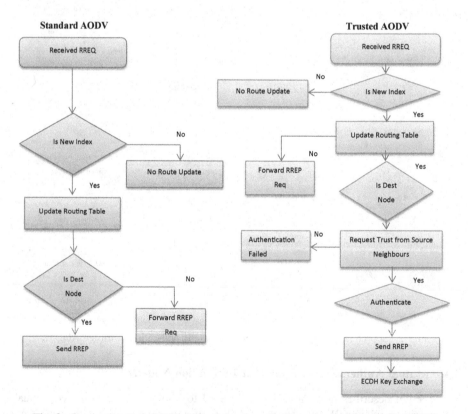

Fig. 3. Destination node DFD standard versus mutually authenticated trusted AODV

4.5 Diffie-Hellman Elliptic Curve Key Exchange

To ensure the data cannot be intercepted by any third party or protect is from eavesdropper, we propose implementing the cryptographic protocol. DHEC algorithm is implemented when Route Request (RREQ) message is received and RREP acknowledgement is sent by the destination node D. This is a novel concept through which peer nodes authenticate one another through trust which is discussed in detail in Sects. 4.3 and 4.4. The authentication using trust ensures that the communicating nodes are trusted and their trust values are endorsed by the neighbour. We believe that trust values calculated by neighbours can have highest level of trust, than trust calculated through other methods. When the trust and mutual authentication schemes are combined they provide a foundation to secure key exchange between any communicating nodes. The secret key could be used to provide security in the following ways;

1. Authentication and authorization
2. Encrypting data exchange between nodes

This could provide protection against the forms of attack that are common in MANET, such as Blackhole, Greyhole, Rushing and Wormhole attack.

The last step of our proposed scheme is the key exchange mechanism to encrypt messages using secret keys. The keys are exchanged using Diffie-Hellman key exchange [31]. This would ensure the data is encrypted and could not be intercepted or tempered with by eaves dropper between source S and destination D.

DHEC scheme allows us to exchange secure information i.e. secret shares between sender and the receiver over insecure channel. This is an example of Asymmetric algorithm [31]. This algorithm states that two nodes exchange public keys and then each performs a calculation on their individual private key and the public key of the other. The result of this whole process gives us an identical shared key. The shared key obtained is used for encrypting and decrypting data between two nodes. The scheme provide a framework about how to perform key generation and exchange between parties or devices that do not yet have secure connection to establish shared keying material (key that can be used with symmetrical keying algorithm such as AES, DES, HMAC) therefore it's more a key-agreement protocol than an encryption algorithm. Elleptic Curve Diffie Hellman is more efficient variant of Diffie-Hellman key exchange algorithm which will be used in our scheme [32]. They are used in Public Key Cryptography for conceiving efficient factorization algorithm.

Public Key cryptography is designed on the principle of hardness of solving the following two problems;

1. Factorization of large integers
2. Discrete Logarithm Problem DLP

The main idea behind the above concept is the trapdoor one way function.

A one way Trapdoor function is such that
Given x, $Y = f(x)$ is easy to compute
Given Y, it's computationally infeasible to calculate x

Elliptic curves are set of points defined by the solution to the following equation

$$E = \{(x,y)|y^2 = x^3 + ax + b\}$$
$$a,b \in K$$
(3)

Where a is an element of field, b is an elements of field and K is a field.
Some of the fields K that Elliptic curves are defined over are

- R: Real numbers
- Q: Rational Numbers
- C: Complex numbers
- Z: Integers modulo p represented as Z/pZ

Following is the example of a graph of elliptic curve over real numbers R (Fig. 4).

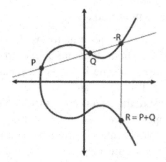

Fig. 4. Elliptic curve over integer modulo p

Also there is a point at infinity represented as O

Point at infinity: O

And there is also a condition that

$$4a^3 + 27b^2 \neq 0$$
(4)

Discrete Logarithm Problem DLP is a type of one-way function as explained above in which exponentiation is easy but logarithm is difficult to compute. The types of cyclic groups used in public key cryptosystem are
Example of DLP in zp^*

- Given the finite cyclic group zp^* of order $p-1$ and a primitive element $a \in zp^*$ and another element $b \in zp^*$
- The DLP is the difficult computation of determining the integer $1 \leq x \leq p-1$ such that

$$a^x \equiv b \bmod p \quad or \quad x = \log_a b$$
(5)

Elliptic curves uses shorter encryption keys hence consume fewer memory and CPU resources. It offers more security per bit in increase in size and is more computationally efficient then the first generation RSA and Diffie-Hellman public key systems [31]. The figure below shows the comparison of Diffie-Hellman and RSA key exchange protocols using elliptic curve (Table 1).

Table 1. Comparative analysis between RSA and Diffie-Hellman using ECC

Symmetric encryption (key size in bits)	RSA and Diffie-Hellman (modulus size in bits)	ECC key size (in bits)
56	512	112
80	1024	160
112	2048	224
128	3072	256
192	7680	384
256	15360	512

The above comparison shows that the Elliptic Curve keys are much smaller [31]. Secondly the ratio of the key lengths utilizing the protocol from multiplicative group using modulus mod p as shown in the middle table to the key length of Elliptic Curve protocol is increased from 6:1 for 80 bits, 12:1 for 128 bits and 30:1 for 256 bits [33]. This implies that the more security is required the more efficient ECC becomes.

In order to keep the shares confidential and secure so it doesn't get into malicious hands or get compromised in any way during exchange process from Source node to the Destination Node as shown in Figs. 1 and 2 above we propose the use of Diffie-Hellman Elliptic Curve Key exchange algorithm.

The following section describes various steps needed to configure DHEC protocol.

Let E be an elliptic curve over a finite field k.

Let P, Q be points on E such that $P = nQ$ for some integer n.

Let $|P|$ denote the number of bits needed to describe the point P.

We wish to find an algorithm which determines n and has runtime polynomial in $|P| + |Q|$. So this problem seems hard. This is also referred to as Discrete Logarithm Problem where "adding is easy on Elliptic Curve but undoing is hard" [34].

Using a multiplicative group of points on an elliptic curve the ECDH protocol works as follows;

1. Node A and Node B agree on an elliptic curve E over a Field Fq and a base-point $P \in E/Fq$.
2. A generates a (random) secret kA and computes $PA = kAP$.
3. B generates a (random) secret kB and computes $PB = kBP$.
4. A and B exchange PA and PB.
5. A and B compute $PAB = kaPB = kbPA$

The secret kA and kB is a random value $\in \{1, ..., n - 1\}$ where n is the order of the group generated by P [36] and exchanged non secure channel without revealing Identity of the secret.

5 Performance Metrics

The performance of the proposed scheme is evaluated using the following metrics:

- **Throughput:** It is the amount of data (bit or packets) transferred between source and destination per period of time (seconds).

$$Throughput = \frac{Size\ of\ Data\ Received}{StopTime - StartTime} \tag{3}$$

- **Packet delivery ratio:** The ratio at which packets are delivered in the network.

$$PDR = \frac{\sum_{\forall i \in D} TPR_i}{\sum_{\forall i \in D} TPS_k} \times 100 \tag{4}$$

The TPRi represents the total number of packets received by the destination node i, and TPSk, represents total packets sent by the source k. Where S, represents source and D, represents destination using Constant Bit Rate (CBR) application.

5.1 Parameters

- **Node Mobility Parameters**

The scheme is tested in a simulated environment using machine specification shown in Table 2 using NS2. Standard AODV and dynamic trusted scheme run in the presence of malicious nodes and the results obtained are presented in the section below.

The Random Waypoint Mobility (RWM) model was used to generate mobility. Parameters listed in Table 3 were used to generate mobility in NS2.

Table 2. Simulation system environment

Machine specification					
Model	CPU	CPU's speed	Memory	Memory speed (Hz)	Operating system
HPProbook 450	Intel Core i5	2.20 GHz	8.0 GB	166 MHz	Ubuntu 16.04

Table 3. Node movement and network size

Mobility model	Node movement scenarios and Network size parameters						
	Network size (node)	Malicious nodes	Topology size (m)	Transmit. range (m)	Node's speed (ms)	Pause time (seconds)	Simulation time (sec)
RWP	100	3	400 × 400	250	5–20	0–100	180

- **Parameters Specifying Traffic Patterns**

The data parameters are shown in Table 4, list all the parameters and their corresponding values used to run the simulation.

Table 4. Traffic pattern parameters 20 nodes

Conn no	Source node	Sink node	Application	Send rate	Layer 4 type	Packet size	Max pkts	Conn time
1	1	2	CBR	0.2 approx.	UDP	512	10000	2.556 approx.
2	4	5	CBR	0.2 approx.	UDP	512	10000	56.333 approx.
3	4	6	CBR	0.2 approx.	UDP	512	10000	146.9651 approx.
4	6	7	CBR	0.2 approx.	UDP	512	10000	55.634 approx.

5.2 Throughput

It is referred to as the number of packets successfully received per unit time. It is an important indicator of the performance and quality of network connection. Figure 5, shows the throughput for nodes ranging between 20–100 nodes and the comparison between trusted and standard AODV. It can be observed the due to malicious nodes introduced in the network, standard AODV having no protection has a lower throughput than the secure AODV.

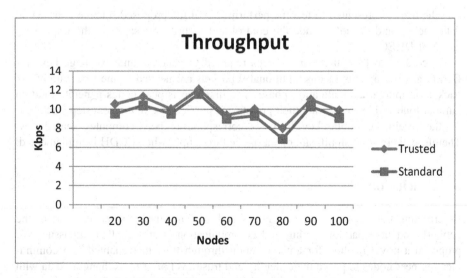

Fig. 5. Network throughput

5.3   Packet Delivery Ratio

The result for packet delivery ratio is shown in Fig. 6 below. This metric indicates the performance of the proposed trusted scheme after analysing all other performance metrics. This metric represent the ratio of the number of packets received by the destination to the number of packets sent by the destination nodes. The comparison is between standard and trusted AODV is presented in Fig. 6.

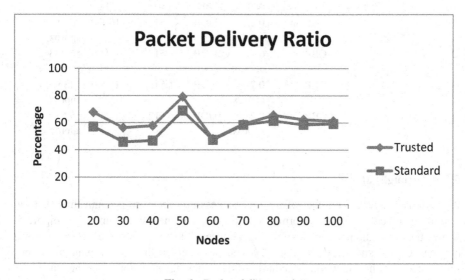

Fig. 6. Packet delivery ratio

The metrics presented to test the performance of the proposed scheme is based on data packets and do not include the control and security message i.e. the implementation of DHEC.

According to [32], there are 9 steps required to generate and exchange keys for DHEC algorithm. This means additional 9 packets are needed to the total number of packets in mutual authentication phase. The first step is peer nodes generate random number followed by generating their private and public keys. In the next step, each peer on the receipt of public key from its corresponding peer computes shared key. Therefore, there is no significant effect on the throughput when ECDH is implemented.

6   Conclusion

Determining the trust level of new nodes and allowing them to become part of the network and take part in routing and communication is still challenging issue. We proposed a novel method for authentication through trust that enabled two communicating peer nodes to prove their identity and trust level prior to exchanging data with each other. The proposed scheme provides a foundation for MANET routing protocol to implement a layer of security that enables a distributed, trusted and secure key exchange algorithm when the network initializes and ensure secure data exchange between peer nodes.

The scheme is implemented in the MANET environment with no predetermined trust therefore all nodes are treated as having no trust at all. The scheme is compatible with any MANET routing protocol and can be implemented in the network using routing protocol other than AODV.

In our proposed security scheme, we utilized common Trust based scheme for authentication and Diffie Hellman Elliptic Curve DHEC for encryption and key exchange. These schemes have some distinctive characteristic that support MANET decentralized and resource constraint environment. The trust based schemes identifies trusted and untrusted nodes while DHEC provides an efficient and secure mechanism for the distribution of key between nodes over insecure network. In our research we also propose an efficient way to support existing and new joining nodes. The scheme offers encryption of data communication using shared secret keys that are generated by the communicating nodes using DHEC algorithm. This ensures that all the nodes whether existing or new joining nodes will undergo the process of trust evaluation and authentication. The dynamic nature of the MANET makes the use of conventional security scheme such as Secret and Public Key cryptography more challenging. Therefore, the scheme proposed in this research is robust and encompasses various aspects of security. The scheme not only allows the nodes to authenticate its self but the security is implemented throughout the network and is scaled as the network grows through efficient Trust based scheme. This signifies that not only the security of individual nodes is important but the security of network as whole is of paramount importance as well and above all the security of the data communicated between is the most important of all.

References

1. Khan, I.M.S., Midi, D., Khan, M.I., Bertino, E.: Adaptive trust threshold strategy for misbehaving node detection an isolation. In: IEEE Trustcom/BigdataSE/ISPA (2015)
2. Al-Roubaiey, A., Sheltami, T., Mahmoud, A., Shakshuki, E., Moufta King Fahd, H.: AACK: Adaptive Acknowledgment intrusion detection for MANET with node detection enhancement. In: IEEE International Conference on Advanced Information Networking and Applications (2010)
3. Botkar, S., Chaudry, S.R.: An enhanced intrusion detection system using adaptive acknowledgment based algorithm. IEEE (2011)
4. Jim, L.E., Gregory, M.A.: AIS reputation mechanism in MANET. In: 28th International Telecommunication Networks and Application Conference, pp. 1–6, January 2019. https://doi.org/10.1109/atnac.2018.8615267
5. Balakrishnan, K., Deng, J., Varshney, P.K.: TWOACK: preventing selfishness in mobile AdHoc networks. IEEE Communication Society (2005)
6. Cai, R.J., Li, X.J., Chong, P.H.J.: An evolutionary self-cooperative trust scheme against routing disruptions in MANETs. IEEE Trans. Mob. Comput. **18**, 42–55 (2019). https://doi.org/10.1109/tmc.2018.2828814

7. Buttyan, L., Hubaux, J.-P.: Enforcing service availability in mobile ad-hoc WANs. In: Proceedings of MobiHoc, August 2000
8. Zhong, S., Chen, J., Yang, Y.R.: Sprite: a simple, cheat-proof, credit-based system for mobile ad-hoc networks. In: Proceedings of INFOCOM, March–April 2003
9. Zapata, M., Asokan, N.: Securing ad hoc routing protocols. In: Proceedings of ACM Workshop on Wireless Security (WiSe), Atlanta, GA, September 2002
10. Jhaveri, R.H.: MR-AODV: a solution to mitigate blackhole and grayhole attacks in AODV based MANET. In: Third International Conference on Advanced Computing and Communication Technologies. IEEE (2012)
11. Anju, J., Sminesh, C.N.: An Improved clustering-based approach for Wormhole attack detection in MANET. In: IEEE 3rd International Conference on Eco-Friendly Computing and Communication Systems (2014)
12. Yu, M., Su, W.: A secure routing protocol against byzantine attacks for MANETs in adversarial environments. IEEE Trans. Veh. Technol. **58**(1), 449–460 (2009)
13. Rifquddin, M.R., Sukiswo, M.: Performance of AOMDV routing protocol under rushing and flooding attacks in MANET. In: Proceedings of 2015 2nd International Conference on Information Technology, Computer and Electrical Engineering (ICITACEE), Indonesia. IEEE, 16–18 October 2015
14. Hinds, A., Sotiriadis, S., Bessis, N., Antonopoulos, N.: Performance evaluation of security algorithm for AODV MANET routing protocol. In: Third International Conference on Emerging Intelligent Data and Web Technologies. IEEE (2012)
15. Juwad, M.F., Al-Raweshidy, H.S.: Experimental performance comparisons between SAODV and AODV. In: Second Asia International Conference on Modelling and Simulation. IEEE (2008)
16. Hu, Y., John, D.B., Perrig, A.: SEAD: secure efficient distance vector routing for mobile ad hoc networks. In: Proceedings of the Fourth IEEE Workshop on Mobile Computing Systems and Applications (WMCSA 2002). IEEE (2002)
17. Perrig, A., Canetti, R., Tygar, J.D., Song, D.: The TESLA broadcast authentication protocol. RSA Lab. **5**(2), 2–13 (2002)
18. Hu, Y.-C., Perrig, A., Johnson, D.B.: Ariadne: a secure on-demand routing protocol for ad hoc networks. Wirel. Netw. **11**(1–2), 21–38 (2005)
19. Yi, S., Naldurg, P., Kravets, R.: Security-aware ad hoc routing for wireless networks. In: Proceedings of the 2nd ACM International Symposium on Mobile Ad Hoc Networking and Computing, pp. 299–302 (2001)
20. Carter, S., Yasinsac, A.: Secure position aided ad hoc routing. In: Proceedings of IASTED International Conference on Communication and Computer Networks (CCN 2002), pp. 329–334 (2002)
21. ARAN (A secure Routing Protocol for Ad hoc Networks) Implementation. http://signl.cs.umass.edu/arand/
22. Johnson, D., Hu, Y., Maltz, D.: The Dynamic Source Routing Protocol (DSR) for mobile ad hoc networks for IPv4. RFC 4728 (Experimental), February 2007. http://www.ietf.org/rfc/rfc4728.txt. Accessed 14 Oct 2008
23. Shakshuki, E.M., Kang, N., Sheltami, T.R.: EAACK—a secure intrusion-detection system for MANETs. IEEE Trans. Ind. Electron. **60**(3), 1089–1098 (2013)
24. Marti, S., Giuli, T., Lai, K., Baker, M.: Mitigating routing misbehavior in mobile ad hoc networks. In: Proceedings of MobiCom, August 2000
25. Nasser, N., Chen, Y.: Enhanced intrusion detection system for discovering malicious nodes in mobile ad hoc networks. Reviewed at IEEE Communication Society Subject Matter Expert for Publication in the ICC 2007 Proceeding (2007)

26. Buchegger, S., Le Boudec, J.-Y.: Performance analysis of the CONFIDANT protocol: cooperation of nodes, fairness in dynamic ad-hoc networks. In: Proceedings of MobiHoc, June 2002
27. Buttyan, K.L., Hubaux, J.-P.: Enforcing service availability in mobile ad-hoc WANs. In: Proceedings of MobiHoc, August 2000
28. Sukiswo, M., Rifquddin R.: Performance of AOMDV routing protocol under rushing and flooding attacks in MANET. In: IEEE 2nd Conference of Information Technology, Computer and Electrical Engineering (ICITACEE), Indonesia, 16–18 October 2015
29. Rajesh, M., Gnanasekar, M.: Consistently neighbour detection for MANET. In: 2016 IEEE International Conference on Communication and Electronic Systems (ICCES) (2016)
30. Carter, S., Yasinsac, A.: Secure position aided ad hoc routing. In: Proceedings of IASTED International Conference on Communication and Computer Networks (CCN 2002), pp. 329–334 (2002)
31. Zhong, S., Chen, J., Yang, Y.R.: Sprite: a simple, cheat-proof, credit-based system for mobile ad-hoc networks. In: Proceedings of INFOCOM (2003)
32. Wong, Y., Ramamurthy, B., Zou, X.: The performance of elliptic curve based group Diffie-Hellman protocols for secure group communication over ad hoc networks. In: IEEE International Conference on Communication (2006)
33. Misic, J.: Traffic and energy consumption of an IEEE 802.15.4 network in the presence of authenticated ECC Diffie-Hellman ephemeral key exchange. Comput. Netw. (2008). www.elsevier.com/locate/comment
34. Gajbhiya, S., Karmakar, S., Sharma, M.: Diffie-Hellman key agreement with elliptic curve discrete logarithm problem. Int. J. Comput. Appl. **129**(12), 25–27 (2015)

A Review and Survey on Smartphones: The Closest Enemy to Privacy

Priyanka Jayakumar, Lenice Lawrence, Ryan Lim Wai Chean,
and Sarfraz Nawaz Brohi[✉]

Taylor's University, Selangor, Malaysia
{Priyankas.Jayakumar, Lenicelawrence,
Ryanwaichean.Lim}@sd.taylors.edu.my,
SarfrazNawaz.Brohi@taylors.edu.my

Abstract. Smartphones have changed the world from a primitive to a high-tech standpoint. However, there have been many incidents where third parties have used confidential data of the users without their consent. Thus, it causes people to be paranoid and distrustful of their smartphones, never knowing which application threatens to expose them. In this paper, we have conducted an in-depth review of the significance of smartphones in human life, and we have discussed the methods used by various authorities to collect and exploit users' data for enigmatic benefits. Moreover, we surveyed the smartphone users to identify the vulnerabilities leading to privacy violation, and to examine their knowledge about the protection mechanisms. We determined that Technology and Human are the two major vulnerabilities that are exploited to invade users' privacy. It is the necessity of the moment for the researchers and developers to formulate solutions that could be used to educate and protect smartphone users from potential threats and exploitation of data.

Keywords: Smartphones · Privacy · Data exploitation · Mobile applications

1 Introduction

Smartphones have revolutionized human life due to features such as connectivity, efficiency, functionality, and entertainment [1–3]. Connectivity: Besides phone calls and text messages, one can access social networking sites like Facebook, Twitter, SnapChat and many more. Advanced connection services like Viber and Skype enable one to save money through free conversation. One can also send and receive emails once their email accounts are set up and synced to their phone. Efficiency: Smartphones are efficient because they speed up processes making it easier for people to go about their business on the move. Applications such as Google Docs and OneDrive allows a person to work and collaborate with other people anywhere and anytime without the aid of computers. Functionality: Other than connectivity and efficiency, there are abundant applications for various purposes that can be installed on a smartphone. Smartphones provide users, the choice of enabling security measures to protect important data on their devices. Entertainment: One of the main attractions of smartphones is the entertainment factor. Latest movies, songs, TV shows and even online

M. H. Miraz et al. (Eds.): iCETiC 2019, LNICST 285, pp. 106–118, 2019.

gaming has been accessible on the move using smartphones. The discussion of smartphones being an invasion of data privacy never ends. Smartphones are great pocket-assistant devices because they contain a variety of sensors [4]. Since smartphones have become a necessity, people rarely go without them. This enables the sensors to gather users' data. These sensors are both a gift and a curse. This is because the sensors could be compromised for malicious intents without users' knowledge. For example, online app store Google Play removed 20 apps because they were abusing their access through sensors found on Android phones. This means before Google discovered the privacy violation conducted by these apps, they could track and keep a record of users' most private data like their current location, pictures, videos, sensitive files and everything else on their devices. Besides providing opportunities for hackers or perpetrators to snoop into users activities via sensors, certain apps on smartphones gather data such as recently searched, most popular search, and download history. The developers have built the apps in such a way that they compile all the raw data and then sell them off to advertising companies, which then convert them into useful information and ultimately, profit. It may seem harmless on the surface, but there may be data that the user would have wanted to keep private and confidential. For example, randomly searching for a product on a search engine could cause pop-ups or e-mails regarding the same searched product at a discounted price. In order to contribute to the domain of smartphones data security, we conducted this research to identify the user and technology related vulnerabilities. The findings from this research could be used as strong foundations to carry out advanced research in the domain especially related to protecting smartphone users from data privacy violation and to make smartphones a trustable next-generation technology. The rest of this paper is structured as follows: In Sect. 2, we discuss the secret methods of data collection using smartphones. Section 3 contains a discussion on the exploitation of the data. The survey results are analyzed in Sect. 4 and critically discussed in Sect. 5. Finally, we have concluded the research in Sect. 6.

2   The Data Collection Methods

Unauthorized data collection is a major concern among the general population in today's age. Due to the vast upgrades and constant improvements in technology, devices are being more necessary than ever in a society. Smartphone devices have become almost like a necessity in today's world, and base models are getting increasingly more affordable [7]. What would have cost thousands of dollars previously, could be only a couple of dollars today. This is one of the many reasons that the use of smartphones is widespread with some users being as young as three years of age. Users of devices like smartphones should be constantly aware of the permission that they grant the phone, if they are not, their data can be collected even without them realizing it. There are many ways through which smartphone users' data can be accessed. The data collection methods are discussed in the following sub-sections.

2.1   Location Sensors

Location sensors determine the exact geographical location of smartphone users with high accuracy. Longitude and latitude coordinates obtain the geographical location, but its accuracy is dependent on the types of applications, operating system and hardware of the smartphone [8]. As more users are using phones for navigational purposes as well as transport services, the majority of smartphones being produced have high accuracy location sensors embedded in them. Some of these location sensors measure not only the latitude and longitude but also an 'x' element, which refers to the height or elevation of the device. This allows for more accurate tracking and data collection. The applications of an iOS and Android device are different. Apple is stricter when it comes to granting location permission to an application, and allows the user to adjust these settings, both via the application, as well as through the device privacy settings [9]. For Apple, users can select between having the location of the device always turned-on, always turned-off or be turned-on only when an application with permission is open and running. However, for Android, users may need to take extra precautions. In an investigation and report by Quartz, it was found that even if the smartphone device is actively turned-off, the device is without a SIM card, is not connected to the internet, and does not have any applications needing location services to be used, Android OS phones can still collect location data to be sent to Google as soon as the smartphone is connected to the internet. When the application has location access or if the device itself has location access turned-on all the time, data is being collected constantly. Certain smartphone applications can even figure out roughly what floor of a high-rise building that you work or stay in based on time and frequency of visits [10].

2.2   Accelerometer and Gyroscope

Most older smartphones have had accelerometers that measure in only one dimension. However, the latest smartphones have accelerometers that measure in three dimensions, with these dimensions being 'x', 'y' and 'z'. This is also known as the three-axis accelerometer. Apart from this, a gyroscope is also available on most devices [11]. This allows not only the speed to be measured but also the relative positioning and direction of travel of the smartphone device. A certain travel company who has monitored these data has found that in their application, the number of visitor's peak and surge around midnight, which is right before most adults head to bed. It was also found that during these times, the devices (mainly smartphones) that are being used had many rotations going on. This indicated that a majority of the users were looking at travel sites while lying in bed, as lying on their side generally causes the phone to rotate to landscape mode.

2.3   Wi-Fi Sensors

Another way of gathering data is through Wi-Fi. The monitoring and data gathering of location-based data via Wi-Fi is one of the lesser-explored uses of Wi-Fi. However, it is a good way to get these location-based data as it uses less battery as compared to GPS or accelerometers [11]. With Wi-Fi sensors, the location of a user can be extracted based on which access points they have connected their device to. Other data that can be gathered from Wi-Fi access points are the speed or if the user is currently traveling. This data is gathered by measuring the speed of the connection changes as it may rapidly connect and drop, thus assuming if the user of the smartphone device is traveling at a relatively high speed. Even if the smartphone device does not connect to a Wi-Fi network, it can still be traced, and data can be collected based on the fact that smartphone devices usually automatically scan for Wi-Fi connections through various access points [12]. These access points can be tracked as smartphone devices can measure various components such as the access point's MAC address, its SSID's, name and signal strengths.

2.4 Virtual Keyboards

A Virtual Keyboard (VK) is a vital part of any smartphone, as the majority of the things we do on a smartphone needs a VK to function. Another reason it is important is that every piece of information from mundane daily memos to private credit card numbers and other passwords go through the VKs [3]. Some VKs require a login account to personalize data such as words and phrases that are commonly used. However, it is highly likely that these VKs sell the data to third-party applications or companies for targeted advertising [13].

2.5 Third Party Tracking Applications

A study has shown that about 70% of applications share the data collected with companies such as Google analytics [14]. Companies like these can obtain data from various applications and combine them to form a scarily accurate and detailed profile of smartphone users [15]. They can combine information to do this even if all applications are granted permissions separately [12]. However, big companies like these have one goal in mind, i.e., profit. The main source of this profit is to create and deliver specific and targeted advertisements based on what the tracking applications have identified to be interesting to the smartphone user.

3 The Exploitation of Data

There are many different purposes for organizations or authorities to obtain users' data. However, most of these reasons lead back to one cause, i.e., profit. [16]. When we say that data is unethically, illegally or inappropriately used, it means that the original owner of the data did not consent to the data being used in that specific manner. This section contains information about the uses of data that are unethical, illegal, or a combination of both.

3.1 Targeted Advertisements

Targeted advertisements are dedicated to specific products or services that interest a user. This is achieved by collecting various user data using many applications, especially social media based apps. Some of the most used categories of data for targeted advertisements are; location, search history, browsing history, posts viewed or interacted with on social media, pictures seen or videos watched, and even certain key terms based on keyboard activities. Location-based advertisements gather location data from GPS of the device to deduce the locations that the user is most often at, as well as locations that have been visited or areas checked in on various social media apps [17]. The advertisements presented may be related to travels, services or goods provided near those locations. For search history and browsing history, the advertisements would be items or services that have previously been searched or looked for. Data from posts viewed or interacted with, pictures looked at or videos watched, will generate data that will produce advertisements of similar topics or items related to recently viewed activities. Finally, it would be keyboard activity, which is the most privacy invading option. The data stored could be anything from credit card information to passwords to words that are often used. This information will be used to find advertisements that are related to these words.

3.2 Selling Data

Numerous third-party firms would buy the data to be analyzed. Companies can also use this data for themselves. For example, The Wall Street Journal has cited two cases relating to this; A travel website charging Mac users' higher hotel prices, and a large multinational office supply chain offering better deals only if there is a competitor within a 20-mile radius. The travel website, Orbitz, found out that Mac users were more likely to spend up to 30% more on a hotel room, and they were 40% more likely to spend on 4 or 5 star hotel rooms as compared to Windows users [18]. Thus, they have started providing Mac users with higher hotel room prices to increase their profits. As for the office supply store Staples, the Wall Street Journal has found out that Staples is tracking the location of online users and only offering discounts and coupons if there is a competitor store within a 20-mile radius from their current location [19]. If no competitors are found nearby, Staples assumes that the users are willing to pay the higher price as they do not have a choice, thus eliminating the discounts and coupons for these users and increasing their profits.

3.3 Candidate and Employees Profiling

New companies tend to do screenings on potential employees or the employees that they feel they may need to worry about. Companies and organizations these days will either look up the employee on social media and various search engines or get investigators to find out more about these employees. Not all companies or organizations will have the resources to hire investigators, nor need to if it is not a high position. Facebook has been found to publicly display users' data even if the user has restricted it to the 'friends only' option [8]. This enables employers to check Facebook pages of potential or current employees. This is unethical on the part of Facebook, as users have restricted these data or contents to specifically their friends only, and not the general public.

3.4 Predicting and Influencing Users Habits

Similar to the targeted advertisement, the data collected is used by marketers to try to influence certain users to purchase certain products or services. The difference from targeted advertisements is that the user may not have shown interest in these products before, and these advertisements are usually decided based on demographics or personal data. The data collected will be used to promoting certain items, which they feel the user may be inclined to buy. A well-known example of this was certain cigarette companies targeting their advertisements towards highly stressed and lower-income users, as it was this group of people that were most likely to start smoking and buy cigarettes [20]. A user dependent on cigarettes is a loyal customer to them, thus increasing their profits constantly.

3.5 Distribution of Confidential Data

There have been multiple cases where personal data had been stolen and published on the internet for everyone to see. A few common cases were the nudes of celebrities stolen via iCloud and published, and when accounts of dating site users were published. In the first case, which happened in 2014, a hacker gained access to the iCloud library of Apple used by celebrities and leaked their personal and private photos online [21]. The hacker gained access to the iCloud accounts via brute force attacks and followed up by publishing a list of 100 celebrity names whose accounts had been supposedly hacked, followed by uploads of photos soon after. In the second mentioned case, occurred in 2015 when a hacking group accessed and stole users' data of a site called Ashley Madison. The Ashley Madison site was a dating site targeted towards individuals who were married or in a relationship. These hackers believed that what they did was ethical as they were exposing cheating and unfaithful individuals. However, the fact that they had hacked into, and stole 60 GB worth of user profiles and data, along with identifying and real-world profiles, is illegal [22]. This data leak has caused many problems towards the affected individuals, ranging from the breakdowns of families, discrimination among their peers, and was even linked to two cases of suicide. Regardless of whether the hackers believe that their stealing of data is for ethical reason, the act in itself is illegal and wrong. The users entrusted the companies with keeping their profiles and data secure and did not consent to their data being openly uploaded online for others to view. It is a serious breach of personal and private data and can have many negative effects on the victims.

4 Survey

This section analyses the survey conducted to identify the user vulnerabilities that could lead to privacy violation using smartphones. Additionally, we aimed to understand how users feel about their privacy concerning smartphones. This survey has 202 responses from participants of different age groups, geographical locations, and opinions on smartphones data privacy. We started with a question to determine the data that participants find the most private to them. 151 participants (74.8%) consider passwords on their devices to be the most confidential data. Coming close to that number, 103 participants (51%) declared photos and videos are most private to them. 90 participants (44.6%) find emails, and a total of 80 participants (39.6%) stated that location is the most sensitive data to them, respectively. The remaining participants have considered documents, banking details, messages, chat history, and contacts as the most private data as shown in Fig. 1.

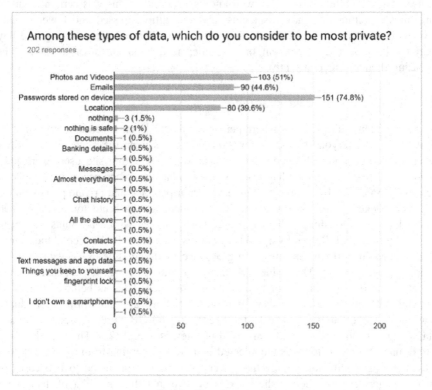

Fig. 1. Data importance.

In the world of smartphones, the application level permissions could potentially lure users into collecting their sensitive information. The second and third question was targeted to understand the users' interaction with the permissions required by the apps. As shown in Fig. 2, 49% participants occasionally, 26.7% participants have never, and 24.3% participants make it a point to read all the required permissions before installing or using an application on their smartphones. This finding is bothersome because only a minority of the participants read all the permissions requested by an application before installing it. This is probably because the permissions are too lengthy to read or the need for the application is greater than data privacy or simply due to lack of knowledge. Moreover as shown in Fig. 3, 62.9% of our participants had refused to install an application when it asked for certain unrelated permissions. Of the remaining participants, 23.8% have never, and 13.4% have refused to install an application once due to the permission it requested, respectively.

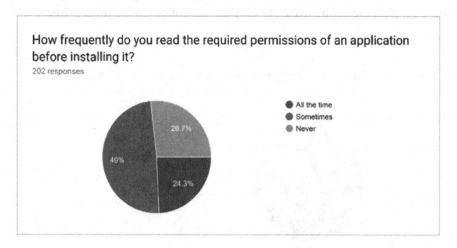

Fig. 2. Users knowledge.

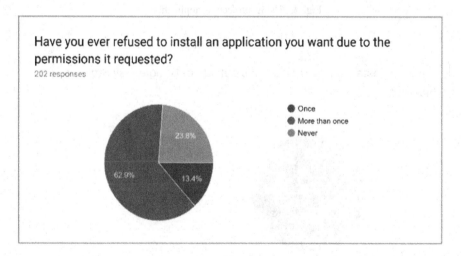

Fig. 3. Application permissions.

The fourth and fifth question was targeted to identify the protection mechanisms and precautionary measures undertaken by the users as a defense mechanism against the privacy-violating Apps. As shown in Fig. 4, we are amazed to determine that 42.6% of participants have never used anti-virus and anti-malware applications on their smartphones, 31.7% are currently using either anti-virus or anti-malware on their devices, whereas 25.7% used to have one of those two types of applications but not anymore since they uninstalled it. Moreover, as shown in Fig. 5, 60.4% participants have not installed applications outside of Google Play Store or Apple App Store, while 38.6% has confessed to having installed applications outside of the certified application installation platforms and trusted sources. This number is worrisome because participants open doors for many malicious applications that can invade their privacy.

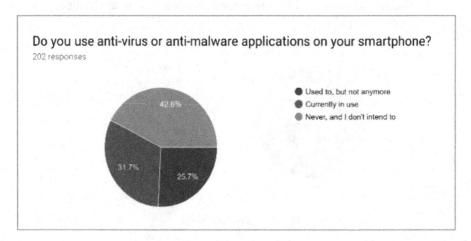

Fig. 4. Using protection application.

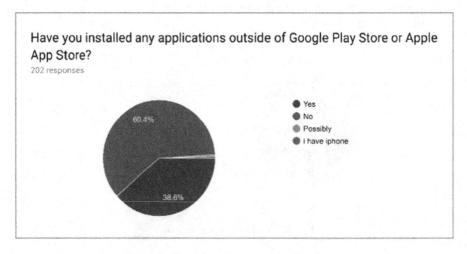

Fig. 5. Trusted and untrusted applications

5   Discussion

From the overall survey results, we observe that smartphone privacy issues occur due to two major vulnerabilities (Human and Technology). The smartphone technology has been developed to enable communication, collaboration and to assist users in a variety of other everyday tasks. However, likewise any other technology, this technology can and has been exploited for malicious reasons. The intruders such as hackers and organizations are spying on user activities, collecting data for personal gains such as advertisement, service improvement, and selling data. The smartphone users are vulnerable to various threats, and in most cases, they are unaware of the effects on their data privacy. However, in certain cases, users indirectly or unintentionally allow access to their sensitive data due to lack of awareness and knowledge of the smartphone technology and the apps. Many of the users are not even aware and well informed of using protection mechanisms such as anti-virus, anti-malware, and other anti-spyware services. Furthermore, the users of smartphones are also not conscious of the permissions that apps require from them during the installation or execution time. In certain cases, the users grant unwanted permissions to the Apps due to their need and convenience to use the required features. The lack of care in granting permissions could lead to privilege escalation, and users' data privacy can be at risk. It is the necessity of the moment for the researchers and developers to formulate solutions that could be used to educate and protect smartphone users from potential threats and exploitation of data.

There are solutions developed to deal with issues regarding the required permissions of a mobile application. When people download an application, they do not read the app's privacy policy because it is tedious and filled with complicated words that they may not understand [23]. To address this issue, the mobile application market should be plastered with application reviews that come from trusted sources. This will give users a sense of relief knowing that their data will be secured from third-party exploitation. Brands also serve their purpose by building a reputation of being responsible for maintaining the privacy of user data so that users will not have any qualms from downloading any mobile application developed by them. A balance needs to be struck between users of apps who want their data to be secured and the app developers who want to boost their revenue by using user profiles for advertisement purposes [24]. To do this, a new model must be developed that will have two distinct flows of information, one from the user to the developer and another from the user to the advertisement network, both vice versa. Both developers and ad-networks will have unique privacy requirements. The application developer has certain privacy requirements that work in conjunction with the application while the ad-network can develop privacy methods that will fully aid the market reliant on advertisements. A solution to privacy risks in the form of an anonymous identifier has been presented [25]. Blockchain can also be used to protect data that users want to keep private [26]. The blockchain system involves two main proceedings, the protection of users' data and the ability for services to retrieve the data after a verification process using digital signatures. To better ensure that users are aware of the available mobile applications that consist of effective privacy and security features, an app recommendation system is a solution [27]. TaintDroid is a system designed to keep track of the usage of private data by third-party applications that may or may not be suspicious on Android [32]. Data from both reputable and non-reputable apps will be tainted. Whenever it is found that the data has been shifted from 1 location to another, TaintDroid will create a log of the event containing the details of the movement of the data, painting a clearer picture as to which apps are credible and which are not.

6   Conclusion

Cyber-criminals who are utilizing a highly sophisticated range of approaches and destructive codes, are aiming conventional operating platforms such as iOS and Android [33]. There is a legion of operating system versions in use to cater to the ever-increasing number of smartphone users on Earth [34]. While conducting this research, we realized that smartphone technology is a double-edged sword. It brings many benefits and makes lives very convenient but also presents several risks to user data stored within it. The privacy problems posed by smartphones are phishing attacks through location tracking, racial profiling, user surveillance and controlling the smartphone camera for spying purposes. Some solutions we have discovered include increasing the number of trusted reviews for applications, blockchain security and app recommendation systems. In our survey, we have discovered that fewer users read the terms and conditions of the application before installation. Almost half of the participants do not have antivirus or anti-malware apps on their phones, leaving them vulnerable to attacks. Finally, nearly 40% have downloaded an app from an untrusted site increases the chances of compromising their phone because these applications might be virus or worm infected.

References

1. John, J.: Why are smartphones so important in daily life? - Trffc Media (2018) Trffcmedia.com. http://www.trffcmedia.com/topics/why-are-smartphones-so-important-in-daily-life/
2. Targetstudy.com: Importance of smartphones in our life (2018). https://targetstudy.com/articles/importance-of-smartphones-in-our-life.html
3. Wang, D., Xiang, Z., Fesenmaier, D.: Smartphone use in everyday life and travel. J. Travel. Res. **55**(1), 52–63 (2014)
4. Temming, M.: Your phone is like a spy in your pocket (2018). Science News. https://www.sciencenews.org/article/smartphones-data-collection-security-privacy
5. DeMuro, J.: 8 reasons why smartphones are privacy nightmare (2018). TechRadar. https://www.techradar.com/news/8-reasons-why-smartphones-are-privacy-nightmare
6. Hoffman, S.: Your smartphone or laptop camera: a window into your private life? (2018). InCyberDefense. https://incyberdefense.com/original/smartphone-laptop-camera-private-life/
7. Weinstein, M.: 13 ways your online privacy was violated in 2016 - and what you can do about it (2018). Mirror. https://www.mirror.co.uk/tech/13-ways-your-privacy-violated-9479084
8. University, S.: Unauthorized transmission and use of personal data (2018). Scu.edu. https://www.scu.edu/ethics/focus-areas/internet-ethics/resources/unauthorized-transmission-and-use-of-personal-data/
9. Ng, V., Kent, C.: Smartphone data tracking is more than creepy – here's why you should be worried (2018). The Conversation. https://theconversation.com/smartphone-data-tracking-is-more-than-creepy-heres-why-you-should-be-worried-91110
10. Baraniuk, C.: Phone sensors can save lives by revealing what floor you are on (2018). New Scientist. https://www.newscientist.com/article/2152366-phone-sensors-can-save-lives-by-revealing-what-floor-you-are-on/
11. Garnett, O.: Beware the power and pitfalls of mobile data collection (2018). Forbes. https://www.forbes.com/sites/forbestechcouncil/2018/04/18/beware-the-power-and-pitfalls-of-mobile-data-collection/#4162ef4c40dc

12. Goode, L., Ceres, P., Pardes, A., Barrett, B., Goode, L., Barrett, B.: App permissions aren't telling us nearly enough about our apps (2018). WIRED. https://www.wired.com/story/app-permissions/

13. Kromtech, S.: Virtual keyboard developer leaked 31 million of client records (2017). Kromtech.com. https://kromtech.com/blog/security-center/virtual-keyboard-developer-leaked-31-million-of-client-records

14. Narseo Vallina-Rodriguez, T.: 7 in 10 smartphone apps share your data with third-party services (2018). Scientific American. https://www.scientificamerican.com/article/7-in-10-smartphone-apps-share-your-data-with-third-party-services/

15. ICSI: The ICSI haystack panopticon (2018). Haystack.mobi. https://www.haystack.mobi/panopticon/

16. Guest, C.: On the ethical use of data vs. the Internet of Things (2018). Forbes. https://www.forbes.com/sites/ciocentral/2016/12/21/on-the-ethical-use-of-data-vs-the-internet-of-things/#3982da7e1247

17. Shermach, K.: Data mining: where legality and ethics rarely meet (2018). E-Commerce Times. https://www.ecommercetimes.com/story/52616.html?wlc=1245363355

18. Mogg, T.: Orbitz travel website directs Mac users to pricier hotel options | Digital Trends (2018). Digital Trends. https://www.digitaltrends.com/apple/orbitz-travel-website-directs-mac-users-to-pricier-hotel-options/

19. Jennifer Valentino-DeVries, J.: Websites vary prices, deals based on users' information (2012). WSJ. https://www.wsj.com/articles/SB10001424127887323777204578189391813881534

20. Connolly, G.: Tobacco companies target poorer neighborhoods with advertising (2010). News. https://www.hsph.harvard.edu/news/hsph-in-the-news/tobacco-advertising-poor-neighborhoods/

21. Cellan-Jones, R.: Apple: celebrity accounts hacked (2014). BBC News. https://www.bbc.com/news/av/technology-29032705/apple-celebrity-photos-targeted-by-hackers

22. Lord, N.: A timeline of the Ashley Madison hack (2017). Digital Guardian. https://digitalguardian.com/blog/timeline-ashley-madison-hack

23. Chin, E., Felt, A.P., Sekar, V., Wagner, D.: Measuring user confidence in smartphone security and privacy. In: Proceedings of the Eighth Symposium on Usable Privacy and Security, p. 1. ACM, July 2012

24. Leontiadis, I., Efstratiou, C., Picone, M., Mascolo, C.: Don't kill my ads!: balancing privacy in an ad-supported mobile application market. In: Proceedings of the Twelfth Workshop on Mobile Computing Systems and Applications, p. 2. ACM, February 2012

25. Beach, A., Gartrell, M., Han, R.: Solutions to security and privacy issues in mobile social networking. In: International Conference on Computational Science and Engineering, CSE 2009, vol. 4, pp. 1036–1042. IEEE, August 2009

26. Zyskind, G., Nathan, O.: Decentralizing privacy: using blockchain to protect personal data. In: 2015 IEEE Security and Privacy Workshops (SPW), pp. 180–184. IEEE, May 2015

27. Zhu, H., Xiong, H., Ge, Y., Chen, E.: Mobile app recommendations with security and privacy awareness. In: Proceedings of the 20th ACM SIGKDD International Conference on Knowledge Discovery and Data Mining, pp. 951–960. ACM, August 2014

28. Liang, X., Zhang, K., Shen, X., Lin, X.: Security and privacy in mobile social networks: challenges and solutions. IEEE Wirel. Commun. 21(1), 33–41 (2014)

29. He, D., Chan, S., Guizani, M.: User privacy and data trustworthiness in mobile crowd sensing. IEEE Wirel. Commun. 22(1), 28–34 (2015)

30. Zhang, K., Yang, K., Liang, X., Su, Z., Shen, X., Luo, H.H.: Security and privacy for mobile healthcare networks: from a quality of protection perspective. IEEE Wirel. Commun. 22(4), 104–112 (2015)

31. Kotz, D., Gunter, C.A., Kumar, S., Weiner, J.P.: Privacy and security in mobile health: a research agenda. Computer **49**(6), 22 (2016)
32. Enck, W., et al.: TaintDroid: an information-flow tracking system for realtime privacy monitoring on smartphones. ACM Trans. Comput. Syst. (TOCS) **32**(2), 5 (2014)
33. Finjan Mobile: Mobile device privacy and security challenges and recommendations (2018). https://www.finjanmobile.com/mobile-device-privacy-and-security-challenges-and-recommendations/
34. Tsavli, M., Efraimidis, P., Katos, V., Mitrou, L.: Reengineering the user: privacy concerns about personal data on smartphones. Inf. Comput. Secur. **23**(4), 394–405 (2015)
35. Kaspersky Lab, Android Mobile Security Threats. Daily English Global. https://www.kaspersky.com/resource-center/threats/mobile
36. Warner, C., Smartphone attacks: 7 reasons why hackers have shifted their target. Wandera. https://www.wandera.com/smartphone-attacks-rise/
37. Security Service MI5, Interception of Communications | MI5 - The Security Service. Security Service MI5. https://www.mi5.gov.uk/interception-of-communications
38. Fagundes, L.: Smartphone use and data confidentiality. Virtual data rooms. https://www.securedocs.com/blog/2014/05/smartphone-use-and-data-confidentiality

Hybrid Rule-Based Model for Phishing URLs Detection

Kayode S. Adewole[1(✉)], Abimbola G. Akintola[1], Shakirat A. Salihu[1], Nasir Faruk[2], and Rasheed G. Jimoh[1]

[1] Department of Computer Science, University of Ilorin, Ilorin, Nigeria
{adewole.ks,akintola.ag,salihu.sa,
jimoh_rasheed}@unilorin.edu.ng
[2] Department of Telecommunications Science, University of Ilorin,
Ilorin, Nigeria
nasirfaruk@gmail.com

Abstract. Phishing attack has been considered as a major security challenge facing online community due to the different sophisticated strategies that is being deployed by attackers. One of the reasons for creating phishing website by attackers is to employ social engineering technique that steal sensitive information from legitimate users, such as the user's account details. Therefore, detecting phishing website has become an important task worthy of investigation. The most widely used blacklist-based approach has proven inefficient. Although, different models have been proposed in the literature by deploying a number of intelligent-based algorithms, however, considering hybrid intelligent approach based on rule induction for phishing website detection is still an open research issue. In this paper, a hybrid rule induction algorithm capable of separating phishing websites from genuine ones is proposed. The proposed hybrid algorithm leverages the strengths of both JRip and Projective Adaptive Resonance Theory (PART) algorithm to generate rule sets. Based on the experiments conducted on two publicly available datasets for phishing detection, the proposed algorithm demonstrates promising results achieving accuracy of 0.9453 and 0.9908 respectively on the two datasets. These results outperformed the results obtained with JRip and PART. Therefore, the rules generated from the hybrid algorithm are capable of identifying phishing links in real-time with reduction in false alarm.

Keywords: Phishing website · JRip · PART · Machine learning · Rule-based model · Rule induction

1 Introduction

The recent development in information technology coupled with the advancement in Internet usage has created an ample of opportunity for online community to communicate and share varieties of resources. There has been an exponential growth in the number of businesses and organization offering web services to improve their customers' experience. Many of these organizations provide online trading including sales of goods and services over the World Wide Web (WWW) [1]. To access these online

M. H. Miraz et al. (Eds.): iCETiC 2019, LNICST 285, pp. 119–135, 2019.

resources, users need to know their Uniform Resource Locators (URLs). URL is an essential identification for all objects on the WWW such as audio, video, hypertext pages and a host of other online resources. Nevertheless, despite the huge opportunities offered by the Internet, accessibility to online resources may expose Internet users to different forms of vulnerabilities and online threats. This can damage financial reputation and lead to loss of private information through various malicious strategies that may be deployed by hackers. Such strategies include the creation of phishing websites to lure legitimate users. Thus, the suitability of the Internet as a channel for secured online communication and commercial exchange posed a serious question. According to Dhamija, Tygar [2], phishing is categorized as a form of online threat that involves an act of impersonating a website or web resources of a reputable organization with the aim of illegally obtaining user's confidential information like social security numbers, usernames, and passwords. Phishing links are sometimes referred to as malicious URLs.

Attackers make use of malicious links in high magnitude to distribute malware over the web and to hijack confidential information from Internet users. If successful, the link can give partial or full control of the system to the attacker [3]. In recent years, there has been an increase in the growth of cybercrime which needs to be critically addressed by network information security authorities. Attackers have targeted many sectors from e-commerce and banking to government, private and many more by inserting malicious codes into a standard webpage to evade detection [4]. Timely detection of such phishing URLs is of great importance in order to reduce the damage it can cause to online community [5].

Early detection approach for phishing website was based on blacklist method, which relies on repository of already classified websites. This approach suffers from inclusiveness due to the fact that any URL or new URL that is not listed in the repository might evade detection [5, 6]. Machine learning approaches have also been deployed to build intelligent models that can separate phishing websites from legitimate ones. For instance, Gupta [7] applied pattern matching algorithm based on word segmentation to identify malicious URL. Thakur, Meenakshi [8] developed a system for detecting malicious URLs in big data environment using JRip rule induction machine learning algorithm. The detection and classification of malicious URLs in cloud environment based on machine learning approach has been investigated by [9]. The authors proposed a method that is based on Markov decision process, Information gain ratio and Decision tree to simultaneously analyzed malicious webpages. Although, a number of studies have applied machine learning algorithms to develop suitable models for phishing URLs detection, however, investigating hybrid predictive model to effectively detect phishing websites still remain an open research issue. Thus, this paper proposes hybrid rule-induction algorithm to address this research area.

The remaining parts of this paper are organized as follows: Sect. 2 discusses related studies on phishing website detection; Sect. 3 focuses on the main methodology deployed to develop the proposed hybrid rule-induction algorithm. Section 4 presents the results obtained from the different experiments conducted in this study, and finally Sect. 5 concludes the paper and presents future direction.

2 Related Work

Rules induction technique is categorized into two, namely, direct and indirect techniques. The direct technique involves rules generation directly from the data while indirect technique deals with rule generation from another classification algorithm. Vijayarani and Divya [10] examined the performance of three rule-based algorithms for breast cancer and heart disease diagnosis. Formally, let k represent an observation from the dataset, then an instance k can be detected by a rule r provided all the conditions in r according to the value of the attribute pair can also be satisfied based on the corresponding value of the attribute for instance k. Let C be a concept (i.e. decision) which represents the consequent of rule r, then a rule set R is said to completely covered the concept C provided every instance k an element of C has a rule r from R that covers k. Furthermore, it can equally be said that a rule set R is complete provided R covers every concept in the dataset [11]. Generally, rule induction algorithms belong to two major classes: global and local. The global rule induction algorithms used the set of all attribute values as the search space, while the local rule induction algorithms used the set of attribute-value pairs to explore the search domain. Many rule induction algorithms have been introduced over the years, which include Learning from Examples Module, version 1 and 2 - LEM1 and LEM2.

This section discussed some of the existing research efforts for phishing URL detection. In the model developed by Lee and Kim [12], the researchers examined the malicious URL's in a twitter stream. The study focused on exploring frequently shared URLs to discover the suspiciousness of correlated URL redirect chains. The authors experimented with various tweets extracted from the twitter timeline and a classifier was built around them. Experimental result shows that their proposed classification method was able to accurately detect suspicious URLs in a tweet. Spam message and spam account detection models on Twitter have also been proposed in the literature [13, 14]. Another model from Bhardwaj, Sharma [15] applied Artificial Bee Colony to detect malicious URLs. The study was able to detect whether target website is genuine or not with the notion that once a user is aware of the safety of any link they want to click, then half of the problem is solved.

The use of lexical analysis has also been proposed in the literature for detecting malicious web pages. In a research carried out by Darling, Heileman [16], lexical analysis of URLs were used to classify malicious web pages. This approach is light weight with the aim of exploring the best classification accuracy of a purely lexical analysis that could be used in real-time. This approach is only based on lexical features. A study on detecting malicious URLs on two-dimensional barcodes was conducted by Xuan and Yongzhen [17]. Their model was based on utilizing a hash function. The system was able to detect malicious URLs by first extracting the eigenvalues of malicious and benign URLs. Using this approach, a black and white list library was built. Safety tips were incorporated to the system for users according to the match rules generated. Their experiment was able to detect malicious URLs in two-dimensional barcodes. In the study conducted by Dewan and Kumaraguru [18], Facebook Inspector is proposed to identify malicious posts on Facebook social network in real-time. Dataset containing over four million public posts in news making event generated on

Facebook were used. They figured out two set of malicious posts, the one that is based on URL blacklists and Human annotations. These posts were run through a two-fold filtering process and this is confirmed through a cross-validation process of the supervised learning models. Using the developed models, a Facebook inspector was built to detect malicious posts in real-time with accuracy of 80%. Abdelhamid, Ayesh [1] proposed a technique based on associative classification to detect phishing websites. In this study, a Multi-label Classifier based Associative Classification (MCAC) was developed to test its capability for phishing detection. MCAC outperformed other intelligent algorithms evaluated in this study. A number of features for phishing website detection has been investigated in the study conducted by [19]. A study carried out by Gupta [7] applied Boyer Moore string pattern matching technique for word segmentation. In this study, the nature of the attack is detected as a phishing link, follows by the use of real-time system to obtain the phishing links from the DNS server. Finally, the word segmentation approach is used to identify malicious URL. A two stage classification system for detecting malicious URLs has been proposed in the work of [5]. The first phase was conducted with the aim of estimating the maliciousness of web pages and then forward to the next phase to identify the malicious web pages.

Although several studies have investigated the possibility of detecting phishing websites with each study proposing specific individual learning algorithm. However, the investigation of hybrid methods for identifying phishing URLs still remains an open research issue. Therefore, this paper proposes a hybrid-rule induction algorithm that is based on the fusion of two widely used rule induction techniques: JRip and PART. The proposed hybrid model guarantee promising results based on the different experiment conducted.

3 Methodology

Rule induction belongs to machine learning domain where formal rules are induced from a set of data instances. These rules represent patterns in the data or a scientific model of the data. It is one of the most essential techniques in data mining and machine learning, which is useful in extracting hidden patterns and relationships in a dataset. The proposed hybrid rule-based model in this study combines rules induced by JRip and PART algorithms as shown in Fig. 1. From this figure, data collected from different servers such as Yahoo, Alexa, Common Crawl, PhishTank and OpenPhish are preprocessed in order to extract meaningful features that can be used for categorizing phishing websites from legitimate ones. Features extracted from the data are provided for rule induction using both JRip and PART algorithms. These rules are evaluated to ascertain their applicability for the classification task. Rules from the two algorithms are merged to produce hybrid rule-based model with strong capability to detect Phishing URLs. The subsequent section discussed the datasets used for evaluating the proposed hybrid rule-based model.

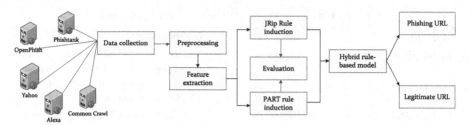

Fig. 1. Proposed hybrid rule-based model for phishing URLs detection.

3.1   Data Collection

This study analyzed two public datasets for phishing URLs detection in order to evaluate the performance of the proposed hybrid rule-based model. These datasets are available on the UCI repository. The first dataset, hereafter referred to as PhishingDataset1, is available at "https://archive.ics.uci.edu/ml/machine-learning-databases/00379/" which contains a total of 1353 URLs. Out of the 1353 URLs, 548 were identified as legitimate URLs as provided from Yahoo website while 702 and 103 URLs were identified phishing and suspicious respectively from PhishTank. This dataset contains ten (10) features for analysis and was donated by [1]. The second dataset, hereafter referred to as PhishingDataset2, is available at "https://archive.ics.uci.edu/ml/machine-learning-databases/00327/". This dataset contains 4898 phishing URLs and 6157 legitimate URLs making a total of 11,055 URLs [19]. Table 1 shows the description of the two datasets considered in this research.

Table 1. Composition of the datasets used in this research.

Dataset name	No. of attributes	Attributes characteristics	No. of instances	Class distribution
PhishingDataset1	10	Integer	1,353	Phishing (702), legitimate (548), suspicious (103)
PhishingDataset2	30	Integer	11,055	Phishing (4898), legitimate (6157)

3.2   Phishing Website Features

To develop effective classification model, it is essential to ascertain the features that can guarantee the prediction of the class label with acceptable level of accuracy. This study utilized 10 and 30 features from PhishingDataset1 and PhishingDataset2 respectively. PhishingDataset2 contains all the features in PhishingDataset1 with addition of 20 features. Therefore, Table 2 shows the description of the features available in the two datasets. Asterisk (*) in the feature name indicates the features that are available in PhishingDataset1. This study uses the two datasets for developing the proposed hybrid rule-based model because they have similar features for analysis.

Table 2. Features in PhishingDataset1 and PhishingDataset2

Feature name	Feature category	Description
*having_IP_Address	Address bar	This is one of the address bar features whose presence in a URL may indicate phishing attack. For instance, http://128.87.2.100/crawl.html
*URL_Length	Address bar	If the length of a URL is long, this may indicate phishing attack. Average URL length of 54 is considered
Shortining_Service	Address bar	Address bar feature that indicates if a URL is shorten or not. Shorten URLs that link to long URL is considered phishing
having_At_Symbol	Address bar	Address bar feature whose presence in a URL indicates phishing attack since @ symbol can cause a web browser to ignore everything after @
double_slash_redirecting	Address bar	Address bar feature whose presence in a URL, excluding the one that follows HTTP, indicates phishing attack. For instance, http://www.normalurl.com//http://www.phishingweb.com
Prefix_Suffix	Address bar	Its presence in a URL indicates phishing attack. This is usually indicated with the use of dash (-)
having_Sub_Domain	Address bar	Multiple sub domains indicating phishing attack. This is usually indicated with the use of dot (.)
*SSLfinal_State	Address bar	URL without SSL indicated by HTTPS is considered phishing while those with HTTPS but with untrusted certificate issuer is considered suspicious
Domain_registeration_length	Address bar	If domain in the URL expires in less than a year, the URL is considered phishing
Favicon	Address bar	If the favicon displayed from the domain is at variant from that in the address bar, such URL is considered phishing
Port	Address bar	If the open port on the server is not within the preferred status, the URL is considered phishing.

(continued)

Table 2. (*continued*)

Feature name	Feature category	Description
HTTPS_token	Address bar	If HTTPS is added to the domain path, the URL is considered phishing. E.g. http://https-www.mypay-pay-creditcard.com
*Request_URL	Abnormal	A link is considered phishing if the percentage of Request URL is high. This deals with the number of external links embedded within the webpage
*URL_of_Anchor	Abnormal	The higher the number of URLs with anchor, the more suspicious the URL is
Links_in_tags	Abnormal	If the percentage links in tags such as <meta>, <script> and <link> is high, the URL is phishing
*SFH	Abnormal	If Server Form Handler (SFH) is empty, blank or refers to a dissimilar domain, the link is phishing or suspicious
Submitting_to_email	Abnormal	If the URL uses mail() or mailto: to submit user's data, it is considered phishing
Abnormal_URL	Abnormal	If the host name is not part of the URL, the link is considered phishing
Redirect	HTML/JavaScript	If the number of redirect of a URL is high such link is considered phishing
on_mouseover	HTML/JavaScript	If onMouseOver event causes the status bar to change, the URL is considered phishing
RightClick	HTML/JavaScript	Disabling right clicking is an indication of phishing
*popUpWidnow	HTML/JavaScript	The presence of popup window with text field is an indication of phishing
Iframe	HTML/JavaScript	The presence of Iframe is an indication of phishing
*age_of_domain	Domain	If age of a domain is less than 6 months, the URL is considered suspicious. This is extracted from WHOIS
DNSRecord	Domain	Absence of DNS record through the WHOIS query indicates phishing URL

(*continued*)

Table 2. (*continued*)

Feature name	Feature category	Description
*web_traffic	Domain	If the website is not ranked among the top 100,000 according to Alexa database rank, the URL is suspicious
Page_Rank	Domain	PageRank is a normalized value from 0 to 1 to measure the importance of a webpage. PageRank less than 0.2 is considered phishing
Google_Index	Domain	Webpage that is not indexed by Google Index is considered phishing due to the short life span
Links_pointing_to_page	Domain	If the number of links pointing to a webpage is less than 2, the URL is considered phishing
Statistical_report	Domain	If a URL is ranked among the top in the statistics from PhishTank or StopBadware, the URL is considered phishing
*Result		Feature indicating the class distribution. The value of 0 is suspicious, 1 is legitimate and −1 is phishing

3.3   Rule Induction Algorithms

As stated in the previous sections, this study considered two rule induction algorithms: JRip and PART due to their simplicity and performance as reported in the literature [20].

JRip

JRip is a rule induction algorithm introduced by William W. Cohen in [21]. JRip is an implementation of a propositional rule learner that is based on a Repeated Incremental Pruning to Produce Error Reduction (RIPPER). The algorithm provides an optimal version for the Incremental Reduced Error Pruning (IREP) algorithm. This rule induction algorithm directly extracts rules from the dataset based on propositional rule learning approach. The algorithm executes four main phases: growth, pruning, optimization and selection. The algorithm is described using the following pseudocode [20]:

Algorithm 1. JRip rule induction algorithm

```
Input: Pos (positive instances), Neg (negative instances)
Output: RS -> set of rules

Module BUILDRS (Pos,Neg)
Pos=positive instances
Neg=negative instances
RS= { }
DL_LENGTH=Desc_length (RS, Pos, Neg)
    DOWHILE Pos is not { }
    //New rule growing and pruning
    split (Pos,Neg) into (PosGrow, NegGrow) and (PosPrune, NegPrune)
    RL = RLGrow (PosGrow, NegGrow)
    RL = RLPrune (RL, PosPrune, NegPrune)
    add RL to RS
    IF Desc_length (RS, Pos, Neg) > DL_LENGTH+64 THEN
        // For pruning the entire rule set. Exit when done
        FOREACH RL R in RS
            IF Desc_length (RS -> R, Pos, Neg) < DL_LENGTH THEN
                remove R from RS
                DL_LENGTH = Desc_length (RS, Pos, Neg)
            ENDIF
        ENDFOR
        return (RS)
    ENDIF
    DL_LENGTH = Desc_length (RS, Pos, Neg)
    remove from Pos and Neg all instances covered by RL
    ENDWHILE
End BUILDRS

Module OPTIMIZERS (RS, Pos, Neg)
    FOREACH RL R in RS
        remove R from RS
        U Posval = instances in Pos uncovered by RS
        U Negval = instances in Neg uncovered by RS
        spilt (U Posval, U Negval) into (PosGrow, NegGrow) and (PosPrune, NegPrune)
        RepRL = RLGrow (PosGrow, NegGrow)
        RepRL = RLPrune (RepRL, PosPrune, NegPrune)
        RevRL = RLGrow (PosGrow, NegGrow, R)
        RevRL = RLPrune (RevRL, PosPrune, NegPrune)
        choose better of RepRL and RevRL and add to RS
    ENDFOR
End OPTIMIZERS

Module RIPPER (Pos,Neg, n)
    RS = BUILDRS (Pos,Neg)
    repeat n times RS = OPTIMIZERS (RS, Pos, Neg)
    return (RS)
End RIPPER
```

PART

Projective Adaptive Resonance Theory (PART) employed partial decision tree approach to infer rules. The specific characteristic of PART is that the algorithm does not need to carry out global optimization strategy as in the case of RIPPER and C4.5 in order to produce the appropriate rules [22, 23]. The algorithm description is as follows:

Algorithm 2. PART rule induction algorithm

Inputs: Dataset S,
        F1 -> dimensions of input vectors,
        F2 -> expected maximum clusters allowable at each clustering level

Initial parameters $\rho_0, \rho_h, \sigma, \alpha, \theta, and\ e.$
Output: RuleSet -> set of rules

Let $\rho = \rho_0$.
L1: WHILE (not stopping condition i.e stable clusters not yet formed)
        FOREACH input vector in S do
            Calculate hij for all F1 nodes Vi and committed F2 nodes Vj. If all F2 nodes are non-committed, goto L2
            Calculate Tj for all committed F2 nodes Vj.
            L2: Select the best F2 node Vj. If no F2 node can be picked, add the input data into outlier O and then proceed with L1
            If the best is a committed node, calculate rj, else goto L3
            If rj >= ρ , goto L3, else reset the best Vj and goto L2
            L3: Set the winner Vj as the committed and update the bottom-up and top-down weights for winner node Vj.
        ENDFOR

        FOREACH cluster Cj in F2, calculate the associated dimension set Dj. Then, let S = Cj
        $\rho = \rho + \rho_h,$ then, goto L1.
        For the outlier O, let S = 0, goto L1
        ENDWHILE

Hybrid Rule Induction Algorithm

The proposed hybrid rule based algorithm leverages the capabilities of JRip and PART algorithms to generate decision rules for detecting phishing URL. The hybrid algorithm is described as follow:

Algorithm 3. Proposed hybrid rule based algorithm

Inputs: Dataset S, with Pos and Neg instances
      F1, F2, ParameterList
Output: RuleSet -> set of rules
    JRipRuleSet = JRip(Pos,Neg)
    PARTRuleSet = PART(S,F_1,F_2,ParameterList)
    HybridRuleSet = JRipRuleSet U PARTRuleSet
    HybridRuleSet = RemoveDuplicateRules(HybridRuleSet)
return (HybridRuleSet)

3.4   Evaluation Metrics

The study employs standard evaluation metrics to ascertain the performance of the proposed approach. These metrics include the total number of rules generated by each rule induction algorithm, accuracy, Kappa statistics, Mean Absolute Error (MAE) and Root Mean Squared Error (RMSE). Accuracy, Kappa, MAE, and RMSE are calculated using the Eqs. 1, 2, 3 and 4 respectively. The number of correctly classified phishing URLs denotes True Positive (TP) while the number of correctly classified legitimate URLs represents True Negative (TN). False Positive (FP) denotes the number of legitimate URLs that were identified as phishing and False Negative (FN) denotes the number of phishing URLs identified as legitimate links. In Kappa statistic calculation, Po and Pe are the probability of observed and expected agreement respectively. MAE is calculated by dividing the sum of absolute errors by the number of samples used during the training stage and similarly, RMSE is computed as shown in Eq. 4.

$$Accuracy = \frac{TP + TN}{TP + TN + FP + FN} \tag{1}$$

$$Kappa = \left(\frac{P_o - P_e}{1 - P_e} \right) \tag{2}$$

$$MAE = \frac{1}{n} \sum_{i=1}^{n} |e_i| \tag{3}$$

$$RMSE = \sqrt{\frac{1}{n} \sum_{i=1}^{n} e_i^2} \tag{4}$$

4 Results and Discussion

To evaluate the performance of the hybrid model for phishing URL detection, different experiments were conducted using PhishingDataset1 and PhishingDataset2 respectively. All experiments were conducted using R statistical package and RWeka library. R is an open source high-level programming language and software development environment that is widely used for algorithm implementation, data analysis, model development and numerical computation. The implementation of the rule induction algorithms was carried out on Windows 8 operating system. The system has a random access memory (RAM) of 4 GB and 2.40 GHz Intel Core i3 CPU with 1 TB Hard Disk. Cross-validation based on 10-fold was utilized to check the behaviors of the selected rule induction algorithms across the different phishing datasets.

4.1 Classification Performance Based on PhishingDataset1

This section discusses the results of the rule induction algorithms based on PhishingDataset1. As shown in Fig. 2, the number of rules generated by PART algorithm is more than the JRip. PART rule induction algorithm produced 41 rules based on PhishingDataset1 while JRip produced 15 rules. The proposed hybrid rule induction algorithm produced 55 rules. The top 10 rules generated by JRip and PART algorithms are shown in Figs. 3 and 4 respectively. From these tables, rule 7 of JRip and rule 3 of PART are the same. The proposed hybrid rule induction algorithm removed duplicate rules from the two algorithms to obtain unique rule set.

Table 3 shows that PART algorithm outperformed JRip according the results obtained during the experiment on PhishingDataset1. Based on the standard evaluation metrics employed in this study, PART produced accuracy, Kappa, MAE, and RMSE of 0.9364, 0.8874, 0.0689, and 0.1855 respectively as compared to JRip rule induction algorithm with 0.9239, 0.8656, 0.0882, and 0.21 respectively. These results demonstrate the superiority of PART algorithm over JRip for phishing URL detection. However, as shown in Fig. 5 the proposed hybrid rule induction algorithm outperformed PART algorithm based on accuracy considered for performance comparison. The hybrid rule induction algorithm achieved accuracy of 0.9453.

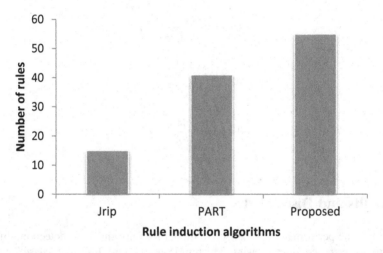

Fig. 2. Number of rules generated by the rule induction algorithms based on PhishingDataset1

1. IF (Request_URL = -1) AND (URL_Length = 1) AND (URL_of_Anchor = -1) AND (SSLfinal_State = 1) => Result=0
2. IF (SFH = -1) AND (URL_of_Anchor = 1) AND (SSLfinal_State = 1) AND (Request_URL = -1) => Result=0
3. IF (SSLfinal_State = 0) AND (URL_of_Anchor = 0) AND (SFH = 0) => Result=0 (14.0/0.0)
4. IF (Request_URL = -1) AND (URL_Length = 1) AND (SSLfinal_State = -1) AND (URL_of_Anchor = 1) => Result=0
5. IF (SSLfinal_State = 0) AND (web_traffic = -1) AND (SFH = -1) AND (URL_of_Anchor = -1) => Result=0
6. IF (Request_URL = -1) AND (URL_of_Anchor = 0) AND (SFH = 1) AND (SSLfinal_State = 1) => Result=0
7. IF (SFH = -1) AND (URL_of_Anchor = -1) AND (SSLfinal_State = -1) => Result=1
8. IF (popUpWidnow = -1) AND (SFH = -1) => Result=1
9. IF (SFH = 0) => Result=1
10. IF (SFH = -1) AND (Request_URL = -1) => Result=1

Fig. 3. Top 10 rules generated by JRip based on PhishingDataset1

| 1. IF SFH = 0 AND Request_URL = 0 AND URL_of_Anchor = 1 => Result=1 |
| 2. IF SFH = 1 AND SSLfinal_State = 1 AND URL_of_Anchor = 1 => Result=-1 |
| 3. IF SFH = -1 AND URL_of_Anchor = -1 AND SSLfinal_State = -1 => Result=1 |
| 4. IF SFH = 0 AND SSLfinal_State = -1 => Result= 1 |
| 5. IF SFH = 1 AND popUpWidnow = 1 AND URL_Length = 0 => Result= -1 |
| 6. IF SFH = 1 AND popUpWidnow = 0 AND Request_URL = 0 => Result= -1 |
| 7. IF SFH = -1 AND popUpWidnow = 1 AND Request_URL = 0 => Result= -1 |
| 8. IF SFH = -1 AND Request_URL = 1 AND popUpWidnow = -1 => Result=1 |
| 9. IF SFH = -1 AND Request_URL = 1 AND age_of_domain = 1 => Result= -1 |
| 10. IF SFH = -1 AND URL_of_Anchor = 0 AND Request_URL = -1 => Result= 1 |

Fig. 4. Top 10 rules generated by PART based on PhishingDataset1

Table 3. Performance evaluation of JRip and PART on PhishingDataset1

	Algorithm		
	JRip	PART	Proposed
Accuracy	0.9239	**0.9364**	**0.9453**
Kappa	0.8656	**0.8874**	
MAE	0.0882	**0.0689**	
RMSE	0.21	**0.1855**	

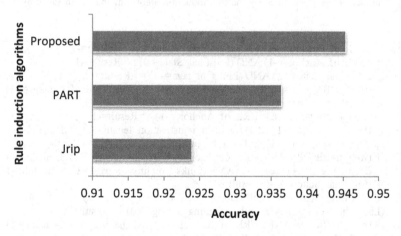

Fig. 5. Accuracy of the rule induction algorithms on PhishingDataset1

4.2 Classification Performance Based on PhishingDataset2

This section presents the results of the rule induction algorithms based on Phish-ingDataset2. As discussed in Sect. 3.1, PhishingDataset2 is a dataset containing 11,055 samples, which is larger than the instances in PhishingDataset1. Similarly, according to the results in Fig. 6, PART algorithm produced more rules than the JRip algorithm. 163 rules were generated from PART algorithm while JRip produces 30 rules. The proposed hybrid rule-based algorithm generated 191 rules. The top 10 rules produced by JRip and PART based on PhishingDataset2 are shown in Figs. 7 and 8 respectively.

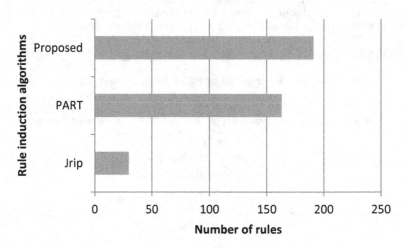

Fig. 6. Number of rules generated by the rule induction algorithms based on PhishingDataset2

1. IF (URL_of_Anchor = -1) AND (SSLfinal_State = -1) => Result=-1
2. IF (URL_of_Anchor = -1) AND (SSLfinal_State = 0) => Result=-1
3. IF (SSLfinal_State = -1) AND (Links_in_tags = -1) => Result=-1
4. IF (web_traffic = 0) AND (having_Sub_Domain = -1) AND (age_of_domain = -1) AND (DNSRecord = -1) => Result=-1
5. IF (web_traffic = 0) AND (URL_of_Anchor = -1) => Result=-1
6. IF (SSLfinal_State = -1) AND (Domain_registeration_length = 1) AND (SFH = -1) AND (Links_in_tags = 1) AND (Links_pointing_to_page = 1) => Result=-1
7. IF (web_traffic = 0) AND (URL_of_Anchor = 0) AND (having_Sub_Domain = 0) AND (having_IP_Address = -1) AND (Links_pointing_to_page = 0) => Result=-1
8. IF (SSLfinal_State = 0) => Result=-1
9. IF (SSLfinal_State = -1) AND (Domain_registeration_length = 1) AND (Links_in_tags = 0) AND (Links_pointing_to_page = 0) => Result=-1
10. IF (web_traffic = 0) AND (URL_of_Anchor = 0) AND (having_Sub_Domain = 0) AND (Links_in_tags = 1) => Result=-1

Fig. 7. Top 10 rules generated by JRip based on PhishingDataset2

1. IF (SSLfinal_State = 0) AND (URL_of_Anchor = -1) => Result= -1
2. IF (SSLfinal_State = 0) AND (Links_pointing_to_page = 1) => Result= -1
3. IF (SSLfinal_State = 1) AND (URL_of_Anchor = 1) AND (Google_Index = 1) AND (having_IP_Address = 1) => Result= 1
4. IF (SSLfinal_State = 1) AND (URL_of_Anchor = 1) AND (Request_URL = 1) => Result= 1
5. IF (SSLfinal_State = -1) AND (Prefix_Suffix = -1) AND (URL_of_Anchor = -1) => Result= -1
6. IF (SSLfinal_State = 1) AND (URL_of_Anchor = 1) AND (Links_pointing_to_page = 1) AND (having_IP_Address = -1) => Result= 1
7. IF (SSLfinal_State = 1) AND (URL_of_Anchor = 0) AND (web_traffic = -1) AND (Google_Index = 1) => Result= 1
8. IF (SSLfinal_State = 0) AND (Links_pointing_to_page = 0) AND (having_Sub_Domain = 0) => Result= -1
9. IF (SSLfinal_State = 1) AND (URL_of_Anchor = 0) AND (web_traffic = 1) AND (SFH = 1) => Result= 1
10. IF (Prefix_Suffix = 1) => Result= 1

Fig. 8. Top 10 rules generated by PART based on PhishingDataset2

According to the results in Table 4, PART rule induction algorithm outperformed JRip with accuracy, Kappa, MAE, and RMSE of 0.9823, 0.964, 0.0281, 0.1185 respectively while JRip algorithm produces accuracy, Kappa, MAE, and RMSE of 0.9547, 0.908, 0.0825, 0.2031 respectively. These results further guaranteed the suitability of the proposed hybrid rule induction algorithm for detecting phishing URL which achieved accuracy of 0.9908 on PhishingDataset2. Figure 9 shows the performance accuracy of the three rule induction algorithms investigated in this research.

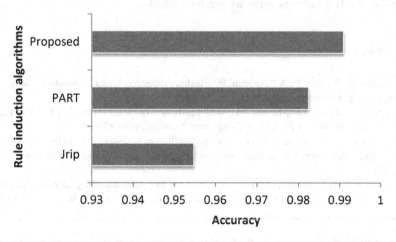

Fig. 9. Accuracy of the rule induction algorithms on PhishingDataset2

Table 4. Performance evaluation of JRip and PART on PhishingDataset2

	Algorithm		
	JRip	PART	Proposed
Accuracy	0.9547	**0.9823**	**0.9908**
Kappa	0.908	**0.964**	
MAE	0.0825	**0.0281**	
RMSE	0.2031	**0.1185**	

5 Conclusion

Phishing detection has been a major challenge to Internet users and the entire World Wide Web (WWW) community at large. A number of strategies based on social engineering have been deployed by attackers to successfully launch phishing attack. This paper explored the possibility of detecting phishing attack at early stage using a combination of rules generated from two widely used rule induction algorithms: JRip and PART. The results of the various experiments conducted indicated that PART algorithm is superior to JRip when it comes to phishing detection problem. Based on two publicly available datasets for phishing detection, PART algorithm produces promising results in terms of the standard performance metrics employed in this study based on accuracy, Kappa, MAE, and RMSE. Therefore, by extension, these results impacted positively on the proposed hybrid rule induction algorithm which fused the rules from the two selected rule induction algorithms. Thus, the hybrid algorithm proposed in this study outperformed both JRip and PART in terms of accuracy. In future, the authors intend to explore phishing detection using adaptive machine learning methods to address zero-day phishing attack.

References

1. Abdelhamid, N., Ayesh, A., Thabtah, F.: Phishing detection based associative classification data mining. Expert Syst. Appl. **41**(13), 5948–5959 (2014)
2. Dhamija, R., Tygar, J.D., Hearst, M.: Why phishing works. In: Proceedings of the SIGCHI Conference on Human Factors in Computing Systems. ACM (2006)
3. He, Q., Ma, X.: A large-scale URL filtering algorithm in high-speed flow. In: Proceedings of 2016 2nd IEEE International Conference on Computer and Communications, ICCC 2016 (2017)
4. Manan, W.N.W., Ahmed, A.G.A., Kahar, M.N.M.: Characterizing current features of malicious threats on websites. In: Vasant, P., Zelinka, I., Weber, G.W. (eds.) ICO 2018. AISC, vol. 866, pp. 210–218. Springer, Cham (2019). https://doi.org/10.1007/978-3-030-00979-3_21
5. Jayakanthan, N., Ramani, A.V., Ravichandran, M.: Two phase classification model to detect malicious URLs. Int. J. Appl. Eng. Res. **12**(9), 1893–1898 (2017)
6. Vanhoenshoven, F., et al.: Detecting malicious URLs using machine learning techniques. In: 2016 IEEE Symposium Series on Computational Intelligence, SSCI 2016 (2017)

7. Gupta, S.: Efficient malicious domain detection using word segmentation and BM pattern matching. In: 2016 International Conference on Recent Advances and Innovations in Engineering, ICRAIE 2016 (2017)
8. Thakur, S., Meenakshi, E., Priya, A.: Detection of malicious URLs in big data using RIPPER algorithm. In: Proceedings of RTEICT 2017 - 2nd IEEE International Conference on Recent Trends in Electronics, Information and Communication Technology (2018)
9. Liu, J., et al.: A Markov detection tree-based centralized scheme to automatically identify malicious webpages on cloud platforms. IEEE Access **6**, 74025–74038 (2018)
10. Vijayarani, S., Divya, M.: An efficient algorithm for generating classification rules. Int. J. Comput. Sci. Technol. **2**(4), 512–515 (2011)
11. Grzymala-Busse, J.W.: Rule induction. In: Maimon, O., Rokach, L. (eds.) Data Mining and Knowledge Discovery Handbook, pp. 249–265. Springer, Boston (2010). https://doi.org/10.1007/978-0-387-09823-4_13
12. Lee, S., Kim, J.: Warning bird: a near real-time detection system for suspicious URLs in Twitter stream. IEEE Trans. Dependable Secur. Comput. **10**(3), 183–195 (2013)
13. Adewole, K.S., et al.: SMSAD: a framework for spam message and spam account detection. Multimedia Tools Appl. **78**, 3925–3960 (2017)
14. Adewole, K.S., et al.: Twitter spam account detection based on clustering and classification methods. J. Supercomput. 1–36 (2018)
15. Bhardwaj, T., Sharma, T.K., Pandit, M.R.: Social engineering prevention by detecting malicious URLs using artificial bee colony algorithm. In: Pant, M., Deep, K., Nagar, A., Bansal, J.C. (eds.) Proceedings of the Third International Conference on Soft Computing for Problem Solving. AISC, vol. 258, pp. 355–363. Springer, New Delhi (2014). https://doi.org/10.1007/978-81-322-1771-8_31
16. Darling, M., et al.: A lexical approach for classifying malicious URLs. In: Proceedings of the 2015 International Conference on High Performance Computing and Simulation, HPCS 2015 (2015)
17. Xuan, J., Yongzhen, L.: The Detection method for two-dimensional barcode malicious urls based on the hash function. In: Proceedings of 2016 3rd International Conference on Information Science and Control Engineering, ICISCE 2016 (2016)
18. Dewan, P., Kumaraguru, P.: Facebook Inspector (FbI): Towards automatic real-time detection of malicious content on Facebook. Soc. Netw. Anal. Min. **7**(1), 15 (2017)
19. Mohammad, R.M., Thabtah, F., McCluskey, L.: An assessment of features related to phishing websites using an automated technique. In: 2012 International Conference for Internet Technology and Secured Transactions. IEEE (2012)
20. Veeralakshmi, V., Ramyachitra, D.: Ripple Down Rule learner (RIDOR) classifier for IRIS dataset. IJCSE **1**(1), 79–85 (2015)
21. Cohen, W.W.: Fast effective rule induction. In: Proceedings of the Twelfth International Conference on Machine Learning (1995)
22. Ali, S., Smith, K.A.: On learning algorithm selection for classification. Appl. Soft Comput. **6**(2), 119–138 (2006)
23. Frank, E., Witten, I.H.: Generating accurate rule sets without global optimization (1998)

Smart Airports: Review and Open Research Issues

Zainab Alansari[1,2（✉)] ⓘ, Safeeullah Soomro[2] ⓘ,
and Mohammad Riyaz Belgaum[3]

[1] University of Malaya, Kuala Lumpur, Malaysia
z.alansari@siswa.um.edu.my
[2] AMA International University, Salmabad, Kingdom of Bahrain
[3] Universiti Kuala Lumpur, Kuala Lumpur, Malaysia

Abstract. Airport exercises and action plans have significantly improved in the last two decades. They help in the development of the worldwide carrier industry. The amendment of the tenets, controls and the deregulation of the new aeronautics period in North America, Europe, Asia, and creative nations have given movement development, enhancement and noteworthy decisions for carrier travelers. In the course of the last few decades, airports have turned out to be more required with more unpredictable tasks. In doing such, they have fortified their capacity to center around and effect instead of productivity. Various factors that can be considered for developing smart airports have been studied so as to address the lackings. The main objectives of this study are to improve the experience of travelers, to make new income streams and to increase operational excellence and enhance security. This research identifies the areas for different sectors supporting the airport management to provide better smart services to the travellers leading to smart world.

Keywords: Smart airport · Smart city · Smart security · Internet of Things

1 Introduction

Variable fuel prices decline in demand, and all the global financial crisis have contributed to the transformation of the aeronautical industry. From the airlines and their international unions to the airports, the broad aviation ecosystem has been forced to implement new strategies for staying today's economic realities. A steep increase in oil prices in 2008 caused unprecedented airline losses [1]. So that fuel costs increased by up to more than 30% from 10% of operating expenses. Airlines, which had bought future's items, faced the enormous amounts of high fuel prices by a sudden price drop. At the same time, business and personal travel were limited by the deterioration of the economic situation. Supply over demand was aggravated by intense competition among many airlines for the trip.

"The International Air Transport Association (IATA)" predicts a 3% drop in passenger traffic in 2019. While a 5% drop in shipments. The prices were also overwhelming when falling demand reduced prices. Only a few Airlines did not get an effect. IATA predicted that airlines would experience net losses of more than $ 9 billion

M. H. Miraz et al. (Eds.): iCETiC 2019, LNICST 285, pp. 136–148, 2019.
https://doi.org/10.1007/978-3-030-23943-5_10

in 2019. The United States shipments account for about 80% of damage and perhaps the worst disaster which was expected by 2020 [2].

The airlines supported an excellent business model while still were profitable. However, dropping the number of passengers would have lower returns and revenue, the impact would not be uniform in all airlines. Nevertheless, large corporations and airline of origins and destinations would have a severe drop in recreational passenger traffic by continuing the experience of the number of passengers dropping down [3].

Traffic and demand may eventually return to its first stage in the next three to four years. As the IATA predicted, the four fundamental changes in the market are likely to have irreversible and lasting changes. Demographic change, new corporate governance conditions, emergence and maturity of communication technology create new patterns that require new business models and strategies [4]. The complexity of the future turmoil of this industry will raise the requirements and needs of the travellers who are always striving and quickly getting adopted to the advanced technology in all the domains. The customers expect real-time aircraft delay information, gates, and special offers from airlines and airports at a more economical and fast pace. Passengers are demanding workflow processes for the delivery of cargo, transportation, and personalized services with a higher level of expectation. This study discusses the evolution of airports with a closer look [5].

1.1 Airport 1.0: Primary Airport Operation

In the airport phase 1.0, airports concentrate on the abilities that are needed to manage efficient and safe landings, outbound flights and other airline operations. They provide essential services, including the delivery of cargo, boarding passengers, security, luggage removal and so on. The airports display evolved activities but do not pay enough attention to the needs of the passengers. While there is always a broader strategy for the airport [6].

1.2 Airport 2.0: Fast-Moving Airports

The highlights of these airports are that they are all around adjusted to natural changes and their working pace is expanded. At these airports, operational technology has been dramatically enhanced and implemented throughout business units and operational environments. Business entities share data rapidly and flawlessly and empower quick airplane terminal stations to react to ecological and operational changes fastly. By utilizing a unified and shared administration system, these airplane terminal stations frequently prevent the utilization of constrained use innovations. Rather, a huge air terminal will share the genius presented interconnected engineering with administrations in standard essential administration. The airports benefit from modest facilities provided and video surveillance [7]. From business value, fast-moving airports offer high-performance operations that can provide airlines with high speed and improve passenger expectations. An example of these airports is "Pearson International Airport Toronto", "London Heathrow Airport", "Changi International Airport", "Hong Kong International Airport", and "McCarran International Airport (Las Vegas)".

1.3   Airport 3.0: Smart Airports

At these airports, the maturity of advanced technologies in the sensory analyzes is steadily evolving. Systems are functioning on the digital platform that often converges with an IP network with classes and in the whole ecosystem, such as airports, city airports, airlines, ports, logistics, government departments, and other sectors, can have a bandwidth Create high-speed traffic [8]. These are the digital networks of the nervous system of the airports that touch and control each point of the interactions and illustrated in Fig. 1. Exchanging the information in the real time environment, deep-seated cooperation, and the integration of extensive airport processes made these smart airports to have improved the efficiency of operations, passenger services, and advanced security capabilities. They have likewise upgraded their movement encounter by giving a scope of customized administrations that can coordinate voyagers' data and foresee the administrations they require in various segments. Expansive incorporated between line applications Littler units, fuel suppliers, prepping and other living community accomplices have made new advantages all through the esteem chain [9].

Fig. 1.   Smart airport [10].

The digital network can create real-time operations and integrate processes and generate a new revenue stream. It will also improve the experience of the passengers.

2   Increasing Experience, Operations, and Values

Smart airports provide an excellent experience for passengers and the airport. Airports, airlines, and partners use technologies, sensors, processors for airports 2.0 and 3.0, and they always provide a framework for communication that can respond and analyze in real time. At these airports, passengers are not checked in different parts, and their crucial information comes in one section. Instead, there is an inclusive continuous connection between the passenger and any place and at any time [11]. The airport may likewise work past the physical limits to upgrade the experience of voyagers at all phases of their excursion. For instance, the airport ought to give data relying on the parameters defined for the traveller to enable them to design their takeoff time and pick ending and different administrations. Currently, some airports are offering Type 2.0 services. For example, the "Baltimore Washington International Airport (BWI)" uses "Twitter" to alert you about airport change, weather conditions, and flight status. While this is simple, innovative work. The airport is trying to use social networks for air travel [12].

These new intelligent airport capacities will make another plan of action, including better and more extensive incorporation and urban biological communities from organizations and associations that altogether communicate with airports. As a result, airport revenues from related departments and affiliates will increase. The increase in these emerging commercial airports will attract new business customers in the new sectors and may even create a brand-new service that delivers excellent services from various industrial clusters with free zones. Accordingly, smart chains will expand their values beyond the boundaries of traditional airports to the smart airport, which can provide innovative services that can create value among business partners [13].

Smart city airports target lots of customers, including travellers, under-handed areas, greetings part, and logistics companies. To do this, they need a broad approach. For example, imagine a traveller arriving by air on an internal flight. He goes to the airport in and meets his customer, a coordination's organization situated in the city of the airport. At all stages of his trip, information is provided in real-time and in person to give a complete and uninterrupted journey from the airport to his workplace. By the use of smart systems, integrated solutions, external and internal airport ecosystem partners, real-time information on the travel status to provide better services, the trip would be more than perfect. Alerts can also be sent to the hotels and the taxi services regarding the delay of flights to enable them to render efficient services. With these facilities, these companies can increase the delivery of services and improve the satisfaction of travellers [14].

With the evolution of airports, virtual airport service providers (VSPs) that integrate value propositions into different markets for different customers, the service portfolio of airports will also change (Fig. 2). Traditional airport service prototypes include IT services, facility management and human resources that can be turned into specific and advanced targeted services, for example, canny transportation, activity administration, and that's only the tip of the iceberg. This up and coming age of airport administrations will produce new income streams for airports, and the part of administration development will progressively be moved in focal airport tasks [15].

Fig. 2. Providing virtual services by airports [16].

3 Opportunity: Turning Business Models into New Revenue Streams

Revenues other than aviation, such as stop, land, unimportant deals, promoting and sustenance and drink, have been a crucial part of the airport's income for a considerable length of time. The airline's recent downturn has led airlines to rely more on revenues other than aviation. Many airports get a more significant part of their income from these sources. The airports combine creativity with good business. The industry is experiencing a new impetus, and new financial profiles, including plant revenue, multi-million-dollar retail expansion, large industrial parks, and land. The development of these sources of new income at airports could reduce airline costs. Competitive conditions between airports would be created to attract passengers by providing air services, which would benefit the entire community [17].

Figure 3 provides further details on revenue generation and the relative position of strategies other than aviation based on the geographic location of airports. Accordingly, there are noteworthy contrasts between income streams in various zones in retail and auto stopping administrations. Airports will get significantly more income from parking areas than central airports, which can undoubtedly exchange travellers starting with one plane then onto the next. Smart airports can take advantage of this opportunity to provide innovative services that enhance the well-being of customers. With this incorporated esteem chain, airports and carriers can go through an offer and strategically pitching procedures and give more customized administrations to fulfill clients and increment their income. Up-selling is one of the techniques where encouraging customers to buy more expensive products. Cross-selling is also a technique in which the customer decides to purchase related products, such as a warranty, etc. after the customer chooses to buy the outcome [18].

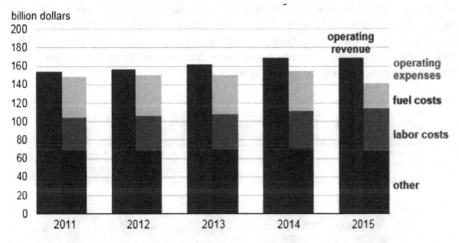

Fig. 3. Percentage of non-aviation revenue by source and region [19].

4 An End-to-End Framework for the Experience of Travelers

Airports can build their non-business income by growing administrations, for example, retail, stopping, and lodgings. With a specific end goal to boost these administrations, they must receive a client-driven approach, concentrating on expanding traveller encounter. As airlines nowadays have a widespread relationship with the client, airports must find ways to have a better travel experience for travellers [20].

Few leading airlines provide an innovative personal experience for travellers, at least for their valued customers, with superior service delivery. With the decline in the economy and the need for security equipment, these airlines will take tolls to enhance the quality and experience of travellers. Increasing security measures means that passengers should be faced with long queues, missed connections, and gate changes. The propensity toward more significant aeroplane delivers more aircraft tasks. But it's likely to cause a lot of passengers in the gates and when boarding aeroplanes [14]. Peer-to-peer expanding the services between passengers and airports has certain benefits such as:

- A more prominent capacity to up-offer and strategically pitch customized administrations in light of ongoing data and travel conditions, for example, giving auto stopping too late entries or in benefits if there should be an occurrence of aeroplane delay [21].
- Additional revenue through the provision of stores and pre-trip information designed for purchases at airports, for example, providing discounts and availability information for goods especially needed for destination or travel [22].
- The ability to utilize the combined knowledge of travellers regarding climatic changes in the weather, congestion to improve the travel experience [23].
- Creating location-based exceptional services, including searching for ways to transfer people at an airport at the right rate and minimizing delays, the ability to provide reliable travel advice [24].

CRM (Airlines' customer relationship management) Specifically, centres around visit and up-offer and strategically pitch projects and highlights of different flight classes. Often little effort has been made to manage and increase overall end-to-end travel for passengers. Airports and airlines have a huge chance to fabricate a decisive and coordinated understanding for explorers from the season of booking to movement through airports until the finish of their trip. In creating such a journey for customers, the role of airports should be shifting from passive landlords to active participants and improve the travel ecosystem as a critical partner. To this end, a bonus system must be built at the airports and airlines integrated. This superior passenger experience is the key to the difference between airports and airlines, and it also improves the loyalty of passengers [21].

As an example of the expansion of Cisco Services, IBSG has introduced five types of smart services that airports can put at the top of their smart structure. The administrations utilize the developing innovation and systems administration capacities to enhance the experience of voyagers, make new income streams, increment operational magnificence and improve security. The needs of every airport rely upon their plan of action. For example, retail revenue for hub airports is vital, and car park services at destination airports are of great importance. By giving top-notch explorers each or these five focuses, airports can gain high incomes, decrease costs, and accomplish their objectives [25].

4.1 Smart Transportation and Parking Services

Travel services in real time inform passengers of all travel problems and offer superior facilities, including parking, changing the route. Smart transportation Administrations, a touchy area variant, can track a traveller through the cell phone and illuminate the explorer before movement, recommending the best course considering activity conditions and flight conditions. Value-added services, including carriers and crew, can be provided to the passenger. A travel guide gives details of flight status at all stages on the smartphone and kiosks at the airport. The guide can also offer positioning services and help to guide travellers to cross the airport to the gateways, retail offers, and hospitality services [26].

4.2 Retail, Hospitality and Entertainment Services

Uncommon traveller retailers and visitor administrations can be offered through cell phones from the basic client data available at the airlines. Based on the passenger's profile, the purpose of the flight (work, leisure, tourism, etc.) or the destination of the passenger, offers can be announced. Smart advertising allows messages about destinations or special conditions to the passengers at different locations. Also, advanced promoting sheets can show travel data or primary data in a crisis. Retail deals to retailers will expand agreements [27].

4.3 Smart Workplace Services

Telecommunication equipment is used to detect radio frequencies for tracking portable apparatus. For instance, an airport can track wheelchairs by these frequencies to help decrease the desires for their asking for travellers. A mobile and a specific locator can tailor the correct data at the opportune time. Furthermore, effectively and rapidly manage airport issues influencing travellers. This incorporates client connections, support, and security issues [28].

4.4 Airport Smart Processes

Location-based services use details of the arrivals and destinations of travellers and, along with location information and airports, will guide travellers to reduce stress, minimize queues and increase retail sales. Check baggage tags based on airport frequencies. It empowers the different proof of gear from a separation or outside of anyone's ability to see, making it less demanding to discover missing and dislodged baggage, and give cutting-edge data to voyagers. Checking tickets without a queue using tagged cards for tracking or using smartphones with activation codes will increase the speed of the passengers to reach their flight. This can be done through tags even from hotels [29].

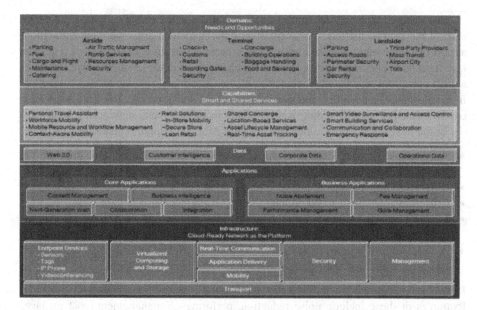

Fig. 4. Structural resources for high-level smart airports [1].

4.5   Smart Business Services

Smart airports provide business customers with a range of value-added services. These administrations incorporate activity administrations and office administration and security administrations. Likewise, in airport urban areas that attention particularly on coordination's suppliers, there is the chance to offer smart chain administrations. Administrations for structures include: advanced signage loads up for promoting, crisis circumstances and data for discovering headings, checking these in the lodging, office or different structures remotely, continuous flight data in the airport urban areas and focal mechanization of structures, observing and enhancing vitality utilization [30]. A very important aspect here is the role IoT is going to play with 5G to still more provide better services as most of the organizations are moving towards industry 4.0, i.e. digitization. And also the authors in [31] have proposed a framework considering the challenges and factors influencing the security for smart cities with smart security paying highest attention towards a safe environment.

5   High-Level Structure for Smart Airport Operations

Intelligent services that support efficient airport operations require a high-level structure. This structure is illustrated in Fig. 4 with the needs and opportunities in each area of the airport, including flight areas, larger airports, and the urban airport environment with the ability to integrate information and applications on the network.

At the highest level, the smart airport landside meets the needs and opportunities to change the experience of the passengers.

The feature layer captures important topics that meet the needs and opportunities in each of the airport districts. These creative services include empowerment throughout airport operations and business units to give better experience for travellers. The data layout outlines important topics for content and support deals [21]. This layer includes airport operations and data companies as well as information gathered about travellers from all angles, landslides, and canals throughout the journey. The data layer also covers extensive and expanding web 2.0 data, including social networking services.

In the next layer, applications that manage data and support capabilities include:

- An example of next-generation applications and optional tools that improve the interactive experience of travellers [32].
- Collaboration programs that enable real-time interactions between all stakeholders.
- Content management to coordinate the upcoming events.
- Smart business to support the continuous improvement of the Smart Airport experience using intellectual resources and newer areas such as social media.
- A series of integrated applications, including intelligent interaction manager that can predict and feel the needs of passengers and respond to them.

Business applications include airport applications, integration and mainstreaming. Examples of these include noise reduction, performance management, cost management, and gate management. Hardware, tools, and software-level services make up the foundation of the higher layers.

6   NFC Mobile Benefits for Air Travel

This section aims to explain the advantages of mobile NFC services based on the work done by the GSMA on NFC services and IATA work to advance the operations of the air travel industry [33].

The objective is to determine how NFC Mobile services based on the UICC can be used for airline industries and improve the convenience and facilities of travel for valuable customers. The UICC is an open source platform with standards that provide multiple NFC services to the customer [34]. Also, it allows space for fair competition between service providers to be created on a joint application. The advantage of this to the customer is that they can choose between services and service providers.

6.1   GSMA's Role

GSMA is a global trading community that has more than 750 GSM mobile operators in more than 200 countries and has over 200 manufacturers and suppliers in the world [35]. GSMA's primary goals is to make sure that the services are available globally in an efficient way through portable devices and play a role in improving the nation's economy by their customers satisfaction, which in turn provides new business opportunities for operators and their suppliers. MNO's cooperation ensures the expansion of mobile NFC services between mobile operators and other sectors involved in this industry [36]. Thus, it improves interoperability and leads to follow common acceptable standard through out the globe and prevents market segregation. Currently, more than 61 organizations from the largest MNOs in the GSMA Pay-Buy-Mobile project collaborated to expand a public view based on the UICC, NFC mobile services. They provide over 50% of the global GSM market and are handling more than 1.5 billion customers [37].

6.2   IATA's Role

Aviation is a standout amongst the most unique enterprises in the world. The International Air Transport Association (IATA) is the business association of this industry [36]. For over 60 years, IATA has extended the norms that have made a worldwide industry. Today, IATA's main goal is to give, oversee and work the aircraft business administrations. Its individuals incorporate around 230 carriers and 93% of worldwide air traffic arranging that offers 2.4 billion travelers [37].

6.3   Performance

IATA tries to improve industry understanding among chiefs and bring issues to light of the advantages that flight has for national and worldwide economies [38]. It likewise battles for the interests of aircrafts around the globe to challenge unreasonable laws and charges, account controller and endeavors to direct sensible costs.

6.4   Governance

IATA likely helps aircrafts by disentangling forms, expanding traveller comfort, lessening costs and improving effectiveness. Likewise, security is the main need of IATA and intends to additionally improve wellbeing benchmarks, specifically through the IATA Safety Inspection (IOSA) [39]. Also, another essential concern is limiting the effect of aeronautics on the earth. IATA budgetary frameworks broadens support in transport and expand travel industry income [40].

6.5   Added Values

For customers, IATA has simplified the carrier and cargo functions at a low cost. Travellers can book a ticket, pay for it and also get a voucher for different airlines to get added benefits. IATA plays the role of an agency between airlines and travellers and serves as cargo agents through the services of the official agency and centralized financial systems [38]. Group of vendors of different industries along with the service providers supported by IATA render their expert services based on their specilizations. For government point of view, IATA makes sure that they make more extended and better decisions in terms of maintaining the airline industry.

7   Conclusions

Nowadays, many airlines and airports fail to meet their customers' expectations. This failure is not easy to reconstruct and requires order, investment and a deeper understanding of the demands of travellers with respect to population, behaviour, requirements and needs [39]. Profound understanding amongst carriers and aeroplane terminals can give a more total and robust recommendation for passengers, which covers the whole adventure rather than the airports by allowing the airlines to share the passengers information with the airports. While sharing traveller data via aircraft does not look an exceptionally great arrangement, but rather it will give a full knowledge into the necessities of the voyager and will enable them to outline and convey new items and administrations which urge the traveller eagerness to pay [40]. The "Cisco Business Solutions Group (IBSG)" trusts this will make a noteworthy open door for income, development and aggressive position [41].

The results of this study increase the knowledge of intelligent airports, recognition of brilliant airports advancement, and support the utilization of innovations as per the feasible improvement paradigm. However, this study has some limitations, since the smart airports' applications are limited, it might impact the inspiration of speculation given prioritization which appears the requirement for specialized and monetary achievability contemplates. Moreover, the administrations are yet not supporting the brilliant aeroplane terminals, its control, and purchaser and maker's rights. Therefore, it could be a future study concern about smart airports implementation.

While this innovative approach has clear benefits for travellers and their experiences, they need to update airport infrastructures such as NFC gateway readers or payment terminals. Additionally, at the time of writing this article, the financing industry standards have not been fully launched, that is why the costs and challenges, the exact details of the aviation industry and business need to allocate credit for this technology and its application in the aviation industry.

References

1. Fattah, A., et al.: Smart Airports: Transforming Passenger Experience to Thrive in the New Economy, pp. 1–16. Cisco Internet Business Solutions Group (IBSG) (2009)
2. Nagy, E., Csiszár, C.: Airport Smartness Index–evaluation method of airport information services. Osterreichische Zeitschrift Fur Verkehrswissenschaft **63**(4), 25–30 (2016)
3. Merelli, E., Paoletti, N., Tesei, L.: Adaptability checking in complex systems. Sci. Comput. Program. **115**, 23–46 (2016)
4. Ghazal, M., et al.: Towards smart wearable real-time airport luggage tracking. In: 2016 International Conference on Industrial Informatics and Computer Systems (CIICS). IEEE (2016)
5. Hussein, D., et al.: Towards a dynamic discovery of smart services in the social internet of things. Comput. Electr. Eng. **58**, 429–443 (2017)
6. Barnett, J.: Smart growth in a changing world. In: Barnett, J. (ed.) Smart growth in a changing world, pp. 5–10. Routledge, New York (2018)
7. de Rubeis, T., et al.: Multi-year consumption analysis and innovative energy perspectives: the case study of Leonardo da Vinci International Airport of Rome. Energy Convers. Manag. **128**, 261–272 (2016)
8. Lee, Y.-K., Park, J.-W.: Impact of a sustainable brand on improving business performance of airport enterprises: the case of Incheon International Airport. J. Air Transp. Manag. **53**, 46–53 (2016)

9. Wang, X., et al.: Exponentially weighted particle filter for simultaneous localization and mapping based on magnetic field measurements. IEEE Trans. Instrum. Meas. **66**(7), 1658–1667 (2017)
10. Ying, X., et al.: TACAN: transmitter authentication through covert channels in controller area networks. In: Proceedings of the 10th ACM/IEEE International Conference on Cyber-Physical Systems, Montreal, Quebec, Canada, pp. 23–34. ACM (2019)
11. Elliott, A., Radford, D.: Terminal experimentation: the transformation of experiences, events and escapes at global airports. Environ. Plan. D Soc. Space **33**(6), 1063–1079 (2015)
12. Grant-Muller, S.M., et al.: Transport policy: social media and user-generated content in a changing information paradigm. In: Nepal, S., Paris, C., Georgakopoulos, D. (eds.) Social media for government services, pp. 325–366. Springer, Cham (2015). https://doi.org/10.1007/978-3-319-27237-5_15
13. Sniukas, M., Lee, P., Morasky, M.: The Art of Opportunity: How to Build Growth and Ventures Through Strategic Innovation and Visual Thinking. Wiley, Hoboken (2016)
14. Barkham, R., Bokhari, S., Saiz, A.: Urban Big Data: City Management and Real Estate Markets. GovLab Digest, New York (2018)
15. Neckermann, L.: The Mobility Revolution: Zero Emissions, Zero Accidents. Zero Ownership. Troubador Publishing Ltd., Verlag (2015)
16. Oldekop, J.A., et al.: 100 key research questions for the post-2015 development agenda. Dev. Policy Rev. **34**(1), 55–82 (2016)
17. Gottdiener, M., Budd, L., Lehtovuori, P.: Key Concepts in Urban Studies. Sage, London (2015)
18. Pogorelova, E., et al.: Marketing Mix for E-commerce (2016)
19. Fasone, V., Kofler, L., Scuderi, R.: Business performance of airports: non-aviation revenues and their determinants. J. Air Transp. Manag. **53**, 35–45 (2016)
20. Bogoch, I.I., et al.: Assessment of the potential for international dissemination of Ebola virus via commercial air travel during the 2014 west African outbreak. Lancet **385**(9962), 29–35 (2015)
21. Taneja, N.K.: Airline Industry: Poised for Disruptive Innovation? Routledge, New York (2016)
22. Birdir, S.S., Dalgic, A., Birdir, K.: Destination marketing and destination image. In: Gursoy, D., Chi, C.G. (eds.) The Routledge Handbook of Destination Marketing, pp. 71–81. Routledge, New York (2018)
23. Buhalis, D., Foerste, M.: SoCoMo marketing for travel and tourism: Empowering co-creation of value. J. Destin. Mark. Manag. **4**(3), 151–161 (2015)
24. Robarts, J.O., Newell, D., Abbott, K.H.: Automated selection of appropriate information based on a computer user's context. Google Patents (2018)
25. Riva Sanseverino, E., Riva Sanseverino, R., Vaccaro, V.: The role of sharing practices and dematerialized services in smart cities. In: Riva Sanseverino, E., Riva Sanseverino, R., Vaccaro, V. (eds.) Smart Cities Atlas, pp. 187–206. Springer, Cham (2017). https://doi.org/10.1007/978-3-319-47361-1_7
26. Peng, G.C.A., Nunes, M.B., Zheng, L.: Impacts of low citizen awareness and usage in smart city services: the case of London's smart parking system. IseB **15**(4), 845–876 (2017)
27. Kuo, C.-M., et al.: SMART SWOT strategic planning analysis: for service robot utilization in the hospitality industry. Consort. J. Hosp. Tour **20**(2) (2016)
28. Brubaker, C.M.: System and method for obtaining revenue through the display of hyper-relevant advertising on moving objects. Google Patents (2015)
29. Alghadeir, A., Al-Sakran, H.: Smart airport architecture using Internet of Things. Int. J. Innov. Res. Comput. Sci. Technol. **4**(5), 148–155 (2016)

30. Wu, D., Zhang, G., Lu, J.: A fuzzy preference tree-based recommender system for personalized business-to-business e-services. IEEE Trans. Fuzzy Syst. **23**(1), 29–43 (2015)
31. Belgaum, M.R., et al.: A framework for evaluation of cyber security challenges in smart cities. In: IET Conference Proceedings, vol. 4, 6 pp.
32. Turban, E., et al.: Intelligent (smart) E-commerce. In: Turban, E., et al. (eds.) Electronic Commerce 2018, pp. 249–283. Springer, Cham (2018). https://doi.org/10.1007/978-3-319-58715-8_7
33. Gamage, M.N., Colombo, S.: Adaptation of Near Field Communication (NFC) technology to enhance the operational efficiency and performance of pre-departure operations of airlinesi. J. Electron. Syst. **5**(1), 23 (2015)
34. Srivastava, A.N., et al.: Unmanned aerial vehicle platform. Google Patents (2017)
35. Raj, P., Raman, A.C.: The Internet of Things: Enabling Technologies, Platforms, and Use Cases. Auerbach Publications, New York (2017)
36. Pourghomi, P.: Managing near field communication (NFC) payment applications through cloud computing. School of Information Systems, Computing and Mathematics, Brunel University (2014)
37. Lobaccaro, G., Carlucci, S., Löfström, E.: A review of systems and technologies for smart homes and smart grids. Energies **9**(5), 348 (2016)
38. Ivanova, M.G.: Air Transport-Tourism Nexus: A Destination Management Perspective. Zangador, Varna (2017)
39. Lovelock, C., Patterson, P.: Services Marketing. Pearson Australia, Sydney (2015)
40. Jiang, C., Zhang, A.: Effects of high-speed rail and airline cooperation under hub airport capacity constraint. Transp. Res. Part B Methodol. **60**, 33–49 (2014)
41. Ylijoki, O., Porras, J.: Perspectives to definition of big data: a mapping study and discussion. J. Innov. Manag. **4**(1), 69–91 (2016)

Context-Aware Indoor Environment Monitoring and Plant Prediction Using Wireless Sensor Network

Sadia Mughal[1(✉)], Fahad Razaque[2], Mukesh Malani[3],
Muhammad Raheel Hassan[4], Saqib Hussain[2], and Ahsan Nazir[2]

[1] College of Computing and Information Science (CoCIS), PAF-KIET,
Karachi, Pakistan
sadiamughal.0092@gmail.com
[2] Faculty of Information Technology, Beijing University of Technology,
Beijing 100124, China
fahad.indus1337@gmail.com,
saqibhussain@emails.bjut.edu.cn,
ahsan_ravian@hotmail.com
[3] Department of Computing, Indus University, Karachi, Pakistan
malaniofcl@gmail.com
[4] Department of Electrical Engineering,
NED University of Engineering and Technology, Karachi, Pakistan
raheel.hassan29@gmail.com

Abstract. Remote sensor networks are a flexible innovation that deals the capacity to observe thorough actual occurrences as well as a wide-range environment where physical frameworks are considered unsuitable and costly. This study presents the context-aware based remote sensing network (remote or wireless sensor networks or WSN uses alternatively in this paper) for indoor ecological observing at home. Indoor environs atmosphere as well as stability among occupant's well-being and predicting plants are the principles of this proposed framework. The introduced framework comprises of various sensor gadgets simultaneously evaluating temperature, relative humidity via mobile sensors, illumination, carbon dioxide CO_2, oxygen O_2 and benzene C_6H_6 levels in separate spaces. This study also exhibits the framework structure, the context-aware lifecycle and the context modeling and reasoning architectures for observing the environment.

Keywords: Pervasive · Context-aware · Wireless sensor networks (WSN) ·
Remote sensor · Acquisition · Reasoning · Schema · Node ·
Air quality monitoring (AQM)

1 Introduction

In 1988, the main innovation officer of Xerox's Palo Alto Research Center, Mark Weiser, has initially instituted the frame of ubiquitous computing. At that time, the advancements in this domain have proceeded for more than 25 years. In the middle of

M. H. Miraz et al. (Eds.): iCETiC 2019, LNICST 285, pp. 149–163, 2019.

this duration, one term in the IT industry has turned into the fundamental style, i.e., "Pervasive Computing," that has the aim of computing gadgets being accessible everywhere at any time. These gadgets, as a feature of our day-to-day lives, enable us to associate with overall systems without any limits and also aims to furnish us with fastening as well as a safe and secure approach to an abundance of data and its directions [1].

An innovation that develops from its sources as scholastic research to a market reality is term as pervasive or ubiquitous computing. This term is not a smooth one and still means distinctive things to various individuals. Pervasive computing, for instance, is about portable information and facilitate the users with providing such networks that allow roaming possibilities. More of it, a space of context-aware environments where humans communicate with their everyday devices to make the environment contextual [2]. All these territories are centered in one Pervasive computing but for sure, pervasive computing in about three core ideas. First, it concerns the portable gadgets from an individual's point of view and perception for utilizing them to act on the environment. Second, it concerns how applications are made and conveyed and to empower the achievement of such undertakings. Third, it relates to the surroundings and how it is upgraded by the development and the fact of appearing everywhere at any time with multi-functionalities. Currently, pervasive computing is more a virtual imagination than the recent innovations. This imagination remains so far as humans keep on viewing handy computing gadgets as smaller than normal work areas, applications as expert programs that keep running on these gadgets and their surroundings as a virtual galaxy that a client enters to implement an action and leaves when the action is done.

Away from the large fixed screen displays and consoles, the interaction between the physical and electronic world through original correspondence has become advanced and embodied along with regular objects such as dresses, rooms, furniture, artistries and so on so forth with the transformation of "invisibility." The artifact is to facilitate these interconnected daily objects to weave them into surroundings even deprived of knowing the existence. Every one of these perceptions presents genuine difficulties to the applied designs of processing, and the related building disciplines in software engineering. Pervasive computing adapts all these circumstances [3].

Even so, Weiser's article evoked genuine emotion that depicted another model for communication between computer and human with having modern difficulties as well as give inspiration for new prototype and designing actions [4]. It opened up new doors by demonstrating how little, specific gadgets could assume a job in more prominent frameworks for individuals who work in equipment structuring. For analysts working in distributed structures, it made new difficulties of scale and revolving the focus on the reciprocal concerns of choosing strategies. At that point, an energizing vision for an extensive variety of software engineering has stepped into research zones famously termed as "Ubiquitous computing" instead of another subject in itself, it provided another way to deal with an extensive variety of research areas with new or old ones.

1.1   Technology Review

A phenomenal chance for bringing up pervasive computing is due to the astonishing progress of portable, distributed computing, wearable, and smart gadgets. Lately, we have envisioned a massive intensification in smartphones, tabs, pads and so forth [1]. While these gadgets are outfitted with numerous CPUs, storages and connectivity gears as well as embedment of GPS or any other sensors.

The third trend in computing [5] which is alluded to as "Ubiquitous Computing" or "Pervasive Computing" has the tendency of turning up the developments, for example on-going shrinking of every object, the expansion of capabilities as well as execution speed [6], lessen the power request and reduction of creation and implementation expenses of innovations, has been portrayed by this no ending trend [7].

The previous term is utilized when the prominence is on the chance of people to approach computing and to use various processing gadgets from anyplace, whenever, and in any shape, additionally nomadically, on the other hand the last term is utilized to direct that computing is undetectably inserted in the whole thing in a comprehensive network. These are considering as making: (a) a sort of computational reasoning, (b) another connection concerning with people, data as well as properties [8], (c) not at all comprehended financial effects, societal or single influences and (d) another circumstance for framework, element and administration engineers and creators.

2   Background Study

A networked of all home electronic apparatuses yet to come soon like phones, coolers, clothe washer as well as computers. Beforehand ACs/heaters were commanded by an on its own, settled or manual indoor regulator would now be able to be overseen by a smart, intellectual command via distant competences [9]. In recent times, the utilization of inhabited atmosphere with expanding expectations for affording mental comforts is growing pervasive. Regulating and observing such indoor atmospheric environments signifies an essential undertaking with the objective of guaranteed appropriate operations and living spaces to individuals.

The thoroughly perceiving of indoor atmospheric conditions that comprise on temperature, CO_2, humidity, pressure, and all others are not being easily examined or measured. A genuine danger to our wellbeing and personal satisfaction is none the other than toxic air. Estimating such toxic atmosphere is indeed noticeable all around the globe for what we inhale and offering the outcomes to our associates is a vital phase in expanding communal attentiveness for making a perfect surrounding. Generally, toxic air estimations are directed utilizing costly observers at settled areas. These estimations are somewhere deficient in giving exact ongoing toxic air data in the vast majority of the profoundly contaminated streets [10]. It is an alluring approach for ongoing estimations to have the capacity to examine and recognize worrying levels of toxins rapidly. The pervasiveness of advanced mobile phones with web network and expanded accessibility of individual air monitoring sensors give a one of a kind chance to create toxic air sensible network of clients for gathering and sharing constant air contamination information.

2.1 Context-Aware in Ubiquitous Computing

To upgrade the urban effective working or timely mannered administration to provide effectiveness, and supportability, the context-aware systems have incredibly fulfilled personal satisfaction. For sure, context-aware applications possess numerous urban applications that are capable of implementing such technologies.

Such areas may be associated via wire, or remote systems are capable of gathering, practicing, and investigating around real-time information. Concerning urban life in connection to the basic frameworks and procedures to cause interpretations, e.g., ecological conditions, 4-D or 3-D locomotion, areas or occasions for taking of predictions step towards implementation of them are needed to appear in a group of context-aware structures, podiums, and applications over a few spatial meters.

One of the significant part to build frameworks for such savvy or urban ecological areas comes under the term of "Context-Aware Computing." Its vital role [11, 12] in assisting decision making is to approach context data in such smart urban applications/structures. It seems progressive that urban conditions dependent on context-aware mechanisms will be typical in urban communities soon to help urban standards from numerous points of view [13].

Paper [14] spoke to the idea of existing WSN devices, gas devices, and soil monitoring screens were utilized for air pollutants observing based on real-time measurements. Java and a toolbox module were used for obtaining sensor information. It gathers the non-meaningful sensor information, explain, excerpt the IAQ data and places them in the sensor data center. The goal that HVAC regulator can access the data by reading daily basis to intrigued IAQ considerations via IAQ factors that are distributed in Context-Aware Framework. Air pollutant Quality directory was computed to realize the wellbeing effect of air contamination on the natural surroundings. Trials were done by utilizing the created indoor air toxins quality observing framework under various ecological conditions. The framework carried on according to the real circumstance and sufficiently gathered measures of continuous air quality information. With the end, the goal is to keep up great indoor air quality record; we mean to build up a DCV framework for occupants in which HVAC regulator algorithm will keep air contaminations inbound. It is required to build a tenant's wellbeing level with vitality investment funds.

The new development in remote sensor equipment made great feasibility to observe the indoor as well as outdoor surroundings of a premises [15]. The article also presents the three distinct goals: (i) the processing and transmission of signals generated from sensors are being customized by these remote sensors and are proficiently fulfilled by a freely available OS, and via particularly remote sensor equipment based computing language, (ii) next, it includes the handling of indicators generated by remote sensor peripherals. At this point by the help of java coding, the remote recipient's conveyed notifications were decoded and sent via PC's sequential ports for keeping them in a record. This may provide the recognition of the vital data sections that are expected to utilize the information, and (iii) last but not the least; the information needs a smooth surface for the assessment is also provided by this observing framework. A client can extract some particular records by providing basic factors, for example, a spatial sensor or correct time of information. It is foreseen that this exploration will show the capability of utilizing remote sensor systems for checking different premises.

A study in [16] portrayed different ecological conditions like humidity, temperature or light is quantified based on TinyOS by implementing nesC language along with SHT 15 remote component as well as photovaristor sensor. This framework gathers, sends and naturally command the information. It also showed the proficient execution of the framework as the client can collect accurate information about the atmosphere with no ambiguity.

ZigBee remote sensor system is posed in [17] for observing the greenhouse atmosphere while conducting the measurements of air moist, CO_2 and temperature values via oretical exploration and exploratory test technique to guarantee framework proficiency. It also facilitates the interconnection of connected nodes with the system, arranges system maintenance as well as a facilitator of hypothetical information and real-time conditions. The framework is turned out to be strong, dependable, and simple for client formation. These days the environmental difference on the planet provoked numerous impacts, for example, ice breaking over the ocean, warm winds, and the heated temperature of lakes or other factors.

Paper [18] proposed a framework that supports in observing such environmental changes that gather real-time information and provide provision of location inquiry based on collected data. They manufactured a framework for climate observing and organizing the location-based demands to deal with keeping remote information. They reserved the received information in different portions by scheming them via timestamp method based on variations in the assisted values. It also shows the updated information if any occurs. They control the portion based strategy to retain the information stream and diminishing the spared dataset with no damaging information. From the question result, the precision of the framework is enhanced, and the strategy that utilized can diminish expense.

3 Challenges of Pervasive System

The "innovation that vanishes" nearly and effortlessly coordinated with consumers, having immersion abilities into computing and in communication has been entitled as "Pervasive or Ubiquitous Computing." Such kind of innovations fundamentally provide portability; as roaming is a basic feature in our daily life span or else, a consumer will be intensely conscious of the innovation by its nonexistence while on the go. Henceforth, Pervasive or Ubiquitous Computing incorporates portable computing with a lot of advances as outlined in the Fig. 1, a couple of challenges standing up to the structure of pervasive computing are mentioned below:

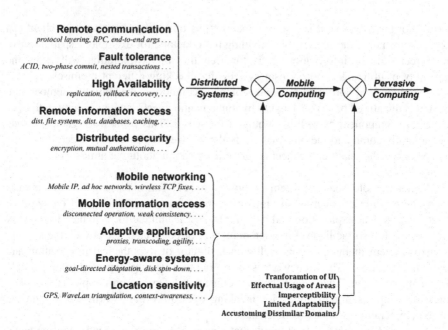

Fig. 1. Taxonomy of computer systems research problems in pervasive computing [19]

Transformation of UI. The coordination of wide-ranging gadgets; including tiny sensors to hand-held, pads or even computer units, altogether with distinct VDUs sizes, is counted as one of the features of ubiquitous computing framework. In the perception of framework engineer's, they pursue such kind of applications that work adequately within the mixed environs, and every element could be governed by consumers having no physical troublesome forced by dimensions. For instance, modest gadgets suggest small demonstrations as well as the finest user interface structure on such a miniature unit necessitates the consumers to explore a sequence of the brisk set of menus. Normal involvements outline such kind of issues with PDAs, frequently stacked with highlights however not once be used, for the reason that they are covered with the unpredictable interface.

To create user interfaces depend on dynamic nature as well as adaptive capabilities of the desired VDUs dimensions, would enable application novelists a much adaptable methodology. Four parts: UI detail dialect, shared device protocol [20], apparatus connectors and the realistic UI generator are expected to fabricate such a framework being extracted by Personal Universal Controller toolbox.

In Ubiquitous Computing conditions, the scope of desire display sizes is more projecting as compare to ordinarily personal computers; subsequently, if the product items keep working on in such situations, the marketplace and possible incomes will be extensively bigger. Though, critical programming obstacles are static in making models as well as essential instruments to create or demonstrate material to the consumer.

Effectual Usage of Smart Areas. The viable utilization of smart areas that might be an encased region like conference area, hallway or might be a clear wide region like plaza or enclosure. A smart area ties two present-awaited disconnected universes by implanting computing structure into building structure [19]. The combination of these universes empowers detecting and being regulated by each other. For instance, in a room dependent on a tenant's electronic profile, a change of warming, freezing as well as illumination levels can be programmed. Additionally, conceivable impact on others is—programming on a consumer's PC may act diversely relying upon where the consumer is presently positioned. Savvy may likewise spread out to singular articles, regardless of wherever positioned in a keen area or not.

Imperceptibility. The Weiser's model is ample vanishing of pervasive technology at the end of the consumer's perception. A sensible guess to this model is insignificant consumer diversion. If pervasive environs constantly encounter consumer desires and once in a while gives him wonders, it enables him to communicate nearly at an intuitive stage [21]. In the meantime, a small portion of expectation might be fundamental to evading huge, repulsive wonders far ahead.

Limited Adaptability. The force of communication between consumers' PC domain and their environments increases due to the complex evolution of smart areas. All these have serious data transfer capacity, vitality and diversion suggestions for a versatile remote consumer. This issue additionally obscure due to the existence of extensive consumers [22]. Therefore, adaptability in the widest think, in pervasive systems is considered a serious issue. Physical separation has been overlooked in past adaptability experiments – a document server should deal with as numerous consumers as expected under the circumstances of though the consumers are positioned nearby or far away.

In pervasive computing the circumstances are quite distinct in manner, the firmly united connections need to decrease as a single step ahead, on the other hand, together the consumer as well as their system will be overpowered via faraway collaborations, assumed to be somehow significant for them [23]. Despite it, a remote gadget consumer not at all near to home will, in any case, produce approximately faraway collaborations accompanied by significant to them, the prevalence of his communications will be a neighborhood.

Accustoming Dissimilar Domains. The speedy of pervasive development into the foundation will fluctuate significantly upon numerous non-specialized aspects, for example, administrative foundation, financial terms, and industrial impacts. A constant entrance is only be accomplished in past eras. In the meantime, there will endure enormous contrasts in the smartness of various conditions. What is accessible in a very much prepared summit room, workplace, or lecture hall might be more advanced as compared to different areas.

This extensive unique scope of smartness can be shocking to a consumer, bringing down the objective of making pervasive innovation undetectable. One approach to decreasing the measure of variety perceived by a consumer is to, let his individualized system area reward for imbecilic surroundings. As a slightly model, a framework that is fit for a separated task can veil the nonappearance of remote inclusion in its condition.

4 Proposed Methodology

The proposed framework comprises of two sections. The initial section controls the environment of the indoor territories including the light, temperature, pressure, and humidity that identifies air toxins and sends cautions to the person. The second section is to predict several indoor plants that are capable of decreasing pollutions present in the indoor air at some degree. This will enable us to connect with indoor atmospheric situations and living space comfort.

The proposed system comprises of different sensor gadgets set in the indoor territories such as a terrace, lounge, and kitchen and resting regions. In this framework, the system uses a set of sensors that enable us to analyze multiple parameters. The demonstrated arrangement gives checking of surrounding humidity, temperature, pressure (gathered from mobile sensors), illumination, and carbon dioxide (CO_2), benzene (C_6H_6) and oxygen (O_2) gas levels.

The inspiration driving creating such a system is that the situation of the present atmosphere portrayed by its dehydrated and exceptionally warm weather conditions, which leads to an increase in the level of global warming. This way, there is a need to give a cutting edge framework that is rapidly adaptable, user-friendly and effortlessly saving executing time. The principal objectives of the proposed concept are to give an appropriate and pleasurable indoor atmosphere, lessen the air toxins, increment the indoor air quality, and to simplify the process of preserving the air conditions. These objectives were put into activities by accomplishing the targets of the concept that includes; building a smooth indoor atmosphere, structuring an independent or intuitive nurturing plants framework, actualizing sensors that screen the plants, adjusting the indoor environment, and installing a notification scheme (Fig. 2).

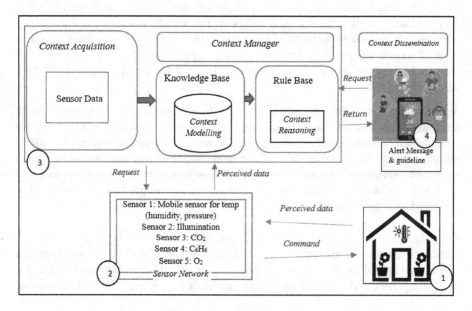

Fig. 2. System architecture

5 Implementation

Sensory information commencing the physical domain is the prime as well as note able dependencies of any smart atmosphere. Such information is being originated by using numerous sensors depending on a particular method or procedures in different spreader areas [24]. Small miniature devices that are used to take ecological parameters like temperature, moisture, sunlight, pressure, CO_2, C_6H_6, O_2 gases and so forth, comprises of numerous cheap, moderate message passing small remote gadgets that team up to construct a remote system.

To gather information about various circumstances from the environment such type of remote sensors are installed into the real domain by providing compact detecting near real environs.

A centralized node is responsible for information analysis as well as decision making on the gathered information from numerous sensors. A typical design of a wireless sensor network is exhibited in the below Fig. 3, through which information is being provided to the consumers. On the other hand, sensor devices may experience numerous confines, and the most commons are infrequent power points, insufficient memory or constrained execution capacities.

Sensors are extensively installed in numerous WSN systems. Therefore numerous different concerns with them, for example, versatility, information consistency, robustness or significant controlling, as well as effective many routing methods. Regardless of all these restrictions, for numerous ecological observing systems, WSN is still considered as the fundamental framework. In this proposed work, the implementation part is further divided into sub-parts, to have the thoroughly understanding of its execution.

The mounting of the sensor is dependable on the indoor structure. For instance, the space is separated by segment dividers from floor-to-ceiling with an average extension of 1.2 to 2.4 m then the analysis zone is just that of the space or room.

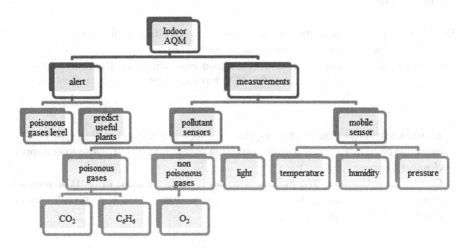

Fig. 3. Hierarchical view of indoor AQM

5.1   Architecture

The proposed system incorporates the following components as multiple sensors are equipped in different spaces for monitoring of humidity, air toxic, gases and temperature values: (i) central node, (ii) multiple air toxic measuring sensors and (iii) information acquiring and preparing and a communication component.

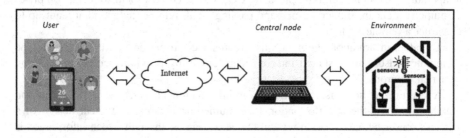

Fig. 4. Atmosphere observing via WSN

Detecting Nodes: Multiple nodes are deliberated and executed to achieve pollutant detection via cheap hazardous gas sensors along with acquiring of temperature, pressure and humidity data. Gas detectors are utilized to guarantee the contamination discovery, C_6H_6 detection, CO_2 and O_2 detections. In the meantime, temperature, pressure and humidity data are attained by using consumer's mobile phones. Self-contained sensors like illumination, temperature, pressure, and humidity are equipped within a large system with additional equipment of gas detectors, e.g., C_6H_6, CO_2 or O_2.

- CO_2: We used BME680 for estimating CO_2 levels that use dispersion valuation of range, from 0–2000 ppm with a precision of 50 ppm or three percent of sensing or either greater.

350–1,000 ppm	Concentrations involved indoor spaces with great air interchange
1,000–2,000 ppm	Illnesses of tiredness as well as bad air
2,000–5,000 ppm	Nuisances, drowsiness, and motionless, smelly air. Bad concentration, carelessness, amplified ECG and minor motion sickness possibly be existed

- *Surrounding Temperature:* The temperature sensor is a silicon bandgap type having the scope of −20 °C–60 °C with the precision of ±0.5 °C (±1 °C close lower/upper closures of scope).
- *Comparative Moisture:* The moistness sensor is having a scope of 0–100% relative humidity with an exactness of ±2% humidity from 20–80% relative humidity (±4% outer this scope).

- *Oxygen:* Typical O_2 is roughly 75–100 mm of mercury (Hg). Qualities below 60 mmHg typically show the requirement for additional O_2. Ordinary heartbeat analyses more often than not go from 95–100%. Qualities below 90% are observed as low.
- *Benzene:* Indoor dimensions of benzene in a home environment and workplaces without solid indoor bases like; oil cookery, warming ovens are commonly under 15 $\mu g/m^3$ every 24-h, which are thriving under the most minimal stages demonstrating a sign of unfriendly wellbeing impacts. Rising high peak in the scope of 100–200 $\mu g/m^3$ is due to the usage of either fragrance scorching or food preparation without vents with twenty-four-hour heights having 10–50 $\mu g/m^3$ scope. Benzene has been connected to unsteadiness, shocks, faintness, retching, cerebral pain as well as laziness subsequently to abnormal states in the scope of 700–3000 ppm [25]. Impacts after sub-constant to unending experiences at very low; i.e., <1 ppm incorporate dynamic worsening including bone marrow harm, variations in flowing platelets and modified invulnerable reaction.

This particular structural design enables us to design separate sensor devices, depend on the specific area. The proposed application is being accessed via a local API system that uses different algorithms for numerous sensors. All the parameters are estimated once at regular intervals.

This paper also tries to notice different hacks and splits that may run periodic interrupts, however security remains a bit of hindsight in an obvious set of applications that make it worse as a result of installing tiny gadgets. Hence, middle ware is a solution that helps to reduce such intrusions and protect the gadgets as well as system while preventing them from such interpolations that turns into the form of great obstruction to originality is among the core challenges (Table 1).

Table 1. Components of context acquisition process in context-aware application

Context acquisition process			
Based on responsibility	Based on frequency	Based on acquisition	Process based on source
Push	Instant (for poisonous gases)	Direct sense	Middle ware
	Interval (for non-poisonous gas and mobile sensors)		

Disposition of Sensors: The proposed system consist of multiple sensors (of each gas) are dispersed on the single story of the building (3 to 5 ft above the floor). Set of sensors are positioned in different areas, e.g., lounge, living room, kitchen, and restrooms. Ad-hoc based sharing is structured to accomplish an effective information passing mechanism. Information passing among the sensors is empowered amidst small scale of span at the standard period of interims. The disposition range for the placement of sensors varies from 5 to 10 m relying upon the closeness of wireless LAN that affect or degenerate sensors motion.

The center node is constantly assembling every information that is being generated by all sensors. All physically generated information by every single sensor is accessible by a collaborative User Interface simultaneously.

Data Analysis: The essential purpose of the proposed system starts with the observing of air pollutants. The excessive energy consuming sensors are typically considered tricky while monitoring toxic in the air and therefore have undesirably influence on sensor duration. This article tries to solve such issues by using implanted BME680 ecological sensor technologically advanced for portable applications as well as wearables having functionalities of size and low energy consumption [26] for the evaluation of indoor air pollutants.

They are dynamic, thin, extensive battery life without repairing (for a short time) capabilities that are persuasive characteristics of any wireless sensor network applications. The article also possesses the concept of delivering immediate information of temperature, pressure, and humidity by using mobile sensors which helps assess the indoor air observing proficiency after some time.

5.2 Context Modelling and Reasoning

After the context acquisition described in Sect. 5, the acquired data afterward will be modeled using database schema with SQL-Query by applying rule-based reasoning. In this paper, the context reasoning is implanted via particular as well as a complete context reasoner at the server side, whose vital role is to execute cognitive jobs because of the distinct areas of sensory devices. The requisition of rule-based thinking methodologies for preparation of context information or knowledgeable rules is required. All the information and rules are explicit to specific areas with separate environments. The provisioning of such thinking over a spread area, there is a need to prototype a model as well as deduce the information and logic associated with overall areas.

This paper proposed a hierarchical structure for context thinking that provides adaptability as well as expandability. A middleware as an individual context medium – at a low level, is implemented to realize the noticeable actions that are taking place in the relating areas. Then the context manager as a high-level reasoner concludes the actions identified with numerous factual areas in particular or distinct spaces. In this manner, the purpose of context thinking is being circulated in the overall system with an increase of adaptability of the framework and reduce the centralized breakdown, and extra load as the amount of cognitive work is divided among numerous reasoner inside various framework portions dependent on their specific logic. The context elements or particular actions generated by any sensor in a specific area becomes the input of high-level reasoner. Sometimes the outcomes generated from top level would become inputs of low level to enhance their thinking condition. The term "circumstance" in this proposed study is a type of realized context element outcome via any two of reasoner in our thinking structure. For example, the high concentration level of toxic gases inside the house is an individual area circumstance (Fig. 5).

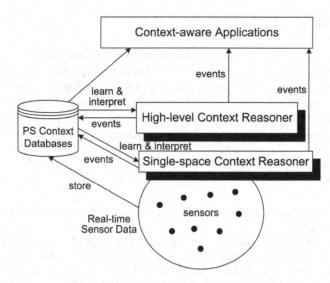

Fig. 5. Structure of context reasoning [27]

The practical illustration of this thinking structure shown in Fig. 4. Every reasoner depicts and executes rule-based prototype and devices. A single circumstance can be followed or anticipated via one single thinking prototype or their mixture specified the particular circumstance delivered by the application. Concurrent information is gathered from overall factual places employing the context information facilities in the indoor environment. The explicitly generated information is stored in the context data-center for further processing by the thinking model at any stage. The unstructured information is first tested and then kept in the data-center for any specific prototype, and afterward utilized to develop as well as periodically upgrade prototype measurable factors. The outcome circumstances of thinking prototype are openly stated to applications at any time or kept in unusual circumstance product stacks in the context data-center for further inquiries. Context data-center presented in Fig. 4 is typically organized in a distributed fashion. The presented framework depicts the execution of rule-based thinking mechanism for the top level reasoner [28]. This dimension of thinking is acknowledged as judgment rules, a vital role of the application semantic (Table 2).

Table 2. Mapping of context life cycle for developing context-aware application

Context acquisition	Context modeling	Context reasoning	Context dissemination
Based on responsibility – "push"	Database schema	Query and rule-based techniques	Ubicomp User Interface (UUI) subscription
Based on frequency – "instant" (for poisonous gases) and "interval" (for non-poisonous and mobile sensors)			
Based on acquisition process – "Direct Sense"			
Based on source– "Middleware"			

6 Conclusion

In this paper, we introduced a simultaneously working remote sensor network establishment for indoor atmosphere checking. The introduced system incorporates diverse sensors situated in rooms, living areas, and kitchen and resting regions. Fully supported sensors are integrated to evaluate the effectiveness of the proposed framework, realize inhabitant well-being. The future work incorporates the expansion of the system with new hubs to cover more space in the house or vicinity.

References

1. Lu, H., et al.: Pervasive computing. Pervasive Comput. **6696**, 188–205 (2011). https://doi.org/10.1007/b96922
2. Godara, V.: Strategic Pervasive Computing Applications. IGI Global, Sydney (2010)
3. Bao, L., Intille, Stephen S.: Activity recognition from user-annotated acceleration data. In: Ferscha, A., Mattern, F. (eds.) Pervasive 2004. LNCS, vol. 3001, pp. 1–17. Springer, Heidelberg (2004). https://doi.org/10.1007/978-3-540-24646-6_1. https://link.springer.com/content/pdf/10.1007%2Fb96922.pdf
4. Dourish, P., Bell, G.: Divining a digital future: mess and mythology in ubiquitous computing (2011)
5. Bell, G., Dourish, P.: Yesterday's tomorrows: notes on ubiquitous computing's dominant vision. Pers. Ubiquit. Comput. **11**, 133–143 (2007)
6. Theng, Y.-L.: Ubiquitous Computing: Design, Implementation and Usability: Design, Implementation and Usability. IGI Global, Hershey (2008)
7. Saha, D., Mukherjee, A.: Pervasive computing: a paradigm for the 21st century. Comput. (Long. Beach. Calif.) **36**, 25–31 (2003)
8. Wing, J.M.: Computational thinking and thinking about computing. Philos. Trans. R. Soc. Lond. A Math. Phys. Eng. Sci. **366**, 3717–3725 (2008)
9. Chung, W.Y., Oh, S.J.: Remote monitoring system with wireless sensors module for room environment. Sens. Actuators B Chem. **113**, 64–70 (2006). https://doi.org/10.1016/j.snb.2005.02.023
10. Sevusu, P.: Real-time air quality measurements using mobile platforms (2015)
11. Al Nuaimi, E., Al Neyadi, H., Mohamed, N., Al-Jaroodi, J.: Applications of big data to smart cities. J. Internet Serv. Appl. **6**, 25 (2015)
12. Solanas, A., et al.: Smart health: a context-aware health paradigm within smart cities. IEEE Commun. Mag. **52**, 74–81 (2014)
13. Bibri, S.E., Krogstie, J.: Big data and context–aware computing applications for smart sustainable cities of the future. Presented at the 2017 (2017)
14. Bhattacharya, S., Sridevi, S., Pitchiah, R.: Indoor air quality monitoring using wireless sensor network. In: 2012 Sixth International Conference on Sensing Technology (ICST), pp. 422–427. IEEE (2012)
15. Jang, W.-S., Healy, W.M., Skibniewski, M.J.: Wireless sensor networks as part of a web-based building environmental monitoring system. Autom. Constr. **17**, 729–736 (2008)
16. Gao, R., Zhou, H., Su, G.: A wireless sensor network environment monitoring system based on TinyOS. In: 2011 International Conference on Electronics and Optoelectronics (ICEOE), pp. V1–497. IEEE (2011)

17. Li, L., Yang, S., Wang, L., Gao, X.-M.: The greenhouse environment monitoring system based on wireless sensor network technology. In: 2011 IEEE International Conference on Cyber Technology in Automation, Control, and Intelligent Systems (CYBER), pp. 265–268. IEEE (2011)

18. Lee, Y.K., Jung, Y.J., Ryu, K.H.: Design and implementation of a system for environmental monitoring sensor network. In: Chang, K.C.-C., et al. (eds.) APWeb/WAIM 2007. LNCS, vol. 4537, pp. 223–228. Springer, Heidelberg (2007). https://doi.org/10.1007/978-3-540-72909-9_24

19. Satyanarayanan, M.: Pervasive computing: vision and challenges. IEEE Pers. Commun. **8**, 10–17 (2001)

20. Nichols, J., Myers, B.A., Litwack, K.: Improving automatic interface generation with smart templates. In: Proceedings of the 9th International Conference on Intelligent User Interfaces, pp. 286–288. ACM (2004)

21. Denning, P.J., Metcalfe, R.M.: Beyond Calculation: The Next Fifty Years of Computing. Springer, New York (1998). https://doi.org/10.1007/978-1-4612-0685-9

22. Alansari, Z., Soomro, S., Belgaum, M.R., Shamshirband, S.: The rise of Internet of Things (IoT) in big healthcare data: review and open research issues. In: Saeed, K., Chaki, N., Pati, B., Bakshi, S., Mohapatra, D.P. (eds.) Progress in Advanced Computing and Intelligent Engineering. AISC, vol. 564, pp. 675–685. Springer, Singapore (2018). https://doi.org/10.1007/978-981-10-6875-1_66

23. Meruje, M., Samaila, M.G., Franqueira, V.N.L., Freire, M.M., Inácio, P.R.M.: A tutorial introduction to IoT design and prototyping with examples. In: Hassan, Q. (ed.) Internet of Things A to Z: Technologies and Applications, pp. 153–190. Wiley, Amsterdam (2018)

24. Cook, D., Das, S.K.: Smart Environments: Technology. Protocols and Applications. Wiley, Hoboken (2004)

25. EPA: VOC Exposures Indoor. https://www.epa.gov/indoor-air-quality-iaq/volatile-organic-compounds-impact-indoor-air-quality

26. Sensortec, B.: Environment Sensor BME680. https://www.bosch-sensortec.com/bst/products/all_products/bme680

27. Pung, H.K., et al.: Context-aware middleware for pervasive elderly homecare. IEEE J. Sel. Areas Commun. **27**, 510–524 (2009)

28. Jena, A.: JENA Rule-based Reasoning. https://jena.apache.org/index.html

Achieving Fairness by Using Dynamic Fragmentation and Buffer Size in Multihop Wireless Networks

Jalaa Hoblos[(✉)]

Penn State, Behrend College, Erie, PA 16562, USA
jxh83@psu.edu

Abstract. Wireless Networks are error-prone due to multiple physical changes including fading, noise, path loss and interferences. As a result, the channel efficiency can be severely degraded. In addition, in saturated multihop wireless networks, nodes with multiple hops away from the destination suffer additional throughput degradation signified by high collisions resulting in high packet loss. It has been shown that packets fragmentation and buffer size play an important role in improving performance. In this work, we propose a technique to dynamically estimate appropriate buffer size and fragmentation threshold for individual nodes across the network in reference of their locality from the gateway and on their traffic load. The results show that nodes far from the gateway incur significantly higher throughput. The technique also results in better fairness across all nodes. Furthermore, it enhances the total network throughput while lowering the end to end and MAC delays.

Keywords: 802.11g · Wireless multihop networks · Throughput · Fairness · Fragmentation · Buffer size

1 Introduction

CSMA/CA (Carrier Sense Multiple Access with Collision Avoidance) [10] protocol used in Wireless Multihop Wireless (WMNs) have been studied mostly on single hop networks, however, their performance on multihop networks is still debatable.

In WMNs the throughput between sender and receiver stations in MWNs depends on several factors. Among them, their location from the gateway, their transmission power, and interferences [17]. In addition, the end to end throughput decreases further more in congested networks.

The work in [28] showed that 802.11 MAC protocol does not work well in MWNs. In [21], the authors showed that, in large ad-hoc networks, if the distance between sender and receiver grows the nodes capacity decreases rapidly. The authors in [8] studied TCP performance over MWNs. They showed that

© ICST Institute for Computer Sciences, Social Informatics and Telecommunications Engineering 2019
Published by Springer Nature Switzerland AG 2019. All Rights Reserved
M. H. Miraz et al. (Eds.): iCETiC 2019, LNICST 285, pp. 164–177, 2019.
https://doi.org/10.1007/978-3-030-23943-5_12

when load increases, links in these networks exhibit high packets drop rate due to increased link contention. As indicated in [12], in WMNs higher rate nodes are adversely influenced by other nodes with low rates thus decreasing their throughput. In addition, they also decrease the entire network throughput.

Research showed that packet size highly affects the network performance [1,25]. Although, researchers [4,5,19,24,26,29] have conveyed the impact of fragment sizes on the entire network, not much is found on the impact of the fragmentation and packet size on the fairness problem on these types of networks.

In this work, we introduce a Fragmentation and Buffer Size Estimation Technique (FBET) capable of assigning dynamically appropriate fragments and buffer sizes to various stations in the network depending on two main factors: their position in distinction to the gateway and their traffic load. Once these two factors become known, FBET then uses them to estimate the blocked and relayed traffic probabilities of each node across the network using Erlang-B [7]. Furthermore, FBET generates fragmentation thresholds and buffer sizes for individual nodes based on the estimated probabilities. Last, FBET sends the suggested values back to the nodes so they can dynamically adjust their attributes. We show that by using FBET, we reduce the unfairness problem, and increase the throughput of underprivileged nodes. Additionally, FBET enhances the network throughput and lowers the end to end and MAC delays.

This article is organized as follows: in Sect. 2, we briefly review previous work done in this area. Section 3 explains the network model and the methodology of the problem. Section 5 presents the simulation outcomes. Last, Sect. 6 examines future work, open questions and the conclusion.

2 Previous Work

The authors in [19] proposed dynamic fragmentation scheme to enhance throughput. The technique was able to increase the network throughput. However, the work only considered uniformly distributed networks where the hidden and exposed nodes problem does not exist. The authors in [23] were able to improve fairness in MWNs by assigning various contention window sizes to stations depending on their rates.

The authors in [27] introduced a protocol that enables stations to find alternative routes to various access points depending on their traffic loads. The protocol however suffered multiple shortcomings as noted in the paper.

The authors in [9] proposed a distributed link layer method on top of the TCP to attain fairness between TCP streams in mesh networks.

In [5], the authors proposed various adaptive fragmentation algorithms able to change the fragmentation size dynamically based on the channel quality in wireless networks. The network throughput was improved but the effect of the proposed algorithms was not studied on individual nodes.

In [20], the authors showed that packet size customization in the application layer may highly increase the channel utilization for wireless networks under harsh conditions.

The authors in [29] created mathematical models, with unlimited traffic loads, to calculate the network throughput in 802.11b using Markov chain. They used in their work packets fragmentation method.

Chang et al. [4] presented an algorithm capable of selecting optimal size packets based on the dynamic channels. The algorithm showed substantial throughput increase.

The paper in [24] introduced an analytical model of the work of 802.11 MAC taking into consideration hidden terminals and interferences. They concluded that by using optimal fragment size, the throughput could be increased significantly.

The authors in [6] discussed a phenomenon they called "symmetrical unfairness". They noticed that stations with the same distance from the gateway also experienced throughput discrepancies. They then presented a distributed routing method capable of enhancing symmetrical unfairness while preserving the overall throughput of the network.

In [18], the authors investigated the advantages and disadvantages of various queuing mechanisms to study the fairness in MWNs.

They observed that without a MAC layer that differentiates priorities, the ideal bandwidth utilization can not be obtained.

Bisnik et al. [2] demonstrated that the largest attainable throughput in ad hoc networks is highly affected by the node distance, its traffic load and its interferences.

In [11], the authors pertained mathematically the existence of deprivation in a simple line topology of two nodes.

In [22], the authors proposed a rate-limiting technique to those nodes closer to the gateway to achieve fairness in MWNs. Their proposal however involves complex computing.

In [13], the authors proposed a method that assigns various contention windows to nodes based on their location from the gateway and on their interferences. However, the method showed only slight improvement in the context of throughput and delay.

In [14], the authors showed that better fairness is achievable by choosing appropriate packet and contention window sizes.

The authors in [16] proposed a distributed scheme to allow nodes to collect information about their neighbors enabling them to make a better decision on staying or leaving the channel.

3   Methodology and Network Model

The authors in [15] studied the throughput decay in a simple linear network of size four. They used Erlang-B to compute the traffic blocking probabilities among nodes in mesh networks. Erlang [3] is a unit of traffic used in telephony as a measure of offered load on telephone circuits or switching. The telephone circuits used in Erlang are comparable to the number of channels available to nodes in a network to transmit their traffic. The blocking probability is shown in

Eq. 1, assuming P_b is blocking probability, m is the number of channels and ρ is traffic load in Erlang. This probability represents the possibility that a customer is denied service due to lack of resources.

$$P_b = \frac{\rho^m}{m!} \bigg/ \sum_{j=0}^{m} \frac{\rho^j}{j!}, \qquad 0 < \rho < 1 \tag{1}$$

The authors also computed the blocking and relay probabilities for individual nodes as shown in Fig. 1. In this linear network, it was assumed that node 1 is the gateway and does not send traffic, only nodes 2, 3 and 4 send traffic. Additionally nodes 3 and 4 forward traffic coming from nodes along the path to the gateway. The computations are represented in Eq. (2)

$$\begin{cases} P_{b(2)} = \frac{3\rho+2\rho^2+\rho^3+1}{3+5\rho+3\rho^2+\rho^3} \\ P_{b(3)} = \frac{2+2\rho+\rho^2}{\rho^2+2\rho+3} \\ P_{b(4)} = \frac{2+5\rho+3\rho^2+\rho^3}{3+5\rho+3\rho^2+\rho^3} \end{cases} \begin{cases} P_{t(2)} = \frac{2+2\rho+\rho^2}{3+5\rho+3\rho^2+\rho^3} \\ P_{t(3)} = \frac{1}{\rho^2+2\rho+3} \\ P_{t(4)} = \frac{1}{3+5\rho+3\rho^2+\rho^3} \end{cases} \tag{2}$$

where the number of channels m is assumed to be 1. Thus the relayed probability is given by $P_t = 1 - P_b$.

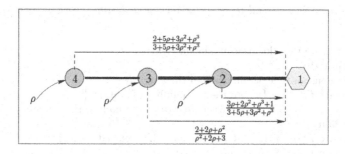

Fig. 1. A Simple linear MWN

4   Fragmentation and Buffer Size Estimation Technique (FBET)

As discussed in Sect. 2, appropriate packet fragmentation and buffer size have positive effect on performance in MWNs. That is because large packets have a better chance of being corrupted and dropped out in congested networks and where interference is factor. Inspired by this phenomenon, we want to be able to award nodes, with multiple hops away from the gateway, with smaller fragments and larger buffer sizes. The intuition behind this idea is as follows: smaller size packets have higher chances to be delivered and in case the transmission fails, nodes are provided with larger buffers to be able to store these packets and retransmit them at a later time. However, we need a to be able to properly estimate these values. One way to do so, is by using the probabilities discussed above. These values without doubt will give us a clearer insight into the degree of throughput disparities between various nodes. Since the equations were generated on a linear network of size four, we decide to use similar scenario as shown in Fig. 2 to test our technique on.

The fact that the unfairness problem manifests mainly in high traffic networks, we compute the blocking probabilities given a high load of $\rho = 0.9$. The values returned for *mobile_node_0*, *mobile_node_1* and *mobile_node_2* are: 0.91, 0.82175 and 0.56750 respectively. Thus, their relay traffic probabilities are: 0.093, 0.178 and 0.432 respectively. The computed values confirm the claim stating that individual nodes' throughput decreases exponentially with the number of hops away from the gateway under heavy traffic. These values are subsequently normalized and used to estimate the fragments and buffer sizes of nodes as described later. In our work, F denotes the default fragment size and B is the default buffer size. In addition, $F(i)$ and $B(i)$ represent the fragment threshold and buffer size, of node i, respectively. The Fragmentation and Buffer Size Estimation Technique (FBET) is described in Algorithm 1.

Algorithm 1. Fragmentation and Buffer Size Estimation Technique (FBET)

Assumption 1. *Nodes are aware of their location from the gateway*

Assumption 2. *Nodes send their traffic load periodically (every window time T) to the gateway*

1: Nodes relegate their location to the gateway
2: **for each** T **do**
3:     Nodes consign their traffic load to the gateway
4:     Calculate $P_t(i) \, \forall \, i$ {where i is the number of stations}
5:     Send F and B to the node with $P_t(min)$ { the node with *minimum* relay traffic probability}
6:     Calculate $R(i)= P_t(i)/P_t(max)$ {normalize relayed values}
7:     Calculate $F(i)= F/R(i)$ and $B(i)= B*R(i) \, \forall i$ s.t $P_t(i) \neq P_t(min)$
8:     Send the computed values back to the nodes
9: **end for**

We claim that the gateway is able to implement FBET. Once the nodes send their locations and traffic loads, the gateway will be able to estimate the appropriate fragmentation thresholds and buffer sizes and sends them back to the nodes.

5   Simulations Results

We apply FBET on the linear network shown in Fig. 2. The number of nodes generating traffic is 3. We assume that *mobile_node_3* is the gateway. *mobile_node_0*, *mobile_node_1* and *mobile_node_2* generate traffic. In addition, *mobile_node_1* and *mobile_node_2* relay their neighbors' traffic it to the gateway. Thus, *mobile_node_1* generates its traffic and forward *mobile_node_0* traffic. The same way, *mobile_node_2* sends and forward both *mobile_node_0* and *mobile_node_1* traffic. We assume that the gateway does not generate any packets and it serves as a router enabling traffic to flow in and out the network.

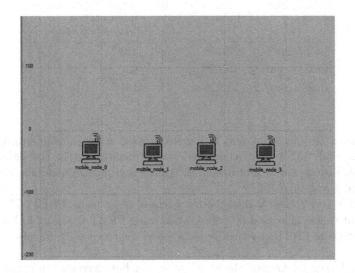

Fig. 2. Multihop wireless network

We call the default scenario *Default* and the scenario that we implement FBET on, is called *Frag*. The buffer size B of all nodes in the default network is set to 1024000 bits and all nodes' default fragmentation threshold F is set to 256 bytes.

For both scenarios (i.e. networks),we use Riverbed Modeler (version 17.5) simulator to assess the conduct of FBET. we utilize IEEE 802.11g protocol. We presume that the traffic is homogeneous. In addition, we also assume that the traffic and the packet size are exponentially distributed. The simulation time is set to 55 min. Table 1 shows other attributes we use in our simulation.

Table 1. Both networks simulation attributes

Attribute name	Value
Data Rate	5.5 Mbps
Inter_arrival time	32 ms
Packet Size	2048 Bytes
On Time	100 s
Off Time	0.01 s

Additionally, Table 2 shows the fragments and buffer sizes obtained by FBET. All other attributes not-shown here are left unchanged (we use the default values set by the simulator).

Table 2. Buffer and fragment sizes returned by FBET.

Nodes	Buffer sizes (bits)	Fragmentation thresholds (bytes)
mobile_node_0	1024000	256
mobile_node_1	422039	621
mobile_node_2	222126	1181

As shown in Figs. 3, 4 and 5, *mobile_node_0* when implementing FBET is able to send ≈21% more compared to its counterpart in the default network. *mobile_node_1* also sent about 10% more and *mobile_node_2*'s sent traffic **decreased** by about 7.5%.

Figures 8 and 7 clearly show better fairness when using FBET. The overall throughput is also increased by ≈24% when using FBET as shown in Fig. 6. The traffic sent using FBET increases by ≈11% and the received traffic also increases by ≈8%.

The end to end delay and the MAC delays are both lower when implementing FBET as shown in Figs. 9 and 10 respectively.

Last, Tables 5, 4 and 3 summarize the major findings described in this Section.

Table 3. Ratios of sent and received traffic across all nodes

Nodes	Default network	Network with FBET
mobile_node_0	0.43	0.52
mobile_node_1	0.557	0.56
mobile_node_2	0.73	0.68

Table 4. Overall network performance when Using FBET

Network parameters	Measurement
Throughput	↑ 24 %
Traffic Sent	↑ 11%
Traffic Received	↑ 8%
Delay	↓ 50.32%

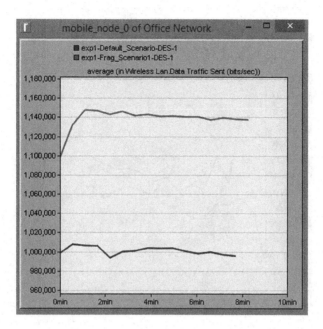

Fig. 3. *mobile_node_0* Traffic Sent

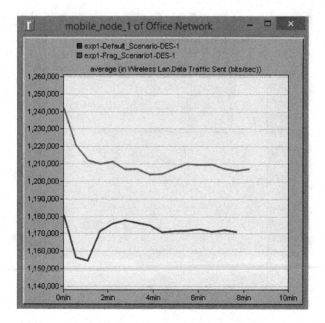

Fig. 4. *mobile_node_1* Traffic Sent

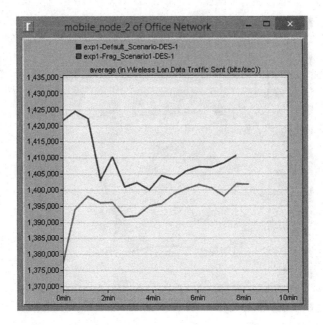

Fig. 5. *mobile_node_2* Traffic Sent

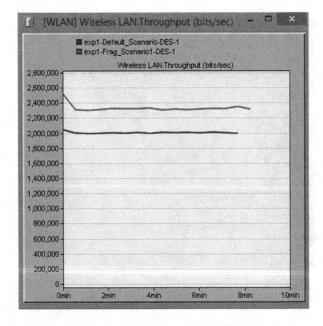

Fig. 6. Throughput w and w/o FBET

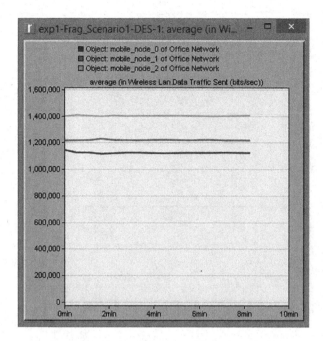

Fig. 7. Traffic Sent by all nodes using FBET

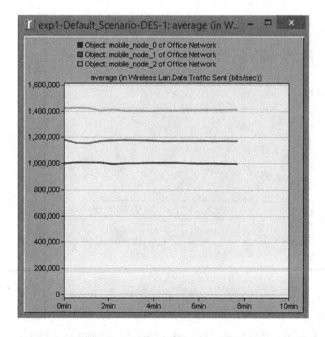

Fig. 8. Traffic Sent by all nodes in the default scenario

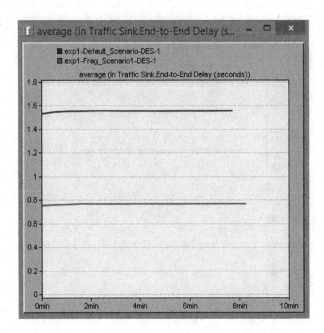

Fig. 9. End-to-End delay in networks w and w/o FBET

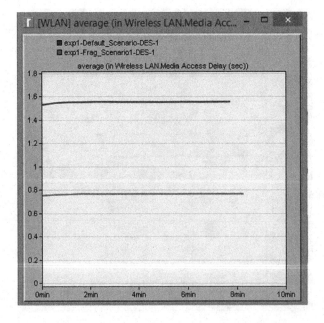

Fig. 10. MAC delay in both networks w/ and w/o FBET

Table 5. Individual nodes throughput when using FBET

Nodes	Traffic sent using FBET
mobile_node_0	↑ 21 %
mobile_node_1	↑ 10%
mobile_node_2	↓ 7.5%

6   Conclusion and Open Issues

Nodes in WMNs suffer from throughput degradation relatives to their locality, interferences and traffic load. To enhance fairness, we propose FBET, a technique capable of estimating fair packets fragmentation thresholds and buffer sizes for all nodes proportional to their physical location and their traffic load. We show that FBET increases fairness and network throughput. It also lowers the end to end and MAC delays. The findings are promising but need further investigation. We acknowledge that FBET was implemented on a simple network of four nodes and needs to be tested on more complicated networks. We also assumed that the nodes are immobile in the network. However, we believe that FBET can be equally implemented on mobile nodes. Since we assume that nodes periodically send their estimated traffic loads to the gateway, they can send their new location, if changed, at the same time. One limitation of FBET is the computation complexity required to be done by the gateway. Analysing the time complexity is part of our future work. In addition, we will be testing FBET on larger, more realistic networks where mobility is also supported.

References

1. Alshakhsi, S.A.A., Hasbullah, H.: Studying the effect of transmission rate and packet size parameters on voip performance. In: 2012 International Conference on Computer Information Science (ICCIS), vol. 2, pp. 814–819 (2012). https://doi.org/10.1109/ICCISci.2012.6297138
2. Bisnik, N., Abouzeid, A.: Queuing network models for delay analysis of multihop wireless ad hoc networks. In: Proceedings of the 2006 International Conference on Wireless communications and Mobile Computing, IWCMC 2006, pp. 773–778. ACM, New York (2006). https://doi.org/10.1145/1143549.1143704
3. Bonald, T., Roberts, J.W.: Internet and the Erlang formula. SIGCOMM Comput. Commun. Rev. **42**(1), 23–30 (2012). https://doi.org/10.1145/2096149.2096153
4. Chang, Y., Lee, C., Kwon, B., Copeland, J.A.: Dynamic optimal fragmentation for goodput enhancement in WLANs. In: 2007 3rd International Conference on Testbeds and Research Infrastructure for the Development of Networks and Communities, pp. 1–9 (2007). https://doi.org/10.1109/TRIDENTCOM.2007.4444673
5. Ci, S., Sharif, H., Noubir, G.: Improving goodput of the IEEE 802.11 MAC protocol by using congestion control methods. I. J. Wirel. Opt. Commun. **1**(2), 165–177 (2003). https://doi.org/10.1142/S021979950300015X

6. Das, S.M., Pucha, H., Hu, Y.C.: Symmetrical fairness in infrastructure access in multi-hop wireless networks. In: ICDCS 2005: Proceedings of the 25th IEEE International Conference on Distributed Computing Systems, pp. 461–470. IEEE Computer Society, Washington, DC (2005)

7. Freeman, R.L.: Fundamentals of Telecommunications, 2nd edn. Wiley-IEEE Press, Hoboken (2005)

8. Fu, Z., Zerfos, P., Luo, H., Lu, S., Zhang, L., Gerla, M.: The impact of multihop wireless channel on tcp throughput and loss. In: IEEE INFOCOM 2003. Twenty-second Annual Joint Conference of the IEEE Computer and Communications Societies (IEEE Cat. No.03CH37428), vol. 3, pp. 1744–1753 (2003). https://doi.org/10.1109/INFCOM.2003.1209197

9. Gambiroza, V., Sadeghi, B., Knightly, E.W.: End-to-end performance and fairness in multihop wireless backhaul networks. In: MobiCom 2004: Proceedings of the 10th Annual International Conference on Mobile Computing and Networking. ACM Press, New York, pp. 287–301 (2004)

10. Gast, M.S.: 802.11 Wireless Networks: The Definitive Guide, 2nd edn. O'Reilly Media, Inc., Sebastopol (2005)

11. Gurewitz, O., Mancuso, V., Shi, J., Knightly, E.W.: Measurement and modeling of the origins of starvation of congestion-controlled flows in wireless mesh networks. IEEE/ACM Trans. Netw. **17**(6), 1832–1845 (2009). https://doi.org/10.1109/TNET.2009.2019643

12. Heusse, M., Rousseau, F., Berger-Sabbatel, G., Duda, A.: Performance anomaly of 802.11b. In: INFOCOM (2003)

13. Hoblos, J.: Improving throughput and fairness in multi-hop wireless mesh networks using adaptive contention window algorithm (ACWA). In: The 7th International COnference on Wireless Commincations, Networking, Mobile Computing and Applications (WiCOM). IEEE Explorer, Wuhan, China (2011)

14. Jalaa, H.: Fairness enhancement in IEEE 802.11s multi-hop wireless mesh networks. In: 2011 IEEE 13th International Conference on Communication Technology, pp. 647–651 (2011)

15. Hoblos, J., Peyravi, H.:: Fair access rate (far) provisioning in multi-hop multi-channel wireless mesh networks. In: Proceedings in International Congress on Ultra Modern Telecommunications and Control Systems (ICUMT), pp. 1577–1586. IEEE Explorer, Moscow (2010)

16. Jembre, Y.Z., Li, Z., Hiroo, S., Komuro, N., Choi, Y.J.: Channel assignment for multi-interface multi-hop wireless networks. In: 2016 International Conference on Information and Communication Technology Convergence (ICTC), pp. 1216–1220 (2016). https://doi.org/10.1109/ICTC.2016.7763411

17. Jiang, L.B., Liew, S.C.: Improving throughput and fairness by reducing exposed and hidden nodes in 802.11 networks. IEEE Trans. Mob. Comput. **7**(1), 34–49 (2008). https://doi.org/10.1109/TMC.2007.1070

18. Jun, J., Sichitiu, M.L.: Fairness and qos in multihop wireless networks abstract. Vehicular Technology Conference. VCT 2003-Fall. In: 2003 IEEE 58th, vol. 5, pp. 2936–2940 (2003)

19. Kim, B.S., Fang, Y., Wong, T.F., Kwon, Y.: Throughput enhancement through dynamic fragmentation in wireless LANs. IEEE Trans. Veh. Technol. **54**, 1415–1425 (2005)

20. Korhonen, J., Wang, Y.: Effect of packet size on loss rate and delay in wireless links. In: IEEE Wireless Communications and Networking Conference, 2005, vol. 3, pp. 1608–1613 (2005). https://doi.org/10.1109/WCNC.2005.1424754

21. Li, J., Blake, C., De, D.S., Lee, H.I., Morris, R.: Capacity of ad hoc wireless networks. In: 2001 Proceedings of the 7th Annual International Conference on Mobile Computing and Networking, MobiCom, pp. 61–69. ACM, New York (2001). https://doi.org/10.1145/381677.381684
22. Mancuso, V., Gurewitz, O., Khattab, A., Knightly, E.W.: Elastic rate limiting for spatially biased wireless mesh networks. In: INFOCOM, pp. 1720–1728 (2010)
23. Nahle, S., Malouch, N.: Fairness enhancement in wireless mesh networks. In: CoNEXT 2007: Proceedings of the 2007 ACM CoNEXT Conference, pp. 1–2. ACM, New York (2007)
24. Park, S., Chang, Y., Copeland, J.A.: Throughput enhancement of manets: packet fragmentation with hidden stations and BERs. In: 2012 IEEE Consumer Communications and Networking Conference (CCNC), pp. 188–193 (2012)
25. Rao, S., Pillai, S.: Impact of IEEE 802.11 MAC packet size on performance of wireless sensor networks. IOSR J. Electron. Commun. Eng. (IOSR-JECE) 10(3), 6–11 (2015). https://doi.org/10.9790/2834-10340611
26. Shih, K., Wang, S., Chou, C., Cheng, L.: A dynamic rate adaptation with fragmentation MAC protocol against channel variation for wireless LANs. In: Proceedings of the 13th IEEE Symposium on Computers and Communications (ISCC 2008), Marrakech, Morocco, 6–9 July 2008, pp. 143–148 (2008). https://doi.org/10.1109/ISCC.2008.4625732
27. So, J., Vaidya, N.H.: Routing and channel assignment in multi-channel multi-hop wireless networks with single network interface. Technical report (2005)
28. Xu, S., Saadawi, T.: Does the IEEE 802.11 MAC protocol work well in multihop wireless ad hoc networks? Communications Magazine. IEEE 39(6), 130–137 (2001)
29. Yazid, M., Bouallouche-Medjkoune, L., Aïssani, D., Khodja, L.Z.: Analytical analysis of applying packet fragmentation mechanism on IEEE 802.11b DCF network in non ideal channel with infinite load conditions. Wirel. Netw. 20(5), 917–934 (2014). https://doi.org/10.1007/s11276-013-0653-2

A Data Science Methodology
for Internet-of-Things

Sarfraz Nawaz Brohi[✉], Mohsen Marjani,
Ibrahim Abaker Targio Hashem, Thulasyammal Ramiah Pillai,
Sukhminder Kaur, and Sagaya Sabestinal Amalathas

Taylor's University, Subang Jaya, Selangor, Malaysia
{SarfrazNawaz.Brohi,Mohsen.Marjani,
IbrahimAbaker.TargioHashem,Thulasyammal.RamiahPillai,
Sukhminder.Kaur,Sagaya.Amalathas}@taylors.edu.my

Abstract. The journey of data from the state of being valueless to valuable has been possible due to powerful analytics tools and processing platforms. Organizations have realized the potential of data, and they are looking far ahead from the traditional relational databases to unstructured as well as semi-structured data generated from heterogeneous sources. With the numerous devices and sensors surrounding our ecosystem, IoT has become a reality, and with the use of data science, IoT analytics has become a tremendous opportunity to perceive incredible insights. However, despite the various benefits of IoT analytics, organizations are apprehensive with the dark side of IoT such as security and privacy concerns. In this research, we discuss the opportunities and concerns of IoT analytics. Moreover, we propose a generic data science methodology for IoT data analytics named as Plan, Collect and Analytics for Internet-of-Things (PCA-IoT). The proposed methodology could be applied in IoT scenarios to perform data analytics for effective and efficient decision-making.

Keywords: Internet-of-Things · Data science · Analytics · Big data

1 Introduction

There was a time when data communication was a challenge between human beings but nowadays due to revolutionized development in the world of standards and network protocols, communication and data exchange has been possible even among the devices/sensors [1]. These devices represent anything literally from our ecosystem such as a wearables accessories, t-shirts, automobile, keychain, sphygmomanometer, chair, game console, air-conditioner, refrigerator, projector, boiler, smartphone, plants, animals, application platforms, humans beings, and bots "connected with smart sensors" to name a few [2–5]. The communication and data generated by these devices (things) come under the world of Internet-of-Things (IoT). Kevin Ashton coined the word IoT in 1999, and its advancement has been directly proportional to the advancement in the internet technology [2]. According to Gartner, there will be 25 billion internet-connectedwired and wireless devices by 2020 and those devices will generate data that could be collected, prepared and analyzed to undertake intelligent decisions [6].

© ICST Institute for Computer Sciences, Social Informatics and Telecommunications Engineering 2019
Published by Springer Nature Switzerland AG 2019. All Rights Reserved
M. H. Miraz et al. (Eds.): iCETiC 2019, LNICST 285, pp. 178–186, 2019.

IoT platforms have been deployed in various domains including healthcare, agriculture, military, food processing sector, energy, security surveillance, and environmental monitoring [7–9]. For example, IoT applications are already serving the community in the weather forecast, monitoring the health and well-being of individuals [10]. The data generated in an IoT environment are processed instantly to enhance the effectiveness and improve the efficiency of the entire service domain. Using IoT applications such as Lenovo smart shoes, one can track and monitor fitness data [11]. Furthermore, the electrical appliances including refrigerators and washing machines can be controlled remotely using IoT. The surveillance cameras installed for securitypurpose could be remotely monitored [12].

Since data plays an integral role in an IoT environment, IoT data could be considered both as a diamond and as dust. Diamond if it is effectively treated using state-of-the-art data science methodology, tools, algorithms and techniques whereas dust if it is improperly or inappropriately analyzed. An IoT system should be able to gather raw data from various networksources and analyze it to produce knowledge. The field of data science could make IoT platforms more intelligent. Data science is amixture of diverse scientific domains. Itusestechniques such as data mining, machine learning and Big Data Analytics (BDA) to identify new insights and patterns from data [1]. Therefore, IoT BDA aims to assist organizations in achieving abetter understanding of data, thus leads to effectualresults that could benefit their business processes [13]. However, likewise any technology, IoT has its limitationsbecause IoT devices generate and collect a huge amount of personal data whose management poses severe legal and ethical issues related to security and privacy. The objective of this paper is to enlighten the role of data science in IoT. In order to contribute to the domain of data science and IoT, we have proposed a data science methodology. The proposed methodology will assist the data scientists to perform an accurate analysis of telemetry to seek effective insights and undertake smart decisions. This paper is structured as follows:the relationship between IoT and data scienceis discussed in Sect. 2. Section 3 contains the discussion on the opportunities of data science and IoT. The concerns of IoT are discussed in Sect. 4. We have discussed the stages of the proposed methodology with details in Sect. 5. Finally, we have discussed the future direction of this research in Sect. 6.

2 The Amalgamation of IoT and Data Science

Huge amount of data have been generating from IoT devices such as RFIDs, sensors, satellites, business transactions, actuators (such as machines/equipment fitted with sensors and deployed for mining, oil exploration, or manufacturing operations), lab instruments (e.g., high energy physics synchrotron), smart consumer appliances (TV, phone, etc.), and social media as well as clickstreams [14]. Figure 1 illustrates the landscape of IoT and Data Science, in which various applications such as smart transportation, smart home andsmart grid, generate data using embedded sensors and objects. These generated data are transferred via networks and stored in the cloud for processing using numerous big data technologies. The data scientists use BDA applications with well-defined data science methods to analyze volumes of structured and unstructured data with various characteristics generated from IoT devices[15]. BDA is used to extract information that assists in identifying trends, discovering correlations, predicting patterns and undertaking effective decisions [16]. However, since IoT data is mostly collected from sensors, it is different from normal big data regarding characteristics such as extreme noise, heterogeneity, and expressevolution. In 2030, the number of sensors will increase by 1 trillion that would eventually upsurge the big data [8, 17].

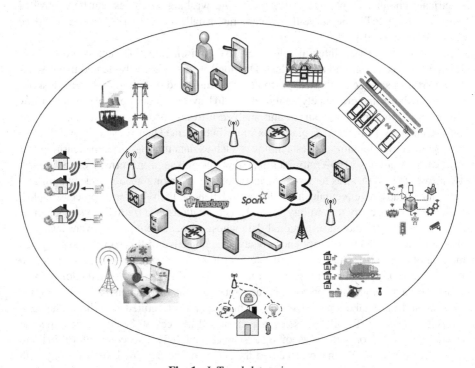

Fig. 1. IoT and data science.

3   Opportunities of IoT and Data Science

IoT is one of the most vital domains of next-generation technology that is obtaining huge attention from the industries widely [18]. IoT technologies offer enhanced data collection, enabling real-time responses, improving the access and control of devices, increasing efficiency and productivity, and connecting technologies [19]. IoT can be considered as a deployment of smart devices which uses data and connectivity [20]. The devices are connected and communicated with each other, and the IoT technologies integrate the collected data from the devices with customer support systems, vendor-managed inventory systems, business intelligence applications, and business analytics tools [18]. The integrated IoT devices produce a huge amount of data rapidly. Hence, data science can play a substantial role in IoT to extract useful information for pattern recognition, trend prediction, and decision-making. Following are some of the opportunities that require IoT and data science to develop more benefits for industry and academia.

3.1 Big IoT Data and Business Analytics

The enormous volume of data is generated by actuators and sensors embedded in IoT machines and devices. This huge amount of data can be transmitted into business analytics and intelligence tools to improve the accuracy of decision-making outcomes. Analyzing markets trends and conditions, and customer behaviors can help business organizations to detect and solve their business issues and increase the level of their customers' satisfaction. Business analytics technologies can be integrated with IoT devices such as wearable health monitoring sensors [18]. This integration provides real-time decision-making possibilities at the source of data. For instance, the health data collected via sensors and monitoring systems such as Humana's Healthsense eNeighbor® remote monitoring system which reports changes in normal activities of its members using in-home sensors can provide opportunities for healthcare providers to analyze the collected data and monitor patients far more regularly and efficiently [18].

3.2 Monitoring and Control System

Monitoring the environmental conditions, the level of energy consumption, and even the performance of equipment require IoT technologies to collect data from available sources and data science to extract useful information for automated controller and managers to monitor the performance and changes of the related objects. Advanced technologies such as smart grid and smart metering offer higher productivity and lower costs by exposing operational patterns, optimizing operations and predicting future changes and trends. One of the well-known IoT monitoring and control Systems is a smart home technology. In this technology, the main intentions are to save energy and also to protect family and property. For instance, the Verizon Home Monitoring and Control network developed remote control applications for home automation using a special wireless communications technology. Users of the applications can monitor and control IoT enabled devices via smartphone, tablet or a computer. They can control the climate, adjust the lights, lock and unlock the doors, manage security systems. The applications also send event notifications to the users automatically. All these functionalities are not possible without analyzing the received data from IoT devices. Another edition of this story is happening in smart cars where IoT technologies are used to monitor and control various parts of smart cars [18].

3.3 Collaboration and Information Sharing

Different types of information sharing can be occurred using IoT technologies. This can be categorizedin human-to-human, human-to-things, things-to-human, and things-to-things. For example, in the human-to-human category, communication and sharing information occurs commonly when a manager assigns a task to staffs using IoT enabled mobile devices. When alerts from sensors embedded in a machine are sent to the person in charge of informing about an event like dropping the temperature of the machine, a things-to-human type of information sharing has been happening. Now a user can send a command to the system and react to the alert as a human-to-things type of collaboration. Sending raw information from a complex machine to a normal user may cause a wrong interpretation. So, the data collected from IoT-enabled devices must be analyzed to take proper actions.

3.4   E-commerce

The real value of IoT for e-commerce platforms is the delivery of intelligent visions which provides new business outcomes. The future of retail is claimed to be e-commerce and shifting to online shopping and marketing is getting the attention of the customers regarding offering more benefits to them. Hence, it is necessary for retailers to adjust their business strategies to embed new technologies such as IoT into their system. Certainly, IoT and big data perform a key role in this ongoing technological disruption. The generated data require to be analyzed to come up with new solutions to improve their business and increase their annual profit. Simultaneously, they should not underestimate the vital impression of their data contribution to gain more benefits by looking for a customized and improved users' shopping experience [20].

3.5   Smart Learning

Activities and behavioral data can be collected from digital sources using IoT devices in various platforms such as social media and online shopping systems. These web-based behavioral data are recorded in different forms such as transactional purchase information or cookies data. IoT devices can observe consumers' habits, preferences, tendencies, and their environments using data science. These IoT enabled devices can learn from the patterns and outcomes extracted from the analytical processes that data science can apply to IoT data. It offers opportunities to markets, providers, and websites to learn more about consumers' needs and interests. This learning process is based on consumers' behaviors in the physical world as opposed to the strictly online world [18].

4   Concerns of IoT: Security and Privacy

Sincetelemetry travels viaseveral hops in a network, a strong encryption mechanism is essential to guaranteedata confidentiality, integrity, and availability. Moreover, the Machine-to-Machine (M2M), Cyber-Physical Systems (CPSs) and Wireless Sensor Networks (WSNs) have progressed as essential components for IoT. Therefore, the security issues related to M2M, CPS,and WSN are rising in relation to IoT. The whole deployment architecture needs to be secured from attacks, which may obstruct the services provided by IoT as well as may pose a threat to privacy, integrity and confidentiality [12]. IoT can bring opportunities for major industries such as healthcare, military, energy, and e-commerce, etc. These opportunities for IoT could also be an encouragement for the hackers to steal a wealth of data generated from IoT sensors due to political and commercial interest [21, 22]. The security of IoT sensors could be violated that could lead to a breach of service integrity [12, 23]. The IoT sensors could retrieve numerous data including the personal information of the users because those sensors can be integrated into a wide variety of things in our entire ecosystem. The hackers could launch a variety of identity theft attacks on the vulnerable IoT devices for malicious purposes. The ownership of personal data is another concern especially when data is collected without the awareness of the users or with their awareness but without the knowledge of how the data related to them is going to be used and who stays the owner of the data? The European Commission also has doubtsregarding data ownership [24]. These challenges related to IoT security and privacy remain the open areas of research. However, efforts have been reported in research and industry standards to make IoT a secure, reliable and trusted platform. Standardization organizations such as IETF and IEEE are also focusedonstrengthening IoT security by developing necessary communication technologies. These technologies are imperative to enhance IoT reliability and power efficiency. IoT has an extraordinarycapability for flexibility and scalability. One of the main goals is to ensure theavailability of authentication mechanisms tothwart any attacks, which could compromise the integrity of dataand services [23].

5 PCA-IOT: Data Science Methodology for IoT Analytics

Although the IoT and data science are frequently discussed research topics nowadays, to the best of our knowledge and findings, we could not find any paper with the systematic description and application of a data science approach to performing analytics on telemetry. To fulfill the gaps, in this paper we have provided a generic data science methodology named as Plan, Collect and Analytics for Internet-of-Things (PCA-IoT) as shown in Fig. 2. The proposed methodology could be applied in IoT scenarios to perform data analytics for effective and efficient decision-making. PCA-IoT initiates with the planning of the project, and it traverses through the collection and analysis of telemetry and ends with the reporting of analytical insights and actions. However, the entire methodology is completely iterative, i.e., there is a possibility to switch backward and forward from one stage to another. For example, a data scientist could switch from analytics to plan stage to modify the initial strategy after the preliminary visualization results. The detailed steps of each stage of the methodology are discussed in the following sub-sections.

5.1 Plan

Since every project has a certain set of goals to achieve, it is imperative for the project to start with the analysis of the requirements. All the stakeholders of an IoT project especially those who require an analytical solution must be involved in the planning stage to ensure that their requirements are being properly understood and analyzed. Furthermore, the main stakeholders such as the domain experts must be involved in every cycle of the project to provide domain knowledge and review and revise the continuous progress as well as the direction of the project to perceive valuable insights and to obtain the required solutions.

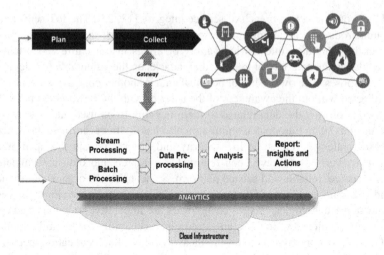

Fig. 2. Data science methodology for IoT analytics (PCA-IoT).

After the successful gathering and analysis of the requirement, a data scientist can formulate the preliminary analytical approaches using statistical techniques and machine learning algorithms to address the problem. With the preliminary findings, team of data scientists, domain experts and appropriate entities from the side of project sponsor could work together to identify and undertake decision on the selection of most suitable analytics tools to be used, algorithms techniques to be applied, the type of models to be generated, and the hosting platform such as in-house or cloud infrastructure. For instance, if the goal is to estimate the relationship between independent and predictor variables, data scientists may choose to generate a regression model. In the planning stage, it is also important to identify the sources of IoT data because telemetry generated from unknown or unreliable sources may lead to inaccurate and invalid analysis.

5.2   Collect

Due to rapidly expanding volume and velocity of telemetry, it would be feasible to perform IoT analytics using third-party cloud services such as Amazon IoT core, IBM Watson IoT, and Azure IoT hub. The gathering of telemetry could initiate after the successful completion of the activities defined at the planning stage. The communication between the IoT hub, i.e., IoT data sources takes places via the gateway which manages all active device connections and implements semantics for multiple protocols to ensure that devices can securely and effectively communicate using various protocols such as MQTT, CoAP, WebSockets, and HTTP. Furthermore, the gateway could apply rules and restrictions to the incoming data using SQL-like statements. A rule can be applied to data from one or many devices. For example, the gateway may filter-out and reject data from certain sensors of the IoT network, or it may accept only certain types of data from specific sensors. The gateway bridge publishes all device telemetry to the cloud that can then be consumed by downstream analytic systems using stream or batch processing.

5.3 Analytics

The data scientist would apply batch-processing techniques to analyze telemetry when analytics takes place on blocks of data that have already been stored over a period. For example, processing all the transactions that have been performed by a major financial firm in a week. However, stream processing will be feasible if real-time analytics is required such as fraud detection and live application monitoring. In an IoT environment, both types of the processing could be useful depending on the requirements and nature of the project especially related to the type of analytics required. Batch processing best fits in the situations where generating real-time analytics results are not the priority andmore importance is given to the processing of large volumes of data than to getting fast analytics results. Streaming processing of telemetry can be performed using platforms such as Apache Kafka, Apache Flink, Apache Storm, Apache Samza, etc. whereas batch processing could be performed using Hadoop. Since the sensors can generate inappropriate or null data values, the next step would be to pre-process the telemetry using typical data science approaches such as removing duplication, filter unwanted outliers, handling missing data, etc. Unlike manual data processing in traditional data analytics systems, in an IoT analytics environment, data processing is fast and automated by writing well-defined program codes. During the analysis of data, if data scientists identified that the data needs to further pre-processed, they will switch to pre-processing before performing the analysis. The prepared data is then analyzed using various machine learning and statistical techniques to generate models by considering the steps decided in the project plan. Finally, the models are visualized to perform various analytics such as descriptive, predictive and prescriptive. Due to real-time analytics, organizations, individuals or governments can undertake efficient as well as effective decisions using telemetry.

6   Future Direction

Likewise, any technology such as cloud, big data, and fog computing, etc., IoT has a bright and dark side. However, the research world is currently focused on eliminating the concerns related to IoT to make it as a trusted, reliable and secure platform to seek incredible insights. The research in the field is rapidly increasing, and we could predict that it will continue because data is of high value for the organizations and IoT is the major source for gathering and generating volumes and variety of data. The relationship between the IoT and data science is eternal because to convert data into diamond, analytical approaches are required. However, there are several opportunities to contribute to the areas of IoT and data science. New systems are required to guarantee the security and privacy of users' data and trustworthiness of IoT sensors. Apart from the developments in the world of technology, there is a need to establish new policies, standards, and guidelines for the entire IoT ecosystem to achieve the trust of all the users and to make IoT analytics an opportunity for all types of organizations.

References

1. Mahdavinejad, M.S., Rezvan, M., Barekatain, M., Adibi, P., Barnaghi, P., Sheth, A.P.: Machine learning for internet of things data analysis: a survey. Digit. Commun. Netw. **4**(3), 161–175 (2018)
2. Ashton, K.: That internet of things. RFID J. **22**, 97–114 (2010)
3. Atzori, L., Iera, A., Morabito, G.: The internet of things: a survey. Comput. Netw. **54**(15), 2787–2805 (2010)
4. Mulligan, G.: The Internet of Things: here now and coming soon. IEEE Internet Comput. **14**(1), 35–36 (2010)
5. Weber, R.H.: Internet of Things-New security and privacy challenges. Comput. Law Secur. Rev. **26**(1), 23–30 (2010)
6. Ray, P.P.: A survey on Internet of Things architectures. J. King Saud Univ. Comput. Inform. Sci. **30**(3), 291–319 (2018)
7. Da Xu, L., He, W., Li, S.: Internet of things in industries: a survey. IEEE Trans. Ind. Inf. **10**(4), 2233–2243 (2014)
8. Li, S., Tryfonas, T., Li, H.: The internet of things: a security point of view. Internet Res. **26**(2), 337–359 (2016)
9. Yuehong, Y.I., Zeng, Y., Chen, X., Fan, Y.: The internet of things in healthcare: an overview. J. Ind. Inf. Integr. **31**(1), 3–13 (2016)
10. Rouse, M., Wigmore, I.: Internet of things (2016). http://internetofthingsagenda.techtarget.com/definition/Internet-of-Things-IoT
11. Heater, B.: Lenovo shows off a pair of intel-powered smart shoes (2016). https://techcrunch.com/2016/06/09/lenovo-smart-shoes/
12. Khan, M.A., Salah, K.: IoT security: Review, blockchain solutions, and open challenges. Future Gener. Comput. Syst. **82**, 395–411 (2018)
13. Marjani, M.: Big IoT data analytics: architecture, opportunities, and open research. Challenges **5**, 5247–5261 (2016)
14. Ranjan, R., Thakker, D., Haller, A., Buyya, R.: A note on exploration of IoT generated big data using semantics. Future Gener. Comput. Syst. **76**, 495–498 (2017)
15. Rollins, J.B., Lin, P., Aklson, A.: Data Science Methodology (2017). https://cognitiveclass.ai/courses/data-science-methodology-2/
16. Golchha, N.: Big data-the information revolution. Int. J. Adv. Res. **1**(12), 791–794 (2015)
17. Chen, M.: Related Technologies in Big Data, pp. 11–18. Springer, Heidelberg (2014)
18. Lee, I., Lee, K.: The internet of things (IoT): applications, investments, and challenges for enterprises. Bus. Horiz. **58**(4), 431–440 (2015)
19. Weinberg, B.D., Milne, G.R., Andonova, Y.G., Hajjat, F.M.: Internet of things: convenience vs. privacy and secrecy. Bus. Horiz. **58**(6), 615–624 (2015)
20. Rottigni, R.: Users' Advantages of Big Data and IoT in E-Commerce (2018). https://readwrite.com/2018/06/05/users-advantages-of-big-data-and-iot-in-e-commerce/
21. Medaglia, C.M., Serbanati, A.: An overview of privacy and security issues in the internet of things. In: Proceedings of 20th workshop on digital communications (2010)
22. Christoph P.M.: Security and Privacy Challenges in the Internet of Things. Electronic Communications of the EASST (2009)
23. Aakanksha, T., Gupta, B.: Security, privacy and trust of different layers in Internet-of-Things (IoTs) framework. Future Gener. Comput. Syst. **2019**, 3 (2018)
24. Janecek, V.: Ownership of personal data in the Internet of Things. Comput. Law Secur. Rev. **34**, 1–14 (2018)

FinTech

A Comparison of the Different Types of Risk Perceived by Users that Are Hindering the Adoption of Mobile Payment

Laure Pauchard[(⊠)]

Solent University, Southampton SO14 0YN, UK
4paucl31@solent.ac.uk

Abstract. Recent research has established that the risk perceived by users is one of the main reasons why, despite offering numerous benefits, the worldwide adoption of mobile payment remains surprisingly low. This pilot study aims to establish more specifically what types of risk have a negative effect on the adoption of mobile payment by proposing a new research model solely focused on the risk dimension. The model is composed of 6 types of risk that were extracted from the existing literature investigating mobile payment adoption. A 5-point likert scale-based questionnaire was used to collect sample data to test the model. The data was subsequently analysed by conducting a reliability analysis of the scale and a regression analysis aiming to quantify the effect of the variables on the users' intention to use mobile payment. The results of the study suggest that Security Risk is the highest deterrent, followed by Financial Risk, Social Risk, Privacy Risk and Time Risk while Psychological Risk was not found to have any negative effect on the users' Intention of Use. These findings potentially have implications for stakeholders such as mobile phone manufacturers and banking organisations as testing the research model on a larger sample of data would identify more precisely what aspects of mobile payment should be improved to increase its appeal to consumers. Furthermore, the proposed model can assist further research aiming to identify what features could reduce the risk perceived by potential mobile payment users.

Keywords: Mobile payment adoption · User acceptance · Hindering factors · Perceived Risk

1 Introduction

Several innovative payment technologies have been developed within the last thirty years, including contactless credit cards which have become extremely popular and are now overtaking traditional payment methods. Mobile payment is a notable example of a new payment technology which is gaining popularity among users as it takes advantage of the ever-increasing number of mobile phone owners [23, 24]. Mobile payment is defined [7] as a purchase of a good or service performed by a mobile device using a mobile communication network. Different types of technologies have been

© ICST Institute for Computer Sciences, Social Informatics and Telecommunications Engineering 2019
Published by Springer Nature Switzerland AG 2019. All Rights Reserved
M. H. Miraz et al. (Eds.): iCETiC 2019, LNICST 285, pp. 189–202, 2019.

designed to perform mobile payment including near field communication (NFC) [3], magnetic secure transmission (MST) and sound base waves technologies. Mobile payment technology offers many benefits for both users and merchants including convenience, mobility, quicker transactions and lower costs [14]. Consequently, mobile payment was expected to become the preferred payment method by the end of the decade [13]. However, research has shown that the world-wide acceptance of mobile payment remains very far from the booming success it was predicted to reach [8]. For instance, the adoption of mobile payment is particularly limited in Western Europe [25] although most of the adult population owns a smartphone.

As a result, research on mobile payment has focused on trying to identify the hindering factors of its adoption. As demonstrated recently [20], several studies have established that the risk perceived by users is a major barrier to their acceptance of mobile payment technologies. Furthermore, [8] the risk perceived by users has been found to diminish the positive impact of the benefits they perceive. However, research has been inconstant as to what types of risk are included in the broad definition of Perceived Risk and as a consequence, the results of recent studies are not easily comparable. This pilot study aims to address this gap by extracting the different types of risk identified in recent research in order to measure and compare their effect on the consumers' intention to use mobile payment.

2   Background

While research aiming to analyse users' attitude towards innovative technology has been based on a variety of models throughout the last decade, mobile payment adoption studies have mainly focused on two particular behavioural intention models: the TAM and UTAUT models [4, 15].

The acceptance model was developed by Davis *et al.* in 1989 to measure the acceptance of information technologies (IT) and information systems (IS) [18]. It was initially composed of two main constructs: Ease of Use and Perceived Usefulness but was later adapted to the study of mobile payment adoption and now includes additional variables such as compatibility, social influence and risk perception depending on the needs of the research. [15]

The Unified Theory of Acceptance and Use of Technology results from the combination of the TAM with seven other models and was designed by Venkatesh *et al.* in 2003 [26, 27]. The UTAUT was initially composed of three main constructs (Expected Performance, Expected Effort and Social Influence) but was also flexibly modified with the addition of relevant variables to suit recent studies on mobile payment adoption [1].

More specifically, in studies investigating the relationship between risk perception and mobile payment adoption, research models have mainly included two variables: Intention of Use and Perceived Risk.

The variable Intention of Use was derived from the Theory of Reasoned Action and the Theory of Planned Behaviour which argues that individuals' actions are decided by their intention to act [2]. Previous studies on social behaviour have demonstrated that Intention of Use is a reliable variable to predict user behaviour. This justifies why Intention of Use has been consistently selected as the dependent variable in research on mobile payment adoption [17].

The variable Perceived Risk in research on payment technology acceptance was defined by Gupta and Kim [11] as "a consumer's perception about the uncertainty and the adverse consequences of a transaction performed by a seller". Several researchers including Yang et al. [30] and Schmidthuber, Maresch and Ginner [25] have demonstrated that Perceived risk has a negative effect of the users' Intention of Use. Nonetheless, the definition of Perceived Risk greatly varies from one paper to another. Some studies broadly define perceived risk as the expectancy of loss while many others include different types of risk within the main variable Perceived Risk. For instance, Ma et al. [16] included Financial Risk and Information Risk in Perceived Risk while Hongxia, Xianhao and Weidan [12] only mentioned Security Risk in their definition of Perceived Risk.

Although all those variations of Perceived Risk relate closely to the fear of a negative outcome, they do not refer to the same aspects of mobile payment and can therefore not be compared or addressed the same way. As a result, it was suggested that the individual testing of each different type of risk as well as a comparison of their effect would be relevant to better understand how mobile payment is perceived and increase its appeal to consumers.

3 Research Method

3.1 Research Model

Most recent studies on mobile payment adoption were based on the TAM or the UTAUT model and included the test of constructs such as Perceived benefits, Perceived Usefulness and Perceived Risk against the variable Intention of Use. This study proposes a new research model based on the TAM, solely focused on the risk dimension to study the impact of different types of risk perceived by users on their intention to use mobile payment.

The main variable Perceived Risk was divided into 6 constructs which correspond to the different types of risk that have been extracted from previous studies investigating the relationship between risk perception and mobile payment adoption. Since recent research has already demonstrated the hindering effect of these constructs, 6 hypotheses were formulated to assume their negative relationship with Intention of Use. This research model provides an opportunity to reinforce or challenge the findings of previous studies while allowing a comparison of the different types of risk to establish which one is the greatest deterring factor.

The first three constructs identified are Perceived Time Risk, Perceived Social Risk and Perceived Psychological Risk which were established by Cocosila and Trabelsi [5] following an investigation of user views on contactless payment via smartphones. Perceived Time Risk corresponds to the perception of users that they may waste time if they subscribe to mobile payment services. Perceived Social Risk refers to their fear of facing judgement or disapproval from their social circle. Finally, Perceived Psychological Risk is the general feeling of anxiety that users might experience regarding the decision of using mobile payment. The findings of Cocosila and Trabelsi [5] established a negative relationship between those variables and Intention of Use. The following hypotheses could therefore be formulated for this study:

H1. Perceived Time Risk has a negative effect on Intention of Use.
H2. Perceived Social Risk has a negative effect on Intention of Use.
H3. Perceived Psychological Risk has a negative effect on Intention of Use.

The 4th construct identified, Perceived Privacy Risk, stems from the combination of constructs identified in different studies which were named differently but essentially described the same concept. Ma *et al.* [16] describe it as Perceived Information Risk while Cocosila and Trabelsi [5] and De Kerviler, Demoulin and Zidda [8] call it Perceived Privacy Risk. Ooi and Tan [19] also include a similar construct named Privacy Concern. All these variables were described as the fear of losing control over one's personal data and were therefore combined into one construct: Perceived Privacy Risk. Surprisingly, only 50% of those studies demonstrated a negative relationship between Perceived Privacy Risk and Intention of Use. In order to test this construct, the following hypothesis was formulated:

H4. Perceived Privacy Risk has a negative effect on Intention of Use.

The 5th construct identified is Perceived Financial Risk which was defined by Liébana-Cabanillas, Sánchez-Fernández and Muñoz-Leiva [15] and De Kerviler, Demoulin and Zidda [8] as the users' expectation of financial loss. Precedent research in mobile payment adoption has established that this construct has a strong negative effect on the users' Intention of Use which justifies the 5th hypothesis:

H5. Perceived Financial Risk has a negative effect on Intention of Use.

Finally, the last construct identified is Perceived Security Risk which was defined by Hongxia, Xianhao and Weidan [12] as the fear that a dangerous outcome might result from the use of mobile payment. They argue that this construct is particularly relevant since the investigation conducted by iResearch company in 2009 showed that 48% of phone users refuse to use mobile payment due to security concerns. Consequently, the following hypothesis was formulated:

H6. Perceived Security Risk has a negative effect on Intention of Use.

The final research model that was designed for this study following the proposed hypotheses can be found in Fig. 1.

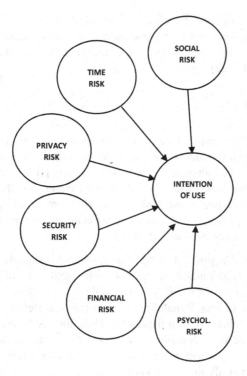

Fig. 1. Research model

3.2   Data Collection

An online survey was conducted to collect data from December 10th 2018 to January 3rd 2019. The survey was based on a questionnaire using a 5-point Likert scale ranging from "strongly agree" to "strongly disagree". This can be justified by the qualitative nature of the question as risk perception is concerned with opinions and therefore requires a metric scale that can measure intangible variables [31]. Furthermore, online questionnaires using 5- or 7-point Likert scales have been broadly used to collect data for the study of mobile payment adoption [20].

The questionnaire used to test the model was designed by combining and adapting questionnaire items from existing literature to fit the research model. The survey was split into two parts: the first part investigated the demographic characteristics of the respondents while the second part measured their opinions about statements directly linked to the constructs tested.

Each variable was tested via 3 statements in the questionnaire with a similar meaning but phrased differently. Cresswell [6] argues that testing a variable using several similar items reduces the risk of bias and allows a better reliability of the scale. The statements were randomly placed in the questionnaire to avoid redundancy for the respondents.

A questionnaire summary including all the questionnaire items can be found in Appendix B. Due to time and cost constraints, the questionnaire-based survey was delivered online only via Google Form which provided the opportunity to collect data efficiently and quickly [22].

3.3 Data Analysis

Respondent Profile Analysis. Once a sufficient number of questionnaires were collected, a profile of the respondents was established in order to identify any unbalanced characteristics that could influence the results of the test [10]. The respondents were then split into two categories: those who use mobile payment and those who do not use it. Since the study is trying to establish what factors are deterring consumers from starting using mobile payment, the answers of respondents who are not currently using mobile payment only were used to test the model.

Reliability Analysis. The program SPSS was chosen to conduct the statistical analysis of the data due to the high number of features it offers and to avoid costs [29]. Prior to analysing the data, a test of reliability of the scale was performed by calculating the Cronbach's Alpha coefficient. Reliability refers to the consistency of results produced by a measure: if the reliability of a measure is high, the results are more likely to be accurate and repeatable under consistent conditions [17]. Tian and Dong [28] argue that the Cronbach's alpha coefficient analysis is the most common reliability test for likert type scales. It aims to verify the internal consistency of the questionnaire by measuring whether similar scores are produced by items testing the same construct.

Regression Analysis. Due to its suitability to small sample sizes, a structural equation modelling (SEM) approach has been favoured to analyse data in recent research on mobile payment adoption [21]. For this pilot study, the relationship of the variables was established by performing a regression analysis. This method aims to measure the direct effect of independent variables on a dependant variable by calculating the path coefficient beta.

The value of the coefficient beta ranges between 0 and 1; the bigger the coefficient is, the higher the effect of the variable is. Additionally, a positive deviation path coefficient indicates that the independent variable has a positive effect on the dependant variable while a negative coefficient indicates a negative effect. This statistical analysis also produces the indicator p which establishes the significance of the relationship. The relationship is considered significant when $p < 0.05$ with the significance level being represented as follows: *$p < 0.1$ **$p < 0.05$ ***$p < 0.01$ [17].

4 Results

4.1 Data Sample

A total of 33 questionnaires were received among which 1 was invalid, leaving a total of 32 valid questionnaires. The characteristics of the sample can be found in Table 1.

Table 1. Profile of respondents

Characteristics of the sample (N = 32)

Item	Type	Frequency	Percentage
Gender	Female	18	56.3
	Male	14	43.8
Age	Under 18	0	0
	18–24	7	21.9
	24–31	14	43.8
	31–38	5	15.6
	Above 38	6	18.8
Education	High School	0	0
	College	3	9.4
	University	13	40.6
	Master/PhD	16	50
Owns mobile phone	Yes	32	100
	No	0	0
Purchase frequency	Once a month	2	6.3
	Once a week	12	37.5
	Once a day	9	28.1
	Several times a day	9	28.1
Uses mobile payment	Yes	12	37.5
	No	20	62.5

The profile shows that the gender of the respondents is relatively equal between male (56.3%) and female (43.8%). While all the respondents are older than 18, the 24-31-year-old category (43.8%) seems to be more represented than the other age categories. This unbalance can be considered acceptable as the majority of technology users tend to be relatively young [16]. However, 90.6% of the respondents indicated they had been in further education which is a strong unbalance compared to the general population and could potentially affect the reliability of the results. Lastly, all the respondents own a mobile phone and the majority of them (93.7%) carry out purchases at least once a day which seems plausible. This suggests that most of the respondents are potential candidates for mobile payment. However, only 37.5% of them use mobile payment which confirms the claim that it is not widely adopted by users.

The questionnaires of the respondents who do not use mobile payment only were used for the next stage of the research as this study is focusing of the factors that are deterring consumers from using mobile payment. A final total of 20 questionnaires were included in the statistical analysis.

4.2   Reliability Analysis

The assessment of reliability of the scale is necessary to ensure that the results are accurate and would be found consistently if repeating the experiment. It is agreed that if the value for the Cronbach's alpha coefficient is equal or greater than 0.7, it indicates that the scale is sufficiently reliable to be used [28].

The coefficient is determined by calculating the covariance of answers for items related to the same variable. As can be seen in Table 2, the results of the Cronbach's alpha coefficient are all above 0.7 which indicates a sufficient reliability of the questionnaire.

Table 2. Reliability analysis results

	Cronbach's alpha coefficient	Number of elements
Intention of use	0.855	3
Privacy risk	0.824	3
Security risk	0.862	3
Financial risk	0.858	3
Social risk	0.861	3
Time risk	0.718	3
Psychological risk	0.750	3

4.3 Regression Analysis

Table 3 shows the results of the regression analysis that was conducted on the answers of respondents not using mobile payment. The standardised coefficient beta quantifies the relationship on the tested variable with the dependant variable Intention of Use.

Table 3. Regression analysis results

Model		Non standardised coefficients		Standardised coefficient	T value	Sig.
		Coefficient beta	Standard error	Beta		
1	Dependant variable: intention of use	5.455	1.783		3.060	0.009
	Privacy risk	−0.172	0.227	−0.216	−0.757	0.462
	Security risk	−0.319	0.339	−0.318	−0.938	0.365
	Financial risk	−0.226	0.284	−0.285	−0.797	0.440
	Social risk	−0.108	0.219	−0.154	−0.493	0.630
	Time risk	−0.021	0.230	−0.022	−0.092	0.928
	Psychol. risk	0.057	0.284	0.076	0.199	0.845

The results indicate that 5 out of the 6 tested constructs have a negative relationship with the dependant variable Intention of Use while one construct, Psychological Risk, has a positive relationship. The beta coefficients are respectively −0.216 for Privacy

Risk, −0.318 for Security Risk, −0.285 for Financial Risk, −0.154 for Social Risk, −0.022 for Time Risk and 0.076 for Psychological risk.

The significance indicators are greater than 0.05 for all the variables which indicates that the relationships are not significant at this stage. However, the statistical significance of results cannot be calculated accurately if the size of the sample is too low [9]. In this case, only a small sample of data was collected due to this pilot study being primarily focused on the research model rather than on the results. The significance of the relationships can therefore not be calculated until a full-scale study is conducted.

5 Discussion

5.1 Analysis

As can be seen in Fig. 2, the results of the study suggest that each type of risk tested has a hindering effect on the users' intention to use mobile payment except from Psychological Risk.

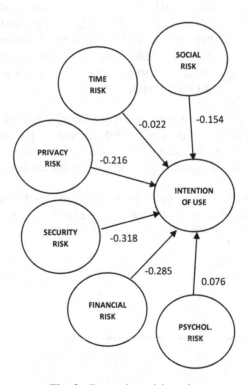

Fig. 2. Research model results

Social Risk and Time Risk have a small to moderate negative effect on the users' intention to use mobile payment. This partially supports the findings of Cocosila and Trabelsi [5]. However, the results also show that Psychological Risk has a positive effect on their intention of use which contradicts their results. Overall, this suggests that H1 and H2 are verified while H3 is not. Privacy Risk has a relatively higher negative effect on the users' intention to use mobile payment which corroborates the findings of several researchers including De Kerviler, Demoulin and Zidda [8], Cocosila and Trabelsi [5] but contradict the results of Ma *et al.* [16]. Nonetheless, these results support H4. Security Risk and Financial Risk both have a substantial negative effect on the users' intention to use mobile payment according to the results. This does not only verify H5 and H6 but also supports the results of multiple studies including the papers of Liébana-Cabanillas, Sánchez-Fernández and Muñoz-Leiva [15], Hongxia, Xianhao and Weidan [12], De Kerviler, Demoulin and Zidda [8], Yang *et al.* [30] and Ma *et al.* [16].

As can be seen in Table 4, it can be concluded that 5 out of the 6 proposed hypotheses have been verified.

Table 4. Hypotheses testing results

Hypothesis	Path	Result
H1	RISK → IU	Supported
H2	SOCIAL RISK → IU TIME	Supported
H3	PSYCHOLOGICAL RISK → IU	Unsupported
H4	PRIVACY RISK → IU	Supported
H5	FINANCIAL RISK → IU	Supported
H6	SECURITY RISK → IU	Supported

This research model does not only aim to clarify the definition of Perceived Risk but also allow a comparison of the effects of the different types of risk perceived by users on their intention to use mobile payment. This provides an opportunity to establish what types of risk specifically have the highest hindering effect on mobile payment adoption.

As can be seen in Fig. 3, the results of this study indicate that Security Risk is the type of risk that has the highest negative effect on the users' Intention of Use, followed closely by Financial Risk which is the second most hindering type of risk. Privacy Risk

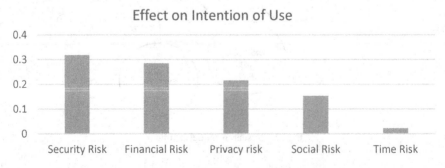

Fig. 3. Comparison of the effects of each type of risk on Intention of Use

and Social Risk respectively rank 3rd and 4th with a more moderate effect while time Risk seems to have the lowest negative effect.

These results do not match the findings of Cocosila and Trabelsi [5] who compared Time Risk, Social Risk, Psychological Risk and Privacy Risk and established that Psychological Risk was the most hindering factor followed by Privacy Risk, Time Risk and finally Social Risk.

However, it corroborates the findings of Hongxia, Xianhao and Weidan [12] and Ma *et al.* [16] who respectively established that Security Risk is the greatest hindering factor and that Financial Risk has a higher negative effect than Privacy Risk.

To summarise, the results of this study have shown that 5 out of the 6 types of risk identified have a negative effect on the users' Intention of Use and are therefore hindering mobile payment adoption. Financial risk, Security Risk have a relatively strong negative effect; Privacy Risk and Social Risk have a moderate negative effect while Time Risk has a minor negative effect which corroborates the results of several studies. However, psychological risk was not found to have any negative effect on the Intention of Use which contradicts the results of Cocosila and Trabelsi [5]. Finally, a simple comparison of the beta coefficients suggests that Security Risk has the highest hindering effect, followed by Financial Risk, Privacy Risk, Social Risk and finally Time Risk.

The findings of this pilot study have several implications for stakeholders within the mobile payment industry including mobile phone manufacturers, retailers and banking organisations. The ranking of the different types of risk perceived by users should be used to effectively prioritise the aspects of mobile payment that need improving. The primary focus should be to implement stronger security mechanisms to increase the safety of mobile payment and thus reduce the risk of dangerous outcomes and financial loss such as hacking, identity theft and financial fraud. Additionally, the marketing of mobile payment should aim to increase mobile device owners' confidence by showing that security is one of the main priorities of the mobile payment industry. Finally, further effort should be made to increase transparency regarding how the data of mobile payment users will be used and protected.

6 Limitations

Although this study proposes a valid research model, the data sample used to test the constructs was not substantial enough to give accurate results. It is therefore suggested that this research model should be tested on a larger sample of data to verify these findings. Cocosila and Trabelsi [5] suggest using the So per size sample calculation to estimate the required size for the sample. A larger sample will also allow an accurate analysis of the significance of each relationship calculated. Furthermore, the larger the data sample is, the better the population is represented. For instance, the characteristics profile of the sample indicated that more than 90% of the respondents had been in further education which does not necessarily reflect the population of the UK and constitutes a risk of bias.

Another major limitation of this study which may affect the accuracy of the results is the possible confusion of respondents regarding the definition of mobile payment.

3 respondents were informally questioned after completing the survey to discuss the clarity of the test, 1 of the respondents explained that they confused mobile payment with the action of purchasing an item or service on the internet from their mobile phone. This suggests that some of the answers may have been biased due to respondents misinterpreting the subject of the questions. It is therefore suggested that a brief definition of mobile payment should be added to the questionnaire to ensure all respondents understand what mobile payment refers to and thus improve the accuracy of the results.

Finally, although the findings of this study bring further insight into the issues associated with mobile payment, they do not provide any solution to improve them. It is therefore suggested that further research aiming to establish what features or security mechanisms can reduce the risk perceived by potential users would be beneficial to further increase the appeal of mobile payment. Additionally, mobile payment acceptance could be further understood by studying the effect of demographics on the types of risk perceived.

7 Conclusions

A new research model including 6 constructs was proposed to investigate the effect of different types of risk perceived by mobile device users on their intention to use mobile payment. A quantitative empirical study was conducted to verify the proposed research model by collecting data via a 5-point likert scale-based questionnaire and conducting a regression analysis to quantify the relationships between the model constructs. The results suggest that Security and Financial Risk are the first and second highest areas of concern for potential users of mobile payment. Privacy and Social Risk also seem to be moderate deterring factors while Time Risk has a minor negative effect on their intention to use mobile payment. Psychological Risk on the other hand was not found to have any hindering effect. However, this study presents a number of limitations such as the size of the data sample and the lack of clarification on mobile payment within the survey. It was therefore suggested that the research model should be tested on a largest sample using an improved questionnaire to verify the accuracy of the results. Nonetheless, the findings of this study provide the mobile payment industry with an interesting insight into the perceptions of mobile device users which can be used to increase the appeal of mobile payment. Finally, new areas of study investigating potential solutions and user demographics were suggested to further increase the users' willingness to adopt mobile payment.

References

1. Abrahao, R.D.S., Moriguchi, S.N., Andrade, D.F.: Intention of adoption of mobile payment: an analysis in the light of the unified theory of acceptance and use of technology (UTAUT). RAI Revista de Administração e Inovação 13(3), 221–230 (2016)
2. Ajzen, I.: The theory of planned behavior. Organ. Behav. Hum. Decis. Proceses 50(2), 179–211 (1991)

3. Almazroa, M., Gulliver, S.: Understanding the usage of mobile payment systems-the impact of personality on the continuance usage. In: 2018 4th International Conference on Information Management (ICIM), pp. 188–194 (2018)
4. Berrado, A., Elfahli, S., El Garah, W.: Using data mining techniques to investigate the factors influencing mobile payment adoption in Morocco. In: 2013 8th International Conference on Intelligent Systems: Theories and Applications (SITA), pp. 1–5 (2013)
5. Cocosila, A., Trabelsi, H.: An integrated value-risk investigation of contactless mobile payments adoption. Electron. Commer. Res. Appl. **20**, 159–170 (2016)
6. Cresswell, J.: Research Design: Qualitative, Quantitative, and Mixed Methods Approaches, 4th edn. Sage publications, London (2013)
7. Dahlberg, T., Mallat, N., Ondrus, J., Agnieszka, Z.: Past, present and future of mobile payments research: a literature review. Electron. Commer. Res. Appl. **7**(2), 165–181 (2008)
8. De Kerviler, G., Demoulin, N.T.M., Zidda, P.: Adoption of in-store mobile payment: are perceived risk and convenience the only drivers? J. Retail. Consum. Serv. **31**, 334–344 (2016)
9. Elston, D.M.: Sample size. J. Am. Acad. Derm. **79**(4), 635 (2018)
10. Geisen, E., Romano Bergstrom, J.: Chapter 2 - Respondent–Survey Interaction, pp. 21–49. Morgan Kaufmann, Boston (2017)
11. Gupta, S., Kim, H.: Value-driven Internet shopping: the mental accounting theory perspective. Psychol. Mark. **27**(1), 13–35 (2010)
12. Hongxia, P., Xianhao, X., Weidan, L.: Drivers and barriers in the acceptance of mobile payment in China. In: 2011 International Conference on E-Business and E-Government (ICEE), pp. 1–4 (2011)
13. Johnson, V.L., Kiser, A., Washington, R., Torres, R.: Limitations to the rapid adoption of M-payment services: understanding the impact of privacy risk on M-Payment services. Comput. Hum. Behav. **79**, 111–122 (2018)
14. Kim, D, Ferrin, D., Raghav Rao, H.: Trust and satisfaction, two stepping stones for successful ecommerce relationships: a longitudinal exploration D-Information systems research pubsonline.informs.org (2009)
15. Liebana-Cabanillas, F., Sanchez-Fernandez, J., Munoz-Leiva, F.: Antecedents of the adoption of the new mobile payment systems: the moderating effect of age. Comput. Hum. Behav. **35**, 464–478 (2014)
16. Ma, L., Su, X., Yu, Y., Wang, C., Lin, K., Lin, M.: What drives the use of M-Payment? an empirical study about alipay and WeChat payment. In: 2018 15th International Conference on Service Systems and Service Management (ICSSSM), pp. 1–6 (2018)
17. Mingxing, S., Jing, F., Yafang, L.: An empirical study on consumer acceptance of mobile payment based on the perceived risk and trust. In: 2014 International Conference on Cyber-Enabled Distributed Computing and Knowledge Discovery, pp. 312–317 (2014)
18. Munoz-Leiva, F., Hernández-Méndez, J., Sánchez-Fernández, J.: Generalising user behaviour in online travel sites through the Travel 2.0 website acceptance mode. Online Inf. Rev. **36**(6), 879–902 (2012)
19. Ooi, K., Tan, G.W.: Mobile technology acceptance model: An investigation using mobile users to explore smartphone credit card. Expert Syst. Appl. **59**, 33–46 (2016)
20. Pauchard, L.: A systematic literature review on the relationship between risk perception of users and mobile payment adoption (2018, Unpublished)
21. Ringle, C.M., Sarstedt, M., Straub, D.W.: Editor's comments: a critical look at the use of PLS-SEM in "MIS Quarterly". MIS Q. **36**(1), xiv (2012)
22. Robson, C.: Real World Research, 2nd edn. Blackwell Publications, Oxford (2002)

23. Sahnoune, Z., Aïmeur, E., El Haddad, G., Sokoudjou, R.: Watch your mobile payment: an empirical study of privacy disclosure. In: 2015 IEEE Trustcom/BigDataSE/ISPA, pp. 934–941 (2015)
24. Schierz, P.G., Schilke, O., Wirtz, B.W.: Understanding consumer acceptance of mobile payment services: an empirical analysis. Electron. Commer. Res. Appl. 9(3), 209–216 (2010)
25. Schmidthuber, L., Maresch, D., Ginner, M.: Disruptive technologies and abundance in the service sector - toward a refined technology acceptance model. Technological Forecasting and Social Change (2018)
26. Venkatesh, V., Morris, M., Davis, G., Davis, F.: User acceptance of information technology: toward a unified view. MIS Q. 27(3), 425–478 (2003)
27. Venkatesh, V., Speier, C., Morris, M.G.: User acceptance enablers in individual decision making about technology: toward an integrated model. Decis. Sci. 33(2), 297–316 (2002)
28. Tian, Y., Dong, H.: An analysis of key factors affecting user acceptance of mobile payment. In: 2013 Second International Conference on Informatics & Applications (ICIA), pp. 240–246 (2013)
29. Weinberg, S.L., Abramowitz, S.K.: Statistics Using SPSS: An Integrative Approach, 2nd edn. Cambridge University Press, Cambridge (2008)
30. Yang, S., Cao, Y., Mao, W., Zhang, R, Luo, L.: Determinants of behavioral intention to mobile payment: Evidence from China. In: 2011 7th International Conference on Advanced Information Management and Service (ICIPM), p. 151 (2011)
31. YusoffS, R., Janor, R.: A proposed metric scale for expressing opinion. In: 2012 International Conference on Statistics in Science, Business and Engineering (ICSSBE), pp. 1–6 (2012)

Proposing a Service Quality Framework for Mobile Commerce

Abdulla Jaafar Desmal[1(⊠)], Mohd Khalit Bin Othman[2],
Suraya Binti Hamid[2], Ali Hussein Zolait[3],
and Norliya Binti Ahmad Kassim[4]

[1] Faculty of Computer Science and Information Technology,
University of Malaya, Kuala Lumpur, Malaysia
a.desmal@outlook.com
[2] Department of Information Systems, University of Malaya,
Kuala Lumpur, Malaysia
[3] College of Information Technology, University of Bahrain, Sakheer,
Kingdom of Bahrain
[4] Faculty of Information Management, Universiti Teknologi MARA (UiTM),
Shah Alam, Malaysia

Abstract. Customer satisfaction influences the profitability of organizations and can keep competitive advantages. One of the critical factors in customer satisfaction is the availability of a quality scale that measures the service. The service quality aims to ensure that the service delivered meets customer expectations. However, with the popularity of using mobile devices, there are many electronic businesses shifted to mobile platforms. Mobile platforms have unique features that differ from Personal computers, such as mobility, portable, wireless. Mobile business is a category of business development refers to new business platforms that enabled by using the technology of wireless and mobile devices. In this case, measuring of service quality of the mobile business is necessary nowadays to ensure the delivered services with the best quality. Due to the lack of a comprehensive framework to evaluate service quality at the mobile business, the business sector uses electronic service quality measurement to evaluate mobile business services, which results in difficulties in identifying accurate results. Using the theoretical base model of offline service quality "SERVQUAL" and the online service quality model "E-S-QUAL," the researchers were able to propose a framework of service quality to evaluate the services provided through mobile commerce. The proposed service quality framework is consisting of six dimensions that are application design, reliability, responsiveness, trust, efficiency, and system availability. The proposed service quality framework helps business providers for better development of business strategies and leads for best customers' expectations due to the compatibility of the proposed model with the unique features of mobile devices with considerations of the environment of business sectors.

Keywords: Mobile commerce · Mobile business · M-service quality

© ICST Institute for Computer Sciences, Social Informatics and Telecommunications Engineering 2019
Published by Springer Nature Switzerland AG 2019. All Rights Reserved
M. H. Miraz et al. (Eds.): iCETiC 2019, LNICST 285, pp. 203–212, 2019.

1   Introduction

The development of ICT has influenced many sectors. Mobile commerce (or Mobile business) is one of these sectors that take attention from researchers practitioners to develop it according to business requirements. The technology of m-commerce provides smart functions and services to meet end-users expectations with attention to service quality and usability's features (Safieddine 2017). Mobile commerce considered as an extension of Electronic Commerce (Ghazali et al. 2018) which referred to monetary value's transactions conducted through mobile devices over a wireless internet connection (Taylor 2016). The popularity of using smartphones among the public, encourage business sectors to use mobile technologies as a platform for business transactions such as providing business services and selling goods (Lin et al. 2016; Santos 2003). Mobile commerce offers the feature of ubiquity, which allows users to reach the information through the smartphones connected with wireless connection regardless of locations (van der Merwe and Bekker 2003; Zhou 2011).

Delivering best service quality through m-commerce to end users is a crucial strategy for business improvement and success with results in understanding end users' expectations and best business profits (Salo and Karjaluoto 2007; Su et al. 2008; Zheng et al. 2015). Measuring service quality at m-commerce requires to identify the dimensions' characteristics of service quality with considerations of unique features of the mobile device and the context of the business sector (Ghazali et al. 2018; Jimenez et al. 2016; Safieddine 2017).

There were many of online service quality evaluation scales that proposed at different fields, but it is difficult to use these models for evaluating the service quality at m-commerce (Choi et al. 2008; van der Merwe and Bekker 2003; Yang et al. 2006). Using different models at m-commerce leads for more complexity and wrong evaluation data (Casaló et al. 2007; Ghazali et al. 2018; Safieddine 2017; Zeithaml 2002; Zheng et al. 2015). However, the main research gap of this paper focused on lack of m-commerce service quality measurement which leads business providers to face issues when launching services into the mobile platform.

Thus, it is necessary to investigate the context of mobile commerce by identifying the service quality dimensions that can improve the business relationship with customers by analyzing and answering the following questions:

1. What are the unique features of the mobile business?
2. What are the service quality's critical dimensions of mobile business?
3. How can service quality influence mobile business?

However, to overcome this issue, the current research aims to analyze and study the service quality context and features of mobile commerce according to offline and online theoretical models. The first model is an offline service quality measurement scale called "SERVQUAL" proposed by the study of (Parasuraman et al. 1988). The second theoretical base model is online service quality measurement scale called "E-S-QUAL", which was proposed by the study of (Parasuraman et al. 2005) which aimed to evaluate the service quality through electronic forms and it focuses on both system and service attributes based on four primary service quality attributes.

This paper consists of five main sections. The first is a general introduction of the discussed topic. The second section is a literature review that is discussing the main relevant area of the topic that is the concept of service quality, electronic service quality, and mobile commerce. The third section is the research methodology. The fourth section proposed the framework for m-commerce service quality by analyzing the relevant dimensions supported by theoretical models of service quality. The fifth section is the research implications and future research, and the last section is the conclusions of the research.

2   Literature Review

2.1   Service Quality

The Service Quality (SQ) is a concept used as an evaluation scale that measuring of organizations' performance in terms of effectiveness and efficiency (Santos 2003; Stamenkov and Dika 2015). It gets attention from researchers and practitioners a variety of fields, including business and marketing. The competitive among organizations leading them to employee service quality to differentiate their performances from other organizations (Ribbink et al. 2004; van der Merwe and Bekker 2003). It means the best service quality provided by organizations leads to a good reputation that results in high profits (Choi et al. 2008; Santos 2003). In the literature of marketing, the general concept of service quality associated with consumer perception of service, the privilege of product, and consumers' satisfaction. (Stamenkov and Dika 2015; Yang et al. 2006; Zhou 2011). The author (Rust and Oliver 1994) describes the concept of service quality as the overall customer's satisfaction based on delivered services from organizations or service providers. Therefore, the general concept of service quality is common among the definitions which measuring the quality of service by comparing the current performance of delivered services with the expectations of the end users (Parasuraman et al. 1988).

Measuring service quality at offline services differ from online services (electronic services). Most popular service quality measurement scale at offline services is the model of "SERVQUAL". It proposed by (Parasuraman et al. 1985). This model aims to study the expectations of customers and the service performance's evaluations from different aspects related to service quality. This model consists of ten dimensions that cover the attributes related to service delivery to customers in terms of quality. The model was developed later in order to measure the two main areas of offline service quality that are the expectations and perceptions based on customers view (Parasuraman et al. 1988).

2.2   Electronic Service Quality

With the development of ICTs, the business service uses the technologies as a channel to deliver their business online to consumers. The website is widely used by the business sector in different fields such as online banking, online payment, and online tickets reservations. There were many of e-service quality evaluation scale proposed by different studies i.e. e-commerce S.Q. that consisting of four main dimensions designed to evaluate the quality of electronic commerce by evaluating the attributes of website (Liu and Arnett 2000). The author (Yoo and Donthu 2001) proposed an e-service quality's model called "SITEQUAL" that focused on "online retailing" based on four main dimensions that are "ease of use, aesthetic design, processing speed, and security".

The well-known e-service quality model is "E-S-QUAL", which proposed by (Parasuraman et al. 2005) contains four main with a total of (22) measured factors. The four main dimensions are "Efficiency", which measures the satisfaction of end users in term of accessing and using the website. The second dimension is "Fulfillment", which measures the availability of items at the website and delivery of the items to the customer. The third dimension is "System Availability", which measures the overall technical functions of the website. The last dimension is "Privacy", which measures the level of protecting the customer's information at the website.

However, there were many of e-service quality models developed to measure the satisfaction of customers through online services, which enable the organization for more improvement weather a technical or service delivery process, to meet the expectation and increase the satisfaction's level of end users.

2.3   Mobile Commerce

Mobile commerce (MC) is a dynamic business opportunity that has unique features to enhance transactions (Safieddine 2017). The concept of MC considered as a business giant due to its ability to reducing costs with increasing and extending the organizations' profit (Cristobal et al. 2007; Gotzamani and Tzavlopoulos 2009; Safieddine 2017). Mobile commerce is an extended type of electronic commerce (Ghazali et al. 2018; Safieddine 2017). The authors (Ribbink et al. 2004; Taylor 2016; Zhou 2011) considered that the transactions at mobile commerce are similar to those who proceeded at electronic commerce. The significant differences between electronic commerce and mobile commerce are the technology used, the kind of business provided, and kind of business model represents (Bhatt and Emdad 2001; Kong and Mayo 1993; Yang et al. 2006). Using smartphones devices encourage business sectors to the use the technologies of mobile commerce due to an effective and efficient way to deliver the business services to end users with saving costs and fewer efforts. MC supported by the variety of advanced techniques such as voice, live chat and live video, which helped business providers and customers for more interactivity and portability. Mobile banking, online shopping, bills payment, are some examples of services provided via mobile commerce platforms, which enable consumers to perform the transactions from anywhere and anytime using smartphones connected with wireless internet connections (Deb and Agrawal, 2017; Salo and Karjaluoto 2007; Shao et al. 2009; Wang and Li 2012).

Study of (Taylor 2016) stated that the applications of mobile commerce are necessary to be simple and easy to use since the education level among consumers is different which required an easy and straightforward m-commerce application to enable them using these types of business services. The main success of mobile commerce mainly depending on consumers buys. Thus, the business's provider focuses on these categories of consumers who are using smartphones' technologies.

However, to ensure continues uses of mobile commerce, it is the responsibility of business' provider to guarantee the best level of service quality through m-commerce, which required a particular service quality framework that can analyze and understand the consumers of mobile commerce.

3 Research Methodology

The service quality dimensions of mobile commerce extracted from previous studies at the area of offline and online service quality. This helps to gain in-depth knowledge of nature and concept of the dimensions associated with service quality. The study uses the theoretical models of "SERVQUAL" by (a Parasuraman et al. 1988; Parasuraman et al. 1985) and the model of "E-S-QUAL" by (Parasuraman et al. 2005), that enhanced the current research for constructing m-commerce service quality model. The evaluation process of the proposed sub-dimensions performed by investigating the mobility characteristics of m-commerce with consideration of the two mentioned theoretical base models. The proposed sub-dimensions are compatible with the basic concept of offline and online service quality models and developed a new model for mobile platforms that meets the requirements and characteristics of business sectors. However, this research uses the systematic literature review that enables researchers to tabulate the data and conduct the analyses.

4 Proposed Service Quality Measurement Scale for Mobile Commerce

The first proposed dimension for mobile commerce is "application design", which refers to overall design appears at the application. This dimension is consistent with the model proposed by (Parasuraman et al. 1988) in term of tangibility. The overall design of mobile business affecting online marketing satisfaction of end users which causes continues using such m-business in the future. The building of a great and interactive interface of m-commerce is a challenge for the service provider since this stage is essential to get an initial acceptance of end users toward m-commerce application. When the application building of interactive elements such as (processing stage, loading and uploading level and time remaining, confirmation of sending and receiving of transactions). These examples are easy to mention at m-commerce, but when there are some interactive elements for each transaction, there will be a satisfaction for m-commerce application (Ghazali et al. 2018). The dimension of "application design" can measure the criteria of usability of such m-commerce application, information architecture, interaction design, wireframe, and visual design (Khoi et al. 2018). In this regards, including the dimension of "application design" into m-commerce service quality, due to its essential that affecting customer perceived S.Q.

The "reliability" considered as a basic service quality dimension at the model of "SERVQUAL", which measures the service performance in term of "dependability, consistency, and accuracy" (a Parasuraman et al. 1988). Other studies in the field of computer technology such as (Cox and Dale 2001; Lu et al. 2009; Ribbink et al. 2004; Zhu et al. 2002), stated that the performance and consistency are basic dimensions of service quality, which is associated with providing best protection to end users against risks at electronic services. In term of the mobile business, the end users are performing their transactions online from issuing the order until received the necessary service (Chiu et al. 2017). In this case, the end users are expecting that the business providers are providing the services with the best reliability, which means that the business provider is taking care of service provision, solving issues faced by end users about services and prices. Therefore, the dimension of "reliability" is necessary to be included at the proposed service quality scale of mobile commerce, which can influence the perceived S.Q.

Responsiveness is one of service quality dimension included at SERVQUAL. It is defined as the desire of employees to serve consumers and dealing with their complaints (Parasuraman et al. 1988). The study of (Santos 2003) stated that the dimension of "responsiveness" aims to measure the ability of an organization to serve consumers and the way of dealing with consumers in case of a problem. The revolution of ICT has to influence the business context to merge the technology with services affecting providing the business through online and mobile platforms. It is critical for business sectors to understand the needs and expectations of end users and adopt modern ICT systems to provide more effective and efficient services (Safieddine 2017). Using the latest technologies in the business sectors can develop the strategies of business and respond quickly to end users with taking care of the expectations and quality of service provided to the audience. Taking action to any issues through mobile business quickly and positively means that the service providers are meeting the quality criteria of responsiveness. Therefore, "responsiveness" affecting perceived service quality and it is essential to include at the S.Q. Measurement scale of mobile commerce.

The fourth dimension is "trust" which is a basic component of SERVQUAL service quality model. The "trust" is associated with providing the best level of confidence at electronic services by taking consideration of security and privacy (Wei et al. 2009). The trust considered as a complex phenomenon due to associated with many other factors. It has been studied and analyzed from different fields of study such as management (Dirks and Ferrin 2002), marketing (Kumar 1996) and sociology (Strub and Priest 1976). The previous studies of trust argued that it has an essential impact on the success of the personal relationship. In this case, the concept of the dimension of trust is essential to evaluate at mobile commerce in order to increase the relationship between the service provider and end users. The studies of (Khoi et al. 2018; Lin et al. 2018) suggested that trust is a success element when considering the transaction based online platforms. The weak trust associated with m-commerce may affect the success and continues uses of m-commerce transactions. The "trust" affecting the user's acceptance of electronic services, which required to translate it into actual processing of electronic transactions. Therefore, trust can influence m-commerce service quality which is vital to include at the service quality model.

The dimension of "efficiency" refers to measuring the satisfaction of end users in term of accessing and using the website, which is a key dimension at the S.Q. model of "E-S-QUAL" that proposed by (Parasuraman et al. 2005). At the context of mobile commerce, the efficiency of mobile commerce application assists consumers inuse mobile commerce in a simple way, well-structured steps, with minimum input requirements required by consumers. These criteria enhanced consumer's satisfactions toward m-commerce and encouraged them for continues use. Mobile devices have unique features that differ from other devices, i.e. personal computer. In this case, there are limitations of end users to perform transactions through m-commerce applications such as touch screen, small screen and keyboard keys (Deb and Agrawal 2017; Ghazali et al. 2018). The processing of transactions through m-commerce applications should be simple and take less time when comparing to performing such transactions through a personal computer. Efficiency at m-commerce increased the quality of the application and encouraged public for more using of this platform.

The last dimension is "system availability", which describes the overall website's technical characteristics and it is part of "E-S-QUAL" (Parasuraman et al. 2005). In term of mobile commerce, ensure availability of m-commerce services affecting consumer's satisfactions toward such services, which affects the reputation of the service provider (Phong et al. 2018). The reasonability of business provider in term of system availability is to ensure that the m-commerce application is working properly and update the necessary technical functions to meet the requirements of service delivery mobile (Khoi et al. 2018; Lin et al. 2018). Some technical issues can be detected by end users, in this case, it is important to allow end users to report on such issues to enable business providers regularly updating the application to meet end users expectations and ensure the satisfaction of them. Hence; the dimension of "system availability" has a relationship with perceived service quality at m-commerce.

However, Fig. 1 illustrates the proposed dimensions of the m-commerce service quality framework which mapped according to the theoretical base model of offline service quality "SERVQUAL" and the online model of e-service quality measurement scale "E-S-QUAL".

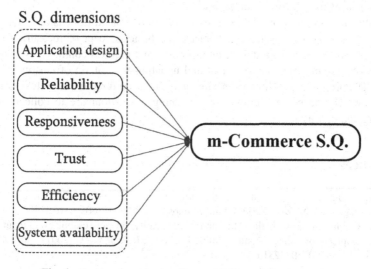

Fig. 1. Proposed service quality model for mobile commerce.

5   Research Implications and Future Research

A service quality framework for m-commerce constructed for use by researchers to conduct further investigation and research. The current paper created a comprehensive m-commerce service quality framework as a base that guided business providers for a better understanding of their consumers through mobile platforms. It helps business providers to evaluate their business service through m-commerce to understand the consumer expectations and for more development on their business strategies. The proposed model consists of six sub-dimensions that cover the critical quality aspects in the context of mobile commerce. Business providers can conduct regularly quality evaluation process of m-commerce application by asking the end users of m-commerce to evaluate the application before closing it. End users are the key to improving in any fields; therefore, the proposed model is designed to evaluate m-commerce based on end users opinion. However, future researches can be conducted to test the ability of m-commerce framework.

6   Conclusions

In this paper, the service quality dimensions for mobile commerce have been analyzed and presented based on the offline service quality model of "SERVQUAL" and online service quality model of "E-S-QUAL". It founds that the unique features of mobile commerce are ubiquity, reachability, personalization, flexibility, and dissemination. The proposed model for mobile commerce consists of six dimensions which are the application design, reliability, responsiveness, trust, efficiency, and system availability. This model is useful for evaluating the service quality at mobile commerce which is more useful to identify the strongest and weakness steps at the service delivery process. It enhanced the business sector to understand the expectations of consumers for more development of their business strategies.

Finally, the proposed model consists of the most related dimensions that can be measured based on end users, which meets the basic concept of measuring service quality. Mobile business is a unique environment that requires continues development in terms of development, improvement and updating the criteria of customers' satisfaction. The proposed sub-dimensions are analyzing according to the context of mobile business which can be measurable by evaluating e-questionnaire to collect the data from targeted end users.

References

Bhatt, G.D., Emdad, A.F.: An analysis of the virtual value chain in electronic commerce. Logist. Inf. Manag. **14**(1/2), 78–85 (2001). https://doi.org/10.1108/09576050110362465

Casaló, L.V., Flavián, C., Guinalíu, M.: The role of security, privacy, usability and reputation in the development of online banking. Online Inf. Rev. **31**(5), 583–603 (2007). https://doi.org/10.1108/14684520710832315

Chiu, J.L., Bool, N.C., Chiu, C.L.: Challenges and factors influencing initial trust and behavioral intention to use mobile banking services in the Philippines. Asia Pac. J. Innov. Entrep. (2017). https://doi.org/10.1108/apjie-08-2017-029

Choi, J., Seol, H., Lee, S., Cho, H., Park, Y.: Customer satisfaction factors of mobile commerce in Korea. Internet Res. 18(3), 313–335 (2008). https://doi.org/10.1108/10662240810883335

Cox, J., Dale, B.G.: Service quality and e-commerce: an exploratory analysis. Manag. Serv. Qual.: Int. J. 11(2), 121–131 (2001). https://doi.org/10.1108/09604520110387257

Cristobal, E., Flavián, C., Guinalíu, M.: Perceived e-service quality (PeSQ). Manag. Serv. Qual.: Int. J. 17(3), 317–340 (2007). https://doi.org/10.1108/09604520710744326

Deb, M., Agrawal, A.: Factors impacting the adoption of m-banking: understanding brand India's potential for financial inclusion. J. Asia Bus. Stud. 11(1), 22–40 (2017). https://doi.org/10.1108/JABS-11-2015-0191

Dirks, K.T., Ferrin, D.L.: Trust in leadership: meta-analytic findings and implications for research and practice. J. Appl. Psychol. (2002). https://doi.org/10.1037//0021-9010.87.4.611

Ghazali, E.M., Mutum, D.S., Chong, J.H., Nguyen, B.: Do consumers want mobile commerce? A closer look at M-shopping and technology adoption in Malaysia. Asia Pac. J. Mark. Logist. 30(4), 1064–1086 (2018). https://doi.org/10.1108/APJML-05-2017-0093

Gotzamani, K.D., Tzavlopoulos, Y.E.: Measuring e-commerce-quality: an exploratory review. Int. J. Qual. Serv. Sci. 1(3), 271–279 (2009). https://doi.org/10.1108/17566690911004203

Jimenez, N., San-Martin, S., Azuela, J.I.: Trust and satisfaction: the keys to client loyalty in mobile commerce. Academia Revista Latinoamericana de Administración 29(4), 486–510 (2016). https://doi.org/10.1108/ARLA-12-2014-0213

Khoi, N.H., Tuu, H.H., Olsen, S.O.: The role of perceived values in explaining Vietnamese consumers' attitude and intention to adopt mobile commerce. Asia Pac. J. Mark. Logist. 30(4), 1112–1134 (2018). https://doi.org/10.1108/APJML-11-2017-0301

Kong, R., Mayo, M.C.: Measuring service quality in the business-to-business context. J. Bus. Ind. Mark. 8(2), 5–15 (1993). https://doi.org/10.1108/08858629310041393

Kumar, N.: Module 6 The Power of Trust in Manufacturer-Retailer Relationships. Harv. Bus. Rev. 74, 92–106 (1996)

Lin, J., Li, L., Yan, Y., Turel, O.: Understanding Chinese consumer engagement in social commerce: the roles of social support and swift guanxi. Internet Res. (2018). https://doi.org/10.1108/IntR-11-2016-0349

Lin, Y., Luo, J., Cai, S., Ma, S., Rong, K.: Exploring the service quality in the e-commerce context: a triadic view. Ind. Manag. Data Syst. 116(3), 388–415 (2016). https://doi.org/10.1108/IMDS-04-2015-0116

Liu, C., Arnett, K.P.: Exploring the factors associated with Web site success in the context of electronic commerce. Inf. Manag. 38(1), 23–33 (2000). https://doi.org/10.1016/S0378-7206(00)00049-5

Lu, H., Yu-Jen Su, P.: Factors affecting purchase intention on mobile shopping web sites. Internet Res. 19(4), 442–458 (2009). https://doi.org/10.1108/10662240910981399

Parasuraman, A., Zeithaml, V.A, Berry, L.L.: SERQUAL: a multiple-item scale for measuring consumer perceptions of service quality. J. Retail. (1988). https://doi.org/10.1016/S0148-2963(99)00084-3

Parasuraman, A., Zeithaml, V.A., Berry, L.: A conceptual model of service quality and its implications for future research. J. Mark. (1985). https://doi.org/10.2307/1251430

Parasuraman, A., Zeithaml, V.A., Malhotra, A.: E-S-QUAL a multiple-item scale for assessing electronic service quality. J. Serv. Res. 7(3), 213–233 (2005). https://doi.org/10.1177/1094670504271156

Phong, N.D., Khoi, N.H., Nhat-Hanh Le, A.: Factors affecting mobile shopping: a Vietnamese perspective. J. Asian Bus. Econ. Stud. (2018). https://doi.org/10.1108/jabes-05-2018-0012

Ribbink, D., van Riel, A.C.R., Liljander, V., Streukens, S.: Comfort your online customer: quality, trust and loyalty on the internet. Manag. Serv. Qual.: Int. J. **14**(6), 446–456 (2004). https://doi.org/10.1108/09604520410569784

Rust, R.T., Oliver, R.L.: Service quality: insights and managerial implication from the frontier. In: RolandRust, T., Oliver, R.L. (eds.) Service Quality: New Directions in Theory and Practice, pp. 1–19 (1994). https://doi.org/10.4135/9781452229102.n1

Safieddine, F.: M-Commerce. In: Innovations in E-Systems for Business and Commerce (2017). https://doi.org/10.1201/9781315207353

Salo, J., Karjaluoto, H.: A conceptual model of trust in the online environment. Online Inf. Rev. **31**(5), 604–621 (2007). https://doi.org/10.1108/14684520710832324

Santos, J.: E-service quality: a model of virtual service quality dimensions. Manag. Serv. Qual.: Int. J. **13**(3), 233–246 (2003). https://doi.org/10.1108/09604520310476490

Shao Yeh, Y., Li, Y.: Building trust in M-commerce: contributions from quality and satisfaction. Online Inf. Rev. **33**(6), 1066–1086 (2009). https://doi.org/10.1108/14684520911011016

Stamenkov, G., Dika, Z.: A sustainable e-service quality model. J. Serv. Theory Pract. **25**(4), 414–442 (2015). https://doi.org/10.1108/JSTP-09-2012-0103

Strub, P.J., Priest, T.B.: Two patterns of establishing trust: the marijuana user. Sociol. Focus. (1976). https://doi.org/10.1080/00380237.1976.10570947

Su, Q., Li, Z., Song, Y., Chen, T.: Conceptualizing consumers' perceptions of e-commerce quality. Int. J. Retail. Distrib. Manag. **36**(5), 360–374 (2008). https://doi.org/10.1108/09590550810870094

Taylor, E.: Mobile payment technologies in retail: a review of potential benefits and risks. Int. J. Retail. Distrib. Manag. **44**(2), 159–177 (2016). https://doi.org/10.1108/IJRDM-05-2015-0065

van der Merwe, R., Bekker, J.: A framework and methodology for evaluating e-commerce Web sites. Internet Res. **13**(5), 330–341 (2003). https://doi.org/10.1108/10662240310501612

Wang, W., Li, H.: Factors influencing mobile services adoption: a brand-equity perspective. Internet Res. **22**(2), 142–179 (2012). https://doi.org/10.1108/10662241211214548

Wei, T.T., Marthandan, G., Chong, A.Y.L., Ooi, K.B., Arumugam, S.: What drives Malaysian m-commerce adoption? An empirical analysis. Ind. Manag. Data Syst. (2009). https://doi.org/10.1108/02635570910939399

Yang, Y., Humphreys, P., McIvor, R.: Business service quality in an e-commerce environment. Supply Chain. Manag.: Int. J. **11**(3), 195–201 (2006). https://doi.org/10.1108/13598540610662086

Yoo, B., Donthu, N.: Developing a scale to measure the perceived quality of an Internet shopping site (SITEQUAL). Q. J. Electron. Commer. (2001). https://doi.org/10.1007/978-3-319-11885-7_129

Zeithaml, V.A.: Service excellence in electronic channels. Manag. Serv. Qual.: Int. J. **12**(3), 135–139 (2002). https://doi.org/10.1108/09604520210429187

Zheng, H., Hung, J.-L., Lin, Z., Wu, J.: The value of guarantee in service e-commerce. Nankai Bus. Rev. Int. **6**(1), 82–102 (2015). https://doi.org/10.1108/NBRI-03-2014-0019

Zhou, T.: An empirical examination of initial trust in mobile banking. Internet Res. **21**(5), 527–540 (2011). https://doi.org/10.1108/10662241111176353

Zhu, F.X., Wymer, W., Chen, I.: IT-based services and service quality in consumer banking. Int. J. Serv. Ind. Manag. **13**(1), 69–90 (2002). https://doi.org/10.1108/09564230210421164

Sentiment Analysis in E-commerce Using SVM on Roman Urdu Text

Faiza Noor, Maheen Bakhtyar[(⊠)], and Junaid Baber

Department of Computer Science and Information Technology,
University of Balochistan, Quetta, Pakistan
noorfaiza84@gmail.com,maheenbakhtyar@um.uob.edu.pk,junaidbaber@ieee.org

Abstract. The usefulness and importance of sentiment analysis task is a widely discussed and effective technique in e-commerce. E-commerce is a very convenient way to buy things online. It saves a lot of time that is usually spent traveling and buying by visiting the shops. E-commerce provides an efficient and effective way to shop sitting right in front of one's computer/mobile at home. For a given product, sentiment analysis captures the users views; their feelings and opinion related to that product. The reviews are categorized into three basic classes i.e. negative, positive, and neutral. This paper focuses on *Urdu Roman reviews* that are obtained by one of the most famous and accessed e-commerce website of Pakistan–Daraz.pk. There are total 20.286 K reviews which are annotated into three classes by three different experts. Vector space model, a.k.a bag of word model is applied for feature extraction which are later passed to Support Vector Machines (SVM) for sentiment classification. Experiments are conducted on MATLAB Linux server. The dataset is kept public for future use and experiments.

Keywords: Roman Urdu · Sentiment analysis · Opinion mining · SVM · E-commerce · Reviews

1 Introduction

Internet has widely become user centric. People are busy in sharing their views by using different platforms. Similarly, online shopping has also become very common and one of the most convenient ways to shop. Products are being purchased online avoiding the real hectic process to visit the shops in person. Customers get the products at their door step and secure payment is made online conveniently. Whenever a people plan to buy a product, they tend to read product respective product reviews provided by other people who have already used the same product. Online reviews provide a way to check product popularity and usefulness prior to buying.

People show their positive or negative attitude towards the products through their comments below the product description. Products are getting hundreds of

© ICST Institute for Computer Sciences, Social Informatics and Telecommunications Engineering 2019
Published by Springer Nature Switzerland AG 2019. All Rights Reserved
M. H. Miraz et al. (Eds.): iCETiC 2019, LNICST 285, pp. 213–222, 2019.
https://doi.org/10.1007/978-3-030-23943-5_16

reviews online affecting the overall perception of the company and their products. We examine the reviews of DarazPK and observe that in Pakistan, customers conventionally post the comments either in English language or Roman Urdu language. Roman Urdu, Urdu being native language of Pakistan, is widely used, making it easy for people to correctly express their feelings. Daraz.pk is an e-commerce website which brings all the cultural aspects of Pakistani nation along with its products. The products being sold belong to the interests of Pakistani customers.

Various other e-commerce sites are available targeting Pakistani users such as symbios.pk, homeshopping.pk, shophive.com, ishopping.pk, and 24hours.pk/. These sites either do not have an option to review the products, hence, unavailability of review data, or the reviews are not filled by the customers most of the times. Daraz.pk is the most commonly used site therefore, the reviews are being filled and thus data is available.

This research deals mainly with sentiments analysis on Pakistani products based on comments/reviews in English and Roman Urdu languages. Reviews are mainly either positive, negative, or neutral and they determines and examines the user perception assisting the sellers to increase and enhance their products availability and quality hence, affecting online shopping positively.

In Pakistan business ideas has completely transformed and people prefer to buy items such as electronics, ladies clothing, gents wear, kids wear, accessories, home appliances, etc. online.

Roman Urdu language is being used now a days. Mostly in Pakistan and India, people express their words by typing in roman Urdu. Even now a days social sites are based on reviews that comprises of Roman Urdu texts. If a person buy any product online, he/she shares the sentiments by writing in their own native language. In English Language the sentiment analysis has been well explored. In every area research has been done any analyzing the sentiments. Machine learning and lexicon based learning has been done at great extent. These can be used in Roman Urdu reviews. Arabic language is vast language and being used in Arab countries. This language has achieved its goals by analyzing the sentiments in Arabic texts. Many research works has been done in Arabic language [1, 9, 12, 20]. Persian language is the old language and the first language in Muslim World which was in competition with Arabic Language. Persian has a very good history in Persian literature. Many great poets has also written in Persian script. Sentiment analysis has been discussed and experimented in Persian language [6, 16, 25]. Local languages have also been making use of sentiment analysis to analyze the user opinions. For example, Pashto language sentiment analysis [19] and Sindhi language sentiment analysis [3, 4] are making use of sentiment analysis approaches.

Roman text is usually very challenging to process. Roman Urdu has no standards and no rules therefore, understanding such language is not so easy. For example word *Mein* میں means I/Me, and can be written in various ways such as, *Mn, Me, Main, Ma, Men, M,* etc. Non-standard word forms make it difficult to process and understand. Further discussions are given in the sections to follow.

Section 2 discusses the related work, Sect. 3 provides the methodology of the framework, and Sect. 3 discusses the experiments and results of the system.

2   Related Work

The aim of sentiment analysis and opinion mining is to differentiate a user like/dislike review on a particular product. Big data was collected from amazon and reviews. Recommendation system was used to check the users reviews priority and qualitative analysis was done to check sentiment analysis on large data reported by [30] Bootstrapping method was used to extract adopter information reviews from site. Maximum likelihood was used to check reviews and matrix factorization for recommendation of product [32]. Data collected from amazon and drawn a distribution curve of the products. Products were divided into categories like product category, number of product, review of product and mean of product. Compared the models and at last proved their work by lemma, proof of proposition and proof of corollary [15]. Gathered data from different platforms which were available easily. And four types of platforms were identified and experimented. A survey was done using Qualtrics, a questionnaire. Data was displayed in the form of table and compared the result [18]. Sentiment analysis was done and the reviews were extracted by preprocessing method, then part of speech tagging was applied and feature score was calculated using opinion mining [24]. Amazon data was collected and positive and negative reviews were extracted. Reviews were tested by test classifier. Logistic regression and L2 regularization was used as baseline of classifier. Drawn ROC curve, F1 measure was also calculated, also measured precision and recall, unigram, n-gram, and histogram [7]. Web crawler (web spider) was used to extract data and collect them from amazon. Locospider was used as a web crawler. Data pre-processing (including segmentation, POS tagger), text analysis (labeling noun, phrases, feature detection), multiple linear regression was used [10]. Data was collected from regarding the reviews of products from cnet.com, ciao.co.uk and shopping.yahoo.com. Three classifiers were used and discussed, 1: Passive Aggressive algorithm 2: Language Modeling, 3: Winnow Classifier. N-gram was also used and high order n-gram improves the performance of classifiers, especially negative instances [11]. Online product reviews data was gathered from amazon. Analysis was done for sentences and reviews with hopeful conclusion. Reviews were about electronics, book, beauty and home and were categorized into tables. Negatives phrases were separated. Sentences were divided into tokens and POS tagger was applied. Histogram was drawn, F1 measure was calculated and ROC curve was shown. Application used is scikit-learn, python open source. Models used were Nave Bayesian, SVM, and Random Forest [13] Polarity of texts was found. They trained the model depending on bootstrap aggregating algorithm and state of art model. This improved F measure result. SentiME system was developed. Stanford sentiment system was used to classify the sarcasm of sentences. Cross validation test was done. Sentiment analysis, precision and recall was measured [28]. Data was gathered about product reviews from Twitter. Opinion lexicon dictionary was used to find polarity of words either positive, negative or neutral. Twitter has its own features like emoticons, abbreviation, hashtags etc, this creates less recall for lexicon based method. Classifier was built to find positive, negative or neutral words. Sentences were detected like declarative sentences, interrogative sentences and imperative sentences. Hashtags words like # fail was included in their lexicon. Score equation formula was used to collect the scores. POS tagger was used for comparative sentences like iPhone is better than Samsung. And also used pearson chi square test for identifying the indicators. F measure, recall and precision was used for evaluation measure [31] Aim was to perform replication using webis source code to see if it produces comparable result. Evaluated sentiMe on amazon reviews. Semantic evaluation was done. Positive, negative, or neutral words were separated from twitter reviews. Top scoring system between 2013–2015 on semEval was discussed in paper. F score was used to compare the pre trained model and retrained model. Selected linear averaging function because it predicts in a very simple way [27]. Twitter is popular communication platform. Blogs were create to communicate between users for variety of topics. Data was collected from twitter API v1.0 and corpus of tweet was related to Justin Bieber brand. Sentiment analysis was done. POS tagger, negative sentences and positive sentences were separated, n-gram was applied. Also focused on sad and happy emoticons because users also comment through their emotions. DAN2 architecture was also discussed and SVM was also implement and at last by comparing the results of DAN2 and SVM, it was concluded that DAN2 produces better recall [14]. Sentiment analysis on twitter to check the reviews on different topics. Sentences polarity was measured including subjective or objective. Emoticons are used to differentiate between positive or negative tweets. Opinion mining was also done. Experiments were performed (NaveBayes algorithm with supervised classification and it was then displayed with map SOM method). Vector space model was applied (stemmer or stopper process). TF/IDF was also calculated at the end [23]. There is a gap between description and review of a product because mostly customers buy a product by reading the reviews written by early users. Data was collected from 63 participants (male/female) both. HOM (high order mean) was calculated and shown by graph (description and experience rating). Online consumer rating and WOM was also discussed [29]. Emotions help a lot in purchasing any product from online stores. Emotions express positive or negative sentiments. Cognitive appraisal theory is discussed which shows that some sentiments are linked with reliability, and some are allied with unreliability. Latent semantic analysis (LSA) was used. Also discussed Tobit regression for analyzing the model [2]. Objects with high rating provides much information about the product. Data was about 4000 books from amazon.com and data was extracted from it. Sentiment polarity was done to check the positive or negative language in text. Feature based sentiment analysis was applied (to check subjectivity or objectivity of sentences) [17]. Customers share their views in their native language. In this paper Roman Urdu and English views were extracted using easy extractor software. Extracted data was then filtered in WEKA2. Also used three different algorithms Nave Bayes algorithm, decision trees, and KNN. And in the end the results of each algorithm was compared. Which has showed that nave Bayes provides good result as compared to decision tree because of its simplicity and easyuse [8]. In this paper the authors have first created a dictionary for Persian words. They have added persian words in it which was the difficult task of their work. Sentiment analysis was done to check the positive or negative reviews by the viewers. Data was collected from the most visited website digikala by using web crawler.dataset contains reviews about different products with different categories. Preprossesising was done by spell checker, lemmitizer, pos, stop words removal etc. they have also used various classification methods like F measure, Bayesnet, KNN, LibLinear, SMO. Results were matched with each classification method. Persian reviews are analyzed just like other languages. FarsNet is the first Persian WordNet containing Persian words, its latest version is also available for researchers. Words are first matched in the dictionary and then the extraction is done. The authors have used n-gram, bi-gram, uni-gram methods, TF/IDF, precision and recall. And in the end they have just compared the results [5] Just like other languages Chinese language reviews are also analyzed by the researchers. They have collected the mobile phone reviews from a known website, www.360buy.com. Java crawler was created to find negative and positive reviews. Then preprocessing is done and Boolean weighting is done to calculate feature weight of the products. Authors have used statistical machine learning methods to find online Chinese reviews. They choose ICTCLASS system for word segmentation and POS tagging. Used DF/IDF algorithm for their experiment on Chinese reviews. At last compared their results and showed it through graph and charts [33] Based on multilingual sentiment analysis. Viewed and worked on different languages like Chinese, English, Spanish, German, Swedish, Romanian, French, Japanese. Investigated both lexicon and corpus based approaches. lemmatization, tokenization, POS tagging, F-measure, unigram, bigram, n-gram, is done and compared. Translation from languages (formal to informal) is also done and results are compared. References from various papers have been pinpointed in their works. Which has helped them a lot. Authors have looked at wide range of tools and methods used in sentiment analysis [21] Sentiment analysis was investigated and reviewed. Total number of published papers on sentiment analysis and number of citations for that papers. Tools used in that papers are analyzed and compared with others. Publications on Sentiment analysis started from 2004. And today it is one of the fast growing field in research area of computer science. Top most cited papers are also discussed. Positive, negative reviews, their polarity, languages, citation, everything has been deeply studied and compared. Qualitative and quantitative analysis has been done. The top most citation from scopus and google scholar and publication venues area also discussed and shown in table. Different areas of research has been discussed like languages, Humans(emotions, interaction, language, behavior etc), tools (nlp, machine learning etc). 20 most cited papers per year in scopus and google scholar has been highlighted and their work has been discussed. How sentiments are analyzed, which tool to use, polarity checking, preprocessing etc. and it has been observed that with the passage of time citations have been increased per year. And it might increase in next few years too [22].

Table 1. Review Dataset description. Total 20285 reviews.

Review sentiments	Training set instances	Test set instances
Neutral ($\mathcal{N}$)	7119	1780
Positive ($\mathcal{P}$)	4880	1220
Negative ($\mathcal{E}$)	4228	1058
Total	16227	4058

3 Methodology

This section explains the methodology for experiments and data generation. Different query terms are used on DarazPK portal and then the reviews of the users are stored in raw text file. The products used for the reviews are listed in the Table 1.

Reviews are represented by vector space model (VSM), a.k.a bag of word model. In VSM, each review is represented by the normalized frequency of the words, known as term frequency (TF), from the set of a vocabulary ($\mathcal{V} = \{v_1, v_2, \ldots, v_d\}$) by its weight ($\mathcal{W} = \{w_1, w_2, \ldots, w_d\}$); inverse document frequency (IDF) is widely used to find the weights $\mathcal{W}$.

The basic flow of the system is shown in Fig. 1.

Fig. 1. Basic flow of the framework

There are total 20285 reviews which are denoted by $\mathcal{R} = \{r_1, r_2, \ldots, r_n\}$, where $n = 20285$. Three post graduate students, who have sufficient knowledge of sentiment analysis, are requested to label each review with either of following sentiments $\mathcal{S} = \{\mathcal{N}, \mathcal{P}, \mathcal{E}\}$; Neutral ($\mathcal{N}$), Positive ($\mathcal{P}$), or Negative ($\mathcal{E}$). Finally, each review r_i is labeled as $s \in \mathcal{S}$ if two of the students voted as s. So, the representation of reviews $\mathcal{R}$ is extended as $\mathcal{R} = \{(r_1, s_1), (r_2, s_2), \ldots, (r_n, s_n)\}$, where $s_i \in \mathcal{S}$. Each review $r_i \in \mathcal{R}$ is feature vector, a.k.a bag of word, which is $\mathbb{R}^d$ dimensions, where d indicates the number of words.

There are total 13662 words taken into account during the experiments. To generate the vocabulary, 25 thousand reviews are randomly crawled from Darazpk, frequency of each word is computed and all words present in at least 80% of the reviews are removed (marked as stop words), such as 'a', 'aaaaa', and 'yar'. Once the vocabulary is chosen, then TF-IDF is applied.

Since, the reviews are mostly short sentences, comprises of few words; that makes r_i very sparse. For example, some of the reviews contains only two words such as 'Bahtareen hai yar' which is labeled as $\mathcal{P}$, in English its mean 'its wonderful buddy', where the word 'yar' (in English buddy) is treated as stop word and removed.

Support Vector Machine (SVM) classifier is used with two kernels: linear kernel and cubic kernel. SVM is inherently a binary classifier. To enable SVM to classify multiple classes, one of the following two approaches are used, namely; (i) one-vs-one (OVO) (ii) one-vs-all (OVA). OVA trains, for q different classes, ($q > 2$,) q different classifiers. For each class i, it assumes i as positive and the remaining as negative. In case of sentiment analysis, for the sentiment $\mathcal{E}$ recognition, there will be 65% which give more weight to negative instances.

Commonly, OVO approach is better in accuracy than OVA [26]. $q(q-1)/2$ binary classifiers are trained in case of OVO approach. In case of sentiment analysis of Roman Urdu would have three distinct binary classifiers. The decision to label the given instance r_j is taken using the ensemble/voting approach. r_j is fed to 21 various binary classifiers, and the label showing the highest frequency selected. Approach of OVO is used in this paper.

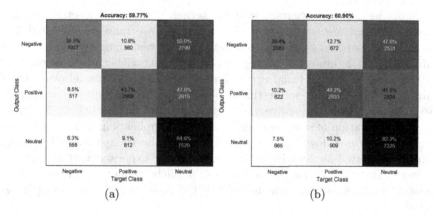

Fig. 2. SVM accuracy on whole dataset. (a) shows the Linear kernel, and (b) shows the cubic kernel.

4   Experiments and Results

Figure 2 shows the accuracy of SVM on whole dataset; dataset is not divided into training set and test set. In literature, cubic kernel out performs linear kernel in multi-class classification, but in current situation, it is just marginally better. In both kernels, the accuracy of sentiment $\mathcal{N}$ is very high, whereas the sentiment $\mathcal{E}$ remains challenging. It is because there are number of ways to show negative feelings for any product, where natural intelligent person can identify

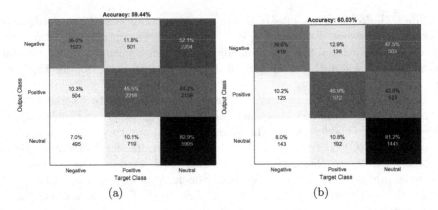

Fig. 3. SVM accuracy using cubic kernel. (a) shows the training set accuracy, and (b) shows the test set accuracy.

but it remains very difficult for artificial intelligent algorithm, unless complex and advance algorithms are not applied such as semantic analysis using natural language processing.

Figure 3 shows the accuracy of cubic kernel, when the dataset is split into training set and test set; 20% of each sentiment are randomly selected from the main dataset and labeled as test set, and the remaining 80% is labeled as training set. It is quite interesting to observe that neither of the kernel over fits the data, in case of facial expression recognition cubic kernel over fits the training set [26]. It is also interesting to observe that $\mathcal{N}$ has highest accuracy and also it has highest false positive scores against rest of the sentiments. Mostly, in live implementation of sentiment analysis on any application, if the score of any unknown reviews is low, then that review should be treated as neutral unless manually reported as negative by any user. In our experiment, this constraint is already intact. The dataset is available publicly online[1] for future use and research. The source code can be provided if requested to the corresponding author.

5   Conclusion

This paper classifies the reviews on DarazPK, an e-commerce portal, into three different classes which are widely known as sentiment analysis. More than 20 K reviews are obtained and annotated by experts into three classes. The dataset is later divided into two sets; training set (80%) and test set (20%). Vector space model is used for feature extraction. Different kernels of SVM are used for classification. Cubic Kernel achieves highest accuracy on given dataset.

---

[1] http://www.maheenbakhtyar.com/links.

References

1. Abbasi, A., Chen, H., Salem, A.: Sentiment analysis in multiple languages: feature selection for opinion classification in web forums. ACM Trans. Inf. Syst. **26**(3), 12:1–12:34 (2008). https://doi.org/10.1145/1361684.1361685. http://doi.acm.org/10.1145/1361684.1361685

2. Ahmad, S.N., Laroche, M.: How do expressed emotions affect the helpfulness of a product review? Evidence from reviews using latent semantic analysis. Int. J. Electron. Commer. **20**(1), 76–111 (2015)

3. Dootio, M., Wagan, A.: Sentiment summarization and analysis of Sindhi text. Int. J. Adv. Comput. Sci. Appl. **8**, 296–300 (2017). https://doi.org/10.14569/IJACSA.2017.081038

4. Ali, M., Wagan, A.I.: An analysis of sindhi annotated corpus using supervised machine learning methods. Mehran Univ. Res. J. Eng. Technol. **38**(1), 185–196 (2019). https://doi.org/10.22581/muet1982.1901.15. http://publications.muet.edu.pk/index.php/muetrj/article/view/754

5. Asgarian, E., Kahani, M., Sharifi, S.: The impact of sentiment features on the sentiment polarity classification in Persian reviews. Cogn. Comput. **10**(1), 117–135 (2018)

6. Basiri, M.E., Naghsh-Nilchi, A.R., Ghassem-Aghaee, N.: A framework for sentiment analysis in Persian. Open Trans. Inf. Process. **1**(3), 1–14 (2014)

7. Bhat, S.K., Culotta, A.: Identifying leading indicators of product recalls from online reviews using positive unlabeled learning and domain adaptation. arXiv preprint arXiv:1703.00518 (2017)

8. Bilal, M., Israr, H., Shahid, M., Khan, A.: Sentiment classification of Roman-Urdu opinions using naïve Bayesian, decision tree and KNN classification techniques. J. King Saud Univ.-Comput. Inf. Sci. **28**(3), 330–344 (2016)

9. Boudad, N., Faizi, R., Thami, R.O.H., Chiheb, R.: Sentiment analysis in Arabic: a review of the literature. Ain Shams Eng. J. **9**(4), 2479–2490 (2018). https://doi.org/10.1016/j.asej.2017.04.007. http://www.sciencedirect.com/science/article/pii/S2090447917300862

10. Chen, X., Sheng, J., Wang, X., Deng, J.: Exploring determinants of attraction and helpfulness of online product review: a consumer behaviour perspective. Discret. Dyn. Nat. Soc. **2016**, 19 Pages (2016)

11. Cui, H., Mittal, V., Datar, M.: Comparative experiments on sentiment classification for online product reviews. AAAI **6**, 1265–1270 (2006)

12. El-Masri, M., Altrabsheh, N., Mansour, H., Ramsay, A.: A web-based tool for Arabic sentiment analysis. Procedia Comput. Sci. **117**, 38–45 (2017). https://doi.org/10.1016/j.procs.2017.10.092. http://www.sciencedirect.com/science/article/pii/S187705091732149X. Arabic Computational Linguistics

13. Fang, X., Zhan, J.: Sentiment analysis using product review data. J. Big Data **2**(1), 5 (2015)

14. Ghiassi, M., Skinner, J., Zimbra, D.: Twitter brand sentiment analysis: a hybrid system using n-gram analysis and dynamic artificial neural network. Expert. Syst. Appl. **40**(16), 6266–6282 (2013)

15. Holleschovsky, N.I., Constantinides, E.: Impact of online product reviews on purchasing decisions. In: WEBIST (2016)

16. Hosseini, P., Ramaki, A.A., Maleki, H., Anvari, M., Mirroshandel, S.A.: Sentipers: a sentiment analysis corpus for Persian. CoRR abs/1801.07737 (2018)

17. Hu, N., Koh, N.S., Reddy, S.K.: Ratings lead you to the product, reviews help you clinch it? The mediating role of online review sentiments on product sales. Decis. Support. Syst. **57**, 42–53 (2014)
18. Hu, N., Pavlou, P.A., Zhang, J.: On self-selection biases in online product reviews. MIS Q. **41**(2), 449–471 (2017)
19. Kamal, U., Siddiqi, I., Afzal, H., Rahman, A.U.: Pashto sentiment analysis using lexical features, November 2016. https://doi.org/10.1145/3038884.3038904
20. Kiritchenko, S., Mohammad, S.M., Salameh, M.: Semeval-2016 task 7: determining sentiment intensity of English and Arabic phrases. In: Proceedings of the International Workshop on Semantic Evaluation, SemEval 2016, San Diego, California, June 2016
21. Lo, S.L., Cambria, E., Chiong, R., Cornforth, D.: Multilingual sentiment analysis: from formal to informal and scarce resource languages. Artif. Intell. Rev. **48**(4), 499–527 (2017)
22. Mäntylä, M.V., Graziotin, D., Kuutila, M.: The evolution of sentiment analysis—a review of research topics, venues, and top cited papers. Comput. Sci. Rev. **27**, 16–32 (2018)
23. Martínez-Cámara, E., Martín-Valdivia, M.T., Urena-López, L.A., Montejo-Ráez, A.R.: Sentiment analysis in Twitter. Nat. Lang. Eng. **20**(1), 1–28 (2014)
24. Pednekar, S., Patil, K., Sawant, R., Shah, T.: Sentiment analysis on online product reviews. Int. Educ. Res. J. **3**(3), 130–134 (2017)
25. Roshanfekr, B., Khadivi, S., Rahmati, M.: Sentiment analysis using deep learning on Persian texts. In: 2017 Iranian Conference on Electrical Engineering (ICEE), Tehran, pp. 1503–1508, May 2017. https://doi.org/10.1109/IranianCEE.2017.7985281
26. Saeeda, S., Baber, J., Bakhtyar, M.: Empirical evaluation of SVM for facial expression recognition. Int. J. Adv. Comput. Sci. Appl. **9**(11), 670–673 (2018)
27. Sygkounas, E., Rizzo, G., Troncy, R.: A replication study of the top performing systems in semeval Twitter sentiment analysis. In: Groth, P., et al. (eds.) ISWC 2016. LNCS, vol. 9982, pp. 204–219. Springer, Cham (2016). https://doi.org/10.1007/978-3-319-46547-0_22
28. Sygkounas, E., Rizzo, G., Troncy, R.: Sentiment polarity detection from amazon reviews: an experimental study. In: Sack, H., Dietze, S., Tordai, A., Lange, C. (eds.) SemWebEval 2016. CCIS, vol. 641, pp. 108–120. Springer, Cham (2016). https://doi.org/10.1007/978-3-319-46565-4_8
29. Wulff, D.U., Hills, T.T., Hertwig, R.: Online product reviews and the description-experience gap. J. Behav. Decis. Mak. **28**(3), 214–223 (2015)
30. Yengi, Y., Omurca, S.İ.: Distributed recommender systems with sentiment analysis. EJOSAT: Eur. J. Sci. Technol. Avrupa Bilim ve Teknoloji Dergisi **4**(7) (2016)
31. Zhang, L., Ghosh, R., Dekhil, M., Hsu, M., Liu, B.: Combining lexicon based and learning-based methods for Twitter sentiment analysis. HP Laboratories, Technical Report HPL-2011, vol. 89 (2011)
32. Zhao, W.X., Wang, J., He, Y., Wen, J.R., Chang, E.Y., Li, X.: Mining product adopter information from online reviews for improving product recommendation. ACM Trans. Knowl. Discov. Data (TKDD) **10**(3), 29 (2016)
33. Zheng, L., Wang, H., Gao, S.: Sentimental feature selection for sentiment analysis of Chinese online reviews. Int. J. Mach. Learn. Cybern. **9**(1), 75–84 (2018)

Prediction and Optimization of Export Opportunities Using Trade Data and Portfolio

Sardar Muhammad Afaq Khan[(✉)] and Adeel Yusuf

Electronics and Power Engineering, Pakistan Navy Engineering College Karachi,
National University of Science and Technology, Islamabad, Pakistan
{skhan,adeel}@pnec.nust.edu.pk

Abstract. The modern portfolio theory targets to achieve a safe investment while extracting maximum profit. Its use in exploring export opportunities is undocumented. Traditionally, the gravity model of trade is widely used to calculate trade flows while the prediction of trade flow was based on application of time-series prediction algorithms on historical trade data. The proposed research introduced the risk involved in the trade opportunity as a quantitative factor determined by product complexity and gravity model of trade, while predicting the optimal export commodities to maximize profit and minimize risk. Improvement in trade prediction accuracy using portfolio optimization methods as compared to other previously documented methods is also reported. The results indicate MSE of 0.161 and 0.239 using Black Litterman model and CAPM against 1.226 and 1.026 using the traditional Holt and Grey models respectively. The results are supplemented by the level of risk attached to each commodity, to classify the optimal products for export investment.

Keywords: Export prediction · Portfolio theory · Product complexity ·
UN COMTRADE data · Gravitational theory · Textile · Black-Litterman model ·
Trade forecasting

1 Introduction

Countries do not remain in isolation, they import commodities to fulfill their requirement which are not produced or in the shortage, and in return they export the commodities/goods which are surplus. Exports of a country are proportional to its economic development and GDP. In order to analyze exports trade data is standardized using the Harmonized Systems (HS) of tariff nomenclature to globally standardize a trade item into number and name to classify the product.

Risk is considered a major component in trade analytics [1]. World Trade Statistical Review 2018 [2] by World Trade Organization (WTO), while forecasting an improvement in trade flows warned for the inevitable consequences in case of triggering of the risk factors. At macro-level, trade risks include national policy changes, tensions between countries, military conflicts etc. These risk factors lead to weak investment spending and consequently lowered world GDP.

Risk is directly related to Product complexity [3] due to the disruption cost of complex items. It has direct and indirect impacts on trade. Dominik et al. [4]

© ICST Institute for Computer Sciences, Social Informatics and Telecommunications Engineering 2019
Published by Springer Nature Switzerland AG 2019. All Rights Reserved
M. H. Miraz et al. (Eds.): iCETiC 2019, LNICST 285, pp. 223–239, 2019.

documented the linear relationship between the product complexity and economic development of the country. Product complexity therefore, poses a more serious risk for developing countries. As we increase the product complexity of a product, we also tend to increase the life cycle cost of that product. The increase in the direct costs due to the increase in product complexity was also documented [5]. The more complex a certain product the costlier and complicated it becomes, which increases the direct costs associated with production and development e.g. time, product analysis etc. GDP of trading countries and the distances between them, explained in the gravity model, define the factors which determine the trade flow between the countries [6]. This was first displayed in 1962 by Jan Tinbergen, who suggested that the span of reciprocal exchange streams between any two nations can be approximated by utilizing the 'gravity equation'. Relative size is dictated by the present GDP, and financial vicinity is controlled by profession costs that the all the more monetarily "distant" the more prominent the trade costs, similarly role of gravity model was defined by different researchers [7, 8] to consider the impacting factors of trade.

The objective of this research was to identify the gaps in the current export investment model of all commodities especially textile industries and introduce a more robust framework which quantitatively evaluates the risk factors involved in trade of specific sector and optimize the system which maximize profits and minimize risk. The modern portfolio theory explains the optimal portfolio concepts that investor will invest on the basis of maximizing their profit for their selected tolerated level of risk to determine the suitable commodities with their weightage in a portfolio. The Fig. 1 explains how the optimal portfolio works. Along the line of the curve the ideal risk portfolio is depicted which shows a perfect trade-off between risk and returns.

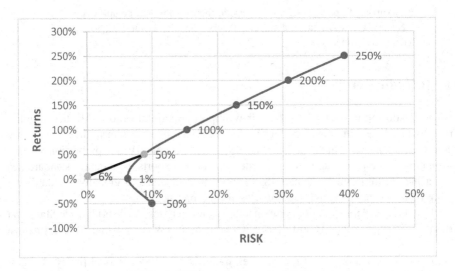

Fig. 1. Efficient frontier of portfolio

The modern portfolio methods used in this research are Markowitz portfolio [9], CAP M. [10] and Black-Litterman [11] model which incorporate qualitative and quantitative analysis on the dataset extracted from UN comtrade [12]. The database is from United Nations international trade statistics. Annual international trade statistic data including details of commodities category with partner country are provided to United Nation static division (UNSD) by more than 170 countries. It is the biggest repository of international trade data. Comtrade data by clause 3 & 16 of United Nation department of economic and social affairs statistic division are permissible to use in research. It contains more than 3 billion trade data record since 1962.

The rest of the paper is classified as follows. Brief background research is provided in Sect. 2 that overviews the related work. Section 3 presents the proposed algorithm used on the dataset. Results and implementation are discussed in Sects. 4 and 5 gives the analysis of results and future work.

2 Background/Related Work

Uribe et al. [13] did an informational approach to forecast of inter-regional trade flows. They used RAS method for trade flow analytics to project features for trade flow forecast of the years 1938 to 1960. Xia et al. [14] worked on China export by using holt model on trade data. They worked on the export of garments & textile products to provide the forecast of textile industry with MAPE of 13.25-34.99. Xie et al. [15] introduced genetic algorithm to optimize Grey modeling to predict the aggregate volume of trade. They presented a technique in view of hereditary calculation to optimize parameters of grey model GM (1, 1) through genetic algorithm. Kong et al. [16] worked on the long-term export prediction of textile industry and discovered the market of clothing still developed quickly in three to five years. Dabin et al. [17] took the trade data of Hubei province of China to forecast custom export and showed increased accuracy of holt model than the traditional econometric model.

In this way researchers [18, 19] forecasted trade data by using different models defined above to increase the prediction accuracy or defining the future potential of the trade commodity. Different researches [3–5] defined the role and impact of product complexity and gravity model [6] on trade. Currently, no published work was available, which could define the opportune commodities for investors to invest with control on the risk parameter. The major factors which are used to calculate the export opportunity include trade data, government policies, gravity equation and product complexity. Expert opinion has a major role to forecast trade of a country. Several researches [20–22] provide theoretical parameters like demographic change, investment, technology, energy and other resources, institution etc. strongly impact on trades. For this problem we used an approach to multiplex all the factors and utilize modern portfolio theory and Black-Litterman model to incorporate expert opinion based on commodity complexity, gravitational theory, law, government policies etc. with past data to present a unique idea to forecast trade and find opportunities for capitalist to invest in trade and gain risk control returns.

3 Proposed Algorithm

In the proposed work Markowitz portfolio optimization [9] and Black-Litterman model [11] was utilized from the perspective to calculate expected return and risk related to each commodity of export using trade data, gravitational theory and product complexity data for the expert to incorporate their views in a model for better accuracy and minimum risk. Figure 2 shows the conventional forecasting model and the proposed model shown in Fig. 3 has classified the trade optimization and asset allocation into 2 main categories. The quantitative method incorporates the algorithms which only use the historical trade data to make asset allocation and risk calculation whereas the quantitative method additionally also employs expert opinion in the form of a numeric matrix to add the expert views in the algorithm.

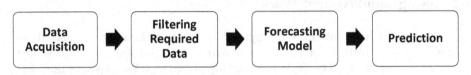

Fig. 2. Conventional forecasting model

3.1 Markowitz Portfolio Optimization

We used Markowitz mathematical framework to diversify investment and finding opportunities in different trade commodities to boost the profit and having the information of risk involved to each trade commodity, to assist investors in decision making of investment to gain high returns and defined risk. The overall return of the portfolio is calculated by Eq. (1), there are N commodities. r_{ct} is the return at time t on an investment in a commodity C; d_{ct} is the rate of return of commodity C at time t and W_c the weightage of investment.

$$R = \sum_{t=1}^{\infty} \sum_{c=1}^{N} d_{ct} r_{ct} W \tag{1}$$

$$R = \sum_{c=1}^{N} W_c \left(\sum_{t=1}^{\infty} d_{ct} r_{ct} \right) \tag{2}$$

$R_c = \sum_{t=1}^{\infty} d_{ct} r_{ct}$ is the return of cth commodity, Therefore

$$R = \sum XcRc \tag{3}$$

In this equation X_c and R_c are independent. Since $X_C \geq 0$ for all C and $\Sigma Xc = 1$ for maximize return.

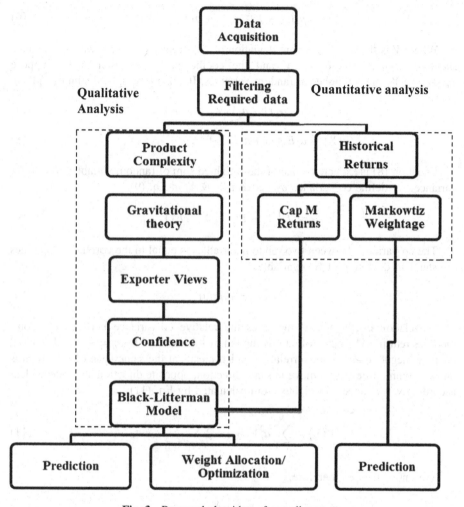

Fig. 3. Proposed algorithm of overall system

$$\sum_{a=1}^{K} X_{c_a} = 1 \qquad (4)$$

For several investments amount $a = 1, \ldots, K$ for maximum returns. The expected value or μ(mean) [23] of X defined by Eq. (5) where X be the random variable of finite number value $x_1, x_2, \ldots, x_N$, the probability that $X = x_1$ is and $X = x_2$ is p_2.

$$E = p_1 x_1 + p_2 x_2 + \ldots + p_N x_N \qquad (5)$$

The Variance of X is defined by Eq. (6).

$$V = p_1(x_1 - E)^2 + \ldots + p_N(x_N - E)^2 \tag{6}$$

Where V is the average square deviation of $\sqrt{X}$ from its μ mean, we can calculate standard deviation as $\sigma = \sqrt{V}$ and the coefficient of variation, σ/E. Suppose $Y_1, Y_2, \ldots, Y_N$ are a number of random variables, If Y is the weighted sum of Y_i then,

$$Y = a_1 Y_1 + a_1 Y_1 + \ldots + a_n Y_N \tag{7}$$

$$E(Y) = a_1 E(Y_1) + a_2 E(Y_2) + \ldots + a_N E(Y_N) \tag{8}$$

Equation (8) is expected value of the weighted sum of random variable, proof 6 for variance; we define co variance σ_{ij} between Y_i & Y_j in Eq. (9).

$$\sigma_{ij} = E\{[Y_i - E(Y_i)][Y_j - E(Y_j)]\} \tag{9}$$

The co-variance between two random variables is equal to the correlation ρ_{ij} times the standard deviation of two variables

$$\sigma ij = \rho ij \sigma i \sigma j \tag{10}$$

Correlation coefficient ρ_{ij} measures the relative co-variance between the commodities returns. The range of ratio is limited by $+1.0$ and -1.0, $\rho_{ij} = +1.0, -1.0$ & 0.0 positive, negative and zero Correlation which means at the same span of time returns on two commodities try to move in same direction, opposite direction and independent accordingly. Variance of weighted sum calculated by Eq. (11):

$$V(Y) = \sum_{i=1}^{N} a_i^2 V(W_i) + 2 \sum_{i=1}^{N} \sum_{i>1}^{N} a_i a_j \sigma_{ij} \tag{11}$$

We know Y_i is σ_{ii} therefore,

$$V(Y) = \sum_{i=1}^{N} \sum_{j=1}^{N} a_i a_j \sigma_{ij} \tag{12}$$

$$R = \sum R c W c \tag{13}$$

where R_c is the return on the cth commodity. μ_c is the expected return of R_c, σ_{cs} = covariance between R_c & R_s; σ_{cc} = variance of $R_c' W_c$ = percentage weightage of investor of R_c. Similarly, R is the random variable and return on the portfolio is a weighted sum of R & R_c. W_c is the percentage of investment. $^P W_c = 1$ represent sum of all investment is equal to 1. Therefore, Expected Return & Variance of the portfolio are calculated by Eqs. (14) and (15)

$$E = \sum_{c=1}^{N} W_c \mu_c \tag{14}$$

$$V = \sum_{c=1}^{N} \sum_{s=1}^{N} \sigma_{cs} W_c W_s \tag{15}$$

3.2   Black-Litterman Model

Trade is influenced by the government policies, current trend, gravity model and PCI [20]. Optimal portfolios are very sensitive to inputs, for the small change in input results in a significant change in asset allocation of portfolio. Black-Litterman (BL) introduced an expert view matrix to the Markovitz mean variance optimization and CAPM to add expert's perspective who has experience based information on the assets which are not modelled and are not reflected from the CAPM alone. Return using the BL model is expressed as

$$U = W^T R - \frac{1}{2} A W^T S W \tag{16}$$

Where, A = Risk Aversion; R = Risk; S = Variance Co-Variance matrix; w = weights $\Sigma w = 1$

$$du/dw = R - ASW = 0 \tag{17}$$

Rather, solving for weights, BL argued that weights are already observed in the market therefore they computed them using market capitalization.

$$R = ASW \tag{18}$$

$$A = \frac{E(r_m) - r_f}{\sigma_m^2} \tag{19}$$

$$M = [(\tau S)^{-1} + P^T \Omega P]^{-1} \tag{20}$$

$$E(R) = [(\tau S)^{-1} + P^T \Omega P]^{-1} [(\tau S)^{-1} \Pi + P^T \Omega Q] \tag{21}$$

τ = Scalar number indicating uncertainty usually range (0.025 to 0.05)

$$\Pi = ASW_{mkt} \tag{22}$$

M = Uncertainty of returns; Π = Implied equilibrium returns; P = Investors views matrix; each row a particular view of the market and each element of the row represents the portfolio weights of each asset (K×N matrix); Q = The expected returns of the portfolios from the views depicted in matrix P (K×1 vector); Ω = A diagonal co variance matrix with elements of the uncertainty inside each view (K×K matrix)

$$S_B = S + W \tag{23}$$

S_B = Variance covariance Matrix of Black-Litterman model. Assumed there are N commodities in the portfolio, this formula will calculate new expected return. We used CAP M weights for reverse optimization to include market capitalization factor and an impact of overall trade covariance with each commodity to gain the minimum error in efficient frontier of Black-Litterman model.

3.3 Product Complexity Index

Berkowitz et al. [21], came up with a quantitative measurement of measuring product complexity through PCI. In this method complexity was based on the number of product functions and the level at which they appear in a decomposed function tree. Accordingly, total complexity is measured by (24).

$$C_T = \frac{w_1 C_m + w_2 C_p + w_3 C_{st} + w_4 C_s}{w_1 + w_2 + w_3 + w_4} \tag{24}$$

C_m = f(material, tooling, geometry, process), C_p = f(geometry), C_{st} = f(number of subassemblies, levels in hierarchy, max number of components/sub-assemblies); C_s = f(number of assembly operations), w_t = numerical constraints, where i = 1, 2, 3, 4.

Most of the variable in this measurement are identified by design and production ratings. From the above, the optimum number of components are calculated by (25)

$$\frac{dC_T}{dn} = \frac{d}{dn} \left(\frac{w_1 C_m + w_2 C_p + w_3 C_{st} + w_4 C_s}{w_1 + w_2 + w_3 + w_4} \right) = 0 \tag{25}$$

3.4 Gravitational Model

General Trade Gravity model is expressed as:

$$Y_{IJ} = G \frac{X_I X_J}{D_{IJ}} \tag{26}$$

$$lnY_{IJ} = \alpha_0 + \alpha_1 lnX_I + \alpha_2 lnX_J + \alpha_3 lnD_{IJ} + \in \tag{27}$$

Where 'I' and 'J' denote the trading nations, X is general is represented by the GDP of the country and D is the distance between the two nations. The conventional Trade Gravity Model proposes that exchange streams between the two nations are emphatically identified with the GDP of the two nations and contrarily identified with the separation between the two nations.

4   Implementation and Results

For implementation, using approach in Fig. 3 various qualitative and quantitative analysis were extracted from the comtrade dataset using the Markowitz portfolio, CAP M. and Black-Litterman model. Each result from the dataset is compared with the actual result to conclude the best model.

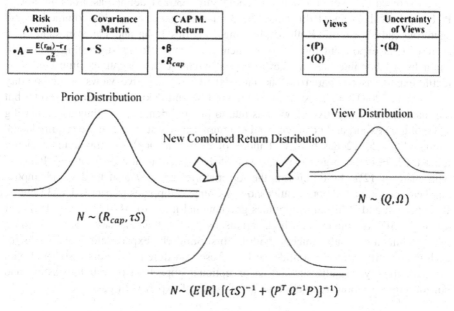

Fig. 4. Prediction approach

4.1   Data Acquisition

HS [6-digit code] dataset of all the commodities from the year 2003 to 2016 was used in this paper. Data of 23 textile commodities was filtered, which were more than 0.5% of the total textile export of Pakistan. The data was acquired from United Nation Commodity Trade Statistics Database [12], their source in Pakistan is Pakistan Bureau of Statistics.

4.2   Qualitative Analysis

Portfolio optimization methods (Markowitz and CAPM) generate risk and return of commodities based on the historical data. Black-Litterman model adds expert opinions and implied equilibrium return to the quantitative methods. We generated implied equilibrium return using CAPM weights. CAPM incorporated the information of the capital pricing and percentage of share of commodity in total export. Expert opinion was derived by the trade specialist who explained the increase or decrease of each commodity by designing a view matrix and giving its corresponding confidence level. The view matrix was obtained on the basis of product complexity index [22], gravitational model [6], government laws, trends [20, 21] and other factors associated with the specific trade. Higher confidence level gives a more assured result of a product. Table 1 Showed each commodity in the view matrix along with its confidence level. Expert showed 0.1% of confidence in commodity 630231 defined as it has the lowest PCI Index of 1.75 and Pakistan is the 3rd largest exporter of this commodity and capturing India's export. Both neighboring countries India and Pakistan share 21% stake of total export but Indian government economic reforms suggesting their transition from labor intensive market to capital intensive has negatively impacted their textile exports as compared to Pakistan. Expert gave negative views on commodity 610590 and 520812. PCI index for 610910 is 1.88 and Pakistan is the top exporter but the main cause of negative views was due to the low demand, continuous decreasing share of total export and negative trend of returns since last 5 year of the acquired data. Commodity 520512 has high PCI index of 2.29 with negative gravitational theory impact. China is the largest exporter with 65% of world total export through Pakistan with share of 12%. Philippines is the top importer with 37% of total world import. Applied gravitational theory results showed China-Philippines impact is 1.1233 billion USD per km and Pakistan Philippines gravitational impact is 0.0145 billion USD per km as the GDP of china is very high and distance is less than Pakistan from Philippines giving China a high advantage in both factors. Similarly, expert defined his views for each commodity with the confidence level based on different factors associated with each commodity. Results showed an exceptional impact on overall forecasting and portfolio optimization by multiplexing the views of expert with past data.

Table 1. View matrix P & confidence matrix Q

Views	Confidence level Q	520512	630260	630231
View 1	0	1	0	0
View 2	0	0	1	0
View 3	0.1	0	0	1

The risk of covariance of each view matrix is shown in the equation. Where Ω is the uncertainty of matrix, S is the covariance and P is the view matrix.

$$\Omega = \tau PSP^T \tag{28}$$

The Covariance matrix S & S_B is shown in Tables 2 and 3.

Table 2. Covariance matrix of covariance S

S Matrix	520512	630260	630231	620322	630239
520512	0.052	-0.010	-0.003	-0.006	-0.019
630260	-0.010	0.017	0.001	0.001	0.019
630231	-0.003	0.001	0.019	-0.017	0.011
620322	-0.006	0.001	-0.017	0.781	-0.013
630239	-0.019	0.019	0.011	-0.013	0.141

Table 3. Covariance matrix of covariance S_B

S_B Matrix	520512	630260	630231	620322	630239
520512	0.038	-0.004	-0.043	0.167	-0.172
630260	-0.003	0.016	0.012	-0.048	0.065
630231	0.001	-0.004	0.029	-0.049	0.037
620322	-0.018	0.004	-0.019	0.986	-0.083
630239	-0.022	0.014	-0.006	0.061	0.073

4.3 Quantitative Analysis Efficient Frontier of Markowitz Model

Using the filtered trade data, calculated expected return from the historical commodities value. Total expected return from the year 2003 to 2016 calculated by Eq. 29.

$$E(R) = \left(\sum_{t=1}^{\tau} \right) \div T \qquad (29)$$

Table 4. Expected returns of year 2015 using different portfolio optimization models

S. no.	Commodities	Historic returns	Cap. M returns	BLM returns	Actual return
1	520512	8.17%	−0.08%	−46.88%	−20.34%
2	630260	7.44%	3.41%	41.80%	−5.33%
3	630231	−1.86%	3.12%	−15.63%	3.81%
4	620322	93.07%	3.71%	314.06%	255.38%
5	630239	26.81%	6.95%	10.16%	10.86%

By using Black-Litterman model in Fig. 4, expected returns of 23 textile commodities of Pakistan for the year 2015 using trade data [12] from the year 2003 to 2014, was shown in Table 4. Figures 5, 6 and 7 represent efficient frontier of expected and the actual returns versus risks of the year 2015 using Markowitz, CAPM & Black-Litterman model respectively, indicating minimization of standard error by incorporating expert views using Black-Litterman model. Figure 8 represent the comparative analysis of historical, CAPM and Black Litterman model using mean square error (MSE) metric. Table 5 represents the expected return for the predicted year 2016 of the 23 textile commodities of Pakistan and the weightage allocation for maximum return, minimum variance and maximum sharp ratio. Figure 9 is the efficient frontier graph of 2016 predicted returns versus risks using Black-Litterman model.

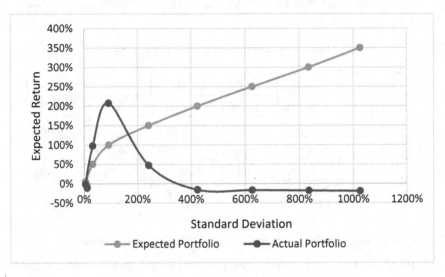

Fig. 5. Efficient frontier of Markowitz model

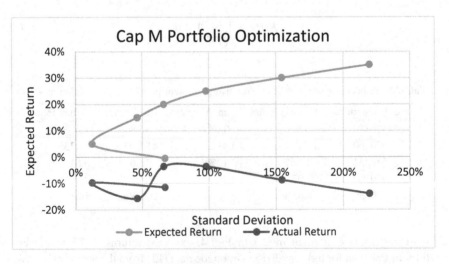

Fig. 6. Efficient frontier of CAP model

Table 5. Expected returns & weightage allocation year 2016 using Black-Litterman model

S. no.	Commodity	Expected return	Weights for max return	Weights for min variance	Weights for max sharp ratio
1	520512	10.67%	0.00%	16.16%	20.24%
2	630260	3.07%	0.00%	24.91%	14.45%
3	630231	−0.61%	0.00%	22.34%	1.60%
4	620322	−19.85%	0.00%	1.54%	0.00%
5	630239	3.47%	0.00%	0.00%	0.00%

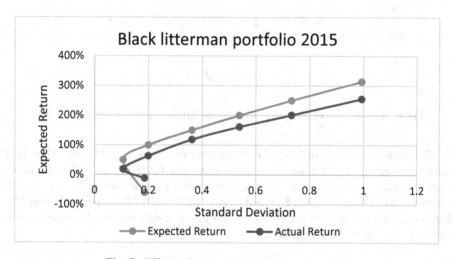

Fig. 7. Efficient frontier of Black-Litterman model

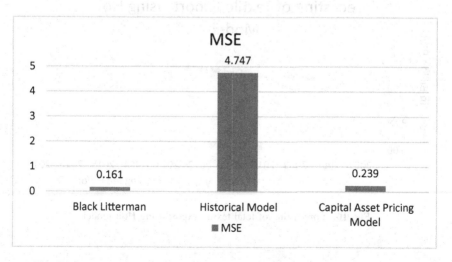

Fig. 8. Comparative analysis of Black-Litterman MSE with Holt & Grey model

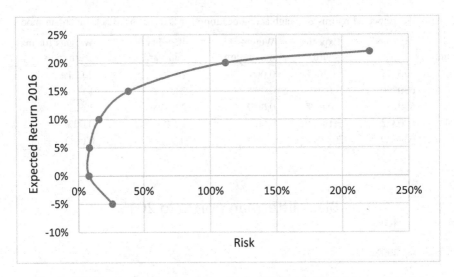

Fig. 9. Efficient frontier for the predicted year 2016 using Black-Litterman model

Comparative analysis of Black-Litterman forecasted with Holt [14] and Grey [17] model showed the Black-Litterman model forecasted better results with risks information of each commodity (i.e. MSE for the specific expected return through Black-Litterman is 0.235 and through Holt and Grey is 1.226 and 1.026 respectively Fig. 12). Figures 10 and 11 showed the predicted and actual textile export of Pakistan using comtrade data from 2007 to 2015.

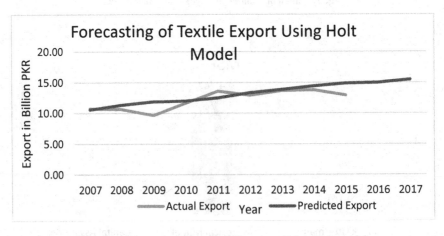

Fig. 10. Forecasting of total textile export using Holt model

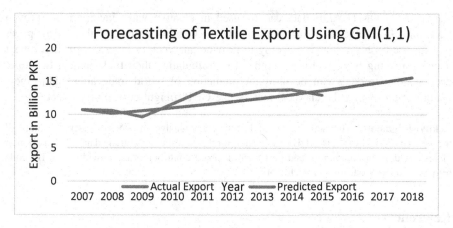

Fig. 11. Forecasting of textile export using Grey model

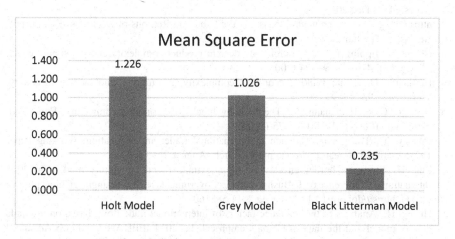

Fig. 12. Comparative analysis of Black-Litterman MSE with Holt & Grey model

5 Conclusion

In this paper, we introduced a portfolio optimization theory which gave the investor control of risks with maximum returns. The risks and returns information was defined for each commodity. The three models, incorporated were Markowitz historical model, CAPM. and Black-Litterman model. As trade data was nonlinear and vary with the overseas demand, expert opinion became crucial for assessment which was utilized by Black-Litterman model.

The efficient frontier of these 3 models using the trade data of the last 13 years was compared. The results indicate that the predicted value of the Black-Litterman model is closest to the actual value and tracks the efficient frontier graph. Later we compared Black-Litterman model with the conventional models Holt and Grey. The results showed Black-Litterman with improved quantitative and qualitative results. We have shown that COMTRADE data can be used in creative ways incorporating proven algorithms from other domains like financial engineering in trade analysis. This paper will inspire further research not only to provide analytics to investors for investment decision making but also for government in formulating their trade policy. In future, deep learning models can be used for prediction of world trade after adding new features representing the classical factors like GDP, freight cost, policy effect etc.

Acknowledgments. The authors would like to acknowledge the Massachusetts institute of technology and UN COMTRADE organization for the contributors of trade dataset, visualization of trade with each commodity and past trade database contributors for providing the HS code resources to carry out this research work.

References

1. WTO Homepage. https://www.wto.org/english/res_e/statis_e/wts2017_e/wts2017_e.pdf. Accessed 12 Dec 2018
2. https://ntc.gov.pk/wp-content/uploads/2016/05/Study-on-Reasons-of-Decline-in-Exports.pdf. Accessed 11th Jun 2016
3. Novak, S., Eppinger, S.D.: Sourcing by design: product complexity and the supply chain. Manag. Sci. **47**(1), 189–204 (2001)
4. Hartmann, D., et al.: Linking economic complexity, institutions, and income inequality. World Dev. **93**, 75–93 (2017)
5. Hidalgo, C.A., Hausmann, R.: The building blocks of economic complexity. Proc. Natl. Acad. Sci. **106**(26), 10570–10575 (2009)
6. Chaney, T.: The gravity equation in international trade: an explanation. Working Paper 19285 National Bureau of Economic Research, August 2013
7. Zhu, H.: Study on border effects for shipping trade based on gravity model. In: 2011 International Conference on E-Business and E-Government (ICEE), Shanghai, China, pp. 1–4 (2011). https://doi.org/10.1109/icebeg.2011.5881602
8. Huang, H.: Analysis of the influence factors of international trade flows based on the trade gravity model and the data of China's empirical. In: 2014 IEEE Workshop on Advanced Research and Technology in Industry Applications (WARTIA) (2014)
9. Markowitz, H.: Portfolio selection. J. Financ. **7**(1), 77–91 (1952)
10. French, C.W.: The Treynor capital asset pricing model. J. Invest. Manag. **1**(2), 60–72 (2003). SSRN 447580
11. Black, F., Litterman, R.: Global portfolio optimization. Financ. Anal. J. **48**, 28–43 (1992)
12. UN Comtrade: United Nations commodity trade statistics database (2010). http://comtrade.un.org
13. Uribe, P., de Leeuw, C.G., Theil, H.: The information approach to the prediction of interregional trade flows. Rev. Econ. Stud. **33**(3), 209–220 (1966)
14. Xia, L., Yaomei, G., Weiwei, S.: Forecast to textile and garment exports based on holt model. In: IEEE 2010 International Conference of Information Science and Management Engineering, pp. 274–277 (2010)
15. Xie, Q., Xie, Y.: Forecast of the total volume of import-export trade based on grey modelling optimized by genetic algorithm. In: 2009 Third International Symposium on Intelligent Information Technology Application, Nanchang, pp. 545–547 (2009)

16. Li, X., Kong, F., Liu, Y., Qin, Y.: Applying GM (1,1) model in China's apparel export forecasting. In: 2011 Fourth International Symposium on Computational Intelligence and Design, Hangzhou, pp. 245–247 (2011)
17. Dabin, Z., Hou, Z., Jingguang, Z.: Forecasting of customs export based on gray theory. In: 2009 International Conference on Business Intelligence and Financial Engineering, Beijing, pp. 630–633 (2009)
18. Wang, C.C., Tu, Y.H., Wong, H.L.: The comparison between multivariate fuzzy time series and traditional time series modeling to forecasting China exports. In: 2009 Fourth International Conference on Innovative Computing, Information and Control (ICICIC), Kaohsiung, pp. 1487–1490 (2009)
19. Wong, H.L., Tu, Y.H., Wang, C.C.: An evaluation of comparison between multivariate fuzzy time series with traditional time series model for forecasting Taiwan export. In: 2009 WRI World Congress on Computer Science and Information Engineering, Los Angeles, CA, pp. 462–467 (2009)
20. WTO Homepage. https://www.wto.org/english/res_e/booksp_e/wtr13-2c_e.pdf. Accessed 12 Dec 2018
21. Berkowitz, D., Moenius, J., Pistor, K.: Trade, law and product complexity. Rev. Econ. Stat. **88**(2), 363–373 (2006)
22. Hausmann, R., et al.: The atlas of economic complexity: mapping paths to prosperity. MIT Press, Cambridge (2014)
23. Uspensky, J.V.: Introduction to Mathematical Probability, pp. 161–181. McGraw-Hill, New York (1937)

AI, Big Data and Data Analytics

Automatic Speech Recognition in Taxi Call Service Systems

Samir Rustamov[1,2(✉)], Natavan Akhundova[3], and Alakbar Valizada[3]

[1] ADA University, Baku, AZ 1008, Azerbaijan
srustamov@ada.edu.az
[2] Institute of Control Systems, Baku, Azerbaijan
[3] ATL Tech, Baku, AZ 1022, Azerbaijan
{natavan.akhundova,alakbar.valizada}@atltech.az

Abstract. In this research, the application of automatic speech recognition system in taxi call services is investigated. In comparison with traditional query handling systems such as live agents, Interactive Voice Response systems, type-base websites and mobile applications, the newest trend of artificial intelligence - speech recognition can be applied to make conversations in more natural way. For developing, training and testing of the system, Kaldi and CMUSphinx open-source speech recognition tools were utilized. Approximately 4 h of speech data in Azerbaijani have been processed for both tools. Testing has been accomplished in two ways; one of which is recognizing dataset from unknown speakers, and the other one is recognizing shuffled dataset. During these tests, variance and speed were investigated, along with accuracy. Kaldi showed accuracy between 97.3 and 99.6 with variance changing between 0.03 and 4.8. On the other hand, CMUSphinx attained accuracy between 95.6 and 97.8 with variance values of 0.2 and 3.8 in relatively less training time. Accomplished results were compared and used to define appropriate parameters for investigated models.

Keywords: Speech recognition · Kaldi · CMUSphinx · n-gram ·
Taxi call service · Speech features

1 Introduction

In the hectic life of big cities where people are always in rush, taxis play a valuable and crucial role. As demand increases, taxi companies see an incentive to improve quality of the service, as well as, enhancing query handling methods in call centers. Nevertheless, there is a still problem of customers waiting in long queues, especially, in peak hours. While call center agents work 24/7 to solve this incompetence, they are left with few or no social life. On the other hand, hiring more agents is a short-term solution for a company. The problem lies in the fact that a gap between the improvement of the service and today's technology exists. In order to eliminate this gap, most of the companies keep up with the latest trends of technology. Some made app and online websites, while others valued conversation more and refined calls with Interactive Voice Response (IVR) systems.

M. H. Miraz et al. (Eds.): iCETiC 2019, LNICST 285, pp. 243–253, 2019.

All of these methods have its own pros and cons, however, this paper will focus on improvement of handling queries via call. By applying IVR to calls, certainly more queries can be handled parallelly without a human factor. The disadvantage of this method is that it quickly annoys customers and even can take more time than talking to a person because of starting over when pressed numbers wrongly.

In comparison with IVR systems, the newest trend of artificial intelligence - speech recognition can be applied to make conversations more natural as it does not limit customers with predefined options to choose. Speech recognition transforms speech to text while listening to a voice, and this is why it speeds up recording of an order, whereas previously agents needed to write it down. Having an automatic machine on 24/7 to handle customer queries can play as a competitive advantage for a company resulting in high revenue and customer satisfaction.

This paper promotes speech recognition as a tool for the use of taxi call centers in Azerbaijani language. It compares two open source tool kits - Kaldi and CMUSphinx for speech recognition with data in that language and discusses their advantage and disadvantages relative to the usability by call centers. Accordingly, Sect. 2 presents literature review, Sect. 3 is for an overview of speech recognition process, Sect. 4 introduces speech recognition using Kaldi and CMUSphinx, Sect. 5 delivers experimental results and Sect. 6 is about the discussion followed by the conclusion.

2   Literature Review

In [1], Matarneh, Maksymova, Lyashenko and Belova compared different close-source and open-source speech recognition tools based on various parameters, such as error rate, speed, response time and API. Authors tested Dragon Mobile SDK, Google Speech Recognition API, Siri, Yandex SpeechKit and Microsoft Speech API for close-source, and CMUSphinx, Kaldi, Julius, HTK, iAtros, RWTH ASR and Simon for open-source tools.

In [2], the statement that speech recognition technology has reached human performance by Microsoft is put under a test. Authors concluded that according to the test results, the statement being wrong is claimed.

Authors of [3] evaluated accuracies of three open-source toolkits: HTK, CMUSphinx and Kaldi based on German and English data. Based on their results, Kaldi outperformed the other tools.

In [4], authors integrate PyTorch, a library for neural network, and Kaldi, an open-source speech recognition toolkit, to obtain more efficient and accurate results. The authors confirmed their hypothesis via experiments with various datasets.

Parthasarathi and Strom in [5] build acoustic model with 7000 h labeled and 1 million hours of unlabeled data and discuss their results. The authors put forward the significance of data volume on recognition and how hyper-parameter tuning can improve accuracy.

Authors in [6] introduce a new system for recognizing a specific speaker in a signal with multiple speakers via training two neural networks. The system met expectations by increasing accuracy of recognition on both multi-speaker and single-speaker signals.

Schatz and Feldman discussed in [7] if one of the key parts of speech recognition - Hidden Markov Model or neural networks is more similar to human behavior and perception of speech, via testing on corpuses in American English and Japanese. They concluded that neural networks have the best understanding of human perception of speech.

Fukuda et al. in [8], emphasized the problem of speech recognition on accepted speech and introduced data augmentation as a method to solve it. The authors modified accented data with three operations which are voice transformation, noise addition, and speed modification and concluded the last one being the most effective.

Jain, Upreti, Jyothi also referred to accented speech problem in [9] and suggested an architecture that learns a multi-accent acoustic model and an accent classifier. Together with speech augmentation, these techniques improved the performance of accent recognition.

In [10] authors experimented on recognition of speech on broadcasts when training data is scarce. The proposed approach was to collect data via related web sources in order to span different and broad domains.

In [11] Rustamov et al. developed speech recognition system for Flight Simulator Cockpit in C# from scratch which performed training with neural networks. In comparison with Microsoft Speech SDK, the tool achieved better results.

The idea of applying speech recognition technology in call centers is not new, and it has already been adopted by some companies in the beginning of a century. Australian company named "Regent Taxis" has implemented such a solution for its call center back in 2000 [12]. Within a few months, positive results have been achieved as automated technology gain popularity among users [13]. A company in New Zealand called "Co-op Taxis" was inspired by that and started to apply the same technology by the same vendor in 2001 [14].

In [15–19], authors applied different combination of hybrid neural networks for Azerbaijani isolated speech recognition systems.

3 Overview of Speech Recognition Process

Speech recognition is not a new term; it was first mentioned in 1930s [20]. Speech recognition, also known as speech-to-text, is a process of turning audio waves into texts. According to Jurafsky and Martin [21], in order to automatically recognize speech, four dimensions are considered: vocabulary, naturality of speech, noise and accent of a speaker. To begin with, the task of recognition becomes easier when vocabulary to be defined is small. Also, words isolated with pauses make the recognition easier, in comparison with continuous speech. This is because transforming continuous speech into text requires an additional tough task as separating speech to words, and this process can lead to errors. Finally, any kind of noise and accent in speech can decrease the accuracy of recognition due to the fact that such speeches do not come align with what the tool was trained.

The process of recognition is mainly based on probability and search. Given an audio input, estimates are defined for possible outputs, and an output with the highest probability is searched. If we define sentences with W, the desirable output with $\dot{W}$, and the audio input with O, then our output can be expressed by

$$\dot{W} = \arg\max_{W \in L} P(W|O) \tag{1}$$

where L is a vocabulary in a given language. It means that, with the given audio input O, we take a sentence out of all sentences W which has maximum probability. By using Bayes' rule, this expression can be changed as

$$\dot{W} = \arg\max_{W \in L} P(O|W)P(W)P(O). \tag{2}$$

During calculation, P(O) does not have any effect on the result because it is the same for each value. We can rewrite the equation as

$$\dot{W} = \arg\max_{W \in L} P(O|W)P(W) \tag{3}$$

which gives us the product of acoustic model P(O|W) and language model P(W).

Language model is a set of probabilities for word sequences in the given language. The length of the sequence is defined by n-grams where n changes as 1, 2, 3 and et cetera. On the other hand, the acoustic model calculates probabilities of phones generating feature vectors at each time frame of audio. Feature vectors are vectors which include information about each time frame. The overall process of speech recognition is described in Fig. 1.

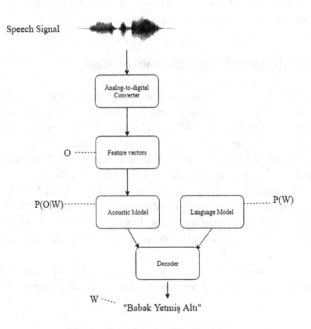

Fig. 1. Speech recognition process

4 Speech Recognition Using Kaldi and CMUSphinx

4.1 Overview of Toolkits

In order to build a speech recognition technology in any natural language, open-source tools will be needed. According to different blogs' top ratings such as LinuxLinks [22] and Silicon Valley Data Science [23], two of the most popular speech recognition tools are agreed to be Kaldi and CMUSphinx, also known as just Sphinx.

To begin with, Kaldi [24] is designed and intended for researchers on the field of speech recognition. It has been compiled on Windows, Linux, MacOs and is continuously updated by a lot of contributors. Therefore, the tool is full of various useful scripts and codes for any appropriate purpose. Currently, Kaldi is developing a new architecture for recognition which is deep neural networks.

CMUSphinx [25], on the other hand, is relatively easy to start with and has a simple documentation. It also has a huge community and in constant update. The toolkit consists of four parts: Pocketsphinx, Sphinxbase, Sphinx4 and Sphinxtrain. These parts are responsible for recognition, its lightweight and supporting libraries and training tools. Sphinx can be compiled on both Windows, Linux and MacOS.

Even though Kaldi was written on C++, while Sphinx on Java, both of the tools have been developed in such a structure where any new module can be easily added or removed [1]. The most accurate out of these two is Kaldi, [3] however Sphinx also will be tested in this paper to compare the results and other performances.

4.2 Data Preparation

The audio data used in this research is in the Azerbaijani language and equals approximately 3.52 h with 152 vocabulary words.

The data contains the most popular 100 addresses of the capital city of Azerbaijan, Baku. There also exist numbers in the names of streets, ranging from one till thousand. The shortest utterance consists of two words, whereas, the longest has eleven words. Examples for the data are: "ABBAS MİRZƏ ŞƏRİFZADƏ OTUZ DOQQUZ" - Abbas Mirza Sharifzada thirty nine; "FÜZULİ KÜÇƏSİ BİR" - Fuzuli street one; "VAQİF PROSPEKTİ" - prospect of Vagif and et cetera.

The audio recordings were recorded via ordinary microphones at 16 kHz with minimal noise and accurate grammar and pronunciation. Speakers, with total number of 62, were students within the age range from 18 till 24. fluent, which means no dialects were used during speaking. Nevertheless, database comprises different speaking styles and tonalities. Each subject pronounced all street names once. Some of the recordings have been removed due to speaker or microphone error, leaving, in total, 6121 utterances. The data was trained as continuous speech.

Data processing for both tools were nearly the same. Sphinx and Kaldi require defining utterance ids, a map of utterance ids to transcriptions and a dictionary with phonetic transcriptions. Additionally, Kaldi needs speaker information like gender and a map of speakers and utterance ids.

When it comes to language model, Kaldi has internal scripts for creating an n-gram, and when the system is put to be trained, an n-gram will be automatically created. To train CMUSphinx based system, an additional command should be executed to create an n-gram, beforehand.

Overall, CMUSphinx has less steps in configuration for training a dataset than Kaldi. This is because Sphinx is aimed at developing practical applications [25], whilst, Kaldi is for researches.

5 Experimental Results

5.1 Overview of Experiments

The experiments comprise of checking accuracies of training and testing on audio data, which are assumed to be useful for taxi call systems. The trainings were conducted using both open-source speech recognition tool kits: Kaldi and CMUSphinx. The environment was the same virtual platform in order to eliminate bias which could have possibly occurred during training and testing the tools. The OS was Kali Linux and was running using single i7 CPU at 1.80 GHz speed.

Accuracy of training is carried out by testing all data against training set, however for calculating the accuracy of tests only ten percent of all data was considered as test, exclusively.

To begin with, different n-grams were used while the trainings, starting from 1 till 5, in order to know how accuracies are changing. This experiment will be conditionally named as "100/100". Both its training and test sets equally have 6121 utterances. The last two tests were performed ten times with random ten percent of data and with 3-grams as a language model. These tests will be named: "90/10 speaker" and "90/10 shuffle". In "90/10 speaker" test, ten percent of all speakers were exclusively given as a test and the rest for a training set. The size of testing set varies within a range of 598 and 612 utterances due to the fact that speakers have different number of recordings, and excluding some accounts for a difference in count. Finally, for conducting "90/10 shuffle" test, ten percent of all data, which is 612 utterances, was excluded from overall database as a testing set.

Accuracies of experiments are defined by Word Error Rate (WER) and Sentence Error Rate (SER). WER is a ratio of inserted (I), deleted (D) and substituted words (S) to the amount of all words (N) within given audio input [21]. It is calculated as

$$WER = \frac{S+D+I}{N} \tag{4}$$

SER is a ratio of errors made while recognizing sentences to all sentences.

$$SER = \frac{E}{N} \tag{5}$$

In this formula, E stands for all sentences with substituted, deleted or inserted words, whereas N indicates all sentences [26].

5.2 Kaldi Results

On Kaldi ASR, training accuracy of "100/100" dataset starts at 3.03% for SER with 1-gram and rapidly decreases afterwards. Even though for WER changes are not so drastic, it can be observed that both error rates decrease till 3-grams and, after, remains stable at 0.36% for SER and 0.1% for WER (Fig. 2).

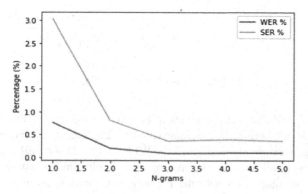

Fig. 2. Kaldi 100/100

Based on the results of training accuracy, the least error prone n-gram, which is 3-grams, was chosen for speaker and shuffle testing.

These tests showed accuracy rates between 97.3% and 99.6%, which are reasonably high results. Variances are all below 1, except for SER in speaker testing. For Kaldi, it took 13 min and 19 s on average to finish a training on the indicted computer above (Table 1).

Table 1. Kaldi test descriptions

	WER %	Variance of WER	SER %	Variance of SER
90/10 speaker	1.020	0.884	2.699	4.750
90/10 shuffle	0.368	0.025	1.363	0.270

5.3 CMUSphinx Results

The next tool, CMUSphinx, starts off with relatively high values: 25.4% for SER and 7.6% for WER. It reaches stability again on 3-grams with "100/100" testing, at 3.7% for SER and 2.1% for WER (Fig. 3).

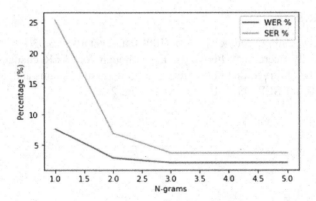

Fig. 3. CMUSphinx 100/100

For "90/10" tests, accuracy changes in between 95.6% and 97.8%, which means WER and SER for both tests are approximately 2% and 4%, respectively. During speaker testing, variance showed 2.147 for WER and 3.821 for SER. The variance is the highest among all tests due to one irregular result. Shuffle testing gave slightly better results, in comparison with the previous one. Sphinx, on average, finished a training in 9 min and 41 s on the indicated computer above (Table 2).

Table 2. CMUSphinx test descriptions

	WER %	Variance of WER	SER %	Variance of SER
90/10 speaker	2.200	2.147	4.350	3.821
90/10 shuffle	2.230	0.227	4.150	0.565

6 Discussion

After performing "90/10 shuffle" and "90/10 speaker" tests 10 times for each, together with testing different n-grams, the following results were obtained.

The most accurate n-grams for the current audio data starts from 3-grams. 3-grams are a common n-gram model for most languages, and based on the results, both tools match on that.

However, differences exist in experimental test results. Kaldi shows better performance on accuracy rates. The fact that Kaldi by far is the most accurate open-source toolkit is claimed also by other sources, including [3]. For variance of WER, Kaldi showed results below 1, whereas, Sphinx attained more than 2 on speaker testing. In terms of SER, variance was higher for both tools on speaker testing, however, Kaldi presented the highest. Furthermore, one of main advantages that CMUSphinx has on above-mentioned results is that the tool performed faster on the same dataset in training process than Kaldi (Table 3).

Table 3. Kaldi and CMUSphinx comparative test results

	Kaldi		CMUSphinx	
	90/10 speaker	90/10 shuffle	90/10 speaker	90/10 shuffle
WER%	1.020	0.368	2.200	2.230
SER%	2.699	1.363	4.350	4.150
Variance of WER	0.884	0.025	2.147	0.227
Variance of SER	4.750	0.270	3.821	0.565

Among all tests, shuffle showed better results than speaker testing. This is because while shuffle testing, tools do not attempt to recognize the voices they were not trained with. All in all, the most accurate result was gained on Kaldi shuffle testing, whereas, the least accurate test was speaker testing on CMUSphinx. Tools perform differently on variance results for WER and SER. Regarding speed, CMUSphinx finished faster than Kaldi.

7 Conclusions

This research paper investigated the application of speech recognition open-source toolkits on taxi call service systems. The toolkits - Kaldi and CMUSphinx were used to train and test a dataset of almost four hours.

The dataset, comprised of 100 addresses in Azerbaijani, was put into "90/10 speaker" and "90/10 shuffle" tests. Additionally, tools were examined in terms of accuracy with different n-grams. Tools coincide with results of n-gram testing, but differ on other two. Kaldi showed lower word and sentence error rates than Sphinx on speaker and shuffle tests. The lowest variances of WER and SER values belongs to Kaldi, however, Kaldi also holds the highest value for variances of SER. Sphinx presented the highest variance in WER values and moderate variance in SER values. It is worthy to note that, with the given hardware, CMUSphinx finished trainings faster than Kaldi.

With given results it could be concluded that for obtaining fast results CMUSphinx can be easy to configure and fast to train. Nevertheless, in order to have an accurate tool with relatively low level of variance, Kaldi should be chosen. Taxi companies will need to consume time and money for applying speech recognition systems to call centers, but will eventually gain return on investment with such an accurate tool as Kaldi.

Acknowledgment. This work has been carried out in Center for Data Analytics Research at ADA University and in Research and Development Laboratory at ATL Tech.

References

1. Matarneh, R., Maksymova, S., Lyashenko, V.V., Belova, N.V.: Speech recognition systems: a comparative review. IOSR J. Comput. Eng. **19**(5), 71–79 (2017). https://www.researchgate.net/publication/320673436_Speech_Recognition_Systems_A_Comparative_Review
2. Saon, G., et al.: English conversational telephone speech recognition by humans and machines, March 2017. https://arxiv.org/pdf/1703.02136v1.pdf

3. Gaida, C., Lange, P., Petrick, R., Proba, P., Malatawy, A., Suendermann-Oeft, D.: Comparing open-source speech recognition toolkits. In: 11th International Workshop on Natural Language Processing and Cognitive Science (2014). http://suendermann.com/su/pdf/oasis2014.pdf

4. Ravanelli, M., Parcollet, T., Bengio, Y.: The pytorch-kaldi speech recognition toolkit, February 2019. https://arxiv.org/pdf/1811.07453v2.pdf

5. Parthasarathi, S.H.K., Strom, N.: Lessons from building acoustic models with a million hours of speech, April 2019. https://arxiv.org/pdf/1904.01624.pdf

6. Wang, Q., et al.: VoiceFilter: targeted voice separation by speaker-conditioned spectrogram masking, February 2019. https://arxiv.org/pdf/1810.04826v4.pdf

7. Schatz, T., Feldman, N.H.: Neural network vs. HMM speech recognition systems as models of human cross-linguistic phonetic perception. In: 2018 Conference on Cognitive Computational Neuroscience (2018). http://thomas.schatz.cogserver.net/wp-content/uploads/2018/11/Schatz2018b.pdf

8. Fukuda, T., et al.: Data augmentation improves recognition of foreign accented speech. Interspeech, September 2018. https://www.isca-speech.org/archive/Interspeech_2018/pdfs/1211.pdf

9. Jain, A., Upreti, M., Jyothi, P.: Improved accented speech recognition using accent embeddings and multi-task learning. Interspeech, September 2018. https://www.isca-speech.org/archive/Interspeech_2018/pdfs/1864.pdf

10. Ragni, A., Upreti, M., Gales, M.J.F.: Automatic speech recognition system development in the "Wild". Interspeech, September 2018. https://www.isca-speech.org/archive/Interspeech_2018/pdfs/1085.pdf

11. Rustamov, S., Gasimov, E., Hasanov, R., Jahangirli, S., Mustafayev, E., Usikov, D.: Speech recognition in flight simulator. aegean international textile and advanced engineering conference. IOP Conf. Ser. Mater. Sci. Eng. **459** (2018). https://iopscience.iop.org/article/10.1088/1757-899X/459/1/012005/pdf

12. Forsyth, A.: Taxi Company Adopts Speech Recognition Technology. Computerworld, 26 October 2000

13. Forsyth, A.: Taxi fleet bets on speech recognition, Computerworld, 18 May 2001

14. Malcolm, A.: Cab firm books speech recognition system, Computerworld, 17 May 2001

15. Aida-Zade, K., Ardil, C., Rustamov, S.: Investigation of combined use of MFCC and LPC Features in Speech Recognition Systems. World Acad. Sci. Eng. Technol. Int. J. Comput. Inf. Eng. **1**, 2647–2653 (2007)

16. Aida-Zade, K., Rustamov, S.: The principles of construction of the azerbaijan speech recognition system. In: The 2nd International Conference "Problems of Cybernetics and Informatics", pp. 183–186 (2008)

17. Aida-Zade, K., Rustamov, S., Mustafayev, E.: Principles of construction of speech recognition system by the example of azerbaijan language. In: International Symposium on Innovations in Intelligent Systems and Applications, pp. 378–382 (2009)

18. Ayda-zade, K., Rustamov, S.: Research of cepstral coefficients for azerbaijan speech recognition system. Trans. Azerbaijan Natl. Acad. Sci. Inform. Control. Probl. **3**, 89–94 (2005)

19. Aida-zade, K., Xocayev, A., Rustamov, S.: Speech recognition using support vector machines. In: 10th IEEE International Conference on Application of Information and Communication Technologies, AICT 2016 (2016)

20. Juang, B.H., Lawrence, R.: Automatic Speech Recognition - A Brief History of the Technology Development, January 2005

21. Jurafsky, D., Martin, J.H.: Automatic speech recognition. In: Speech and Language Processing, pp. 285–291. Pearson Education (2008)

22. Emms, S.: Best Free Linux Speech Recognition Tools – Open Source Software, LinuxLinks 3 March 2018
23. Thompson, C.: Open Source Toolkits for Speech Recognition, Silicon Valley Data Science, 23 February 2017
24. Kaldi ASR. kaldi-asr.org. Accessed 16 April 2019
25. CMUSphinx Open Source Speech Recognition. cmusphinx.github.io. Accessed 16 Apr 2019
26. Bagiyev, A., Gurbanli, K., Mammadova, N., Nuriyeva, S.: Development of limited-vocabulary ASR for Azerbaijani. ACM Celebration of Women in Computing womENcourage 2018, October 2018. https://womencourage.acm.org/2018/wp-content/uploads/2018/07/womENcourage_2018_paper_26.pdf

Accuracy Comparison of Machine Learning Algorithms for Predictive Analytics in Higher Education

Sarfraz Nawaz Brohi[1(✉)], Thulasyammal Ramiah Pillai[1],
Sukhminder Kaur[1], Harsimren Kaur[2], Sanath Sukumaran[1],
and David Asirvatham[1]

[1] Taylor's University, Subang Jaya, Selangor, Malaysia
{SarfrazNawaz.Brohi,Thulasyammal.RamiahPillai,
Sukhminder.Kaur,Sanath,David.Asirvatham}@taylors.edu.my
[2] Hilti Asia IT Services, Petaling Jaya, Malaysia
simyaulekhl0@gmail.com

Abstract. In this research, we compared the accuracy of machine learning algorithms that could be used for predictive analytics in higher education. The proposed experiment is based on a combination of classic machine learning algorithms such as Naive Bayes and Random Forest with various ensemble methods such as Stochastic, Linear Discriminant Analysis (LDA), Tree model (C5.0), Bagged CART (treebag) and K Nearest Neighbors (KNN). We applied traditional classification methods to classify the students' performance and to determine the independent variables that offer the highest accuracy. Our results depict that the data with the 11 features using random forest generated the best accuracy value of 0.7333. However, we revised the experiment with ensemble algorithms to reduce the variance (bagging), bias (boosting) and to improve the prediction accuracy (stacking). Consequently, the bagging random forest outperformed other methods with the accuracy value of 0.7959.

Keywords: Predictive analytics · Machine learning · Higher education

1 Introduction

Likewise, most industries, data also plays an important role in higher education. Apart from traditional data, nowadays the education organizations are collecting data from social media and location-based streams. The collected data can be used to mine and construct predictive analytical models to enhance students' success rate. The data mining and analytics software can be utilized to provide immediate outcomes to the instructors about the learner's academic performance. Such tools can analyze patterns and predict outcomes such as potential cases of dropping out, requiring extra assistance or demanding challenging assignments [1]. Each learner has different behavior in different modules due to varying strengths and weaknesses. Predictive analytics in education can assist in differentiated learning [2]. Nowadays, higher education institutions are investing in building predictive analysis tools. A prediction model was built in the Nottingham Trent University (NTU) [3]. The application pointed out the four

M. H. Miraz et al. (Eds.): iCETiC 2019, LNICST 285, pp. 254–261, 2019.
https://doi.org/10.1007/978-3-030-23943-5_18

important factors such as library usage, attendance on campus, attendance in the tutorial and the use of the study portal. The software triggers the NTU instructor when the student's rate of engagement is decreasing. The use of predictive analysis can be useful for institutions to raise their profit, revenue, and financial planning. Education organizations are adopting data science practices to predict enrollment trends and operational needs [4]. Moreover, the number of dropouts has become a serious issue for the education organization. Completion and persistence rates are important because they measure how well an institution is serving its students.

According to the National Student Clearinghouse Research Center (2016), the persistence rate from year one to year two is 72.1%. Persistence rates continue to decline during and after the second year of colleges. The total completion rate of students who start college and completed within six years is 54.8% nationally. The persistence and completion rates are lower for part-time students. Rates of completion and persistence vary between two and four-year colleges, public and private, full-time versus part-time students [5]. In order to contribute to the domain of predictive analytics in higher education, in this research, we carried out an in-depth review of the research in the area and compared machine learning algorithms to evaluate their accuracy rate. The rest of this paper is structured as follows. Section 2 elaborates the predictive analytics models and other approaches developed using machine learning algorithms to achieve a wide variety of goals in the education sector. Section 3 briefly describes the methodology of this research. Section 4 contains a detailed discussion of our experiment results. Finally, we have discussed the future direction of this research in Sect. 5.

2   Related Work

A predictive analysis system was built to measure student satisfaction level towards an online course program based on data collected from students who enrolled in the summer-session at western university [6]. Each of the learners was given a survey that included questions on demographics, student satisfaction, and five predictor variables. Correlation, regression, and anova analysis were used to build the prediction model. The study found that the interaction framework with the inclusion of two predictors is internet self-efficacy and self-regulation. Instructors are encouraged to design more collaborative activities to enhance learners' interaction, and student satisfaction level can be improved by performing internet related-tasks. Furthermore, student retention is one of the major issues in higher institutions, especially in the online course program. Several researchers found that the rate of dropouts is increasing [7–9]. Shimin et al. [10] built prediction models using RapidMiner 5.3 that can predict whether a student will engage further after registering to a specific course. The prediction variables are built using J-48 and J-Rip decision tree [10]. The two algorithms tested resulted in producing a high-performance model that provides indicators for predicting the future of a student who has registered in a specific course program. A study was conducted in Delhi Technological University on building predictive analytics model based on the data collected from the National Informatics Center Delhi with the goals of predicting which students will enroll in the particular course and what is the current demand, which programs are trending, and which are becoming obsolete? [11]. The prediction models were built using the decision tree and neural network techniques. The outcomes show that the highest precision indicators were found in decision tree modeling.

The Social Networks Adapting Pedagogical Practice (SNAPP) is a predictive analytics software that is used by University of Wollongong to generate data visualization of user interaction, activity patterns of behavior on the forum [12]. SNAPP is used to map learners' level on engagement and activity to identify learners who are at risk of failing a subject due to lower participation. The tools are used to generate data reports, which include monitoring login frequency, dwell time and number of downloads. Connect for Success is another example of predictive analysis software used by Edith Cowan University (ECU), the system works based on enrolment data, and it is an early warning tool that is used to improve learner success and to improve graduation rates [13]. Automated Wellness Engine (AWE) is an alert system that is designed and built to improve learner engagement and retention rates at the University of New England. AWE is a software-based prediction model that is using emoticons to identify activity embedded in the student portal (myUNE) and another system that identify learners' interaction with the university and instructor. Based on the data collected by AWE, it is smart enough to predict learners who are at high-risk or struggling or may be experiencing disengagement from their course [14]. Open University Australia (OUA) developed Personalized Adaptive Study Success (PASS). PASS is a software tool that is used for predictive analysis to enhance student engagement and retention in an online environment. The model was built based on the individual characteristic, social web, curriculum and physical data collected from some systems [15]. The software assists learners to be aware of their upcoming academic performance and suggests what the students could do better to improve their performance.

3 Methodology

The data was obtained from the Kaggle [16, 17]. It contains 480 student records in rows and 16 features in the columns. The features are classified into three major groups such as Demographic Features (DF), Academic Background Features (AF), and Behavioral Features (BF). The demographic features are nationality, gender, place of birth, and parent responsible for the student. The academic background features consist of the educational stage, grade level, section ID, semester, topics and student absence days. The behavioral features are discussion groups, raised a hand in class, opening resources, viewing announcements, answering the survey by parents and parent school satisfaction. We have utilized these features using traditional classification methods such as random forest and Naive Bayes. Moreover, we applied ensemble algorithms to choose the correct features and to predict the students' performance with high accuracy. The data provider already pre-processed the data. There were no missing fields. The data was pre-processed again before the analysis using R software. The data was split into 75% for training and 25% for testing.

4   Results and Discussion

We used a combination of ensemble techniques that will improve the accuracy of machine learning algorithms results by reducing the variance (bagging), bias (boosting) and improve the accuracy of the prediction (stacking). However, we have compared the results using traditional methods such as random forest and naive Bayes. We tested the behavioral features such as group discussion and resources visited to determine whether these features are contributing factors in students' performance. Firstly, we checked the importance of the features of the dataset. The variables are shown in Fig. 1 circular bar chart and valued by importance in Table 1.

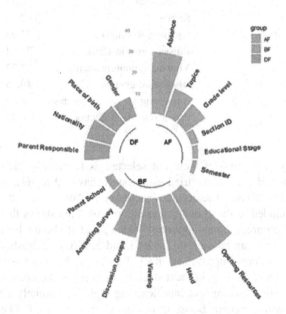

Fig. 1. The categories of the features.

We conclude that behavioral features are the most important features among the three groups of the features from the circular bar chart as shown in Fig. 1. Secondly, academic background features and finally demographic features. We used traditional classification methods to classify the students' performance and to determine the independent variables that offer the highest accuracy. The students' performance was classified using the random forest and Naive Bayes using all the independent characters. The most important 10 features are highlighted with bold font in Table 1. The best (10, 11 and 12) features were selected to classify the performance of the students. The data with the 11 features using random forest gave the best accuracy value (0.7333) as shown in Table 2. The more features taken does not promise higher accuracy. However, we must choose the correct features to improve the accuracy of the algorithms.

Table 1. The importance of features.

Features category	Feature	Importance	Place
Demographic Features	**Parent responsible for student**	**11.95**	**7**
	Nationality	**11.84**	**8**
	Place of birth	**10.10**	**10**
	Gender	9.42	11
Academic Background Features	**Student absence days**	**29.02**	**3**
	Topics	**13.64**	**6**
	Grade level	**11.38**	**9**
	Section ID	3.55	14
	Educational stage	2.73	15
	Semester	2.02	16
Behavioral Features	**Opening Resources**	**32.96**	**1**
	Raised hand in class	**32.94**	**2**
	Viewing Announcements	**27.77**	**4**
	Discussion groups	**19.16**	**5**
	Answering survey by parents	8.69	12
	Parent school satisfaction	4.20	13

All six behavioral variables were not selected as features to classify the performance in this case. However, we tried using one behavioral feature either group discussion or visited resources. The accuracy increased to 0.6917 when the feature visited resources was included in the classification algorithms. This shows that the behavioral variable visited resources is an important feature, and it should be included in the feature selection. This can be seen in Tables 1 and 3. It has established that the better importance of the features improves accuracy. Finally, we have utilized three ensemble methods namely boosting, bagging and stacking to improve the accuracy using all the sixteen features. The boosting machine learning algorithm namely basic tree model (C5.0) and stochastic gradient Boosting model (gbm) were used. The bagging algorithms such as bagged CART (treebag) and random forest (rf) were used. The results are given in Table 4. The ensemble stacking sub-models namely random forest, gbm, K Nearest Neighbors (KNN) and Linear Discriminant Analysis (LDA) were used and the results can be seen in Table 5. The accuracy of bagging random forest had outperformed the other methods with the accuracy of 0.7959. In this study, the ensemble bagging random forest had given the best result. We need to take more combination of features to increase the accuracy of the performance of the student. We can also improve the result by including more features such as hours spent in the module and the students' interest in the particular module to classify the students' performance in the future study.

Table 2. Accuracy using Random forest and Naive Bayes based on the importance of the features.

			95% Confidence interval	
		Accuracy	LB	UB
All 16 Independent variables	Random Forest	0.725	0.636	0.8025
	Naive Bayes	0.625	0.532	0.7117
10 Best Independent Variables	Random Forest	0.7	0.6096	0.7802
	Naive Bayes	0.6583	0.5662	0.7424
11 Best Independent Variables	Random Forest	**0.7333**	0.6449	0.8099
	Naive Bayes	0.6667	0.5748	0.7501
12 Best Independent Variables	Random Forest	0.7083	0.6184	0.7888
	Naive Bayes	0.5917	0.4982	0.6805

LB = Lower boundary UB = Upper boundary

Table 3. Accuracy with and without behavioral features using Random forest and Naive Bayes.

			95% Confidence interval	
		Accuracy	LB	UB
Without all behavioral variables	Random Forest	0.6583	0.5662	0.7424
	Naive Bayes	0.6	0.5066	0.6883
Behavioural variables *group discussion*	Random Forest	0.6583	0.5662	0.7424
	Naive Bayes	0.5417	0.4483	0.6329
Behavioural variables *visited resources*	Random Forest	**0.6917**	0.6009	0.7727
	Naive Bayes	**0.6917**	0.6009	0.7727

Table 4. Accuracy using boosting and bagging ensemble algorithm.

		Min	1st Qu	Median	Mean	3rd Qu	Max	NA's
Boosting	**C5.0**	0.6327	0.7262	0.7732	0.7771	0.8084	0.9375	0
	gbm	0.6531	0.7500	0.7708	0.7626	0.7917	0.8367	0
Bagging	**treebag**	0.6596	0.7372	0.7836	0.7749	0.8154	0.9167	0
	rf	0.6809	0.7672	0.8125	**0.7959**	0.8333	0.8750	0

Table 5. Accuracy using an ensemble stacking algorithm.

		95% Confidence interval	
	Accuracy	LB	UB
Random Forest	0.7396	0.64	0.8238
GBM	0.7188	0.6178	0.8058
LDA	0.7500	0.6512	0.8328
KNN	0.6354	0.5309	0.7313

5   Future Direction

Likewise, most of the recent research trends of technology such as Big Data, Cloud Computing, and Edge Computing, predictive analytics has several barriers to its implementation in education organization and various other sectors where security, privacy, quality and transparency of data play a critical role. Both instructors and students have raised data privacy and ownership concerns. The management must undertake the initiative to ensure ethics and permissions are maintained at all levels. As an example the University of California has addressed the concern of how students data privacy is violated, as the institution use a third party service platforms to gather data, the management realized that the vendors were using the student data to commercialize or sell their product [18]. There is an utmost need to formulate secure and privacy preserved data collection as well as analysis techniques. Most importantly, users of the data must be aware of the fair usage and treatment of their records. In education organizations, predictive analytics must be carried out in compliance with legal standards such as FERPA. Another concern raised on predictive analytics is the ethics, transparency and legal compliance on the use of data. Furthermore, data must be gathered from trusted sources, and systems must be in place to ensure that data is reliable, and analyzing such data would lead to suitable insights and appropriate actions. Predictive analytics also requires domain experts as well as data scientists [15]. The human brain has to make the decision, not analytic tools, hence the number of experts, background and wisdom do matter in making a decision. Data is just a help to produce a result. Lack of vision and familiarity is considered as the major barriers to predictive analytics.

Formulating predictive analysis modeling requires a lot of thought process to address the problem and the goal of predictive analytics modeling. The lack of data warehousing among institution makes the process of predictive analysis as a challenge. An institution cannot get the right type of data if there is no central repository of data that is accessible and transparent. The lack of data warehousing is also affecting the complexity of analytical tools. One of the major barriers to implementing data analytics in higher education is cost. Management tends to view analytics as an investment as the tools are expensive and tend to think it will not return the investment. To come up with predictive analysis, the first spending would be in human resources such as hiring a data analyst. The second comes to the data warehousing which includes the infrastructure, platform and services that are being purchased to build predictive analytics [19]. Apart from these barriers, the accuracy of the predictive model is also very important to make better decisions. Depending on the features of the dataset, a predictive model should be generated by trying a combination of various machine learning algorithms, and the model should be validated to obtain optimum accuracy. For example, in this research, based on our experience of data analytics, first, we found that random forest and naive bayes gave the accurate results, and then we enhanced the accuracy by using ensemble techniques with random forest. In the future direction of this research, we plan to use advanced deep learning algorithms to build a predictive analytics model for higher education.

References

1. Harel, E., Sitko, T.: Digital Dashboards: Driving Higher Education Decisions. Educause Center for Applied Research, Boulder (2003)
2. Johnson, L., Levine, A., Smith, R., Stone, S.: The 2010 Horizon report. The New Media Consortium, Austin, TX (2010). http://wp.nmc.org/horizon2010
3. Watson, H.J.: Business analytics insight: hype or here to stay? Bus. Intell. J. **16**(1), 4–8 (2011)
4. Burke, M., Parnell, A., Wesaw, A., Kruger, K.: Predictive analysis of student data (2017). https://www.naspa.org/images/uploads/main/PREDICTIVE_FULL_4-7-17_DOWNLOAD.pdf
5. Shapiro, D., et al.: Completing College: A National View of Student Completion Rates – Fall 2011 Cohort (Signature Report No. 14), December 2017. National Student Clearinghouse Research Center, Herndon, VA (2017)
6. Long, P., Siemens, G.: Penetrating the fog: analytics in learning and education. EDUCAUSE Rev. **46**, 30 (2011). http://net.educause.edu/ir/library/pdf/ELI7079.pdf
7. Willging, P.A., Johnson, S.D.: Factors that influence students' decision to dropout of online courses. J. Asynchronous Learn. Netw. **13**(3), 115–127 (2009)
8. Boston, W.E. et al.: Comprehensive Assessment of Student Retention in Online Learning Environments. School of Arts and Humanities, APUS. Paper 1 (2011)
9. Hoskins, S.L., Van Hooff, J.C.: Motivation and ability: which students use online learning and what influence does it have on their achievement? Communications **36**(2), 177–192 (2005)
10. Kai, S., et al.: Predicting student retention from behavior in an online orientation course
11. Hawkins, B.L.: Accountability, demand for information, and the role of the campus IT organization. In: Katz, R.N. (ed.) The Tower and the Cloud, pp. 98–104. Educause, Boulder (2008). www.educause.edu/thetowerandthecloud/PUB7202j
12. Bakharia, A., Dawson, S.: SNAPP: a bird's-eye view of temporal participant interaction. In: Proceedings of the 1st International Conference on Learning Analytics and Knowledge, pp. 168–173 (2011)
13. Jackson, G., Read, M.: Connect 4 success: a proactive student identification and support program, pp. 1–5. ECU, Australia (2012). fyhe.com.au/past_papers/papers12/Papers/9B.pdf
14. Leece, R., Hale, R.: Student engagement and retention through e-Motional intelligence. UNE, Australia (2009). http://www.educationalpolicy.org/events/R09/PDF/Leece_E-Motion.pdf
15. Atif, A., Richards, D., Bilgin, A., Marrone, M.: A panorama of learning analytics featuring the technologies for the learning and teaching domain. In: Carter, H., Gosper, M., Hedberg, J. (Eds.) Electric Dreams. Proceedings ascilite 2013, Sydney, pp. 68–72 (2013)
16. Amrieh, E.A., Hamtini, T., Aljarah, I.: Mining educational data to predict student's academic performance using ensemble methods. Int. J. Database Theor. Appl. **9**(8), 119–136 (2016)
17. Amrieh, E.A., Hamtini, T., Aljarah, I.: Preprocessing and analyzing educational data set using X-API for improving student's performance. In: 2015 IEEE Jordan Conference on Applied Electrical Engineering and Computing Technologies (AEECT), November 2015, pp. 1–5. IEEE (2015)
18. Nissenbaum, H.N.: Privacy in Context: Technology, Policy, and the Integrity of Social Life. Stanford Law Books, Stanford (2010)
19. Denley, T.: How predictive analytics and choice architecture can improve student success. Res. Pract. Assess. **9**(2), 61–69 (2014)

Generic Framework of Knowledge-Based Learning: Designing and Deploying of Web Application

Awais Khan Jumani[1(✉)], Anware Ali Sanjrani[2],
Fida Hussain Khoso[3], Mashooque Ahmed Memon[4],
Mumtaz Hussain Mahar[5], and Vishal Kumar[1]

[1] Faculty of Science and Technology, ILMA University, Karachi, Sindh, Pakistan
awaisjumani@yahoo.com, hit.vishal@outlook.com
[2] Department of Computer Science, University of Baluchistan, Quetta, Pakistan
anwar.csd@gmail.com
[3] Department of Basic Sciences, Dawood University of Engineering
and Technology, Karachi, Pakistan
fidahussain.khoso@duet.edu.pk
[4] Department of Computer Science, Benazir Bhutto Shaheed University,
Layari, Karachi, Pakistan
pashamorai786@gmail.com
[5] Department of Computer Science, Shah Abdul Latif University Khairpur,
Khairpur Mir's, Sindh, Pakistan
mhmahar@salu.edu.pk

Abstract. Learning technology was used as standalone software to install in a particular system, which needs to buy learning software of a particular subject. It was costly and difficult to search CD/DVD of the particular program in the market. Nowadays the trend of learning is changed and people are learning via the internet and it is known as Electronic Learning (E-learning). Several e-learning web applications are available which are providing more stuff about students and it fulfills requirements. The aim of this paper is to present a well-structured, user-friendly framework with the web application for e-learning, which does not need any subscription. The experiment was conducted with 691 students and teachers, the result shows 91.98% of participants were satisfied with the proposed E-learning system.

Keywords: Distance learning · Web applications · Graphical user interface

1 Introduction

The Internet was implemented and more established for educational organizations in the 1970s for communication system [1], instructors have been aware of its enormous perspective as a learning tool. Nowadays underdeveloped nations are excited to avail possibilities of online learning to convey actual cost, easily accessible and modern education of all ages and people backgrounds and geography. In the modern era, where the workers with good education are preferred as compared with workers with less

M. H. Miraz et al. (Eds.): iCETiC 2019, LNICST 285, pp. 262–272, 2019.

knowledge and lifetime learning is realized as key to the nonstop achievement of modern civilization [2, 3]. E-learning is compared by many as the feasible solution to the problem providing the funds mandatory to smooth lifetime learning [4, 5].

However, present practices and theories of e-learning are not lucid, significance and scalable [6, 7]. Although most distinguish learning frameworks are available and it's likely to enhance prominent learning and experience of learning at all stages, people have realized its hitches and presently still too boundless to commit it seriously [8]. While several works have been revealed as well as written for e-learning strategy, but it still looks incapable to really express how, when or where eLearning should best be used [9, 10]. This paper shows that when it can be using E-Learning and what kind of eLearning should be used in our schools and colleges. Some successful results have been taken from different schools while using eLearning management. E-Learning considered as a globally that impacts much more of board learning [11, 12].

E-Learning activities collaborating technologies and communication system is more progress in the learning involvement [13]. It has been impending to renovate the way to learn and teach transversely the board [14]. It can increase values and enlarge participation in lifetime learning. It cannot swap lecturers and teachers, besides prevailing methods it can improve the quality and reach of their teaching and decrease the time consumed on administration. It can facilitate every beginner to accomplish his or her perspective and help to construct an educational workforce endowed to change. It makes imaginable a truly aspiring system for a future learning civilization.

1.1 Web Applications

Evolution of web application is using everywhere and these are dynamic websites, which is combination of server-side and client-side programming [15, 16]. Some of the facilities, for example, interacting with users, linking to back-end databases, and creating results to browsers. Web Application Frameworks are a group of many libraries programs, modules, and tools structured in an architecture system so it allows developers to construct and maintain complex web application program projects with their efficient methodology [17]. Some of the web application is updating programming and stimulate code reuses for common functions and classes. Those can be created dynamically website that can be taking JavaScript for making dynamically webpages. ASP.NET user can use object-oriented programming with C sharp, it can give a lot of facilities to the user for making practical or useful web application [18].

Entity Framework Fundamental is the newest version of the lightweight Entity Framework designed to work with .NET Fundamental applications. Suppose, ASP. NET Essential has been revised from the ground up and contains several new ways to perform. One of those is the introduction of the Track Graph technique for controlling multifarious data in disconnected situations such as Model View Controller (MVC) or Web API applications. The Track Graph technique is new in Entity Framework Essential and offers a simple way to repeat over a graph of objects that the perspective to begin tracking and to apply personalized code based on the type of entity and other benchmarks [19]. Early traditional web applications have not given the guarantee

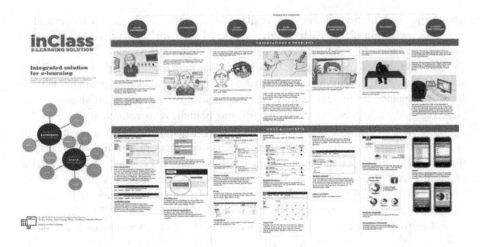

Fig. 1. Traditional web applications

of and also additional plug-in required for viewing the lectures on flash player. Figure 1 shows a traditional application interface where videos or audio lectures are not available.

2   Literature Review

Many researchers have provided research work regarding this work. Nagarajan and Jiji have introduced that online education has three major activities: Design, application and proper post-implementation assessments [19]. It reduces the cost and time efficiency, which is the main factor of our education and this framework have improved the quality of e-learning. But it gives the particular subjects knowledge environment and that efficiency.

Kumar et al. have proposed an E-learning framework for disabled persons whose arms are disabled to access systems. The technique of this framework is that disable student can use a computer by their voice control and learn by the e-learning software. ICT gives a lot of features for them but still, the framework has limitation for disabled persons to access [20].

Gopalan et al. have discussed in his research about the student of rural areas, which did not attend schools intermittently due to less source of income and working. E-learning education makes it possible if a student could not attend classes than they can learn these all thing from smartphones having e-learning app for students and they can interact with the teacher by using an application as like real environment [21]. Another research work given by Zhang and Goel, they have compared that e-learning technology usually used in higher education institutes. During the comparisons, they make two possibilities of results, first e-learning synthesized by identifying a relevant framework and second theoretical results. After getting results of e-learning it shows that it is more appropriate as compared to theoretical learning [22].

Similarly, Wu et al. were reviewed that e-learning is growing from 2005 and many of the research papers on their efficiency on their better effectiveness, a lot of the ratio of using e-learning in Croatia. It shows the relationship between user and perceptions of user characteristics; it gives limited atmosphere in web application and security issues concerned [23]. Similarly, Mosharraf et al. have applied the learning management system for the elementary schools and achieved successful results during the implementation. In the learning management system for kids, it gives more accurate results and students get more serious interest to learn through-out learning management system [24].

Further, Patel et al. has been explored that influence of e-learning in the life of learner that is a brilliant way to teach students using e-learning tools. Using e-learning tools they can enormously increase the learning process. The important remunerations of e-learning are that they can make it always on and update through connect the organizations [25]. Hence, Noesgaard and Ørngreen [26] have revealed that e-learning is more effective as compared to face to face learning methods. After the analysis of the student's perspective e-learning gives more good result and teachers should apply the method e-learning. Furthermore, Jumani et al. [27] have designed an application for kids to measure their mental approach using web application thus that application shows the interest of kids in learning with traditional and game-based learning using web application. He has taken their results which are overcome to traditional learning methodology.

3   Design and Development of Proposed Framework

Initially, the intranet environment is created for application testing. Inbounds of the firewall involved with the port exception, which enable to send and receive the request and response from the centralized server. Moreover, SQL Server has installed for storing, retrieving and manipulating records accompanied with Data Definition Language (DDL) and Data Manipulation Language (DML). Furthermore, C# integrated development environment along with ASP.Net technology has used for calling the classes. Namespaces and different libraries are used to accomplish the task. Cascade style sheet is played a crucial role in designing the application interface. Proposed application based on a few tabs which are given below with its description.

1. Video: This tab provides all the lectures of their subjects in the form of Videos and these can run on any media player or built-in flash player and these are special peculiarities. These videos also able to download and store on a computer drive. Once it reaches on end different thumbnail suggested the other related videos and these are similar to available media sites but different in functioning.
2. Documents: In this tab, more than 8000 doc or docx files have already stored and it is also related to their selected subjects. Document viewer control is used for getting a preview of the document and have feature, which enables to share this one with their friends. Moreover, the document can be stored and send via Bluetooth device to their mobiles.

3. PDF Document: This tab provides to students approximately 9000 pdf documents on different topics based on their subjects. Students are able to download the document and take a snapshot as well. Furthermore, all functionalities of zooming and rotating along with a quick search are integrated with the portable document viewer.

4. PowerPoint Presentations: Several pptx or ppt has already stored in that tab for providing different lectures slides with pictorial representation and it also enables to students to convert these presentations into a compact disc. Different themes and styles accompanied by slides have installed predefined and these are constant nobody can change it but only are able to download it or directly print through-out the printer. Users can also view these slides directly by clicking on the required topic or author name. For this, Microsoft office built-in components and libraries have been used from visual studio 2013 and some online other packages.

Some snapshots of the web application are given in Figs. 2, 3 and 4. Allah Dino Jumani (ADJ) E-learning application provide better platform for teachers and students In Fig. 2 user can first, sign-up an account and after it sent an activation link to the user email address. Once the user clicks on provided on link account successfully done with that process and the user can log in with a credential such as a user name and password. Moreover, easy and connect process with ADJ E-learning System gives notifications as well with the passage of time. After the login approvals, the user can easily access many different services.

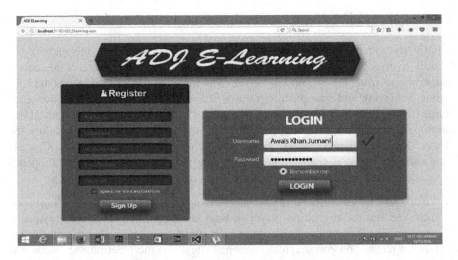

Fig. 2. Illustrates login and signup screen

In Fig. 3 user can see four tabs in front of their screen. In video tab user can easily watch any video of their concerned subject, it can be synchronized and bookmark of that video. Also, it can be downloaded directly and that can share it with the social network. This tab will offer some different aspect of e-learning any user can be upload video with concerned lectures and give online comments.

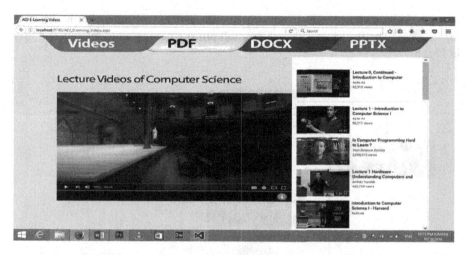

Fig. 3. Displays video lectures

In Fig. 4 user can see the pdf lectures of their related subject and it can be downloaded or directly view in Adobe Acrobat reader. It can be shared online in any social network with other users; every pdf lecture is updated with new technologies and close with authenticating references.

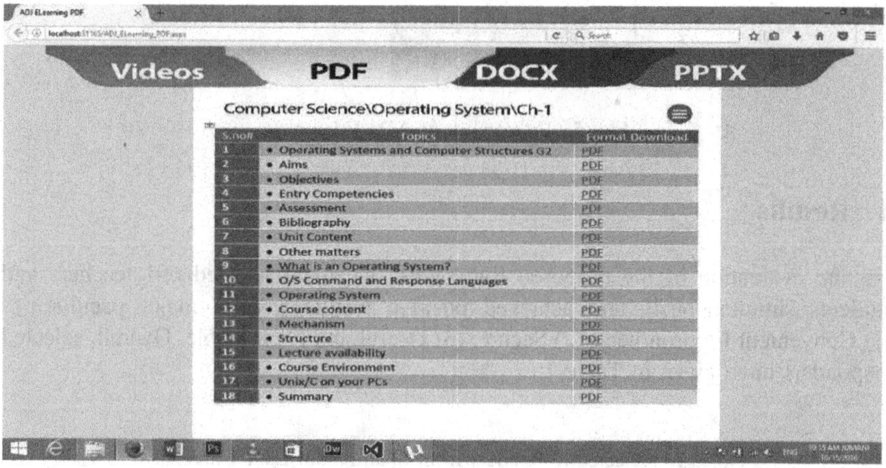

Fig. 4. Displays PDF lecture topics

In the proposed framework, initially, the user should have their email address of an account. The user can sign up their account, it requests to server and server sends the activation account link to their given email address. If an account activation link acknowledges from the given email account, it will be activated. After confirmation user can sign in from the inbox of ADJ E-Learning web application similar to Yahoo and Gmail and then user interact with all present functionalities. If a link which has sent will not confirm by the user it will expire and ADJ has resent option is available for next use. The flowchart shows the overall process of sign up to log out of a user in Fig. 5.

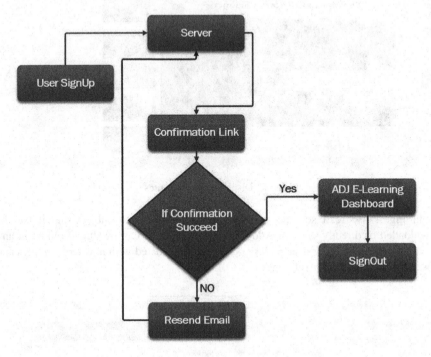

Fig. 5. Framework of ADJ E-learning

4   Results

For the evaluation of the proposed framework, we have selected 691 teachers and students simultaneously and achieved positive results from 4 major peculiarities (1) Convenient Environment, (2) Secure, (3) Useful and (4) Reliable. Overall, selected responders have given in Table 1.

Table 1. Selected responders from Shah Abdul Latif University

Teacher	
Male	67
Female	54
Student	
Male	235
Female	335

Table 1 shows that 67 male (M) teachers were chosen from SALU and given 60 responds from M teachers accompanied with 89.55% positive satisfaction response. From the side of female (F) teachers, 54 were chosen and 49 has given respond with positive satisfaction accompanied with 90.74%.

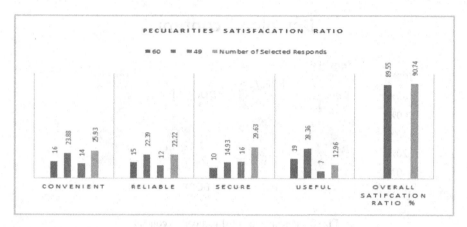

Fig. 6. Teachers peculiarities satisfaction ratio

On the other side, 235 M students have chosen and 225 students have given respond along with 95.74% satisfaction, 335 F students were chosen and 295 has to respond along with 88.06% satisfaction.

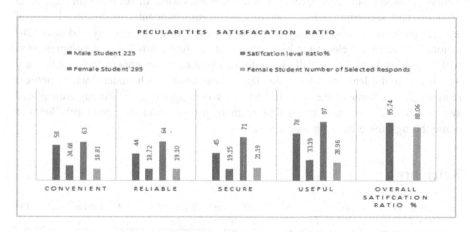

Fig. 7. Student peculiarities satisfaction ratio

Figures 6 and 7 represents that among the four aspects, respondents have given reviews that, presented application more convenient, useful for students and will give fruitful results to up-coming generation.

During testing of the proposed application by selected responded it is observed, the majority of responded were interested to download videos in contrast to a text document. Figure 8 illustrates focused contents while testing.

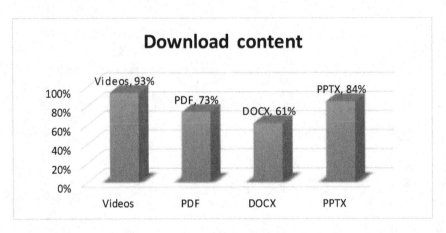

Fig. 8. Percentages of downloaded content

5 Conclusion

We have presented a convenient framework wrapped with several peculiarities for providing academic stuff regarding their subjects. There are several e-learning platform available, based on the users expectation features are varied. In our platform there is no need for any subscription by using this application student can download several lectures presentation without any cost. Technology grows day by day and also educational institutes use electronic learning system. In future this E-Learning application will be used in institutes, it will give a lot of facilities to students in their studies and with the help of e-learning, technology teacher can easily teach students with graphical representations. Some of the students can take advantages from E-learning educational system which did not give much time to their institutes and they can easily learn at home through the e-learning web application.

References

1. Dewath G.: An introduction to e-Learning a study of the current state of e-Learning in the United Kingdom (2004). http://idp.bl.uk/4DCGI/education/e_learning/index.a4d. Accessed 23 Mar 2019
2. van der Molen, H.F., et al.: Interventions to prevent injuries in construction workers. Cochrane Database Syst. Rev. **2**(2), 12, CD006251 (2018)
3. Machin, S., Vignoles, A.: What's the Good of Education?: The Economics of Education in the UK. Princeton University Press, Princeton (2018)

4. Lo, K.W.K., Ip, A.K.Y., Lau, C.K., Wong, W.S., Ngai, G., Chan, S.C.F.: Integrating majors and non-majors in an international engineering service-learning programme: course design, student assessments and learning outcomes. In: Shek, D.T.L., Ngai, G., Chan, S.C.F. (eds.) Service-Learning for Youth Leadership. QLA, vol. 12, pp. 145–163. Springer, Singapore (2019). https://doi.org/10.1007/978-981-13-0448-4_9

5. Moore, J.L., Dickson-Deane, C., Galyen, K.: e-Learning, online learning, and distance learning environments: are they the same? Internet High. Educ. **14**, 129–135 (2011)

6. Lin, C.Y., Huang, C.K., Zhang, H.: Enhancing employee job satisfaction via E-learning: the mediating role of an organizational learning culture. Int. J. Hum. Comput. Interact. **35**, 1–12 (2018). https://doi.org/10.1080/10447318.2018.1480694

7. Donnell, E.O.: Students' Views of E-Learning: The Impact of Technologies on Learning in Higher Education in Ireland. Dublin Institute of Technology ARROW@DIT IGI Global, pp. 204–226 (2012)

8. Stepanyan, K., Littlejohn, A., Margaryan, A.: Sustainable e-Learning: toward a coherent body of knowledge. Int. Forum Educ. Technol. Soc. (IFETS) **16**(2), 91–102 (2013). https://www.j-ets.net/ETS/journals/16_2/9.pdf

9. Klašnja-Milićević, A., Vesin, B., Ivanović, M., Budimac, Z.: E-learning personalization based on hybrid recommendation strategy and learning style identification. Comput. Educ. **56**(3), 885–899 (2011)

10. Liebowitz, J., Frank, M. (eds.): Knowledge management and e-learning. CRC Press, Boca Raton (2016)

11. Kingsley, O.S., Ismail, M.Z.: Web based E-learning system for pre-school kids. Int. J. Educ. Learn. Train. (IJELT) **1**(1), 1–14 (2015)

12. Gu, X., Wu, B., Xu, X.: Design, development, and learning in e-Textbooks: what we learned and where we are going. J. Comput. Educ. **2**(1), 25–41 (2015)

13. Chan, T.W., et al.: Interest-driven creator theory: towards a theory of learning design for Asia in the twenty-first century. J. Comput. Educ. **5**(4), 435–461 (2018)

14. Tam, V., Lam, E.Y., Fung, S.T.J.: Comput. Educ. **1**, 335 (2014). https://doi.org/10.1007/s40692-014-0016-8

15. Colton, P., Sarid, U., Lindsey, K.E., Haynie, J.G., Langston, M.D.: System and method for exposing the dynamic web server-side. US Patent 9,798,524, 24 October 2017

16. Vassilakis, C., Lepouras, G.: Controlled caching of dynamic WWW pages. In: Hameurlain, A., Cicchetti, R., Traunmüller, R. (eds.) DEXA 2002. LNCS, vol. 2453, pp. 9–18. Springer, Heidelberg (2002). https://doi.org/10.1007/3-540-46146-9_2

17. Zhou, D., Djatej, A., Sarikas, R., Senteney, D.: Framework and guidelines to industry web portal business. In: Idemudia, E.C. (ed.) Handbook of Research on Technology Integration in the Global World, pp. 407–421. IGI Global, Hershey (2019)

18. Al-Farsi, A., Al-Mahruqi, A., Vrindavanam, J.: Application system for file uploading using ASP.NET. Int. J. Appl. Inform. Syst. (IJAIS) **7**(5), 11–15 (2014)

19. Nagarajan, P., Jiji, G.W.: Online educational system (e- learning). Int. J. u- e-Serv. Sci. Technol. **3**(4), 37–48 (2010)

20. Kumar, K.A., Ravi, S., Srivatsa, S.K.: Effective e-learning approach for students with learning disabilities. Int. J. Sci. Eng. Res. **2**(11), 1–5 (2011)

21. Gopalan, A., Karavanis, S., Army, H., Payne, T., Sloman, M.: Smartphone based e-Learning. In: International Conference on Computer Supported Education (CSEDU), pp. 161–170 (2011)

22. Zhang, P., Goel, L.: Is e-Learning for everyone? An internal-external framework of e-Learning initiatives. MERLOT J. Online Learn. Teach. **7**(2), 193–205 (2011)

23. Wu, B., Xu, W., Ge, J.: Experience effect in e-Learning research. In: International Conference on Applied Physics and Industrial Engineering, pp. 2067–2074 (2012)

24. Mosharraf, M., Taghiyareh, F., Nasirifard, P.: Developing a child-centered LMS to enhance learning and creativity of students in elementary school. Bull. IEEE Tech. Comm. Learn. Technol. **15**(3), 10–13 (2013)
25. Patel, H., Patel, A., Shah, P.: Impact of e-learning in the development of student life. Int. J. Res. Eng. Technol. (IMPACT: IJRET) **2**(4), 235–238 (2014)
26. Noesgaard, S.S., Ørngreen, R.: The effectiveness of e-Learning: an explorative and integrative review of the definitions, methodologies and factors that promote e-learning effectiveness. Electron. J. e-Learning **13**(4), 278–290 (2015)
27. Jumani, A.K., Memon, M.A., Kartio, M.A.: A technique to measure students' mental approach using web and game based e-Learning application. Ann. Emerg. Technol. Comput. (AETiC) **2**(3), 19–26 (2018)

The Bearing of Culture upon Intention to Utilize D-learning Amongst Jordanian University Students: Modernizing with Emerging Technologies

Saleem Issa Al-Zoubi[1] and Maaruf Ali[2(✉)]

[1] Department of Computer Science, Irbid National University, Irbid, Jordan
[2] IAER, Kemp House, 160 City Road, London EC1V 2NX, UK
maaruf@ieee.org

Abstract. An investigation into the variables that have a bearing on the acceptance of D-learning (Digital-learning) services such as Electronic-learning and Mobile-learning, in two universities of Jordan is presented along with a discussion on modernizing in particular m-learning with emerging technologies. The study fuses the Unified Theory of Acceptance and Use of Technology (UTAUT) model with the cultural paradigm. 100 valid questionnaires distributed to random Jordanian students in two cities were used to collect the primary data. The IBM SPSS® (Statistical Package for the Social Sciences) software platform was used to analyze the data. The validity of the overall model was proven statistically with an acceptable data match with the measurement model. The findings show that the factor with the greatest bearing on "*Intention to use M-learning*" is the "*Attitude toward using M-learning*". Whilst the influence with the greatest indirect bearing on "*Intention to use M-learning*" is "*Compatibility*". The conclusions are that the: *cultural factor* has a significant and positive impact on the "*perceived usefulness*" and "*perceived ease of use*". "*Perceived usefulness*" and "*perceived ease of use*" have the greater impact on the "*customers' attitude*", which consequently influences the students' "*intention to use M-learning services*". Emerging technologies such as the Cloud, AI (Artificial Intelligence) and the Blockchain and how they may be utilized to enhance the delivery of M-learning is discussed throughout the paper.

Keywords: Unified theory of acceptance and use of technology model ·
UTAUT · D-learning · Mobile learning services · Mobile learning ·
M-learning · Culture · E-learning

1 Introduction

1.1 M-learning

M-learning (Mobile-learning) is a type of learning which can potentially happen anytime or anywhere through the use of a portable electronic computing device [1], which can be either online or offline. Furthermore, this method of learning creates a more personalized learning experience [2]. Additionally, through the use of portable,

M. H. Miraz et al. (Eds.): iCETiC 2019, LNICST 285, pp. 273–282, 2019.

networked mobile and cellular devices, the users access learning applications in a selection of diverse contexts when interacting within their environment or with other users. Moreover, m-learning is increasingly growing and moving from asynchronous to synchronous instructor-to-learner communication and content delivery, owing to the rapid advances in computer networking and multimedia technology. Specifically, asynchronous learning encompasses gaining information without instructor-learner interaction; such as reading and understanding an online article on a mobile device solely by the user. On the other hand, synchronous learning comprises of active back and forth instructor-learner interaction, such as the learner participating in an online webinar by posting questions or making comments using video conferencing tool or a smartphone. M-learning is not restricted by time-and-space limitation, as it has now become a method that allows both educators and students to communicate utilizing a variety of learning tools through the use of mobile gadgets [3]. Even synchronous m-learning can be asynchronous in the sense that the human lecturer may be replaced by a synthetic AI entity performing the rôle of the peripatetic. The student may access this virtual person anytime. The Cloud will also offer more flexibility in delivery and access to the learning material. The use of mobile devices being many, are still traditional voice only and increasingly real-time video calls, internet browsing/shopping and social networking site access, email exchanges, capturing and sharing multimedia files (pictures/videos) and playing ever increasing amount of interactive networked games. Thus, the handheld devices function with one of these three common modes and qualities, namely that of: utility, communication or fun/leisure [4, 5].

2   Literature Review

According to [6], m-learning is a significant alternative platform for learning services in which having the knowledge on the influencing elements for m-learning acceptance amongst higher education learners is crucial. Apart from that, as stated in [7], an individual's volition and conscious participation in m-learning activities are some of the success keys for m-learning.

Further, when factors associated with acceptance of mobile learning are identified, the universities implementing this learning method can improve on the delivery of services to the students. Apart from that, when these factors are incorporated into the business process, education and learning will become more efficient and there will consequently be an increase in the loyalty of the students [5–8]. However, according to [9], the university would have to take into careful consideration the potential factors that may influence the students' intention and understand how these factors could entice them to use it in order to invest in the development of university delivered mobile services and content properly. Nonetheless, it would be difficult for the students to acquire the pedagogical information if they fail to accept the new technology designed to deliver it in the first place. Reassurances must be offered such as privacy and security. This may be enabled by the use of the blockchain technology. Payment processing in cryptocurrency will also open up m-learning to an even greater audience and consumers beyond just university students, with a potential transnational market base.

Aside from that, considering that the market for mobile learning has gradually become global, cultural difference also becomes an important factor. Thus, universities or training organizations should have the knowledge of cultural difference so that they can earn a significant competitive edge [8, 10, 11]. According to [10], the cultural perspectives of m-learning in Malaysia is an aspect that has yet to be covered. However, it must be pointed out here that m-learning needs to be cognizant of both mobile users and nomadic users. Nomadic users make use of the computing nodes, devices and platforms around them, whilst mobile users carry their own devices. M-learning needs to be deployable, accessible and functional across all types of devices, ensuring operationality when a user is offline too. Content may be downloaded for future offline use. There is thus a need to be a universal accessibility learning approach for the mobile and nomadic computing age. Inasmuch as to embrace the often, primary rôle of the user's mobility and communication to m-learning. So, the effectiveness of existing models still needs to be enhanced, to which researchers have pointed out parameters that must be considered with culture being one. With the widespread proliferation of Internet of Things (IoT) objects, it must be appreciated that m-learning devices are themselves also IoTs which may be networked to other IoTs. This study is paramount in consolidating the chasm in the development of services in order to create more efficiency and relevance in the education environment – all of which could be achieved through the expansion and use of the UTAUT model.

3 Theoretical Background

3.1 UTAUT (Unified Theory of Acceptance and Use of Technology) Model

[12] had formerly conducted a study to draw a comparison between the similarities and differences amongst established models and theories of user acceptance and from their studies they formulated the UTAUT. The steps to deriving this model involved comparisons utilizing the: technology acceptance model (TAM) [13], theory of planned behavior (TPB) [14], theory of reasoned action (TRA) [15] and several others. The resultant UTAUT model was made to counter the problems being faced by researchers in the sphere of IT during the construction of their study framework as an attempt to create understanding towards the usage of technology amongst the users [12].

Further, [13] added that acceptance models established in the past had some successful records in an estimate of 40% in their prediction accuracy of the adoption of IT (Information Technology). By contrast, [12] reported that the use of their UTAUT model helped prediction of the uptake of IT in the region of 70%, in their study of the users' intention. The UTAUT model is also appropriate in predicting equally, for a large range of groups, the individual acceptance of IT. Scales that have been adopted in previous acceptance models were brought together to develop new scales and tested for further enhancements [12].

For predicting the users' behavioral intention and the behavior of use, four constructs are used by UTAUT. These constructs are [12]:

(a) social influence;
(b) expectancy of effort to be expended on the task;
(c) performance expectancy;
(d) conditions that will facilitate undertaking the job.

With respect to the linkage between these constructs, behavior intention and behavior of use is moderated by four primary factors including the [12]:

(a) age;
(b) gender;
(c) voluntariness and
(d) experience [12].

Figure 1 illustrates the UTAUT model, whilst Fig. 2 illustrates the proposed modified model.

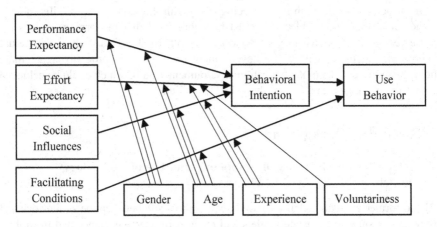

Fig. 1. The original UTAUT model [12].

3.2   Research Model Factors

Culture Factor (CF)
The word "culture" herein is understood to be this definition, "the collective pro-gramming of the mind which distinguishes the members of one group or category of people from another" [16] or basically expressed, "culture is" [any] "shared values of a particular group of people" [17]. Further, according to [18], culture indicates the individual's "core values and beliefs which" [were] "formed" [during] "childhood and reinforced throughout life", while [19] define culture being, "the beliefs, philosophy, shared values, attitudes, customs, norms, rituals, common practices, and traditions which govern the ways of living of a group of people." Culture may also be expressed in terms of norms and values, where values, according to [20], are what is worth acting upon and acquiring, and are shaped by involvement and familiarity with parents, school life, personal religion, and the media, while norms as highlighted by [21–23], encompass any shared beliefs with regard to behavior. On the other hand, [24] observes

culture as discrepancies that occur between the beliefs, values, and motivations of groups that are dissimilar from one another, while other scholars such as Samovar [25] perceive culture as the sum of values, beliefs, attitude, experience, knowledge, religion, meanings, hierarchies, spatial relationships, rôles, universal concepts, notions of time and possessions and material objects attained along the timeline of generations by the group and individuals.

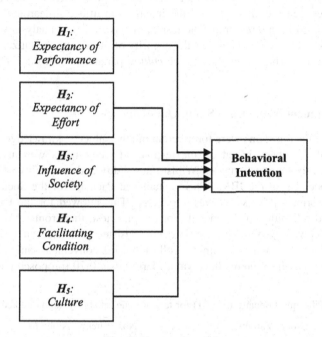

Fig. 2. Proposed model.

3.3 The Hypotheses

The following are the research alternative hypotheses factors for this case study, as shown in Fig. 2:

H_1: The *expectancy of performance* has a correlation with *intention* to utilize mobile learning.

H_2: The *expectancy of effort* to be expended has a correlation with the *intention* to utilize m-learning.

H_3: The *influence of the society* (*social influence*) has a correlation with the *intention* to use m-learning.

H_4: *Facilitating conditions* has a correlation with the *intention* to utilize mobile learning.

H_5: *Culture* has a correlation with the *intention* to use m-learning.

4 Research Methodology

This research employed 100 Jordanian university students (of both genders) aged 20 years and above as the respondents. The data was extracted from participants filling in online questionnaires from www.surveyshare.com. This contained one part which represented several constructs. The Likert scale (with five points) was used to score the user's acceptance level. This was then statistically post-processed to calculate the correlation between the elements and the intention to utilize m-learning. Regression analysis was used in this research. The results of this statistical analysis were used to create a framework that encompassed the capacity of measuring the citizens eagerness to mobile learning. Thus, validation to the *culture* parameter with the UTAUT model was ascertained.

4.1 Development of the Case Study Questionnaire

The writing of the questions were for ascertaining the subjects' knowledge of access to the e-material. Feedback based on the respondent's comments were used to make minor changes to the questionnaire. Whilst the validity and readability of the content were confirmed. Using the IBM SPSS® (Statistical Package for the Social Sciences) software platform, a pilot study was conducted. This allowed for the testing of the validation and reliability of the model. For the pilot test, the Cronbach's alpha reliability measure was used to test for internal consistency. Factor analysis was also conducted on the data, with the samples collected using convenient sampling. Table 1, below, shows that all the items have values larger than 0.70 (proposed cut-off).

Table 1. Pilot questionnaire ($n = 31$) for test of scale reliability, alpha ranked in order.

Order	Variable	No. of items	Alpha (a)
1st	*Culture*	4	0.897
2nd	*Behavioral intention*	4	0.874
3rd	*Expectancy of effort*	4	0.811
$=4^{th}$	*Expectancy of performance*	4	0.784
$=4^{th}$	*Influence of society*	4	0.784
6th	*Facilitating conditions*	4	0.747

5 Data Analysis and Results

The assessment of the structural model with respect to the model being measured was undertaken using SPSS analysis including towards the inner model. The proposed requirements in [26] were investigated. The hypotheses were tested by the method of bootstrapping for determining the path coefficients' significance levels.

The interactions between the parameters of the research model was determined using multiple regression analysis. The test indicated some influences between the factors. Three regression models, containing the five hypotheses, were used for the analysis, as shown in Table 2.

Table 2. Summary of the research alternative hypotheses.

Hypotheses	Variable		β	Supported
H_1	*Expectancy of Performance*»»»	Behavioral intention to use (BI)	0.387**	Yes
H_2	*Expectancy of Effort*	»»» Behavioral intention to use (BI)	0.411*	Yes
H_3	*Influence of Society*	»»» Behavioral intention to use (BI)	0.217**	Yes
H_4	*Facilitating Conditions*	»»» Behavioral intention to use (BI)	0.342**	Yes
H_5	*Culture*	»»» Behavioral intention to use (BI)	0.477**	Yes

$*p < 0.1$; $**p < 0.05$; $***p < 0.01$.

6 Discussion

The readiness to utilize mobile learning services amongst Jordanian students was positively identified. The parameters or factors identified and tested were: *culture, expectancy of effort, expectancy of performance, facilitating conditions, influence of society* and *intention*. As mobile learning service usage amongst students should be maximized, the educational providers must consider them carefully regarding their optimization. The collection of the data must, however, cover a broader spectrum of the population in order to be more nationally representative. The model for Jordanian university m-learning students took in constructs from the UTAUT model. With respect to *culture*, optimizing *expectancy of effort, expectancy of performance, influence of society, intention* and *facilitating conditions* will all contribute to an increase in m-learning in universities. The intent to utilize internet delivered services was positive if the participants were convinced that the use of the internet would result in an increase in their efficiency of learning.

For the widespread uptake of D-learning (Digital-learning) which are: m-learning and e-learning - it is essential that it embraces and utilizes emerging technologies. These pioneering technologies include, viz.: cloud delivery; artificial intelligence; the blockchain for added security, and integration with diverse IoT devices. Mobile as well as nomadic users must be catered for, taking into account transnational cultural aspects that need to modify the user interface. Thus, the plasticity of the user interface must also be carefully approached.

7 Conclusions

The last decade has seen exponential growth in d-learning (e- and m-learning) in the developed nations. This has not gone unnoticed in the rest of the world, especially in the rapidly developing and lucrative emerging nations of the Middle East. This is because of the governmental plans of many of these oil rich nations to increase the digital literacy of their national subjects. These countries must employ the technology of the Internet coupled with emerging technologies such as the Cloud, Artificial Intelligence, Deep Learning and the Blockchain - to make it appeal to a wider consumer base beyond just the academia sector. Unfortunately, internet penetration amongst the population is still lagging for nearly all the Middle Eastern countries, compared to the rest of the world. In fact, comparatively few mobile learning websites exist in the Arabic speaking world compared to the Western World.

The outcomes generated by this study has positively identified that to increase the intention to use d-learning in two Jordanian universities, the students must:

(i)   be immersed in a conducive culture to internet usage for education delivery;
(ii)   have the intention to follow through the online program;
(iii) see that their effort expended must not be seen to be too onerous compared to using traditional non-Internet based learning;
(iv)   meet their performance expectations after using the d-learning technology;
(v)   be in an environment that has a positive social influence to using this technology;
(vi)   find the technology easy to use and furthermore, that it must help facilitate their learning process.

As such, the increase in the number of Arabic university websites delivering d-learning is expected to grow exponentially, especially once coupled with emerging technologies such as the Cloud with its various xAAS (x-As-A-Service) offerings.

References

1. Behera, S.K.: E- and M-learning: a comparative study. Int. J. New Trends Educ. Their Implic. **4**(3), 65–78 (2013). http://www.ijonte.org/FileUpload/ks63207/File/08.behera.pdf. Accessed 17 Apr 2019
2. Kim, D., Rueckert, D., Kim, D.J., Seo, D.: Students' perceptions and experiences of mobile learning. Lang. Learn. Technol. **17**(3), 52–73 (2013). https://scholarspace.manoa.hawaii.edu/bitstream/10125/44339/1/17_03_kimetal.pdf. Accessed 17 Apr 2019
3. Goundar, S.: What is the potential impact of using mobile devices in education? In: GlobDev 2011, vol. 16 (2011). https://aisel.aisnet.org/globdev2011/16. Accessed 17 Apr 2019
4. Mockus, L., Dawson, H., Edel-Malizia, S., Shaffer, D., An, J.S., Swaggerty, A.: The impact of mobile access on motivation: distance education student perceptions. In: 17th Annual Sloan-C Consortium International Conference on Online Learning, Lake Buena Vista, FL (2011). https://dissem.in/p/25066345/the-impact-of-mobile-access-on-motivation-distance-education-student-perceptions. Accessed 17 Apr 2019

5. Alzubi, M.M., Alkhawlani, M.A., El-Ebiary, Y.A.B.: Investigating the factors affecting University students' e-commerce intention towards: a case study of Jordanian universities. J. Bus. Retail. Manag. Res. **12**(1), 189–194 (2017). http://www.jbrmr.com/cdn/article_file/content_80576_17-10-04-22-20-41.pdf. Accessed 17 Apr 2019

6. Alzaza, N.S., Yaakub, A.R.: Students' awareness and requirements of mobile learning services in the higher education environment. Am. J. Econ. Bus. Adm. **3**(1), 95–100 (2011). https://core.ac.uk/download/pdf/25831726.pdf. Accessed 17 Apr 2019

7. Liu, Y., Han, S., Li, H.: Understanding the factors driving m-learning adoption: a literature review. Campus Wide Inf. Syst. **27**(4), 210–226 (2010). https://doi.org/10.1108/10650741011073761

8. Pimpaka, P.: Mobile learning: designing a socio-technical model to empower learning in higher education. LUX J. Transdiscipl. Writ. Res. Claremont Grad. Univ. **2**(1), 23 (2013). https://doi.org/10.5642/lux.201301.23

9. Al-matari, A.Y., Iahad, N.A., Balaid, A.S.: Factors Influencing Students' Intention to Use M-learning. J. Inf. Syst. Res. Innov. **5**, 1–8 (2013). https://seminar.utmspace.edu.my/jisri/download/Vol5/Pub1_Factors_to_Use_Mobile_learning.pdf. Accessed 17 Apr 2019

10. Ariffin, S.A.: Mobile learning in the institution of higher learning for malaysia students: culture perspectives. Int. J. Adv. Sci. Eng. Inf. Technol. **1**(3), 283–288 (2011). https://doi.org/10.18517/ijaseit.1.3.59

11. Alzubi, M.M., Al-Dubai, M.M., Farea, M.M.: Using the technology acceptance model in understanding citizens' behavioural intention to use m-marketing among Jordanian citizen. J. Bus. Retail. Manag. Res. **12**(2), 224–231 (2018). http://www.jbrmr.com/cdn/article_file/content_35965_18-01-19fac10-55-36.pdf. Accessed 17 Apr 2019

12. Venkatesh, V., Morris, M.G., Davis, G.B., Davis, F.D.: User acceptance of information technology: toward a unified view. Manag. Inf. Syst. Q. **27**(3), 425–478 (2003). https://aisel.aisnet.org/misq/vol27/iss3/5/. Accessed 17 Apr 2019

13. Davis, F.D.: Perceived ease of use, and user acceptance of information technology. MIS Q. **13**(3), 319–340 (1989). https://doi.org/10.2307/249008

14. Ajzen, I.: The theory of planned behavior. Organ. Behav. Hum. Decis. Process. **50**(2), 179–211 (1991). https://doi.org/10.1016/0749-5978(91)90020-T

15. Ajzen, I.: From intentions to actions: a theory of planned behavior. In: Kuhl, J., Beckmann, J. (eds.) Action Control. SSSSP, pp. 11–39. Springer, Heidelberg (1985). https://doi.org/10.1007/978-3-642-69746-3_2

16. Hofstede, G.: Cultures and Organizations: Software of the Mind. McGraw-Hill, NY (1991)

17. Erez, M., Earley, P.C.: Culture, Self-Identity, and Work. Oxford University Press, NY (1993)

18. Shore, B., Venkatachalam, A.R.: Role of national culture in the transfer of information technology. J. Strat. Inf. Syst. **5**(1), 19–35 (1996). https://doi.org/10.1016/S0963-8687(96)80021-7

19. Hasan, H., Ditsa, G.: The impact of culture on the adoption of IT: an interpretive study. J. Glob. Inf. Manag. **7**(1), 5–15 (1999). https://doi.org/10.4018/jgim.1999010101

20. Van Maanen, J., Laurent, A.: The flow of culture: some notes on globalization and the multinational corporation. In: Ghoshal, S., Westney, D.E. (eds.) Organization Theory and the Multinational Corporation. Palgrave Macmillan, London (1993). https://doi.org/10.1007/978-1-349-22557-6_12

21. Hill, C.E., Loch, K.D., Straub, D., El-Sheshai, K.: A qualitative assessment of arab culture and information technology transfer. J. Glob. Inf. Manag. **6**(3), 29–38 (1998). https://doi.org/10.4018/jgim.1998070103

22. Straub, D.W.: The effect of culture on IT diffusion: E-Mail and FAX in Japan and the U.S. Information Systems Research. **5**(1), 23–47 (1994). https://doi.org/10.1287/isre.5.1.23

23. Straub, D., Keil, M., Brenner, W.: Testing the technology acceptance model across cultures: a three country study. Inf. Manag. **33**(1), 1–11 (1997). https://doi.org/10.1016/S0378-7206 (97)00026-8
24. Goodman, S.E., Green, J.D.: Computing in the Middle East. Commun. ACM **35**(8), 21–24 (1992). https://doi.org/10.1145/135226.135236
25. Samovar, L.A., Porter, R.E., McDaniel, E.R.: Communication Between Cultures. Wadsworth Publishing Company Inc., Boston (2009)
26. Hair, J.F., Black, W.C., Babin, B.J., Anderson, R.E.: Multivariate Data Analysis, 7th edn. China Machine Press, Beijing (2011)

Tracking, Recognizing, and Estimating Size of Objects Using Adaptive Technique

Fazal Noor[1(✉)] and Majed Alhaisoni[2]

[1] Islamic University of Madinah, Madinah, Kingdom of Saudi Arabia
mfnoor@gmail.com
[2] University of Hail, Hail, Kingdom of Saudi Arabia
majed.alhaisoni@gmail.com

Abstract. The detection and tracking of object in a video is an important problem in many applications. In surveillance and in robotic vision tracking and recognition of objects and it's size is desired. In this paper, an algorithm to obtain size of an object in image or video is presented based on pixel relationship to actual size. The object is mainly tracked by the Kalman filter and Log Polar Phase Correlation method is used to more precisely recognize objects in a video. The tracking of objects is performed from frame to frame. As the image of an object gets deformed in a video due to motion of either the camera or the motion of an object a dynamic template for matching is proposed to minimize the error. Simulation results are presented showing the errors in determining the size of objects in an image.

Keywords: Arduino microcontroller · Object size · Kalman filter · Log-polar phase correlation · Robotics · Sonar

1 Introduction

In robotics, tracking and recognizing objects is a common task [1]. The Kalman filter has been used in numerous applications and in object detection and tracking [2–5]. Similarly, in self driven cars computer vision object tracking requires processing in real-time [6–8]. Many different types of sensors are used in the self-driven cars, each having their own capabilities and limitations. Sensors such as Sonar, LiDAR are used to measure distances and mapping of the surroundings very precisely [8]. In certain applications, robots need to know an object's size, such as width and height [13]. In case an object is stationary it is less difficult to calculate the object's dimensions, however, in case when an object is moving it is very challenging to calculate an object's size. This is so because as the camera moves or as the object moves in the field of view, the object's image changes or deforms. Recognizing an object may help in determining an object's original size. However, there are situations in which prior information about the object is unknown and therefore determining objects dimensions from tracking in a video becomes even more challenging. Also, there are situations when a moving object of a specific dimension has to pass through pathways openings of another dimension so care must be taken not to collide if the pathway opening is smaller.

© ICST Institute for Computer Sciences, Social Informatics and Telecommunications Engineering 2019
Published by Springer Nature Switzerland AG 2019. All Rights Reserved
M. H. Miraz et al. (Eds.): iCETiC 2019, LNICST 285, pp. 283–291, 2019.

In this paper a reference image with known dimensions is used within a video to obtain dimensions of unknown objects. The number of pixels of an object is camera dependent and varies with precise distance to an object. Practical experiments are performed using Arduino microcontroller, with camera and sonar assembled to it.

The paper is presented as follows, in Sect. 2, the Kalman filter, Log polar phase correlation, and object size determination methods are presented. In Sect. 3, experimental setup of hardware is presented and in Sect. 4 results and discussions are presented and last in Sect. 5, conclusion and future directions are discussed.

2 Methods

2.1 Kalman Filter

In 1960, Rudolph E. Kalman published a paper describing a recursive solution using state space methods, later called a Kalman filter [2–5]. Many applications use Kalman filtering such as tracking, navigation, and estimation. Given a linear stochastic difference equation shown as,

$$\hat{x}_{t|t-1} = A_t \hat{x}_{t|t-1} + B_t u_t + v_{t-1} \tag{1}$$

and a measurement equation given by

$$z_t = H x_t + w_t \tag{2}$$

where A is defined as the state transition matrix, B is defined as a control matrix, H is the measurement matrix, $\hat{x}$ is the estimated state, and u is the control variables. The variables w, and v are assumed to be random, independently distributed with Gaussian white noise. The variables w, and v denote the process and measurement noise, respectively. Assuming the time dependent matrices A, B, and H to be constant, the two part Kalman filter can be written in two parts, the predictor and measurement as shown below.

Predict (process time update equations):

$$\hat{x}_{t|t-1} = A_t \hat{x}_{t|t-1} + B_t u_t \tag{3}$$

$$P_{t|t-1} = A_t P_{t-1|t-1} A_t^T + Q_t \tag{4}$$

The predicted state is given by Eq. (3) and the predicted estimate covariance is given by Eq. (4). Update (measurement or correction update equations):

Feedback

$$\hat{z}_t = y_t - H_t \hat{x}_{t|t-1} \tag{5}$$

$$S_t = H_t P_{t|t-1} H_k^T + R_t \tag{6}$$

$$K_t = P_{t|t-1}H_t^T S_t^{-1} \tag{7}$$

$$\hat{x}_{t|t-1} = \hat{x}_{t-1|t-1} + K_t \hat{z}_t \tag{8}$$

$$P_{t|t} = (I - K_t H_t)P_{t|t-1} \tag{9}$$

where in Eq. (5), $\hat{z}_t$ denotes the measurement residual and y denotes the measurement variables. In Eq. (6), S gives the innovation covariance and R is the measurement variance matrix. In Eq. (7), K_t is the Kalman gain, P is defined as the state variance matrix. In Eq. (8), $\hat{x}_{t|t-1}$ is the updated (a posteriori) state estimate and in Eq. (9), $P_{t|t}$ is the updated (a posteriori) estimate covariance.

2.2   Log Polar Phase Correlation

A powerful signal processing technique is the correlation filter and has been used in object detection and registration problems. The use of correlation filter appears in numerous applications such as signal matching, automatic target detection, missile guidance systems, in medical imaging, and many others [4, 5]. The basic idea of the phase correlation method is to see the similarity between two images. Phase correlation is used in methods such as motion estimation, image registration, object tracking by template matching. In particular the log polar phase correlation technique has been shown to be robust to image scaling, rotation, and translation and provides a good solution to image recognition.

Suppose f(x, y) represents a scaled, translated, and rotated version of an original image h(x, y), given by [4, 5, 12],

$$f(x,y) = h(s \cdot x \cos\theta - s \cdot y \sin\theta - x_0, \\ s \cdot x \sin\theta + s \cdot y \cos\theta - y_0) \tag{10}$$

After taking the Fourier transform of f(x, y) transforms it in frequency domain as,

$$F(u,v) = \frac{1}{|s^2|}H(u' \cos\theta - v' \sin\theta, u' \sin\theta + v' \cos\theta) \rightleftarrows \cdot \\ e^{-j(ux_0 + vy_0)} \tag{11}$$

where u' = u/s and v' = v/s. Taking the magnitude of F(u, v) results in the following,

$$M_F(u,v) = w \cdot M_H(u' \cos\theta - v' \sin\theta, u' \cos\theta + v' \sin\theta) \tag{12}$$

where w is defined as a weighting factor. Utilizing the polar coordinates (r, φ) and using the relation $u = r \cos \varphi$ and $v = r \sin \varphi$. Inserting in Eq. (12) above will result in,

$$M_F(u, v) = w \cdot M_H(r' \cos \varphi \cos \theta - r' \sin \varphi \sin \theta, \tag{13}$$
$$r' \cos \phi \sin \theta + r' \sin \phi \cos \theta).$$

and using trigonometric identities results in the following,

$$M_F(u, v) = w \cdot M_H(r' \cos(\varphi + \theta) - r' \sin(\varphi + \theta)) \tag{14}$$

which can be denoted by,

$$M_F(r, \varphi) = w \cdot M_H(r', \varphi + \theta) \tag{15}$$

Transforming the above Eq. (15) to log-polar form, by using the logarithm results in

$$M_F(\log r, \varphi) = w \cdot M_H(\log r', \varphi + \theta) \tag{16}$$

where $r' = r/s$ and $\log r' = \log r - \log s$.

It is seen by the use of the Fourier properties, a phase shift is produced by a positional shift. Also, a linear scaling of the variables x, and y causes an inverse scaling of the spatial frequencies u and v. Using the log-polar transform and applying it to the magnitude spectrum, the scale and rotation are obtained by using the phase correlation. This is possible because the scaling and rotation in the Cartesian system become pure translation in the log-polar system.

2.3   Variation of Objects with Distance

The object appearance changes due to angle of viewpoint, change in shape, occlusion, daylight, etc. [7, 9, 10, 11]. For example, as the road sign comes in view of a camera the image of it changes with relationship to motion, becoming larger as camera is moved toward it and smaller as the camera moves out [10]. The size of a slanted image is more involved and needs the angle of camera or angle of object or both to determine the size of an object [9]. For an object forming a 90° angle to a camera, the size relationship of an object is:

$$\text{Size} = \text{Object size in pixels} / (\text{Number of pixels/cm}) \tag{17}$$

Where pixels/cm is obtained by Object size/Actual size. The pixels/cm in the equation is Camera dependent and needs to be determined beforehand, the distance to an object can be determined using either ultrasonic sensors or LiDAR [8]. A known object size can be inserted in an image and use it to calculate the pixels/cm relationship (Fig. 1).

The algorithm to determine the size of an object from a video can be summarized as follows:

Algorithm:

Preliminary Steps: Calibrate the pixel relationship to actual object size.

1. Assume original object dimensions are known for comparison and determining the error.
2. Given a video frame.
3. Detect an object of interest.
4. Calibrate the relation of object size to number of pixels in frame with distance obtained by sonar. Move object back and forth and left and right for obtaining the precise relationship of object scaling to number of pixels.

Track, freeze frame, perform log polar phase correlation.

5. Keep track of the object using Kalman filter, predicting the object's position.
6. Freeze the frame and use log polar phase correlation to recognize the object by matching a reference template of an object. If match is greater than a threshold then object is recognized else if match is less than threshold then object is not recognized.
7. If object is detected and recognized, approximate the dimensions using the pixel relation.
8. Compare the calculated size with original size to obtain the error.

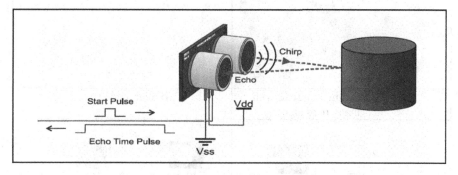

Fig. 1. Using sonar to measure the distance to an object.

Fig. 2. Arduino microcontroller with a camera and sd card connected with wiring.

3 Experiment Setup

An Arduino micro-controller board with a camera, sonar, motor, and a sd card were assembled in the experiment setups. The sonar measures the range to an object, while the camera is used to take a video. Matlab 2017 was used to write a script to capture video and the Kalman Filter was used to track a moving object while the Phase correlation method was used to match an object within the image of a frame video. The algorithm uses the size to pixel relationship to calculate the size of an object and is camera dependent.

Figure 2 shows a sd card connection and a camera assembled to an Arduino microcontroller. The software is downloaded from the pc usb port via wire connection to the board.

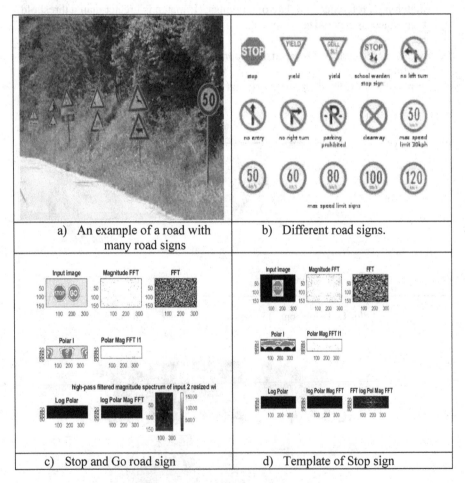

a) An example of a road with many road signs

b) Different road signs.

c) Stop and Go road sign

d) Template of Stop sign

Fig. 3. Road signs and template matching using LPC.

4 Results and Discussion

4.1 Moving Camera with Stationary Objects

In this scenario, a car is mounted with a camera and road signs are detected under clear weather (not foggy weather) while the car is moving. As the video is captured, in real time the road signs are tracked from frame to frame. Ideally, an angle of 90° would give the best results for recognition, however practically it is not possible when the vehicle

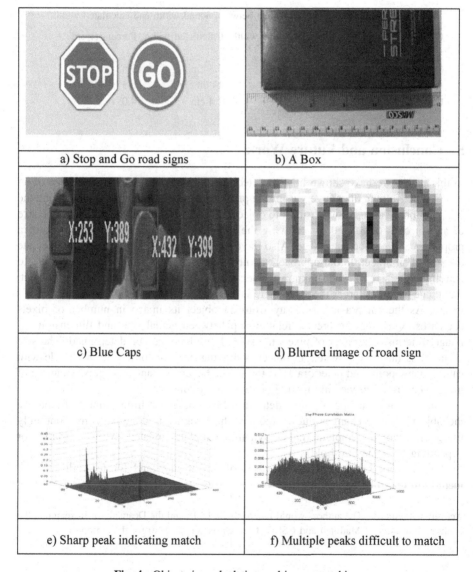

a) Stop and Go road signs	b) A Box
c) Blue Caps	d) Blurred image of road sign
e) Sharp peak indicating match	f) Multiple peaks difficult to match

Fig. 4. Object size calculation and image matching.

is moving. Using the log polar phase correlation method discussed above results in good recognition when the sign is at a 90° angle. However, in case the camera is in motion the view of the road signs will appear to change with distance and angle. Objects will appear to scale, and/or rotate. The log polar phase correlation is robust to image scaling and rotation. Figure 3 shows the result of LPPC for a 90 snapshot of with image template with a scaled and rotated version. Figure 3a, b shows an image with many road signs and objective is to detect them and recognize them (Fig. 4 and Table 1).

Table 1. Comparison of objects size between actual width and calculated width.

Object	Direction	Distance (cm)	Actual width	Calculated width	Percent error%
Stop sign	90	15	5.5 cm	5.3 cm	3.63
Box	90	15	14 cm	14.08 cm	0.57
Cap	90	15	2.5 cm	2.4 cm	4.0

5 Conclusion and Future Work

In this paper, we have shown how to detect, track, recognize, and find the size of an object. The Kalman filter is very useful in predicting the movement of an object and the log polar phase correlation is robust to object scaling, translation, and rotation. The size of an object is calculated by knowing the image scaling relationship due to camera properties and a reference image. Also the distance and angle can be used to calculate the size of an object. In our approach, a known image is inserted in an image to use to determine the size of other unknown objects. As the camera moves toward an object, the image becomes larger therefore there is an increase in number of pixels of object's image. As the camera moves away from an object its image in number of pixels decreases. Knowing the precise relationship between actual size and dimensions of image in terms of number of pixels the size of an object can be determined. The size accuracy is fairly good when an object is moving back or forth with 90° angle with camera view point and deteriorates as the image becomes slanted. A good example of image slant is when viewing road signs from a moving car.

The size of a moving object is determined by tracking it from frame to frame. As the object's image changes due to motion, the tracking is done by correspondingly using an adaptive template (i.e. a dynamic template updated every N frames or depending on some threshold).

Future work involves work for cases of object slant and for feasibility of the method in real-time applications.

Acknowledgement. The authors would like to thank FCIS and the Deanship of Research at the Islamic University of Madinah and CSSE at the University of Hail for their support.

References

1. Vargas, H., et al.: Human-robot interface using face detection and recognition, for the service robot, Donaxi. In: Workshop Proceedings of the 8th International Conference on Intelligent Environments. IOS Press (2012)
2. Raja, T.V., Tirupathamma, M.: Object detection and tracking in video using Kalman filter. Int. J. Res. Adv. Eng. Technol. 5(5), 102–106 (2016)
3. Saravanan, S., Parthasarathy, K.A.: Video object detection and tracking using Kalman filter and color histogram-based matching algorithm. Int. J. Eng. Res. Dev. 9(7), 31–39 (2014). www.ijerd.com. e-ISSN: 2278-067X, p-ISSN: 2278-800X
4. Jain, R.: Phase Correlation Algorithm for Video Tracking: Phase Correlation Algorithm with Kalman Filtering. LAP LAMBERT Academic Publishing (2012). ISBN 10 9783659210730. ISBN 13 978-3659210730
5. Noor, F., Alhaisoni, M.: Distinguishing moving objects using Kalman filter and phase correlation methods. In: 17th IEEE International Multi-topic Conference, Karachi, Pakistan, December 2014
6. Comaniciu, D., Ramesh, V., Meer, P.: Real-time tracking of non-rigid objects using mean shift. In: 2000 Proceedings IEEE Conference on Computer Vision and Pattern Recognition, vol. 2, pp. 142–149 (2000)
7. Object detection and tracking in video. https://towardsdatascience.com/object-detection-and-tracking-in-pytorch-b3cf1a696a98. Accessed 19 Apr 2019
8. Hwang, S., Kim, N., Choi, Y., Lee, S., Kweon, I.S.: Fast multiple objects detection and tracking fusing color camera and 3D lidar for intelligent vehicles. In: Proceedings of 13th International Conference on Ubiquitous Robots and Ambient Intelligence (URAI), pp. 234–239 (2016)
9. Hou, L., Wan, W., Lee, K.-H., Hwang, J.-N., Okopal, G., Pitton, J.: Deformable multiple-kernel based human tracking using a moving camera. In: Proceedings of International Conference Acoustics, Speech and Signal Processing (ICASSP), pp. 2249–2253 (2015)
10. Sankaranarayanan et al.: Object detection, tracking, and recognition for multiple smart cameras. In: Proceedings of the IEEE, vol. 96, no. 10, October 2008
11. Henriques, J.F., Caseiro, R., Martins, P., Batista, J.: High-speed tracking with kernelized correlation filters. IEEE Trans. Pattern Anal. Mach. Intell. 37(3), 583–596 (2015)
12. Srinivasa Reddy, B., Chatterji, B.N.: An FFT-based technique for translation, rotation, and scale-invariant image registration. IEEE Trans. Image Process. 5(8), 1266–1271 (1996)
13. Noor, F., Swaied, M., AlMesned, M., AlMuzini, N.: A method to detect an object's width using an ultrasonic sonar. In: Proceedings of IEEE ICCECE 2018 Conference, UK (2018)

Analysis Filling Factor Catalogue
of Different Wavelength SODISM Images

Amro F. Alasta[1]($\boxtimes$), Mustapha Meftah[2], Rami Qahwaji[1],
Abdrazag Algamudi[1], and Fatma Almesrati[1]

[1] Electrical Engineering and Computer Science,
University of Bradford, Bradford, UK
Amr_hard@yahoo.com, R.S.R.Qahwaji@bradford.ac.uk,
gamudi@yahoo.com, enas199990@yahoo.com
[2] French National Centre for Scientific Research, Paris, France
Mustapha.Meftah@latmos.ipsl.fr

Abstract. The Solar Diameter Imager and Surface Mapper's (SODISM) recording of data on the PICARD satellite in five different wavelengths has increased the need to extract features such as Sunspots. This paper analyses the overall sunspot detection performance, examines the correlation between the filling factor of different SODISM wavelengths and the Solar and Heliospheric Observatory (SOHO) filling factor, and compares them with the USAF/NOAA catalogue. Four months of data from SODISM and SOHO, obtained for the period Aug–Dec 2010, are analysed and compared. This comparison identifies the best wavelength for sunspot detection in SODISM, and compares the overall detection performance of three wavelengths; 535.7 nm, 607.1 nm and 782.2 nm. Furthermore, the study proposes a novel SODISM catalogue summarising SODISM data details including the Filling Factor, area, and the number of sunspots.

Keywords: SODISM · Sunspots · Wavelengths · SOHO · PICARD ·
Filling Factors catalogue

1 Introduction

The 15th June 2010 saw the successful launch of the PICARD satellite; onboard was the Solar Diameter Imager and Surface Mapper (SODISM), the imaging telescope taking solar images at a rate of one image per minute to provide wide-field images of the sun in five bands centred at 215.0 nm, 393.37 nm, 535.7 nm, 607.1 nm, and 782.2 nm, usually abbreviated as '215', '393', '535', '607', and '782' [1]. However, there is no uniformity in the quality of SODISM images captured at various wavelengths; the difference in image quality is evident in the slightly higher degradation in wavelengths 215 nm and 393 nm, because of the combination of solar irradiation and instrumental contamination where the W.L. 215 nm channel lost more than 90% of the normalized intensity, and W.L. 393 nm lost about 80% [2]. Figure 1 shows a pronounced decomposition in the UV channels. Meanwhile, the visible and near-infrared channels present a temporal oscillation but remain relatively constant [3]. However,

M. H. Miraz et al. (Eds.): iCETiC 2019, LNICST 285, pp. 292–304, 2019.

according to the previous degradation reasons, the comparison in this paper will be between visible and near-infrared constant wavelengths (W.L. 535 nm, 607 nm and 782 nm). Detecting sunspots as individual elements is equivalent to determining which pixels belong to each sunspot, thus determining which pixels are active points by using the accurate threshold intensity level to isolate these points from the background [4].

The method presented here detects solar disc edges, then it detects sunspot candidates, and by iterative threshold on the gradient image which has been previously normalized counting the number of the connected regions. Figure 3 charts the fundamentals of the applied segmentation method to detect sunspots [1].

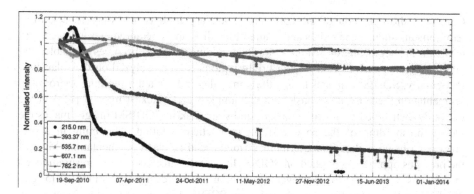

Fig. 1. Integrated intensity normalized time series of PICARD during his mission (Meftah et al. 2015).

Segmentation method was applied to images of 535 nm, 607 nm, and 782 nm wavelengths, which were available at level 1B. Level 1B data products include a number of corrections for any instrumental issues, all images were downloaded, which amounted to a total of 206 for W.L. 535 nm, and each image had a size of 2048 × 2048 pixels. The data obtained was from 5th August 2010 to 4th January 2014 besides 306 images taken at wavelengths of W.L 607 nm, and 300 images at 782 nm; these were collected between 2010 and 2014.

It is notable that many researchers use observatory images from the SOHO and SDO satellites to detect sunspots, but the five SODISM wavelengths have been relatively underused, and this prompted an interest in working with the SODISM images. This article makes the following contributions:

- Applying an automated method to detect Sunspots from SODISM images in W.L. 782 nm with verification.
- The provision of a filling factor of W.L. 782 nm and comparisons with SODISM W.L. 535 nm, 607 nm and SOHO images.
- Analysis of the correlation between SODISM wavelengths and USAF/NOAA catalogue, in number and size of sunspots.

The paper provides statistical means of characterising SODISM data and novel FF catalogue to summarise hundreds of experiments in a more concise manner, including

FF ratio, location and area of sunspots, this information will be the cornerstone in future for any new comparison with SODISM data.

This research study is presented as follows: Sect. 2 summarizes the literature; Sect. 3 presents the Pre-processing detection technique including verification and comparison with USAF/NOAA catalogue, Sect. 4 presents Filling Factor computation and catalogue; Sect. 5 discusses the results obtained from the previous sections; Finally, Sect. 6 summarizes the conclusions.

2 Literature Survey

Generally, the detection of the solar disk boundary limb is necessary to determine requirements such as the radius and centre of the disk, these requirements are necessary to obtain the segmentation features [4]. Once this information becomes available, any interior features such as Sunspots or bright regions can be analyzed on the solar disk. Particularly, SODISM images follow the same rules and use a thresholding approach to segmentation, because it is considered the simplest and quickest method [4]. But the unevenly distributed light of the background solar disk in SODISM images makes the global thresholding of the solar disk an impractical solution. Correcting in a pre-processing to normalize image brightness might lead to better segmentation. Most of the previous approaches applied on SODISM to detect sunspots have been summarized in previous papers, see [3] However Alasta et al's most recent papers in 2017 [5] and 2018 [3] on the topic of sunspot detection on SODISM images applied to 535 nm and 607 nm W.Ls described their methods as follows:

For the 535 nm W.L.

- Detect the solar disk border and record its centre and radius.
- Convert scale of the image from a signed 32 bit, to 8 bit.
- Remove noise by using Kuwahara and à Trous filters.
- Correct pixel brightness outliers and employ a Bandpass filter to display the sunspots on a normalized background.
- Finally, locate the sunspot by the use of the threshold method.

A comparison between the filling factor results produced by this method and the results produced by the SOHO method has established a correlation coefficient of 98.5%.

And recently, in 2018 Alasta et al. provided a new method for 607 nm W.L [3]; their methods were as follows:

[i]   The Solar limb is extracted
[ii] The sunspot gradient is calculated
[iii] Use a closing operation to fill the holes.
[iv] Compute the image obtained in the gradient image and the original image
[v]   Isolated noise from the sunspot gradient,
[vi] Use the Kuwahara filter to remove the unwanted noise.
[vii] Only those sunspots where the difference between the maximum and minimum grey values of a pixel is greater than 5 are verified.

Finally Fig. 2 shows an example of the result by applying a binary overlay in red colour and superimposing the original image. Their result is the first automated method to achieve 99% correlations between SOHO and SODISM.

Fig. 2. The recognised sunspots on the original image (Color figure online)

3 Preprocessing and Detection of Sunspots

Detecting sunspots as individual elements are equivalent to determining which pixels belong to each sunspot, thus establishing which pixels are active points by using the accurate threshold intensity level to isolate these points from the background [4]. The threshold should be computed for each image because it varies from image to image. This method applied on SODISM images for W.L 782 nm to compare results with WLs, 535 nm and 607 nm from previous work [5, 6].

In total, 300 images were obtained at a wavelength of 782 nm. They were the same size as the images from the other wavelengths (2048 × 2048 pixels). The images at this wavelength are free from visible noise, and ghosting artefacts were not observed.

The pre-processing is applied on SODISM images by using Alasta et al's. method [7] to prepare data to the next stage. The method detects solar disc edges then sunspot candidates, and by iterative threshold on the gradient image which has been previously normalized, counting the number of the connected regions. Because the method is automated, it does not invite the problems associated with the pressure of time, and can, therefore, be used on large data for W.L. 782 nm. The method is developed to automatically detect sunspots in 782 nm SODISM L1 images, and is programmed in MATLAB; it adopts the following steps; Fig. 3 shows the flowchart diagram for the basic fundamentals of the applied segmentation method to detect sunspots. The preview method for detecting sunspots by Meftah et al. [8] has limitations because a manual threshold has to be entered. Furthermore, these procedures take the most time, and the method applies only to 393 nm W.L. images, so does not apply to large data, while this study's method can be applied to 535 nm and 607 nm.

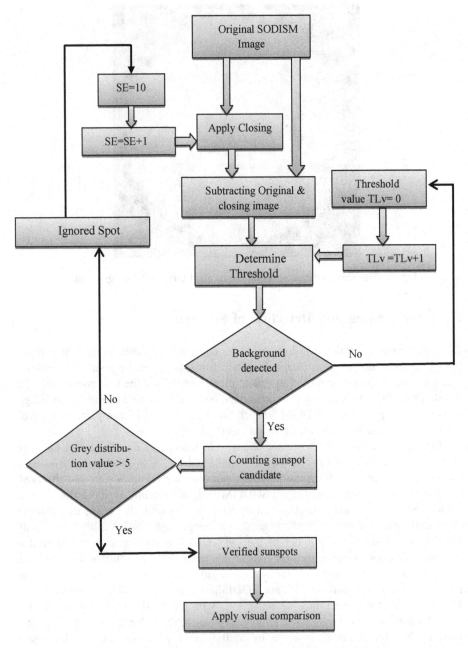

Fig. 3. Chart diagram of the sunspot detection procedure

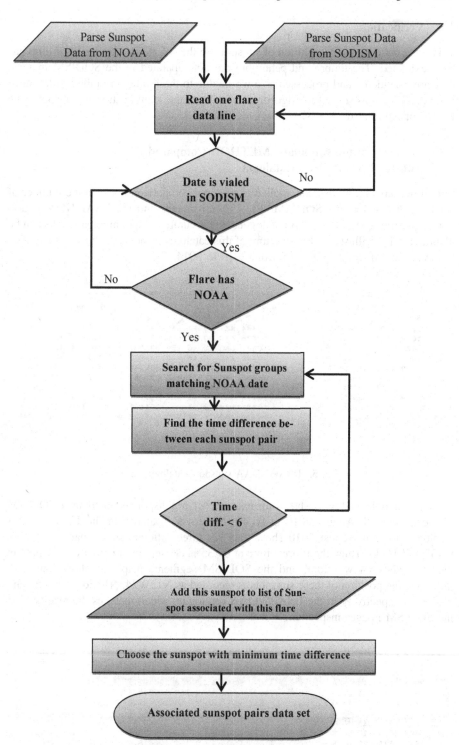

Fig. 4. Comparison between the numbers of sunspots

3.1   Verification

This stage includes the recognition of sunspots on the solar disk after the solar limb has been extracted. The umbra and penumbra are not separated in the SODISM images; they are considered and processed as a whole due to the limitation in the resolution of the data. The steps set out in Algorithm 2 facilitate the identification of sunspots (see Fig. 3 for the related images).

3.2   Accuracy of the Automatic METHOD Compared with the USAF/NOAA Catalogue

The Flowchart Fig. 4 has been applied to obtain a comparison between the number of sunspots detected in the SODISM WL 782 nm images and the USAF/NOAA catalogue. Depending on the NOAA catalogues, the accurate sunspot number results can be identified; Fig. 5 illustrates the structure of this catalogue. The algorithms were applied to the sunspot data for the period from 2010 to 2014.

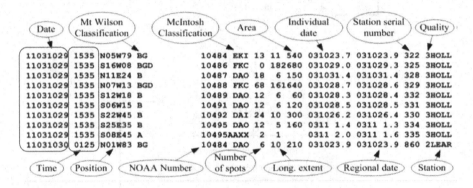

Fig. 5. USAF/NOAA sunspots catalogue data

The example in Fig. 6 shows an example of a sunspot recorded in a SODISM image on the 5th August 2010 at 04:49. Moreover, searches in the USAF/NOAA catalogue for 5th August 2010 show data for three different times, namely: 02:36, 07:35 and 16:35. Thus, the nearest time at 07:35 is chosen, the number of sunspots in the USAF/NOAA was four, and the SODISM segments map also show four; furthermore, the position of these sunspots is recorded as N13W24, N11E67, S19E56 and N25W49 respectively in the USAF/NOAA catalogue, which matches the results from the SODISM images inspection.

```
11100805 0236 N12W21 A        11092 HHX  1  3 200 100803.5 -------.- 062 2LEAR
11100805 0236 N10E68 B        11093 DAO  4 10 160 100810.2 -------.- 063 2LEAR
11100805 0236 N25W46 B        //// CSO   8  4  40 100801.5 -------.- 064 2LEAR
11100805 0735 N13W24 A        11092 HHX  1  3 170 100803.5 -------.- 054 3SVTO
11100805 0735 N11E67 B        11093 CAO  4  8 150 100810.4 -------.- 055 3SVTO
11100805 0735 S19E56 A        //// AXX   2  0  10 100809.6 -------.- 056 3SVTO
11100805 0735 N25W49 B        //// DSO   5  5  50 100801.5 -------.- 057 3SVTO
11100805 1635 N13W30 B        11092 CSO  2  4 230 100803.4 -------.- 063 4HOLL
11100805 1635 S18E50 B        //// BXO   2  1  90 100809.5 -------.- 065 4HOLL
11100805 1635 N12E62 B        11093 CSO  4  8 190 100810.4 -------.- 066 4HOLL
11100805 1635 N25W55 B        11094 CSO  6  4  60 100801.4 -------.- 067 4HOLL
```

Fig. 6. Example, Aug., 5th 2010 for USAF/NOAA catalogue shows time chosen

The sunspot detection and grouping algorithm was tested on the SODISM archived images for the period August 2010 – January 2014 for W.L. 535 nm. Figure 7 shows the comparison with the USAF/NOAA catalogue has been made and the correlation accuracy is 95.17%. Figure 8 shows the plot.

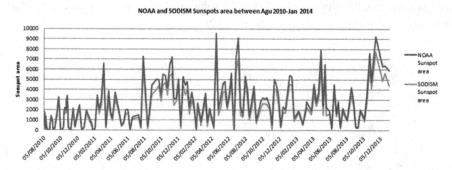

Fig. 7. USAF/NOAA sunspot numbers vs SODISM automated sunspot numbers.

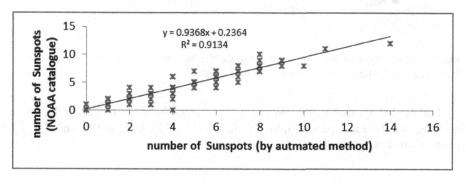

Fig. 8. Showing the plot of sunspots VS the time for SODISM (2010-2014).

The sunspot areas calculated by the automated sunspot detection method were compared to those recorded by the USAF/NOAA. More than two hundred individual images were compared, from August 2010 to January 2014, and results are summarized in Fig. 8. With the exception of regions with images from 2013 and 2014, where there was degradation in the images, there is a strong correlation between the automated sunspot area and the USAF/NOAA sunspot area. A visual inspection of the SODISM images seems to confirm that the automated procedure works well and confirms the results

3.3 Visual Sunspot Verification

In order to verify the detection results, a few randomly selected images of recognized sunspots were chosen. The detected areas are magnified and compared with the original images, and Fig. 9 shows an example of the results.

4 Filling Factors Computation

The filling factor (FF) is a function of the radial position on the sun disk. Thus, the calculated FF for any chosen feature reflects the fraction of the solar disk covered by that feature. For identification purposes, the system generates and assigns a synthetic spectra reference. [9] Eleven rings divide the solar disk beginning with an inner radius (RI), and concluding with an outer radius (RO).

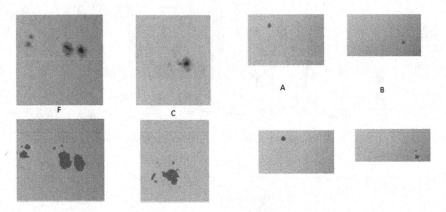

Fig. 9. Enlarge most of the recognised sunspots: the top images show the original sunspot images and the bottom images show the zoomed images.

For the SODISM WL 782 nm images, a correlation of 93% with SOHO was achieved for the same period (from 22 Sep. 2010 to 25 Dec. 2010), and Fig. 10 illustrates this comparison.

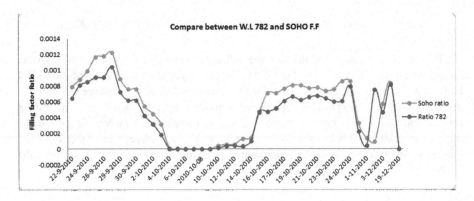

Fig. 10. A comparison of sunspot FFs ratio calculated from SOHO and SODISM images from 22 September 2010 to 25 December 2010.

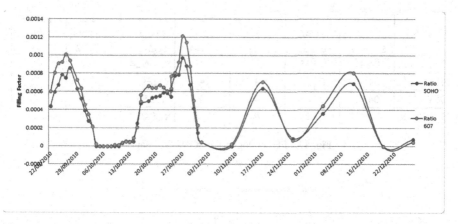

Fig. 11. FF calculation of sunspot from SOHO and SODISM images from 22th Sept. 2010 until 25 Dec. 2010 [3].

The researchers' previous paper [3] clearly mentions the data obtained for the 607 nm W.L. were 306 images collected between 22nd Sep. 2010 and 1st Jan. 2014. The FF of this data sharing with SOHO has been calculated and compared with SODISM over the same period (i.e. Sep., Oct. Nov. and Dec. 2010). The correlation coefficient was 99%. While the correlation coefficient of WL 535 nm FF with SOHO was 98% [5] (Fig. 11).

4.1   Filling Factor Catalogue

In the literature, the FF, specified as a function of radial position on the solar disc, is calculated and then tabulated for each image. However, this process does not provide extensive conclusive data concerning the experimental research carried out on the many hundreds of these images. To provide a means of tabulating these findings such that a single glance at a table would give an overall picture of the work done, a cataloguing procedure was proposed. The FF catalogue holds records of SODISM images information; this catalogue will be organized as follows:

The first column records the sunspot date in the dd/mm/yy format, the second column will record the time of the sunspot in SODISM, and the third column is the equivalent time in the USAF/NOAA catalogue. The fourth and fifth columns show the number of sunspots in SODISM images, and the equivalent number of sunspots in the USAF/NOAA catalogue, the location of SODISM catalogue sunspots is shown in the sixth column and their size in the seventh. The filling factor ratio is recorded in the eighth and final column. Figure 12 shows an example for the FF catalogue. It is notable that the SODISM data is available from August 2010 to January 2014, and that explains that Fig. 13 shows only one month in 2014.

Date	Time of Sunspot in SODSIM	Time of NOAA Sunspot	number of sunpots SODISM	number of spots NOAA	Loction of Sunspot SODISM	Size of Sunspots SODISM	Total FF Ratio
05/08/2010	04:49	07:35	4	4	N13W24		
05/08/2010	04:49	07:35	4	4	N11E67	530	0.000531
05/08/2010	04:49	07:35	4	4	S18E56		
05/08/2010	04:49	07:35	4	4	N25W49		

Fig. 12. FF catalogue for SODSIM images

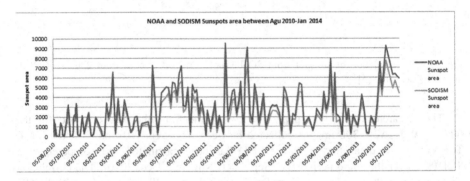

Fig. 13. Sunspot areas extracted from SODISM by the automatic method; and sunspot areas provided USAF/NOAA in Aug. 2010 – Jan 2014

The comparison is made of daily sunspots (illustrated in Fig. 13) extracted by the automatic method from SODISM images from August 2010 until January 2014, with those available as TXT files at USAF/NOAA catalogue. The horizontal axis represents the date of image capture; the vertical represents the sunspot area, in units of millionths of a solar hemisphere. The correlation coefficient in the same tendency is 93% shown in Fig. 14.

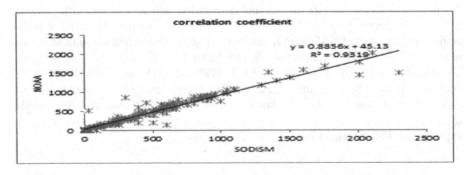

Fig. 14. The correlation coefficient between USAF/NOAA and SODISM Sunspot area

One aim of this study is also to obtain solar spectral variation on SODISM images at 782 nm (Fig. 15). We can check with the SES sensor onboard PICARD, which measured the solar spectral irradiance at 782 nm during the same period, and on the same spacecraft. When we will confirm the Alasta et al. method at 782 nm between SES data and SODISM images, we will make the analysis for the other wavelength in the solar continuum (535 and 607 nm). For this analysis with PICARD/SODISM images, we need to correct the data with the limb darkening function of the Sun [10].

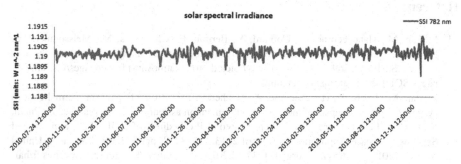

Fig. 15. Solar spectral variation on SODISM images at 782 nm

5 Results

The correlation between SOHO and SODISM data, or measure of dependence between the two quantities, is calculated as Pearson's correlation coefficient, which is 93% in 782 nm while it is 99% in WL 607 nm [6] and 98% nm in WL 535 nm [5]. Figure 7 shows sunspot numbers coverage from October 2010 until the end of life for the Picard satellite on 1st January 2014, also Fig. 10 shows a comparison between the filling factors calculated for the SODISM 782 nm images from the Picard satellite and the MDI intensity-gram images from the SOHO satellite over a similar period. This result leads us to concede that WLs 535 nm and 607 nm are the best bands to detect sunspots in SODISM images.

The comparison has been made between the SODISM catalogue and the USAF/NOAA catalogue in the number of sunspots detected and their location and size over the same period of time. The accuracy comparison for the period August 2010 to January 2014 shows a correlation coefficient of 95.17% (Fig. 13). Moreover, the sizes of sunspots match 93% in the USAF/NOAA catalogue (Fig. 14).

6 Conclusions

The proposed segmentation method has been applied to the entire image data downloaded for 782 nm to detect sunspots and calculate their filling factors. A comparative analysis of the proposed segmentation method in relation to the USAF/NOAA catalogue has been completed. An automated method is used to detect sunspots on SODISM images, despite the image degradation throughout the lifetime of PICARD.

Perhaps the most significant contribution of this research is the SODISM FF catalogue; the novel catalogue summarizes information and details of available SODISM images including size, number and location of sunspots.

The proposed and implemented cataloguing procedure gives a clear representation of the SODISM data. It is hoped that researchers will use the proposed technique in their future work.

References

1. Meftah, M., Hauchecorne, A., Corbard, T., Bertran, E., Chaigneau, M., Meissonnier, M.: PICARD SODISM, a space telescope to study the Sun from the middle ultraviolet to the near infrared. Sol. Phys. **289**, 1–38 (2014). http://picard.projet.latmos.ipsl.fr/webpages/instrument_pages/SODISM_instrument_web.html
2. Meftah, M., Irbah, A., Hauchecorne, A., Hochedez, J.F.: PICARD payload thermal control system and general impact of the space environment on astronomical observations. In: Pham, K.D., Cox, J.L., Howard, R.T., Chen, G. (eds.) Proceedings of SPIE 8739, Sensors and Systems for Space Applications VI, April 2013, vol. 8739, pp. 87390B. Baltimore, United States (2013). https://doi.org/10.1117/12.2010178, https://hal.archives-ouvertes.fr/hal-00838139/document
3. Alasta, A.F., Algamudi, A., Ipson, S.: Identification of sunspots on SODISM full-disk solar images. In: International Conference on Computing, Electronics & Communications Engineering (iCCECE 2018), Univ. Essex, Southend, UK, pp. 23–28. IEEE (2018). https://doi.org/10.1109/iccecome.2018.8658432
4. Curto, J.J., Blanca, M., Martínez, E.: Automatic sunspots detection on full-disk solar images using mathematical morphology. Sol. Phys. **250**(2), 411–429 (2008). https://doi.org/10.1007/s11207-008-9224-6
5. Alasta, A.F., Algamudi, A., Qahwaji, R., Ipson, S., Nagern, T.A.: Automatic sunspots detection on SODISM solar images. In: 2017 Seventh International Conference on Innovative Computing Technology (INTECH), Luton, pp. 115–119 (2017). https://doi.org/10.1109/intech.2017.8102429doi
6. Alasta, A.F., Algamudi, A., Almesrati, F., Meftah, M., Qahwaji, R.: Filling factors of sunspots in SODISM images. Ann. Emerg. Technol. Comput. (AETiC) **3**(2), 1–13 (2019). https://doi.org/10.33166/aetic.2019.02.001. http://aetic.theiaer.org/archive/v3/v3n2/p1.html, Print ISSN: 2516-0281, Online ISSN: 2516-029X
7. Alasta, A.F., Algamudi, A., Qahwaji, R., Ipson, S., Hauchecorne, A., Meftah, M.: New method of enhancement using wavelet transforms applied to SODISM telescope. Adv. Space Res. **63**(1), 606–616 (2019). https://doi.org/10.1016/j.asr.2018.08.002
8. Meftah, M., et al.: Main results of the PICARD mission. In: Proceedings SPIE 9904, Space Telescopes and Instrumentation 2016: Optical, Infrared, and Millimeter Wave, pp. 99040Z, 29 July 2016. https://doi.org/10.1117/12.2232027
9. Ashamari, O., Qahwaji, R., Ipson, S., Schöll, M., Nibouche, O., Haberreiter, M.: Identification of photospheric activity features from SOHO/MDI data using the ASAP tool. J. Space Weather Space Clim. **5**, 15 (2015). https://doi.org/10.1051/swsc/2015013. https://www.swsc-journal.org/articles/swsc/pdf/2015/01/swsc130048.pdf
10. Yeo, K.L., Krivova, N.A., Solanki, S.K., Glassmeier, K.H.: Reconstruction of total and spectral solar irradiance from 1974 to 2013 based on KPVT, SoHO/MDI, and SDO/HMI observations. Astron. Astrophys. **570**, A85 (2014). https://doi.org/10.1051/0004-6361/201423628. https://www.aanda.org/articles/aa/pdf/2014/10/aa23628-14.pdf

Building Energy Management System Based on Microcontrollers

Fazal Noor[(⊠)], Atiqur Rahman, Yazed Alsaawy,
and Mohammed Husain

Islamic University of Madinah, Madinah, Kingdom of Saudi Arabia
mfnoor@gmail.com, fmatiq@yahoo.com,
yalsaawy2@gmail.com, mohd.husain90@gmail.com

Abstract. In this research, a platform is proposed based on optimization algorithms for Energy Management System for buildings. Building energy consumption can be minimized based on Artificial Intelligence and user requirements of power supplied therefore allowing comfort to consumer with efficient operation and functioning of the building. A prototype using SMART devices with a microcontroller is implemented and tested. It is observed with proper management of the operation of devices efficiency increases and therefore consumer costs reduced. A master controller communicating with multiple apartment controllers is proposed with massage passing interface.

Keywords: Energy management system · SMART devices ·
Optimization algorithms

1 Introduction

In today's energy management system, there is the need for consumer participation in demanding comfort and partial management of which appliances should be powered on or off [1]. Commissioning of buildings has many benefits such reducing power wastage, operating of equipment HVAC efficiently, and many others [2]. The Organization for Economic Cooperation and Development (OECD) consisting of 34 countries have shown in their report the building sector accounts for 25 to 40% consumption of energy [5]. In [6], it was predicted that the amount of power required for lighting would be 80% higher in year 2030. It also mentions efficient lighting would reduce the amount of CO2 emissions. It has been shown building energy management systems are required for the increasing demand for energy [8, 9]. Performance studies on energy management systems have shown by proper control of HVAC in buildings lowers the costs to the owners [3, 4, 7, 10, 11]. Artificial intelligence using neural networks have been studied to even further reduce energy consumption in the Smart buildings [12].

The owner of the building and the tenants may agree on abiding by their agreed upon rules and have fixed and flexible scheduling of their own for how long or when the appliance may be used during which time of the day. The basic idea is to have a microcontroller system using either wired ethernet connections or wireless access points at the apartment level. There is another microcontroller system at the building level called the Master Premises energy management system and which is connected to

M. H. Miraz et al. (Eds.): iCETiC 2019, LNICST 285, pp. 305–313, 2019.

a substation layer. Internet of Things (IoT) is a useful platform to achieve this control. It is observed the IoT devices continue to increase in numbers and therefore efficient energy management for IoT in Smart Cities is highly desired. Another important thing in energy management software is the security aspect and the applications must have high level of authentication and security built into them.

There are many vendors producing Smart devices and are available in the market now a days. One of the main problems among the vendors is the compatibility issue and users or developers need open source building automation platforms. Two open source platforms discussed in this paper are the OpenEMS and BEMOSS.

2   OpenEMS and BEMOSS Open Source Platforms

An electrical power management system (EPMS) is defined as an electronic system that provides detailed information about the transmission of power in an electrical power generation system or power substation. PMS record and provide data about power systems and power-related events. That information is used to manage power generation efficiencies, batteries and capacitor banks, gas or steam turbine relays and other systems in power generation stations and power substations. EPMS can visually display real-time or historical data. The system ties together the essential data that formerly had to be checked on numerous readouts and gauges by equipment operators. Supervisory control and data acquisition systems (SCADA) systems often use EPMS, especially those used in power plants.

Besides power generation stations, EPMS can be found in manufacturing plants, on large ships' generators and in similar high power demand locations. Some EPMS are their own systems, while others integrate with supervisory control and data acquisition (SCADA) and yet others are hybrid systems.

EPMS that include generator protection and control (GPC) relays and those that are integrated with SCADA can automate many power-related relays. This control helps increase power efficiency, especially in times of high draw. Some products claim they can help reduce peak power draw by 50%. Applied to the power grid, this reduction could theoretically alleviate concerns of a power crisis resulting from peak demand.

Better power management is helpful in terms of smoothing power demands. Smoothing out peak and low demand is often very beneficial and lower in cost as the problem in energy systems is often not that overall average power is too high but that peak draw times exceed momentary power production. In North America, this is true of the power grid as well as many power generation stations large and small.

2.1   OpenEMS

OpenEMS was developed by FENECON GmbH, a German company specializing in manufacturing and project development of energy storage systems [13]. It is a modular platform for energy management applications and is widely used in private, commercial, and industrial applications. OpenEMS is useful in applications which control, monitor, and integrate energy storage systems, complementary devices, and renewable energy sources. OpenEMS has Internet of Things (IoT) stack which consists of the following 3 main components. OpenEMS Edge controls the devices and executes on the site.

OpenEMS UI is the generic user interface component, and OpenEMS Backend executes on a server (e.g. cloud) and connects the decentralized Edge systems [14]. It also provides aggregation, monitoring, and control through the internet.

The main features of the OpenEMS are wide range of supported protocols and devices (meters, battery inverters; modern web based real-time interface, extendable with the use of modern programming languages and its modular architecture.

2.2 BEMOSS

BEMS stands for building energy management system, which monitors and controls building's power requirements [14]. It can control, fire alarm system, lighting, security, ventilation, air conditioning, and heating in residential or commercial buildings. BEMS is similar in some ways to OpenEMS as it also has a centralized control center from which to control other systems.

BEMOSS stands building energy management open source software built upon VOLTTRON which is a distributed agent platform developed by Pacific Northwest National Laboratory (PNNL) [15]. BEMOSS is a middleware having a seamless interface to variety of devices manufactured by various companies and also has the interface to the application layer where the software developers can develop modules which can be integrated with a variety of functionalities. It has the following features, open source, plug & play, interoperability, scalability and ease of deployment, local and remote monitoring, security, and support.

3 Experiment Results

3.1 Hardware Setup

The testbed is shown in Fig. 3 which is setup in our university lab and consists of hardware having SMART devices such as plugs, inverters, lights, and controllers. These devices are compatible with the BEMOSS system installed on our main PC. As currently there is no integration of BEMOSS with Arduiono microcontroller. In our lab, the Arduino using a webserver communicates wirelessly with the PC and transfers data read from the sensors. The main controller consists of an Arduino microcontroller. The Arduino microcontroller is open source and easily available in the market. The Fig. 1 below shows a Smart home environment. The Smart residential building environment can be thought of multiple stacks of Smart home environments.

The main distinction in this research is the customer demand of power and device management. For example, a customer may demand the home heating, air conditioning, and ventilation (HVAC) be at comfortable levels or at the level of their desire. Multiple apartment controllers communicate with master building controller for power demand. The communication occurs between master and apt controller via message passing interface. The Master controller is connected to grid station and receives information such as time when power cost is minimum and load is peaking. This information is conveyed to apt controller notifying the occupant when is the best time to use appliance such as washing machine or clothes dryer, or best time to iron clothes. Also, the user may demand which appliances to be powered on for their comfort such as A/C or heating.

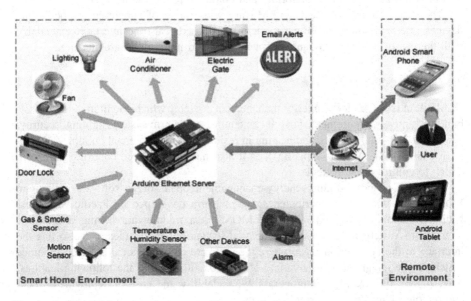

Fig. 1. A SMART home environment with master arduino ethernet server and remote environment based on android systems [16].

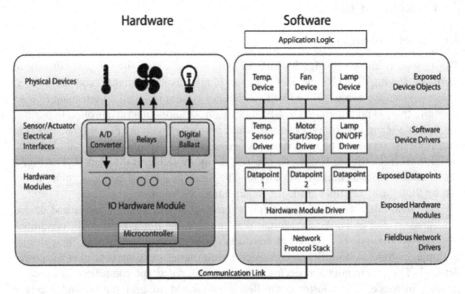

Fig. 2. An overview of hardware and software for a smart building with master controller and communication with multiple apartment controllers [16].

As it is seen in Fig. 2 a microcontroller is useful in controlling devices via a communication link. For residential buildings air conditioning, heating, and ventilation are the items most desired by customers to control. Therefore, sensors installed would be constantly monitoring the environment and communicating with the Building Energy management systems. The communication channels may be wired or wireless. In our experiments, wireless modules were used with an Arduino microcontroller. Arduino is an open source microcontroller and comes with IDE software for programming. The sensors monitor outside temperature, occupancy of apartment whether it is occupied or not, also sensors to monitor inside temperature of apt, and whether lights are on or off. As more sensors are installed to monitor the environment and control the devices the more precisely power efficiency is achieved. A common scenario is when in winter time a sudden cold front occurs and the tenants of a building increase the heat at the same time. In this situation, the power company will have to provide more power and a peak in power output will occur and therefore a rise in cost to the owner and tenants of the building. Too much rise in peak power are the usual cause of blackouts. Table 1 below shows how information from sensors will help provide power efficiency. Neural networks can be incorporated to read in sensor data and classify power usage depending on the device, hour of the day, temperature, daylight, etc. Using Artificial intelligence in studying the behavior of tenants, climate change, receiving data from sensors, etc. may also lead to systems with overall cost savings to tenants and building owners. The major savings comes when the sensors notify the master controller whether the apt is occupied or not occupied. If not occupied then there is no need to increase the temperature and hence less heating therefore will be a decrease in power consumption. Also, in this case of no occupancy there will be no need for lights therefore further reduction in power consumption. The heating of building may also be controlled by opening or closing of blinds of windows, closing of open doors by automatic controlling of motors. The lighting system of a building is also controlled by an Arduino micro-controller based system. Table 2 below shows typical appliances which are controlled by the building owner, and those controlled by the tenant. The hours of operation those controlled by the tenant are flexible compared those controlled by the owner of building. The Master controller may communicate with the apartment controllers and notify it of the best price offered by the utility company at which hours of the day the power is cheapest. Consumer having this information then will be able to program their devices or use them at the hours which are cheapest cost to them.

The monitoring and control of devices utilizing the BEMOSS platform and integrating it with multiple Arduino microcontrollers is studied for reliability of operation. The energy saving = energy cost (without algorithm) − energy cost (with algorithm) where the algorithm is used to properly manage the devices based on energy cost savings, and based on user demand priority settings. The algorithm is based on optimization algorithms such as the Genetic algorithm. The bottom line is to minimize power usage under the constrained of user demand, comfort, priority of appliance operation, hour of the day, and minimum cost times. Table 2 shows the typical types of power loads, KiloWatss (KW), and number of hours the appliance is typically on. Different tenants may differ slightly in their hours of usage.

The function to minimize is

$$f(\mathbf{x}) = E_c(\mathbf{x}) + E_h(\mathbf{x}) + E_f(\mathbf{x}) + E_L(\mathbf{x}) + E_p(\mathbf{x}) + E_o(\mathbf{x}) \tag{1}$$

where E_c is the energy consumption for A/C, E_h is the energy consumption for heating E_f is the energy consumption of the fans, E_L is the energy consumption of lighting, E_p is the energy consumption of pumps, and E_o is the energy consumption that includes other appliances such as washing machine, clothes dryers, and iron. The genetic algorithm consists of the following phases, 1. Initial population, 2. Fitness function, 3. Selection, 4. Crossover, and 5. Mutation. The prediction of energy consumption is a difficult problem and varies with outside temp, user demands, occupancy, sunlight, etc. The daily power consumption continuously varies ups and down as shown in Fig. 4. However, when climate changes it becomes more predictable the demand will increase such as cold front kicking in. Another scenario is when there is no tenant and apt is unoccupied then power consumption is more predictable to be less.

Furthermore, to minimize power is to incorporate SMART devices communicating and recommending the tenant on time of day to operate an appliance when the cost of utilities providing power is minimum. For example, if the user is informed of best time to operate washing machine or clothes dryers, or the best time to iron clothes. The building owner is informed automatically to turn off lights in areas of building where not required. Figure 5 shows the energy savings on average of a typical apartment. Series1 is without using any algorithm and series2 graph is the result of using algorithm. It is seen minor savings can add up when considering large residential buildings. Energy savings of 10% to 30% were obtained in lab simulated environment.

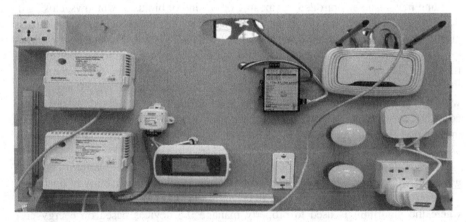

Fig. 3. A testbed of SMART devices used in experiments with BEMOSS and Arduino micro controlled sensors in our university lab.

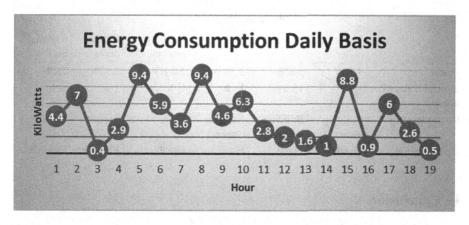

Fig. 4. Power consumption on average daily basis with fluctuates randomly in a residential building.

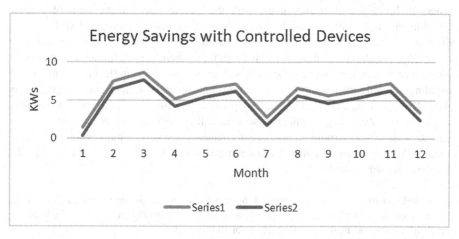

Fig. 5. Power consumption on average on a simulated monthly basis, series1 is without using any algorithm and series2 is with using algorithm.

Table 1. Power efficiency based on temp and occupancy sensors.

Apt	Lights	Heating	Occupied	Outside temp before 12 °C	Outside temp now 5 °C	Power
				Heat before	Heat demand	
1	25	20	Yes	22	27	Increased
2	40	30	Not	24	24	No change
3	75	10	Yes	23	28	Increased

Table 2. Appliances load

	Water boiler	Heating	AC	Washing machine	Clothes dryer	Clothing iron
Power	4 KW	5 KW	2.5KW	2.0 KW	3 KW	2KW
Typical hours of operation	12 h	15 h	15 h	½ h	1 h	½ h
Controllable by	Building owner	Building owner	Building owner	Tenant	Tenant	Tenant
Operating time	Fixed	Fixed	Fixed	Flexible	Flexible	Flexible

4 Conclusion

With the year over year increasing demand for energy in residential or commercial buildings. It is seen that power efficiency is necessary when user demands a certain level of comfort, for example due to a sudden cold front kicking in. It is necessary for owners of buildings to communicate with the tenants and inform them of energy reduction and its benefits to both in cost savings. Also, installation of SMART devices will help in energy savings and usage of certain types of Led lighting. Timers and power strips are also helpful in energy reduction and therefore recommended. It is seen open source microcontrollers can be used with sensors for sensing the environment and providing valuable information to the energy management system and integrating to robust BEMOSS platform and therefore providing a more versatile power efficient system. In the future, large number of sensors will be utilized with microcontrollers to simulate a realistic environment and a performance study will be made with integration to the BEMOSS system. A robust communication and security are also necessary in such large sensor systems.

Acknowledgement. This work is funded by the Deanship of Scientific Research, Islamic University of Madinah (Tamayyuz Project #20/40 titled: "An Intelligent Software Platform for Energy Efficiency and Peak Load Reduction for Buildings").

References

1. Windapo, A.O.: Managing energy demand in buildings through appropriate equipment specification and use. In: Energy Efficient Buildings, Eng Hwa Yap. IntechOpen, 18 Jan 2017. https://doi.org/10.5772/66363. https://www.intechopen.com/books/energy-efficient-buildings/managing-energy-demand-in-buildings-through-appropriate-equipment-specification-and-use. Accessed 2 Feb 2019
2. Claridge, D.E., Liu, M., Turner, W.D.: Commissioning of existing buildings - state of the technology and its implementation. In: Proceedings of the International Short Symposium on HVAC Commissioning, Kyoto, Japan (2003)
3. Levermore, G.J.: Building Energy Management Systems; Application to Low-Energy HVAC and Natural Ventilation Control, 2nd edn. E&FN Spon, Taylor & Francis Group, London (2000)

4. UK DTI. The Energy Challenge: Energy Review. http://www.dti.gov.uk/energy/review/page31995.html. Accessed 2 Feb 2019
5. OECD. Environmentally sustainable buildings: Challenges and Policies. http://www.oecd.org/env/consumption-innovation/2715115.pdf. Accessed 3 Feb 2019
6. IEA. Light's labours lost, OECD/International Energy Agency, Paris, France (2006)
7. IEA. Technical Synthesis Report: A Summary of Annexes 16 & 17 Building Energy Management Systems. Energy Conservation in Buildings and Community Systems (1997). http://www.ecbcs.org/annexes/annex17.htm. Accessed 2 Nov 2010
8. MOD. Building Energy Management Systems. Ministry of Defence: Defence Estates Design and Maintenance Guide, vol. 22 (2001)
9. Levine, M., et al.: Residential and commercial buildings. In: Metz, B., Davidson, O.R., Bosch, P.R., Dave, R., Meyer, L.A. (eds.) Climate Change 2007: Mitigation. Contribution of Working Group III to the Fourth Assessment Report of the Intergovernmental Panel on Climate Change. Cambridge University Press, Cambridge, United Kingdom and New York (2007)
10. Birtles, A.B., John, R.W.: Study of the performance of an energy management system. BSERT, London (1984). http://bse.sagepub.com/content/5/4/155.abstract. Accessed 3 Feb 2019
11. Roth, K., Llana, P., Detlef, W., Brodrick, J.: Automated whole building diagnostics. ASHRAE J. 47(5) (2019). http://www.ashrae.org/publications/page/424. Accessed 3 Feb 2019
12. Álvarez, J.A., Rabuñal, J.R., García-Vidaurrázaga, D., Alvarellos, A., Pazos, A.: Modeling of energy efficiency for residential buildings using artificial neuronal networks. Adv. Civ. Eng. 2018, 10 pages (2018). Article ID 7612623
13. OpenEMS. https://openems.github.io/openems.io//openems/latest/introduction.html. Accessed 3 May 2019
14. BEMOSS platform. http://www.bemoss.org/. Accessed 3 May 2019
15. https://www.researchgate.net/publication/260127438_Ubiquitous_Smart_Home_System_Using_Android_Application/figures?lo=1. Accessed 3 Mar 2019
16. https://www.google.com/search?q=hardware+software+%2B+communication+link+%2B+fan+%2B+temp+%2B+control&tbm=isch&source=hp&safe=strict&sa=X&ved%20=2ahUKEwjalMON4dzhAhVLzIUKHSFgDcYQ7Al6BAgJEA0&biw=1121&bih=530#imgrc=%20EJ9mdUU5aWBbsM. Accessed 3 Mar 2019

Author Index

Printed in the United States
By Bookmasters

Printed in the United States
By Bookmasters